John D Griffin
8th September 2005

St. John's College. 1957/59 & 60.

The Leeds Pottery
1770 - 1881

To Perpetuate the Memory
of
John Green, Master Potter (1742 – 1805)
A founding partner and the manager of the Leeds Pottery 1770 to 1801
Manager of the Swinton Pottery 1785 to 1801
and
The founder of the Don Pottery in 1801

Frontispiece. - Although the Leeds Pottery is justly famous for its creamware it did produce some fine examples of decorated pearlware, which this vase admirably represents. The principal decoration of this piece can be seen, when viewed from the other side, at Plate 288 and which is named under the base in script, "Jerusalem in its present State". The vase measures 10¼ in. (260mm) in height without the lid. It is impressed HARTLEY GREENS & CO./ LEEDS POTTERY on the outside surface of one side of the square base. *Leeds Museums & Galleries, 1928/10.*

The Leeds Pottery
1770 - 1881

To which is Appended an Illustrated Account
of the Work of the Revivalists,
J. & G.W. Senior and J.T. Morton
1880s to c.1950

John D. Griffin

"The town of Leeds, so universally
and justly famed 'all the world o'er'
for its woollen manufacture ...
- has produced some of the most exquisite
examples of the ceramic art
which are to be found in the
cabinets of the collector."
Llewellynn Jewitt, FSA., *The Art Journal*, 1865.

Vol. I

Published in Two Volumes
by
The Leeds Art Collections Fund
2005

British Library Cataloguing-in-Publication Data
A catalogue record for this book is available from the British Library

Typeset in Monotype Baskerville and designed and printed by
J. W. Northend Ltd., Sheffield

Photography, scanning and colour balancing by
John R. Griffin, London, unless otherwise credited

CITY ART GALLERY • THE HEADROW • LEEDS LS1 3AA

Contents

Preface

THE PROJECT to publish a history of the Leeds Pottery and its wares was initiated during my chairmanship of the Leeds Art Collections Fund and I am grateful to Benedict Read, my successor as Chairman, for his support and for enabling me to see the book to publication.

The founding purposes of the L.A.C.F. include the promotion of education in the fine and decorative arts. One means by which this is achieved is the publication of detailed catalogues of the Leeds collections. Subjects covered include: Leeds Creamware and other English Pottery (1976), Furniture (three volumes 1978 and 1998), British Silver (1992) and Textiles at Temple Newsam (2000). *The Leeds Pottery 1770–1881* represents a new development in that although it draws heavily upon the Leeds City collection it is not a catalogue.

Such has been, and still is today, the popularity of Leeds Pottery that to provide a comprehensive survey it has been necessary to research collections across the U.K. and overseas. John Griffin has been tireless in his efforts to check and amplify the history of the pottery and to trace a wide range of the wares for illustration. We are grateful to the Victoria & Albert Museum and to Leeds City Libraries for making the design, shape and pattern books available for reproduction, now brought together in their entirety for the first time.

A publication on this ambitious scale needs financial support if it is to be marketed at an accessible price. The international appeal of ceramics is evidenced by the major financial support given by CERAMICA-STIFTUNG of Basel, Switzerland which has been a key factor. Project team members have been heartened by the encouragement and generous support of Leeds Philosophical and Literary Society and that of several other Leeds-based charities and companies. We are also glad to acknowledge the help of other U.K. charitable trusts, many of which have supported previous L.A.C.F. publications.

Tangible evidence of the enduring appeal of Leeds creamware is provided by the ongoing manufacture of reproduction ware. Hartley Greens Leeds Pottery Limited have revived an early name and were happy to demonstrate production techniques at their Stoke-on-Trent Works. Their interest in the original pottery and financial support are much appreciated.

A full list of supporters is printed below.

April 2005

James S. Fox.
Trustee, Leeds Art Collections Fund.

AUDREY & STANLEY BURTON
1960 CHARITABLE TRUST

CERAMICA-STIFTUNG, BASEL

MARC FITCH FUND

JAN FLETCHER PROPERTIES LTD

JAMES S. FOX

HARTLEY GREENS LEEDS POTTERY LTD

THE IDLEWILD TRUST

LEEDS ART COLLECTIONS FUND

LEEDS & HOLBECK BUILDING SOCIETY

LEEDS PHILOSOPHICAL & LITERARY
SOCIETY LTD

LINDEN CHARITABLE TRUST

THE PAUL MELLON CENTRE
for Studies in British Art

THE SCOULOUDI FOUNDATION,
in association with the
INSTITUTE OF HISTORICAL RESEARCH

SKIPTON BUILDING SOCIETY

TENNANTS AUCTIONEERS
Leyburn, North Yorkshire

PATRICK and MAVIS WALKER

Introduction

MY INTEREST in Yorkshire Ceramics was first aroused in the 1950s by the late Mr. and Mrs. Eaglestone, to whom I was related, when they began to collect and study the products of the Rockingham Pottery. The pioneering research carried out by Arthur A. Eaglestone and his son-in-law Terence A. Lockett into the Wentworth Archives led to the first monograph on that pottery and its wares. Thus my wife and I began our ceramic-collecting interest by acquiring wares from that pottery.

However my earlier interest, from my mid teens, in the history of south Yorkshire, was soon linking up with this new passion for ceramics and from the early 1960s this led me to research another local pottery, neglected by most of the twentieth century writers, namely the Don Pottery. The Doncaster Museum and Art Gallery very magnanimously published the results of my research, with the aid of several generous grants, in 2001.

Shortly after my Don Pottery book had appeared I was approached by Simon Lawrence who, with the support of other members of his family, asked me if I would consider carrying out research towards the publication of a well-illustrated and extended version of his mother's book *Yorkshire Pots and Potteries*. This was a project that I had been thinking about for some time so, needless to say, I was delighted to receive the support of the Lawrence family for this venture. However, in discussing the project with Simon we both agreed that justice could not be done to the Leeds Pottery in such a general work. Shortly after our discussion we arranged a meeting with Dr. Adam White, Keeper of Ceramics, at Temple Newsam House, Leeds, from whom the project received strong and enthusiastic support. It was not long before The Leeds Art Collections Fund had agreed to act as publishers and fund raisers for the necessary finance needed to see it realised. A Committee was then formed consisting of myself, Adam White, Simon Lawrence and Jim Fox, Chairman of the L.A.C.F., himself keenly interested not only in matters relating to the City of Leeds, but also an erstwhile enthusiastic collector of Yorkshire ceramics. Thus the project was launched which has resulted in the publication of these two volumes.

Simon's mother, the late Heather Lawrence, more than any other person in the twentieth century, advanced our knowledge of the history, wares and indeed the existence of so many Yorkshire potteries and her research was published in 1974 in the above-mentioned book. Anyone who wishes to collect or study in the field of Yorkshire ceramics must start by referring to *Yorkshire Pots and Potteries* before embarking on any more detailed studies of an individual pottery. I was privileged, not only to count Heather Lawrence as a friend but also to contribute information from my research to her book. I shall always treasure the letters from her on matters relating to Yorkshire potteries and remember the many hours spent on the telephone discussing recent discoveries or trying to resolve problems encountered in her research.

Reverting now to my earlier interest in both the Swinton Pottery/Rockingham Works and the Don Pottery. Both these potteries had very strong links with the Leeds Pottery through the person of John Green (1742-1805), Master Potter – the founder of the Don Pottery in 1801 and one of the founding partners in the Leeds Pottery in 1770 where, as the reader will discover, he held the most important and influential position until his personal bankruptcy of 1800. Thus my earlier research had revealed to me much about both John Green and the Leeds Pottery; I had also been able to note several fruitful avenues for later research.

From quite an early stage I became aware of the inadequacy of the published works on the Leeds Pottery and, as more source material was discovered and examined, realised that the standard works, by the Kidsons in 1892 and Donald Towner of 1963, each a worthy contribution in its day, gave inadequate and at worst totally inaccurate accounts. Unfortunately with only meagre source material available to them they had indulged in the delusive luxury of conjecture which successive writers, except Heather Lawrence, have accepted as being factual.

The quantity and quality of previously untapped archives has enabled me, for the first time, to present an authoritative account of the Leeds Pottery from its foundation through to its demise. If this account is, in some areas, at variance with what has previously been assumed and published, then so be it; I have had to face up to it and accept it.

Not only has the history of the Pottery and its proprietors been previously often based on conjecture or written in such a way as to support some personally held beliefs but, I believe, the attribution of wares to this pottery has also often been misleading. Thus the Leeds Pottery has become both a generic term and a convenient factory to which much unmarked creamware of the late eighteenth and early nineteenth centuries has been ascribed by dealers, auction houses, museums, collectors and writers.

Unfortunately I am not aware of any complete and detailed extant factory ledgers or day books which, if they had survived, would have told us precisely what was made and when, at Hunslet. I have accepted this problem head on and dealt with it by adopting the following procedure :

The attribution of unmarked wares can only be based on their having details which are the same as features on :

1. Factory-marked wares.
2. Shards of proven Leeds Pottery origin.
3. Published or manuscript Leeds Pottery Design or Drawing Books in which objects and details illustrated can be shown to be peculiar to the Leeds Pottery.
4. Transfer-printed decoration which appears on 1, 2 and 3, above.
5. Extant sprig moulds and some master moulds.
6. Objects, unmarked, and very few in number which have contemporary supporting documentation certifying that they were made at the Leeds Pottery, for example, see Plates 438 – 442.
7. Wares which correspond to the six known registered designs, preferably also having the appropriate 'kite' mark for their registration date, (see Plates 430–432).

I would be very wary indeed of relying on painted or enamelled decoration in the absence of a match with a proven Leeds Pottery shape.

In compliance with the above self-imposed parameters I have restricted the wares chosen for illustrations to factory-marked examples together with wares, *en suite* with such pieces. A selection of shards is also included. Of great interest to students of ceramic design, as well as those eager for information on the range of products made at the Leeds Pottery, will be the reproduction of the published Design Books (45 pages and 7 pages of index, reduced four to a page), together with all the known surviving Drawing, Design and Pattern Books (12 books plus 23 pages of original drawings and patterns bound with a copy of the 1794 published *Design Book* amounting to 676 pages in all – reduced, some one, some two and some four to a page). In short as comprehensive a collection as possible of currently known primary source material as will enable those interested to base their own attributions and without the present work being in any way clouded with 'probables' or 'possibles'.

The decision has also been taken to include, as a lengthy Appendix IX and by way of a warning as well as information, an account of the 'Revivalists', J. & G.W. Senior and J.T.Morton.

The wares made by the Seniors, invariably in creamware and often made using original moulds from the old Leeds Pottery – usually marked LEEDS POTTERY impressed – are frequently offered for sale by those who cannot tell the difference, as genuine old Leeds Pottery wares. The wares of J.T. Morton, while at Filey, are usually marked in a way which could not deceive. All such pots were made during the period 1880s to c.1950. Once the collector can identify the above they do present a very interesting collecting area in their own right and, as will be seen from the illustrations, are frequently very well potted.

In summing up it can be said that the Leeds Pottery was perhaps the largest of Yorkshire's commercial factory potteries employing, in 1851, four hundred hands and capable of drawing nine glost kilns per week. In the early years of the nineteenth century its coal consumption was, for two years, over nine thousand tons in each year. These figures show that it must have produced an enormous quantity of wares, some for the home market but the majority going for export, covering a vast area, from Russia in the north down through the Scandinavian countries into the Netherlands, Germany, France, Spain, Portugal, Italy and the Greek Islands. It also exported to North America and South America into Brazil. As the illustrations will show, its product range was equally wide both in variety of goods and in quality. Previous writers have mainly concentrated on its creamwares which is unfortunate because its pearlwares and other bodies, drab ware and black basalt, for example, were equally fine. It is however, regrettable that so little is known about the middle to late nineteenth century wares, although some were very fine indeed.

It has been my endeavour to relate the account as objectively as possible using the archives available to me and illustrating it with a selection of the marked wares which I have recorded. Alongside this material will be found portraits, views of the pottery, two letter heads and a plan of the Pottery as it was c.1840 and on which all the buildings are named – much of this material never having been published before. This knowledge is capable of being greatly extended as a wider range of marked examples are discovered and if more factory archives eventually come to light.

September 2004.   John D. Griffin

"Whoever thinks a Faultless Piece to see,
Thinks what ne'er was,
nor is,
Nor e'er shall be."
Alexander Pope

Acknowledgements

ONE OF the most pleasant aspects of researching, studying and writing about a subject such as the Leeds Pottery is the contacts made with other collectors, both private and public, many of whom become true and trusted friends. The vast majority of these people are usually generous to a fault in opening up their collections and assisting in so many ways. Without such an attitude the task of research leading to the acquisition of the necessary knowledge would be severely curtailed.

It is, therefore, with pleasure that I now give my acknowledgements to those who have indicated their willingness to be acknowledged by name. There are, of course, others who have been equally generous but who wish to remain anonymous. These deserve equal gratitude and I proffer to them the same as to those listed below.

First. To the following museums and private collectors I give my sincerest thanks for allowing pots and other items from their collections to be recorded, photographed and reproduced in this work or who own archive material which I have been able to consult :

Antique Collectors' Club, Ltd; Astbury Hall Museum, Preston; Garry Atkins, London; Bank of England Archives; Harold Blakey; Borthwick Institute of Historical Research, The University of York; Bryan Bowden; Mac Bramley; The British Library; Keith Docker; Doncaster Archives Service; Doncaster Museum Service; The John Goodchild Collection; Guildhall Library and Archive Service, London; Royal Pump Room Museum, Harrogate; Hartley Greens Leeds Pottery Ltd; Hull Local Studies Library; Indianapolis Museum of Art, Indiana, USA; Laing Art Gallery, Newcaste-upon-Tyne; The Lancashire Record Office; Law Fine Art; Leeds Local Studies Library; Leeds Reference Library; Leeds Museums and Galleries, Temple Newsam House and Lotherton Hall; Liverpool Record Office; Alan & Wynn McGuinness; The National Archives, Public Record Office; The National Art Library, Victoria & Albert Museum; Office of National Statistics; Andrew D. Naylor; The Nelson-Atkins Museum of Art, Kansas City, Missouri, USA; Northamptonshire Record Office; Norwich Castle Museum; Graham Oliver; Penrith Farmers' & Kidd's PLC; Principal Registry of the Family Division; The Registrar General of Births Deaths & Marriages; Royal Botanic Gardens Kew – The Botanic Library; Salford Museum & Art Gallery; Sheffield Archives Service; Sheffield Science & Technology Library; Sheffield Reference Library; Smithsonian Institution, Washington, DC, USA; The Library of the Society of Genealogists, London; Stoke-on-Trent Archives & Local Studies Library; The Thoresby Society, Leeds; J & F.C. Upton; Victoria and Albert Museum, London, Dept. of English Ceramics, Print Library the Word & Image Dept. and the Picture Library; Tom Walford; John & Mavis Walsh; The Wedgwood Manuscripts, Keele University; Ordnance Survey; Colin & Robbie West; The Witt Library, London; West Yorkshire Archive Service, Leeds and Wakefield; Yorkshire Archaeological Society, Leeds; Yorkshire Museum, York.

Secondly. The following individuals who have helped me in so many ways :

Hugh Alexander; Francesca Altman; David Atkinson; John S. Atkinson; Melanie Baldwin; Craig P. Barclay; Graham Beck; John Beckerson; Gaye Blake Roberts; Ken Bowers; David Bradbury; Helen Burton; Philip Carrol; Frances Chambers; Clive Cheeseman; J. & J. Cockerill; W.J. Connor; Rosie & Harold Cooke; Barbara C. Cooper; John Croft; Jean Duke; Martin Durrant; Diana Edwards; Joyce Epps; James Fell; A.E. Fields; Geoffrey Foster; Greg. Freear; Gaye and the late Richard Freeman; Sue Freestone; Robert L. Frost; Christopher Garibaldi; Dorothy Gibson; John Goodchild; Suzan Griffiths; Robin Gurnett; W.W. Hamilton-Foyn; Rodney Hampson; Ken Hawley; Robin J.C.Hildyard; Maurice Hillis; Alan Hitchcock; Jeremy Holmes; John Howard; Ken. Jackson; Joan Jones; James Kay; Dr. W. Keizer; Trevor Kentish; Mary Kershaw; Elizabeth S. Kilgour; Emma Kirby; Ken. Knapton; Anthony Knight; Michelle Lefevre; Terence A. Lockett; James Lomax; Jiří Louda; Liz Miller; Philip Miller; Ron. Morley; Joan Newiss; Charles Newton; Peter Ogilvie; R. C. Parkin; Ingrid Phillips; J. Michael Phillips; Roger Pomfret; Geoff. Preece; Jonathan Y. Rae; Liane Richards; Adrian A.G.Robertson; Connie Rogers; Kitty Ross; Marie Theresa Russell; Susan Ryall; Peter Scott; John Shepherd; B. Sitch; Barbara Tomkins; Vera Lucia Bottrel Tostes; David Turner; Peter Walton; Ros Watson; Anna Wolsey.

Thirdly. To members of the Committee :

– Adam White, Curator of Lotherton Hall and Keeper of Ceramics at Temple Newsam House, Leeds for chairing the meetings and for his support and encouragement throughout.

– James S. Fox who, on behalf of the Leeds Art Collections Fund of which until recently he was the Chairman, has shouldered the responsibility of applying for the necessary financial support, acknowledged elsewhere, which has enabled this work to be published.

– Simon Lawrence for his advice, strong support and friendship throughout – also for reading the text and for proof-reading before publication.

Fourthly. To Keith Stubley and the very professional team at J.W. Northend, Limited, for producing the work before you.

Lastly. To my immediate family – to James and Jan who have always shown an interest in my work and have accommodated me when working in London. To John for his skill, high standards and patience when undertaking virtually all the photography except that from America and the Victoria & Albert Museum. He has also scanned, and colour adjusted, all the transparencies onto CD ready for the printer and has designed the dust wrappers. Finally to Dorothy for her unwavering support, advice, interest and enthusiasm in every aspect and at every stage from the initial conception through to the printing. All of which has ensured that my work has at all times been enjoyable.

January 2005   John D. Griffin.

Dimensions, Abbreviations, Transcriptions, Illustrations and Present-day Values of Money

Dimensions

These are given, first in imperial units to the nearest eighth of an inch followed by the nearest metric equivalent in brackets. All pots which have lids have their heights given without their lids. On such pots handles and spouts, if they project above the body of the pot, are not included in the given height. The following abbreviations are used :

D — diameter.
Ht. — height.
L — the longest dimension when viewed from above.
W — the shortest dimension when viewed from above.
OA — means over all when prefixed to one of the above, e.g. OAL means 'overall length' and would indicate that any handles and spouts have been included.

Abbreviations

DNB — Dictionary of National Biography.
ECC — English Ceramic Circle.
FOBB — Friends of Blue Bulletin.
IGI — International Genealogical Index.
LG — London Gazette.
NCS — Northern Ceramic Society
OED — Oxford English Dictionary. The compact edition, complete text reproduced reprographically, 1971.
OS — Ordnance Survey.
PCY — Prerogative Court of York.
PRO — Public Record Office. From the 2nd of April 2003 renamed "The National Archives".
UYBIHR — University of York, Borthwick Institute of Historical Research.
WRRD — West Riding Registry of Deeds.
WWM — Wentworth Woodhouse Muniments.
YAS — Yorkshire Archaeological Society.

Transcriptions from other authors and from original documents.

All transcriptions have been made without any alterations to spelling, punctuation, the use of upper or lower case letters or underlinings. Portions of text deliberately omitted are indicated by three stops, thus ... and any words which are included in square brackets are mine which have been added to summarize a lengthy passage or to make the text more easily understood. A question mark within square brackets [?] indicates that the word(s) in the original is/are illegible or missing.

Illustrations

The primary function of the chosen wares for illustration is to show shapes and decoration. I have therefore, in some instances, had to use imperfect examples in order to show the range of wares recorded when perfect specimens have not been available.

Present-day Values of Money

The researcher or student of a subject such as the Leeds Pottery cannot avoid coming across frequent references, in documents and earlier publications, to sums of money which are quoted, quite naturally, in their contemporary values. During the latter half of the twentieth century an unprecedented rate of inflation caused the value of the pound to be greatly reduced; thus making very difficult any meaningful appreciation of what the present-day value of earlier sums of money are now worth.

Several attempts have been made to provide tables which show the value of the pound for each year over a long period; for example, Brown and Hopkins in 1956[1] ventured such a table going back to the year 1290. The most recently published set of tables, back to 1750, was published by Jim O'Donoghue and Louise Goulding, of the Office for National Statistics, and

Grahame Allen, of the House of Commons Library, in the March 2004 issue of *Economic Trends*, "Consumer Price Inflation since 1750". It is from this publication that I have included the present-day values of a selected number of sums mentioned in the text, my purpose being to confront the reader with a meaningful appreciation of what such sums of money may now be worth.

The tables are based on "consumer priced inflation and the purchasing power of the pound" – they do not take account of property and land values or wages. The tables show that:

"between 1750 and 2003, prices rose by around 140 times – most of the increase in prices has occurred since the Second World War: between 1750 and 1938, a period spanning nearly two centuries, prices rose by a little over three times; since then they have increased more than forty-fold. Put another way, the index shows that one decimal penny in 1750 would have had greater purchasing power than one pound in 2003."

I am indebted to David Bradbury of the Office for National Statistics for bringing this work to my notice.

---

1. Phelps-Brown and Hopkins (1956) "Seven Centuries of The Prices Of Consumables" *Economica*, November 1956, pp. 311-314.

The Chronology of the Proprietors of the Leeds Pottery

1770 August — The Leeds Pottery in the process of being built. See p. 16.

1770 12th November — Jeremiah Dixon and his wife conveyed Rushy Pasture to Richard Humble. See p. 16.

1770 22nd November — In the Articles of Partnership, agreed on the 1st of January 1776, the partners agreed to compute their term of partnership, of ninety-nine years, from this date. We may therefore accept this as the precise date of the foundation of the Leeds Pottery.

1770 26th November — Richard Humble leased Rushy Pasture to Joshua Green, John Barwick, Henry Ackroyd and John Green. See p. 17.

1771 5th November — The first Articles of Co-Partnership agreed between the above mentioned first partners who would now trade as **Humble, Greens & Co**. See p. 18.

1776 1st January — The second and final Articles of Partnership agreement were signed.
The partners would now trade as **Humble, Hartley Greens & Co**. See p. 27, and Appendix I.

1781 19th February — Richard Humble, aged 64, retired from the partnership. The firm now traded as **Hartley Greens & Co.** See p. 33.

1827 2nd June — The Co-Partnership, trading as **Hartley Greens & Co.**, was dissolved, following a ruling by the High Court of Chancery, and therefore *ceased to exist* from this date. However the Pottery continued, trading as **The Leeds Pottery Co.,** with Samuel Wainewright as its tenant until his death on the 19th of October 1834. See p. 71.

1840 28th July — After a lengthy Chancery Suite **Stephen Chappel** agreed to purchase the Leeds Pottery. See p. 72.

1842 25th January — By an Indenture of this date the Leeds Pottery was conveyed to Stephen Chappel who took his younger brother, James, as his only partner. The Firm now traded as **Stephen & James Chappel.** See p. 72.

1847 26th March — **Stephen & James Chappel** were declared bankrupt and on the 8th of July 1848 Stephen Chappel died. See p. 78.

1850 1st March — **Richard Britton & Samuel Warburton** agreed to become partners in the Leeds Pottery for a term of 15 years. See p. 80.

1851 5th June — **Richard Britton** contracted to purchase the Leeds Pottery from the **assignees of the late Stephen and James Chappel.** See p. 80.

1861 September — **Samuel Warburton** died and was succeeded, as a partner, by his son **William Henry Warburton.** See p. 80.

1863 1st July — The partnership between **Richard Britton & William Henry Warburton** was dissolved by mutual consent. See p. 80.

1874 1st October	**The Middleton Estate & Colliery Co.** took over the mortgages on the Leeds Pottery and **Richard Britton** thereby became a tenant. See p. 81.
By 1876	**Richard Britton's** two sons, **Alfred** and **John Broadbent** had joined in partnership with their father. See p. 82.
1878 15th June	**Richard Britton & Sons** filed a petition under the Bankruptcy Act of 1869 for the liquidation of their affairs. See p. 82.
1878 24th December	The Leeds Pottery Estate, or part of it, was let to the brothers **James, Joseph and Charles Taylor,** all of Hunslet and all potters. See p. 82.
1881 3rd April	In the Census Return, **Charles Taylor**, aged 49, Master Potter employing 250 men and women, was living at the Pottery with other members of his family. See p. 82.
1882	*The Post Office Directory* does not list the Leeds Pottery and shows the "Taylor brothers, potters" living at Hillidge Road, the site of the Hunslet New Pottery. See p. 82.

CHAPTER ONE

The Leeds Pottery –
Its Foundation and Early History
1770-1800

SOMETIME before August 1770 a group of businessmen, namely Richard Humble, Joshua Green, Henry Ackroyd and John Barwick together with the Master Potter, John Green, had agreed to form a partnership to establish a pottery in Hunslet, a chapelry within and on the south side of the parish of Leeds.

Before embarking on an account of the establishment and development of the Leeds Pottery it will be helpful if we pause for a while and remind ourselves of the period from which the pottery emerged. The styles and fashions then prevailing would have been self evident to the founding partners who would realise the need to produce wares in the latest 'taste' in order to ensure their ready sale to customers at home and abroad eager for such goods.

Anyone interested in historical design knows that when studying a period one must begin by examining the architecture of that period as virtually all objects were designed to be in, part of, or outside, buildings. In 1770 the fashionable style was what we now refer to as 'Neo-Classical'. The great exponent of this style, Robert Adam, had returned from his four-year Grand Tour in 1758 and rapidly became sought after by the aristocracy to design new, or to modify existing, country and town houses in this new style. Thus the rococo, or as it was then known 'the French taste' became *passé*. In Robert Adam's own words, when furnishing Luton Hoo in 1764 "...an attempt to banish the absurd French compositions of this kind heretofore so servilely imitated...". Three houses in close proximity to Leeds were in the hands of Robert Adam at this time – Nostel Priory from 1766, Newby Hall from 1767, and the interior of Harewood House from 1765 and where, from 1767 – 78, the Yorkshire-born cabinet maker Thomas Chippendale was supplying furniture in the 'new taste'.

In the field of art Joshua Reynolds and Thomas Gainsborough, who in 1770 had exhibited his famous 'Blue Boy' painting at the Royal Academy, were the leading artists and Angelica Kauffman, who had arrived in England in 1766 was, in 1769, exhibiting history paintings on classical themes at the Royal Academy. John Flaxman, who would work for Josiah Wedgwood from 1775 modelling classical sculptures for jasper ware, had entered the Royal Academy School in 1769.

Mention of Josiah Wedgwood reminds us that by 1763 he had lightened the colour of his creamware, known as Queen's Ware from 1766, and had perfected both its body and glaze by 1768.[1]

Not only were the fine and decorative arts exciting and stimulating, but also in the field of science the discoveries being made stimulated the minds of men of an enquiring nature. The Lunar Society, so called because its members met on the first Monday following the full moon, attracted among others, Josiah Wedgwood, Erasmus Darwin, Matthew Boulton, Joseph Banks and Joseph Priestley who, in 1767, became minister of the Mill Hill chapel in Leeds and also a member of the Leeds Library where Joshua, Savile and Ebenezer Green, all sometime partners in the Leeds Pottery, were also members. In 1770 the above-mentioned Joseph Banks was on board James Cook's ship *Endeavour* along with Charles Green, assistant Astronomer Royal – Joshua Green's youngest brother – who had been sent by the Royal Society to observe the transit of the planet Venus in the Southern Hemisphere. Unfortunately Charles Green died on the return journey and was buried at sea.

Hunslet's proximity to the river Aire, (see the map Plate 1), which had been navigable out to the river Humber and the important port of Kingston-upon-Hull, since the early years of the 18th century, gave the site of the pottery a great advantage. Journeys by land although speeding up, through improvements in the roads, were still slow. In 1768 a coach called 'The Fly' commenced running between Leeds and London the journey taking two and a half days which time would be reduced to thirty-nine hours in 1776.

By 1770 the Industrial Revolution was well under way with cottage industries and small family manufacturers giving way to larger industrial undertakings where the individual members of the workforce had to be specialists – the beginnings of what we now call 'mass production'. The English overseas trade had grown[2] from £6.47m in 1700 to £14.3m in 1770 and would increase to £40.81m in 1800, with the bulk of the Leeds Pottery's products forming a part of this rising flow of exports. Finally, whilst on the subject of exports, it is worth recording that the number of pieces of earthenware exported through the port of Hull rose from 1,624,700 in 1768 to 13,287,000 in 1783. Unfortunately we may never know how many of these came from the Leeds Pottery as Staffordshire manufacturers were also exporting through this port.[3]

Thus the year 1770, in which the Leeds Pottery was founded, was in a very vibrant and exciting period of changing fashion and style and also of scientific discovery and industrial transformation and expansion – the period we now call both the Georgian Period and also the Industrial Revolution. The seeds of this new pottery were therefore sown in very challenging soil which could prove to be very rewarding for those with confidence, ability and vision who were prepared to seek markets both at home and abroad for new products in demand by an ever increasing and discerning market.

The Foundation of the Pottery, its Early History and its Founding Partners

On the 12th of November 1770 Jeremiah Dixon, of Allerton Gleadhow, Yorkshire, and Mary his wife conveyed a close of land called Rushy Pasture containing approximately five and a half acres to Richard Humble of Middleton, Gentleman, for the sum of £600.[4] Two days later Richard Humble leased to Charles Brandling Esq., (see Plate 3), Lord of the manor of Middleton:

> "All that Waggon Way Road and such branches from the same as is or are now made set out and used in upon
> over and through that close of Meadows or Pasture Ground of the said Richard Humble called Rushy Pasture
> situate lying and being in Hunslet..."

granting him free access on foot, horse or carriage and for its maintenance – to clean ditches and drains, for a full term of 48 years paying the rent of £7 on 1st of May and the 11th of November.[5] There is no mention of any pottery buildings in this lease. This would appear to be somewhat misleading in the light of an item of news reported in both *The Leeds Mercury* and *The Leeds Intelligencer* of the 28th August 1770 :

> "On Tuesday last, a melancholy accident happened at the pottery now building near this town, owing, as we are
> informed, to the master bricklayer hurrying up one of the tall hovels too expeditiously, by which, one Moses
> Hawkhead, a boy, was kill'd, and three others ill bruised."

The visitor to Hunslet in the second half of 1770 would have seen great activity on Rushy Pasture and on Jack Lane. Horses and carts conveying bricks, stone, timber, sand and lime with craftsmen and labourers digging foundations and the array of buildings which would become the Leeds Pottery gradually emerging from, what local people had hitherto known as, a tranquil green pasture with only an earlier stable or holme standing there. The only feature remaining being the regular passage of horse-drawn waggons from the Middleton Colliery, *en route* to the Leeds coal staith, which had been crossing this land for over ten years.

1. A section from a "MAP OF THE COUNTY EXTENDING TEN MILES ROUND LEEDS". Originally surveyed by Joshua Thorpe in 1819, 1820 and 1821, it was re-surveyed and corrected to the 1st of January 1831 by S.D. Martin of Leeds. The proximity of the Pottery to the River Aire and also the course of Charles Brandling's Waggon Way passing between the main Pottery buildings and the windmill are clearly shown. *Yorkshire Archaeological Society, Leeds. ref. 96 C 60.*

1 mile

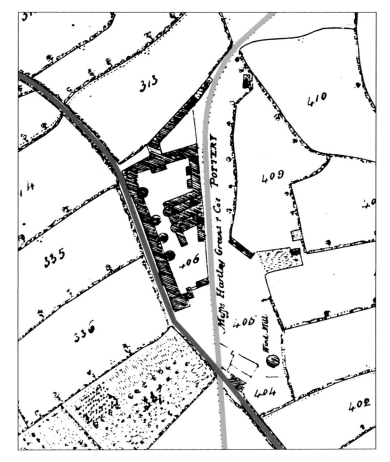

2. PLAN OF THE POTTERY. Surveyed in 1791 it shows the Pottery surrounded by open fields. The blue line shows the course of Brandling's Waggon Way and Jack Lane is coloured red. *WYAS (Leeds) ref. Acc 1849.*

3. CHARLES BRANDLING (1733 – 1802). Portrait in oils by Joshua Reynolds c.1760. Robert Wallace, photographer. *Reproduced by courtesy of the Indianapolis Museum of Art, USA. – Gift of Mrs. Thomas Chandler Werbe in memory of her husband.*

The following extracts from the indenture of the 26th of November 1770[5] supply us with precise details regarding the foundation of the Pottery. It was made between :

Richard Humble of Middleton in the parish of Rothwell, Gentleman, of the one part AND

Joshua Green of Middleton Gentleman
John Barwick of Leeds Surgeon
Henry Ackroyd of Leeds Fulling Miller } - Of the other part
John Green of Leeds Potter

[From this indenture we learn that Richard Humble leased to the four other partners] "...All that Close of Meadow or pasture commonly called or known by the name of Rushy Pasture containing five acres and a half ALSO a stable or Holme standing in the same close ... in the Township of Hunslet and late was in the tenure of Charles Brandling Esq. now in the tenure or occupation of the said Joshua Green John Green Henry Ackroyd and John Barwick together with the said Richard Humble their partner and now Erecting and Building in the said close now an Erection and buildings for the purpose of making Pots and other Earthen Ware TOGETHER with all other Barns Stables Outhouses Commons ..." [Except Chas. Brandling's Waggonway.] "...To have and to hold the said close of ground from 22nd November for 99 years ... YIELDING AND PAYING yearly and every year during the said term unto the said Richard Humble his heirs and assigns the Rent or sum of fifty-three pounds on the 1st of May and the 11th of November each year... [A further clause stipulated that they should pay a further rent of £7 on the same dates in the event of Chas. Brandling giving up the use of the Waggon Way.] AND the said Richard Humble agrees with [the other partners] that he will with all convenient expedition expend and lay out in Building and erecting such messuages dwellinghouses upon the said close of ground for the convenience of the said John Green and others who shall or may be employed in carrying on the said Trade and business the sum of four hundred and sixty pounds over and above his share or proportion therein as a partner in such manner as the said Joshua Green John Green Henry Ackroyd and John Barwick shall direct and appoint without having or receiving any further or other satisfaction for the same other than the reserved rents AND the said Joshua Green John Green Henry Ackroyd and John Barwick for themselves severally and jointly agree to pay the above mentioned rents and to keep in repair all the buildings and erections etc and also pay all Taxes, Assessments, Impositions whatsoever...".

Thus the Leeds Pottery was founded and built. It is of interest that one of the witnesses to this indenture was Savile Green who was the pottery's book-keeper, (see Plate 16) and who also, some years later, became a partner, see page 32.

We now have, for the first time in a published account, an accurate date for the Pottery's foundation and also an unambiguous list of the founding partners of the concern who, we learn, had " ... previous to the time of making and executing [the above indenture of 26th November 1770] agreed to become copartners together and jointly to carry on the trade and Mystery of making Earthen Ware for the term of 99 years ...". Unfortunately the legally drawn up first Articles of Co-Partnership which were dated 5th November 1771 do not appear to have survived. We know that such did exist as they are mentioned in the Deed of 19th February 1781, see page 33, and also in the early 19th century Chancery Court proceedings of 1811-1819.

It would appear that building work was far enough advanced by January 1771 to warrant the partners taking out an insurance on it with the Sun Insurance Office[6]

"10th January 1771
Humble Greens &
Manufacturers of Earthenware On their Buildings
adjoining each other situate in Hunslet in the Parish of
Leeds Brick & Slated/ and for the aforesaid Manufactory
not Exceeding One Thousand Pounds   £1000
£2-10   Xmas 1771"

A second policy was taken out before the above policy's renewal premium was due[7] :

"12 Oct 1771
Humble Green &
Manufactures of Earthenware On their Utensils
& Stock in their Manufactory in One Building
not Exceeding Five Hundred Pounds   500
Eight Cottages under One Roof not finished
near but separate from the above intended
to be Occupied by their Servants not
Exceeding Twenty five Pounds on Each   200
On a Building not finished near but
separate intended for two Dwelling to
be Occupied by the said M[rs] Green not
Exceeding Three Hundred Pound   300
All Brick & Slated & situate in Hunslet   -------
in the Parish of Leeds   £1000
£1-15-0   Mich[s] 1772"

4. THE TWO HOUSES BUILT BY RICHARD HUMBLE, at his personal expense, for John Green and Savile Green. Photograph by Alf. Mattison, 1904. *The Thoresby Society, Leeds.*

5. ENTRANCE TO THE LEEDS POTTERY FROM JACK LANE. Notice the bell turret on the right-hand building. From Plate 2 of the Kidsons' *Historic Notices of the Leeds Old Pottery*, 1892.

6, 7 & 8. THREE VIEWS INSIDE THE POTTERY YARD. Notice the standing figure in one of them which gives some scale to the image, emphasising the size of the hovels near to him. From Plates 2 and 3 of the Kidsons' *Historic Notices of the Leeds Old Pottery*, 1892.

9. THE FLINT MILL showing the old windmill building still standing, c.1892, with the steam-engine chimney close by. From Plate 2 of Kidsons' *Historic Notices of the Leeds Old Pottery*, 1892.

10. VIEW DOWN JACK LANE. This shows a row of low pottery buildings with the remains of a hovel just visible above the roof line. Photograph by Alf. Mattison, 1904. *The Thoresby Society, Leeds.*

11. A CLOSE-UP VIEW OF THE BASE OF ONE OF THE HOVELS. Worth noting are the well-worn stone steps winding round the base of the hovel, the gib of a hoist and on either side of the young man seated on the wheelbarrow can be seen two casks with their cleft-hazel bands. It was in such casks that the wares were packed. However, the general impression made by this and the previous photographs is of a once substantial pottery in a state of dereliction. It was however, from these buildings that the wares to be seen and discussed in this work emanated which, when at full production, would have produced a pall of black smoke constantly clouding the atmosphere of the pottery and the surrounding area.

The building and establishment of the pottery, with all its necessary equipment and materials and workforce requiring weekly wages, was obviously a very expensive matter. It must also be true that it would take some time before sales could be made and payment received for the first wares produced. Were orders sought before pots were produced or wares produced and buyers then sought? The answer is that we do not know. What we do know however, is that in the last quarter of 1770 the pottery purchased only 66 tons of coal from the Middleton Colliery and that in 1771 and 1772 respectively 1284 tons and 2098 tons were purchased, (see pages 84-88 for an account of the pottery's affairs with this colliery and the amounts of coal purchased). Ready money and cash flow must have been a constant anxiety for the early partners. It should not therefore come as a surprise to find the four partners, other than Richard Humble, taking steps to raise some working capital and this is recorded in an indenture of the 30th of May 1772.[5]

> "And whereas the said Joshua Green John Barwick Henry Ackroyd and John Green ... in the Trade and Business of making Pots and other Earthen Ware have Erected and Built several Erections and Buildings at a considerable expense upon the void ... whereof the said Leasehold Tenements are become very valuable NOW having occasion to borrow money for the purpose of carrying on the said Partnership Trade and Business have requested the said Samuel Ellis to advance and lend 'em the sum of One Thousand Pounds upon an assignment to be made him of the said Leasehold Tenements to which the said Samuel Ellis has consented...".

Apart from the four partners this document was also signed by Richard Humble and witnessed by Savile Green. Samuel Ellis, described as "of Middleton Yeoman", was the brother of Richard Humble's wife Ann. Samuel Ellis died and was buried at Rothwell on the 7th of March 1773, just ten months after the date of the above agreement – followed in May of the same year by Ann, Richard Humble's wife. By one of those strange acts of fate Samuel Ellis, by his will, had bequeathed his estate, including the leasehold of Rushy Pasture to Richard Humble.

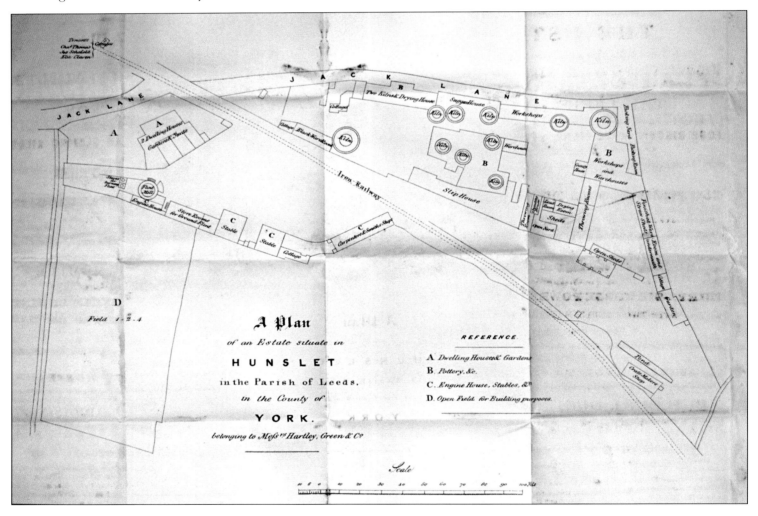

12. PLAN OF THE POTTERY IN 1834. This is the most detailed plan known of the Leeds Pottery. *The John Goodchild Collection, Wakefield.*

This extra injection of cash would therefore have been of great assistance in furthering the plans and aspirations of the founding partners and evidence that plenty of work was being undertaken may be presumed by the steady increase in its coal consumption, see page 87 and also by the fact that the Pottery kept its flint-grinding windmill and, presumably, some of its staff working on Sundays, a practice which was brought to an abrupt end in 1774 as reported in the local newspaper :

> "On Sunday, July 31st, the sails of the windmill belonging to the Leeds Pottery fell down with a tremendous crash, which, being looked upon as a judgment for desecrating the Sabbath, the proprietors resolved that the mill should never be allowed to be worked afterwards on the Lord's Day."

There may well have been a lengthy period without adequate wind to drive the windmill resulting in the pottery running short of the essential ground flint which had persuaded the partners to work the mill as and when weather permitted. Orders might have been increasing resulting in the mill, even with six days working, being unable to produce enough ground flint for the Pottery's needs. Nevertheless although there was much relaxation of Sabbath observance, beginning in the early 18th century, the act of 1677 "... for the better observance of the Lord's Day" which forbade all work and travel by horse or boat on Sundays, was still applicable although it would appear that a blind eye was obviously the order of the day in Hunslet in 1774. Bearing in mind that Richard Humble was a Roman Catholic[8] and that both Henry Ackroyd and John Green were members of the congregation at the White Chapel in Hunslet one can only conclude that the decision to work the windmill on Sundays must have been taken after a great deal of heart searching for them to break the fourth Commandment – "Remember that thou keep holy the Sabbath day. Six days shalt thou labour, and do all that thou hast to do; ...".

Llewellynn Jewitt[9] records :

"Mr Wilson has found the draft of an agreement, dated November 11, 1775, whereby 'Joshua Green, of Middleton Gent., John Green of Hunslet, potter, with divers others, under the firm of Humble Green & Co.,' agree with Messrs. Hutchinson and Evers to erect and maintain in repair at their mill a water-wheel, with all necessary machinery for grinding flints. For thirteen years the wheel was to be used exclusively by the Greens, who were to supply burnt flints and to pay 10s. for every 100 pecks of well ground and levigated flints, the workmen's wages being first deducted."

A copy of this agreement was loaned for the 1926 Leeds Tercentenary Celebrations Exhibition and is recorded in the Exhibition Catalogue page 216, No.696 – "Copy of an Agreement for letting water wheel or mill to Humble Greens & Co., Potters, Hunslett, for the grinding of flints, 11th November, 1775. *Aire & Calder Navigation Co.*" A search has been made in the archives surviving from this company, unfortunately the agreement has not been located.

The windmill was not, therefore, deemed adequate or reliable enough to cope with the increasing demands of the Pottery and the more regular and therefore reliable mechanism of a water-driven mill would be a great improvement. See page 34.

The Founding Partners, trading as 'Humble Greens & Co'

It will be noticed that in the name of the partnership it is 'Greens' and not 'Green' – the plural signifying that Joshua and John Green were from different families.

Before continuing the account of the progress of the Leeds Pottery further it is appropriate and necessary at this juncture to give an account of the first partners – their backgrounds and families. The share holding of each of the founding partners was as follows, the total shares being divided into fourteen parts or shares :

Richard Humble	7 shares.	Henry Ackroyd	2 shares.	John Barwick	1 share.
Joshua Green	2 shares.	John Green	2 shares.		

Richard Humble

Born c.1717, he married Ann, daughter of Samuel and Rebecca Ellis, on the 12th of July 1757 by whom he had six sons, one of which died an infant, and three daughters. His wife died within a few days of the birth of their daughter Grace and was buried on the 1st of June 1773. Richard was buried at Rothwell on the 27th of July 1798, aged 81.

He was obviously a man of some ability and business acumen living, certainly after his marriage, at Middleton Hall. From his will[10] we learn that he had a farm, a brewery and malt kiln, windmill and several closes of land and also collieries held in partnership with Chas. Brandling. Mention is also made of his Keels and part-shares in Keels. Among monetary bequests were £2000 to each of his three daughters.

In the Ledgers and Journals of the Middleton Colliery Estate references are made to the salary that he was paid in respect of his duties as Charles Brandling's agent, e.g. :

31 Dec. 1772 "For Rich[d] Humble for one y[rs] Salary due this day £125."[11]

From his will it is obvious that he had a financial interest in some of the collieries in and around Middleton along with his employer Charles Brandling. It must, therefore, have been in his interest as well as that of his employer, to sell as much coal as possible; the Leeds Pottery became the largest single customer for the coal produced from these collieries in the last quarter of the 18th century.[12] What better reason for Richard Humble to become the leading partner in the establishment of the Pottery – and, as we have seen, he had ample financial resources to enable him to take the lead until the Pottery and its other partners were able to 'go-it-alone'. He felt able to withdraw in 1781.

Finally a contemporary account of his character and personality is found in the diary of Thomas Butler of Kirkstall Forge, near Leeds :[13]

>   p.177, Nov. 1797 – "... Mr Humble is a very passionate; unreasonable man ...".
>   9 Dec. 1797 – "... accidentally and unexpectedly met with Mr Humble – I told him my Errand he flew into a desperate Rage – and swore we should never more do any work for him, and he went on at a furious rate – but I let him go on till 'Self Mettle Tired him.' I reasoned with him coolly – he still raged and persisted in what he had said before ...".

Obviously Humble by name but not by nature.

Joshua Green

Contrary to what earlier writers, except Heather Lawrence, have written – Joshua was not the brother of John Green, nor was he, so far as I am aware, related to him in any other way (see pedigrees in Appx. VI and the notes under John Green page 24). Joshua was baptised 19th of April 1720, the second son of Joshua and Ann Green of Barrow, parish of Wath-upon-Dearne, farmer and butcher.

On the 11th of November 1735 Joshua Green began an apprenticeship with George Batty of Barnbrough, Yorkshire to learn the "Trade Mistery and Profession of a Skinner & Breeches Maker" for the usual term of seven years.[14] His indenture fee of £4 was paid by The Rt. Hon. Thomas Earl of Malton of Wentworth House, who, in 1746, was created 1st Marquis of Rockingham. I have not found any material to indicate if, or for how long, he followed the trade to which he was apprenticed, neither can I say precisely when or for what reason he settled in the area to the south of Leeds. The earliest reference that has come to my notice is the burial of his first wife Ann at Rothwell on the 3rd of August 1756. The following year, on the 12th of July, he was a witness to the marriage of Richard Humble and Ann Ellis thus showing an early friendship between these two founding partners. On the 11th of December 1758, at Rothwell, Joshua married a second time – Judith, the sister of John Barwick who would become one of his fellow partners in the Leeds Pottery.

In the same year, 1758, Joshua Green gave evidence to a Parliamentary Commission regarding the supply and price of coal in Leeds and the advantages which Charles Brandling's proposed waggonway would bring to Leeds, see page 84.

The Leeds Mercury of the 11th of May 1761 carried an advertisement for the sale, by Joshua, of a close of freehold land, "near four acres", situated on the west side of the Leeds to Holbeck road. In the Hunslet Rate Books for 1763[15] and 1770[16] he was recorded as occupying land in Hunslet belonging to Charles Brandling. He was a member of the Leeds Library, No. 145 on the register.[17]

When searching the Ledgers and Journals of the Middleton Colliery Estate Co., I came across frequent references to payments to Joshua Green for leading waggons of coal from Middleton Colliery to the Hunslet staith, e.g., :

>   "28 March 1783
>   For leading 2182 waggons of Coals to Hunslet Staith
>   from 31 Dec 1782 ... at 10½ pr wag. pd Jos Green   £95-9-3
>   21 Oct . . . . . . .ditto . . . . . 4297 waggons   £187-19-10½
>   31 Dec . . . . . . .ditto . . . . .3197 waggons   £139-17-4½"

Joshua therefore had a coal hauling business with plenty of work from Charles Brandling and a very close friendship with Richard Humble.

Before the partners joined together to found the Leeds Pottery, Joshua had entered into another partnership with Benjamin Russell by an Indenture dated the 15th of March 1770[18] whereby Joshua Green of Middleton Gentleman and Benjamin Russell of Holbeck, parish of Leeds, Lime Burner, leased from Hans Busk a close of land in Hunslet for the purpose of digging clay for a period of 21 years at a rent of £25-4-0, and that :

>   "... the said Joshua Green and Benjamin Russell their Executors Administrators and assigns shall not nor will make use of more clay to be got in the said Demised Close in any one year of the said term than wod be sufficient to make five Hundred Thousand Bricks ..."

Holes or pits from which the clay was dug were to be left level :

>   "... and covered all over on the surface with good earth full six Inches thick and neatly drained so as the water falling thereon may be prevented standing and be readily conveyed into the proper Ditches ...".

The indenture also mentions a close which they already rented on the north or north west side of the highway leading from Leeds to Holbeck Moor and which was rented from Mr. John Smith.

Heather Lawrence, in *Yorkshire Pots and Potteries* page 60, describes "Russell's Pottery, Meadow Lane Pottery and Holbeck Pottery" in a position which seems to correspond with Joshua Green's and Benjamin Russell's holdings as outlined above. If this is the case one would have to be very careful in attributing any shards found on this site as they were most likely conveyed there from other local potteries as drainage material.

The Leeds Intelligencer of the 5th of January 1786 announced the dissolution of the "partnership betwixt Joshua Green of Middleton and Benjamin Russell of Holbeck, Potters ..." by mutual consent from the 31st of December 1785. Thus Joshua Green was not a newcomer to the clay and coal-consuming business when he became a partner in the Leeds Pottery. Was it just a coincidence that Joshua had commenced this brick making business shortly before the founding of the Leeds Pottery or was it deliberate, bearing in mind that the new Leeds Pottery would require thousands of bricks for the construction of its buildings ? As will be seen, as the history unfolds further, the Leeds Pottery did itself make bricks, see page 37.

Joshua died in June 1799 and I have reproduced his will at Appendix III. His widow, Judith, survived him by nearly ten years and so far as I am aware there were no children from either of his marriages.

Henry Ackroyd

Very little is known about Henry Ackroyd, neither his parentage nor his date of birth. He married Sarah Metcalf at St. Peter's Church Leeds on 26th of January 1763. They had three daughters – Sarah, who married the Rev. Edward Parsons, Dissenting Minister,[19] in 1789, (see Plate 13), unfortunately died shortly after her marriage; Ann, born 1766, married Ebenezer Green, Joshua Green's nephew and brother in law of Savile Green; and Mary who did not marry. Henry Ackroyd described himself variously as: Miller in 1756, & 1759; Yeoman in 1758; Fulling Miller in 1770 & 1776, and Gentleman in 1781.

On of 22nd of January 1778 he became an "Old Trustee of the Hunslet Workhouse" indicating that he had held positions earlier.[20] Henry was also closely involved with the White Chapel in Hunslet Lane, where the Rev Ed. Parsons was sometime the minister. Part of a touching letter from John Green, himself also a member of the same congregation, to John Brameld at the Swinton Pottery is given at page 39, in which he comments on the death of Henry Ackroyd. He left no will and his shares in the Leeds Pottery (four 24ths at the time of his death) eventually passed to his "legal representatives" – his widow, his daughter Mary and his son-in-law the Rev. Ed. Parsons.

REV.ᴰ EDWARD PARSONS.

13. THE REV. EDWARD PARSONS (1762 – 1833). He was the minister of the Salem Chapel (Independent) in Hunslet Lane and became a shareholder in the Pottery through his first wife Sarah, the daughter of Henry Ackroyd, one of the founding partners of the Pottery. Portrait from a painting by J. Northcote, R.A., engraved by T. Lupton and published in London, 10th of May 1819. *Leeds Library & Information Services, Local History Library.*

John Green 1742 - 1805

14. JOHN GREEN (1742 – 1805), master potter and the only practical potter among the original partners who entrusted him with " ... the Direction and Management of the said Work and appointment of the Workmen and Labourers to be employed therein ...". This conferred upon him not only their trust but a considerable responsibility. The portrait is by John Russell, RA., "Painter to the King and Prince of Wales" and who was the leading pastel portrait artist of his day. It is signed, top left, "Russell, RA pinxit/1802". Unfortunately the present whereabouts of the original portrait are not known. George C. Williamson in his work *John Russell, RA.*, informs us that Russell was so highly regarded as a portrait artist in his day that his fees were the same as those charged by Sir Joshua Reynolds, for portraits of the same size. Williamson also records the size of this portrait as being 30 inches x 24 inches; for a portrait of this size Reynold's fee would have been thirty-five pounds. See also Plates 16 and 21. *Leeds Library & Information Services, Local History Library.*

In my previous book, *The Don Pottery 1801 – 1893*, I stated that John Green, Master Potter, "was perhaps the most influential person in the history of the Yorkshire ceramics industry of the late 18th and early 19th centuries". In the light of the wealth of archive material which I have examined in my research for the present work I can now alter the above statement by deleting "perhaps" and inserting "undoubtedly". Readers who are *au fait* with my Don Pottery book will have to forgive me for repeating here some of the material from Chapter One of that book.

In 1854 Sir Henry de la Beche, director of the Museum of Practical Geology, Jermyn Street, London, wrote to Thomas Wilson of Crimbles House, Leeds, seeking information on the Leeds Pottery. In his reply, dated 20th of March 1854, the following statement occurs: "I understand the Pottery was first established in 1760 by two brothers of the name of Green ...". This statement was subsequently accepted and quoted by: W, Chaffers, Llewellynn Jewitt, Oxley Grabham and Donald Towner, until Heather Lawrence published her *Yorkshire Pots and Potteries* in 1974. In her book she corrected the date to 1770 and accurately dismissed the 'brotherhood' of Joshua and John Green. It is a strange irony that the correct date of 1770 was published by Joseph Marryat in his *A History of Pottery and Porcelain*, second edition revised and enlarged, 1857: "The pottery was established as we have before mentioned about 1770 ...". Of a much more recent date is the suggestion that John Green may have been related to a certain John Green who had a colliery on the Wentworth Estate. This statement has been made without any supporting evidence other than the name itself – possibly one of the commonest names in England. Neither is there any shred of evidence to support another claim – that he came from an old Swinton family. His sons however could and did make this claim, obviously via their mother Elizabeth, neé Scorah,[24] whose paternal ancestors were yeoman farmers of Swinton.

In order to disprove John Green's relationship to Joshua Green and therefore the other Greens of the Leeds Pottery it is necessary to examine some genealogical facts. John Green died and was buried in the church yard of Wath-upon-Dearne in south Yorkshire, his death being recorded in *The Leeds Mercury* of Saturday the 5th of January 1805 :

"On Wednesday last Mr. John Green, one of the proprietors of the Don Pottery, near Doncaster, and formerly a partner in the extensive pottery concern, near this town."

His age, both in the burial registers and on his gravestone, (see Plate 15), is given as 62 and since he died on the 2nd of January 1805 it is reasonable to assume, that unless his birthday was the 1st of January, that he must have been born sometime in 1742. The second genealogical fact is that his mother's death was recorded in *The Leeds Intelligencer* for the 27th of August 1792 as occurring on the 21st of August :

"On Tuesday died in an advanced age, Mrs Green, mother of Mr John Green of the Pottery, in this town."

Remembering these two facts, namely that he was born in 1742 and that his mother lived until the 21st of August 1792; if the reader now turns to the pedigree on page 594 it will be seen that such a person cannot be fitted into the pedigree of that Green family.

The short pedigree which I illustrate at Appx. VI, shows that John Green was baptised in Rotherham Parish Church on the 30th of December 1742, the son of John and Elizabeth Green of Greasbrough, linen weaver.[21] Greasbrough was then a chapelry within the parish of Rotherham and was very close to the chapelry of Swinton, being separated by the parish of Rawmarsh. In my Don Pottery book, at page 18, I illustrate a number of specimens of John Green's signature – one when he witnessed his sister Grace's marriage to Francis Avison and another when he witnessed his cousin John Sharpe's marriage to Elizabeth Howarth – also his signature from an invoice from the Swinton Pottery to Wentworth House and dated c.1768.[22] The last signature is evidence of his having worked at the Swinton Pottery prior to his move to Leeds; as is the fragment of a salt-glazed profile forming tool excavated by A. and A. Cox and which is inscribed "...hn/..reen".[23]

On the 31st of October 1769 John Green married, by license, Elizabeth Scorah, aged 18, at Mexborough Church. One of the witnesses was William Fenny a partner with William Malpass in the Swinton Pottery. William Fenny had previously been a partner in the Rotherham Pottery, until April 1767, and was the son of William Fenny, the founder of the Catcliffe Glass House, who had died in 1761 and was buried at Rotherham. One is tempted to speculate regarding when the friendship between William Fenny and John Green started. Was it at the Swinton Pottery or perhaps earlier at the Rotherham Pottery? Unfortunately we may never know the answer.

In order, however, to complete the proof that I had found the true family of John Green I realised that I must, if at all possible, find the burial of his mother, Elizabeth, for the date given in the Leeds newspapers. I believe that I have now discovered this; she was buried at St. Mary's Hunslet; see Appendix VI for the reasoning to support this claim.

Exactly how John Green, in his 28th year and the year after his marriage, became a partner in the Leeds Pottery is not known. Obviously the other partners would need someone whom they could trust and who had both practical skills as a potter as well as the personality and ability to act as a manager. Two pieces of evidence have already been given to support such credentials. First the discovery of the shaping tool mentioned above bearing what appears to be his name is evidence that he had worked as a journeyman potter at Swinton and also the strong probability that he had held some form of managerial/book-keeping position in the Swinton Pottery, evidenced by his signature on an invoice to Wentworth House. As both Joshua Green and Savile Green both originated from the Swinton area it is reasonable to assume that they would both know of the Swinton Pottery and almost certainly know John Green personally. It will be seen as the account of the development of the Leeds Pottery unfolds that their choice of John Green, to hold the position that he did from its foundation, was fully vindicated.

In 1785 the Leeds Pottery entered into a 21 year partnership with the Swinton Pottery and John Green was the partner who had the oversight of this merger; Llewellynn Jewitt stated as "manager".[25]

The skill and ability of John Green, which undoubtedly led to the success of the Leeds Pottery, brought a not inconsiderable degree of wealth to the partners and especially to John Green. Thus we find him styling himself "Merchant " and "Gentleman". His income from the two potteries gave him money to invest in other concerns for example, a quarry at Idle, various properties at Sowerby, Gomersall, Birkenshaw, Hemsworth, Leeds and Clifford and the Old White Cloth Hall in Leeds with an adjoining cottage, some of these properties he held in Partnership with others. From 1785, with other partners, he invested £7,766 and borrowed £5,300 with which to build two ale and porter breweries[26]– one in Hunslet and the other in Westgate, Rotherham. Near to the Hunslet Brewery he built for himself a new mansion house, which with its contents he insured as follows :

> "22 December 1792
> John Green of Hunslet near Leeds in the County of York
> Maltster Brewer & Merchant On his Mansion House only
> situate as aforesaid not exceeding fifteen hundred pounds –   1500
> Household Goods therein only not exceeding three hundred pounds – 300
> Wearing Apparel therein only not exceeding Sixty pounds –   60
> Plate therein only not exceeding forty pounds –   40
> Coach house Stables Cowhouse Granaries & Offices adjoining &
> Communicating near not exceeding three hundred pounds –   300
> Utensils & Stock therein only not exceeding Two hundred pounds –   200
> Duty £1-16"   All Brick Stone & Slated   £2400

The two breweries were, at the same time, insured for £7,000. Unfortunately as will be shown later, page 42, tragedy struck John Green and his partners in the 1790s as it did so many other businessmen, through no fault of their own, as a result of the vagaries of the weather. The following notice, which appeared in *The Leeds Intelligencer* of the 26th of March 1798, before his personal bankruptcy which was announced in the Leeds newspapers in March 1800, is the fullest description I have found of the Hunslet Brewery[27] :-

> "*Hunslet, near Leeds.*
> ALE and PORTER BREWERY.
> To be LETT, by Private Contract,
> *(To Enter to Immediately,)*

THE REMAINDER of a TERM of YEARS under a LEASE, Thirty-four Years of which are unexpired of and in an Extensive ALE and PORTER BREWERY, now carrying on and situate in the Township of Hunslet, near Leeds; together with Four Malt Houses, capable of turning off Two Hundred and Thirty Quarters per Week, with Seven Drying Kilns; the Ale Brewery is capable of brewing One Hundred Quarters per Week, and the Porter Brewery One Hundred and Thirty Quarters a Week. There are on the Premises a good Steam Engine capable of grinding the Malt, pumping the Liquor and Worts for the use of the same; also a Cooperage, Blacksmith's and Carpenter's Shops with every other Convenience for carrying on the above Business to the greatest Advantage. The Utensils, which are nearly new, will also be disposed of on reasonable Terms. – The Brewery is well established, and none exceeds it in making a good article.

If the whole together is not soon lett, it is purposed to divide the same in Parcels, as several of the Malt Houses may be lett off without interfering with any other Part of the Premises, and the Breweries may at an easy Expense be converted into Distilleries, or places proper for carrying on the Manufacture of Cotton, Woollen, or Flax, as there is Water on the Premises sufficient for the supplying of Steam Engines of any Magnitude.

The Situation is not only eligible for the above Purposes, but particularly so for a Merchant wishing to manufacture his own Goods who may be accommodated with a capital Mansion-House, Coach-House, and Stabling for Twenty-seven Horses, a large Garden, walled round, well stocked with Fruit Trees, and a good Hot House; also Houses for Agents and Servants; together with any quantity of Land, not exceeding Thirty-two Acres, all in high condition, and most eligibly situated for Tenter Grounds, or various other Purposes.

N.B. The whole of the Premises lay together in a ring Fence, within less than a Mile of the Town of Leeds, and near Coal.

For further Particulars apply to Mess. Nicholson and Upton, Attorneys, Leeds; or Mr. John Green, on the Premises."

Before leaving the account of John Green's period in Hunslet, mention must be made of another of his activities, namely his service to the community through the committee of the Hunslet Workhouse and where Savile Green, Henry Ackroyd and later William Hartley also served. The following extracts are taken from the accounts of the Hunslet Overseers of the Poor and the Workhouse which I have examined from the year 1770 :[28]

"16th Dec. 1773 Ordered that Thos Rainforth[29] be putt out apprentice to Mr John Green.

1st May 1777 – Mr John Green – an officer of the Workhouse as an overseer. . . . that Mr John Green be desired Particularly as a Committee Mann."

15th May 1778 He became an "Old Trustee"

"19th Aug. 1779 Ordered that Thos Hutchinson's 2 children serve Mr John Green and that Mrs Green receives from their wages 18d per week for Purposes agreed with Hutchinson.

17th Feb 1780 Ordered that Jonathan Crowfoot Have 6/- per month to commence January 1st 1780 and the money to be lodged in Mr Green's hand.

15th June 1786 Ordered that the overseers of poore Inquire of Mr John Green what Potters belong this Town and not to forget widow Ball."

John Green had moved back to Swinton by late 1801 and, with his eldest son John, together with Richard Clark of Leeds, Wharfinger and Rope Maker, and John and William Brameld of the Swinton Pottery, he founded the Don Pottery. Unfortunately no detailed papers regarding his bankruptcy are presently known to have survived but the fact that, so soon after this event, he was able to outlay money on this new pottery may indicate that the realisation of all his assets had left him with enough surplus for this new venture. Sadly, as mentioned earlier, he died on the 2nd of January 1805. His two sons, John and William carried on the Don Pottery until their bankruptcy in 1834. An indication that John Green, senior, had soon managed to turn around his financial disaster is that in 1802 he could afford to have his portrait painted by the very eminent artist John Russell, R.A., (see Plate 14).

15. GRAVESTONE OF JOHN & ELIZABETH GREEN on the west side of Wath-upon-Dearne Parish Church, the inscription reads :

In Memory
of JOHN GREEN who departed
this Life 2nd January 1805.
Aged 62.
Also of Elizabeth his Wife
who died 8th September 1825
Aged 74 Years.

John Barwick

John Barwick was an apothecary and surgeon in Leeds and the brother of Joshua Green's second wife Judith. Very little is known about him except that his wife's name was Margaret and that they had no children, his estate passing to his nephew William Barwick who, at the time his father made his will, 13th of October 1798, was a merchant in St. Petersburg, Russia.

One item is worth recording with respect to John Barwick and that is that in July 1796 he appeared before the Quarter Sessions in Bradford as the appellant against the Overseers of Hunslet appealing against an Indenture signed by two Justices of the Peace requiring him to take a poor girl being put out to him as an apprentice. The following are from the records of the Court:[30]

"That the appellant is a Partner with eleven other persons in a Manufacty of earthenware in the Town of Hunslett Two of the partners are resident in Hunslett and now have had each an apprentice bound and indentured to them by the overseers of Hunslett which they took without objection.... The apprentice was appointed and tendered to the appellant to be his apprentice individually ... The Appellant is not resident in the Township of Hunslett but at Leeds the adjoining Township the Partnership is rated for Buildings and Land in Hunslett to the amount of 270£ a year of which 23£ a year [there are several persons living in Leeds who have had apprentices from Hunslet] is the appellant's share and there is not any person living in Leeds or Hunslett who is rated for the Poor of Hunslett to that amount who has not had a Parish apprentice from that Town...

The other partners are resident at a distance viz: Manchester [George Hanson] Ferrybridge [Thomas Wainewright] etc. ... The Justices were of the opinion that the appellant was in every respect a proper person to take an apprentice if bound by Law to take one."

The above gives us a fascinating glimpse into the workings of the Poor Law at this time and how it must have intruded in a very obvious and personal way into the lives of so many families. One is bound to wonder what training the poor girl got in either of his callings, or was she just used as an extra 'maid-of-all-work' in the household ?

The Partnership Articles of Agreement

Perhaps the most important document to have survived in this collection[5] is the 'Articles of Agreement' made between the partners just described, together with William Hartley and dated the 1st of January 1776. A full transcript is given at Appendix I. As stated earlier, page 18, we know that the founding partners had had an earlier agreement. The following extracts are particularly relevant to the account being given, the bracketed numbers refer to the appropriate paragraph in the full Agreement:

"That Richard Humble William Hartley Joshua Green Henry Ackroyd John Green and John Barwick in consideration of the Trust Confidence and Good Opinion which they have and do repose in each other have mutually agreed to and with each other to become Partners and Joint Traders in the Art Trade Mystery and Business of Making Earthen Ware and Vending the same ... for the Term of Ninety-nine Years to be Computed from the Twenty-second day of November ... one Thousand seven Hundred and Seventy ... and ... agree to these Presents in Manner Following (that is to say)

(1) That the said Partnership shall consist of fourteen shares to be Divided amongst the said Partners in manner following (to wit) The said Richard Humble five shares William Hartley two shares to the said Joshua Green two shares to the said John Green two shares to the said Henry Ackroyd two shares and to the said John Barwick the remaining one share

(2) That the Capital Stock ... shall be at least seven thousand Pounds which sum is now advanced by the said Parties according to their several respective shares and proportions ...

(5) That all Gains and Profits arising from the said Partnership Trade and Business shall be Divided amongst the said Partners in Proportion to their several Shares above Specified ...

(6) [The partners, their agents or attorneys shall at any time(s) in daytime have access to the letters and books belonging to the partnership.]

(7) [An annual meeting of the Partners to be held on the first Wednesday in February to settle up the accounts and also at 11 o'clock on the first Wednesday in April and then at two-monthly intervals to hold meetings to discuss and consult with each other] " ... the most beneficial and advantageous manner of conducting the said Business"

(9) "That none of the said Partners ... without the consent of all the other Partners shall enter into or engage himself in any other Earthen Manufactory"

(11) " ... and whereas the said Richard Humble Joshua Green John Barwick Henry Ackroyd and John Green have already Erected and are now erecting and Building several Erections and Buildings at the expense of the said Partnership for the purpose of carrying on the said Trade and Business there to which the said William Hartley

hath paid his proportional share of the expences It is therefore by all the said Parties to these Presents agreed and declared that the said Partnership Trade and Business shall be carryed on in such Erections and Buildings as already built or which may hereafter be built by them in the said Close called Rushy Pasture and at no other Place or Places whatsoever without the consent of all the other Partners ...”

(12) “That the said Richard Humble shall during his Natural Life have the appointment of all Stewards Agents Book keepers Managers and other necessary Supervisors to be employed in the said Partnership Trade and Business and shall after the Decease of the said Richard Humble the said Stewards Agents Book-keepers Managers and Supervisors shall be appointed by the said Partners or the Major part thereof by Vote according to their respective Interests in the said Partnership (that is to say) every Partner to have as many votes therein as he is possessed of Shares in the said Partnership Trade and that the said John Green shall have the Direction and Management of the said work and appointment of the Workmen and Labourers to be employed therein which said John Green shall in consideration thereof have the Salary or Wages of Seventy two pounds per Annum so long as the said Partners shall Judge him able to Conduct the same the said Sum of Seventy two Pounds to be paid him over and above his Share or Proportion as a Partner and that such Partnership Trade and Business shall be carryed on in the name of Humble Hartley Green’s and Company”

(15) [Following the death of a partner any who may, by virtue of inheritance or by a will, find themselves entitled to any shares in the Leeds Pottery shall be at liberty to continue as partners of the business.]

(16) “ ... that if any doubt or controversy shall happen to Arise amongst the said Partners or between any of them of or concerning the said Partnership ... the same shall be referred to two arbitrators each of the contending Parties choosing one who shall adjudge and Determine the same within Thirty days next after such Arbitrators shall be appointed and in Case the said Partnership cannot agree in the making of their award that then it shall be Lawful for them the said Arbitrators to choose a third Person who shall be added to them as an Arbitrator and then to the award or determination of the said three Arbitrators or any two of them who shall determine the same within Ten days next after such Election of such third Arbitrator and all the said Partners their respective Executors Administrators and Assigns shall stand to abide and Perform the award of such Arbitrators or two of them and none of the said Partners ... shall commence an Action or Suit at Law or in Equity against the others or other of them ... before such Doubt or Controversy shall have been first referred to Arbitrators as aforesaid”

From the above extracts together with reference, when and where necessary, to the complete text at Appendix I it is now possible, for the first time, to know precisely not only the date of the foundation of the Partnership and the respective shares of each partner but also to get some idea of the organisation and the responsibilities of some of the partners. Such knowledge therefore corrects and nullifies much of what has been published by previous writers where often biased assumptions have been written as ‘facts’ which in turn have been elaborated on and exaggerated by successive writers.

The first point which is worth stressing is the division of shares between the partners which at this early date, and most likely from the foundation, had been worth £500 each. Richard Humble, holding the majority of shares, retained the right to appoint all senior, managerial staff; such appointments after his death were to be made by the other partners, their voting powers being in proportion to the number of shares which each partner held. Of particular importance is the position of William Hartley who had purchased two shares thereby giving himself the same voting rights as Joshua Green, John Green and Henry Ackroyd. It can be further stated that his proportion of shares in relation to the other shareholders did not vary throughout his time in the partnership. There are, therefore, no grounds for the popular belief that he brought significant funds into the Leeds Pottery thereby securing for himself a privileged and senior position.

John Green is the only other partner mentioned in the Agreement with specific responsibilities and as he was the only partner who was a ‘potter’ it is not surprising that he should have, apart from the appointment of the workmen and labourers, the “Direction and Management of the said work”. Thus was bestowed upon him the most important and pivotal roll in the Pottery. It is therefore to <u>his</u> credit, vision and skill backed up by the support of the other partners, that the success both financially and artistically of the Leeds Pottery was based. For this position he had a house provided and remuneration over and above his share of the profits. In order to put his salary of £72 per annum in context, which equalled £1.385p per week, the following wages of pottery workers in Staffordshire as recorded by Arthur Young in 1770 are relevant:[31]

Throwers	– between 9/- and 12/- (45p and 60p)
Engine Lathe men	– between 10/- and 12/- (50p and 60p)
Gilders (men)	– 12/- (60p)
Gilders (women)	– 7/6 (35p)
Painters	– between 10/- and 12/- (50p and 60p).

John Green’s salary was therefore at least double and even treble that of the individual ‘hands-on’ workers at that period when, in the north of England, a skilled craftsman in the building trades was receiving 10/- (50p) a week.[32] In the same year Josiah Wedgwood in a letter to his partner Thos. Bentley stated:[33] “I can have hands in plenty [*i.e.* painters of useful wares] at 12/- to 14/- a week (60p to 70p).”

John Green with a newly-built house, a comfortable salary and dividends as a shareholder would therefore have every inducement to see that the Leeds Pottery would turn out to be a success. To hold such a position was a privilege and indicates that the other partners, all of whom were older and experienced businessmen, obviously trusted him to have the skills and qualities necessary to fulfil his roll on their behalf in this venture in which all had invested considerable amounts of capital, each one fourteenth share being equivalent to almost seven years of John Green's salary.

It is also interesting to note that the Agreement describes William Hartley as being " ... of Bradley in the parish of Colne in the County of Lancaster Gentleman ..." thus indicating that he was not then resident in the Leeds area. Article 11 also states that the original partners " ... have already Erected and are now Erecting and Building several Erections and Buildings at the expense of the said Partnership ... to which the said William Hartley hath paid his proportional share of the expenses ...". This statement shows that the Pottery was expanding and the inclusion of the reference to Wm. Hartley indicates, as stated earlier, pages 27-28, that his input of capital was not above that invested by the other partners, in proportion that is to his two fourteenth shares.

One article of agreement which on the face of it must have seemed quite reasonable when drawn up was to prove a millstone round the necks of future partners, namely No. 15. As partners died and their shares descended to their heirs it is obvious that the surviving partners would have no control over who could become partners. Moreover, as time went by, it would also be obvious that the number of parties who had acquired an interest in the shares of the partnership would increase the difficulty of making any sensible management decisions. By 1842 there were no fewer than 46 persons who had some claim, as trustees or by descent, from the 18th century partners. The saying: "you can choose your friends but not your relations" would certainly reverberate through the minds of many of the partners in the 19th century.

Most eventualities, however, seem to have been adequately covered including the requirement to hold regular bi-monthly meetings – on the first Wednesdays in the specified months at 11 o'clock. Unfortunately there is presently no knowledge that any minute books from such meetings have survived. Llewellynn Jewitt does record that he had examined such books and reported that they were meticulously kept.[34]

From the date of this Agreement the partnership traded under the firm of Humble, Hartley Greens & Company. A full transcript of the Articles of Agreement will be found at Appendix I.

William Hartley 1751 - 1808

So much praise and acclaim has been written about William Hartley by recent writers that it is essential to publish the facts so far as they are evident from extant archive material. From the Articles of Agreement, dated 1st of January 1776 it is obvious that he had become a partner either at that date or shortly before by purchasing his two one-fourteenth shares from Richard Humble, William being only 24 years of age.

In reading through all the known publications which mention the Leeds Pottery it is interesting to note that he is barely mentioned by the early writers, save to record his name as a partner :-

Joseph Marryat – 1850.   Llewellynn Jewitt – 1865 & 1878.   Arthur Hurst – 1922.
Wm. Chaffers – 1863.   Oxley Grabham – 1916.

The Kidsons, in 1892, were the first to write comments about him: page 18, – "... Mr. William Hartley, a man of much energy and business ability, had joined the concern ..." – a statement made without giving any inkling of a source of evidence for making such an assertion; more was to flow from their pens :- "At the death of William Hartley, which occurred sometime about 1818 – 20, the whole business, which he had so carefully built up, collapsed ...". And page 26, " ... After the death of Mr. Hartley, the firm appears to have lost the old spirit of artistic emulation which it once possessed and things appeared to go a little wrong; disputes were frequent among the numerous partners, and about 1820 the concern was thrown into Chancery." That there were disputes among the partners and that it was involved with the Court of Chancery is quite correct, see page 53 *et seq*. The date of William Hartley's death is wrong by at least ten years, he died on the 30th of January 1808. The Kidsons, by giving the date 1818–20 and following it with their assertion that after it the pottery declined, therefore wrongly assumed that its success must *ipso facto* have been solely due to his influence. By now correctly giving the date of his death, the prop to their assumptions has been removed and they fall unsupported. Unfortunately when unsupported 'statements' are published these may then be quoted and elaborated still further by successive writers, causing them to become an accepted component within the literature of the Pottery.

I have been very fortunate in finding and using previously untapped sources of archive material and it is from these, together with accurate fully-sourced material already published, that I am now able to lay before the reader the following. William Hartley was born in August 1751, the third offspring of George and Esther Hartley of Bradley Hall, parish of Colne, Lancashire. For many generations the Hartleys had been copyhold yeoman farmers on the manor of Colne and Ightenhill in Lancashire.[35] We know nothing about William's early life until, in his 22nd year, on the 20th of March 1773, William Hartley, gentleman, of Marsden in the Diocese of Chester, a bachelor, obtained a license from the Archbishop of York's Surrogate to marry Miss Sarah Booth of Parkhill in the parish of Calverley aged "21 years and upwards a spinster",[36] but the marriage did not take place. I have been unable to discover any material which explains why this marriage did not take place; I will leave it to the reader to ponder on the following events.

Sarah's father, Jonathan Booth, had died and was buried at Calverley on the 28th of October 1772, just 5 months prior to when the marriage should have taken place. The obituary notice in *The Leeds Intelligencer* of 3rd of November 1772 described him as "an eminent woolstapler at Idle near Bradford". Jonathan died intestate. Assuming that the above marriage should have taken place on the 21st of March 1773 it is interesting to find that on the 25th of March, Mary (Polly) Booth, Sarah's mother "renounced the taking forth of Letters of Administration in and for the Goods and Chattels rights and credits of the said late Jonathan Booth". On the 7th of May "Admon. of the Goods etc., of Jonathan Booth late of Calverley deceased was granted to Sarah Booth daughter and only child above the age of 21 years, Mary Booth widow and relict renouncing."[37]

Mary Booth, widow aged 40 of Calverley married Richard Brooke aged 40 of Baildon at Baildon on the 13th of October 1775 and William Hartley, now "of the Pottery near Leeds, Merchant" obtained another license to marry the same Sarah Booth on the 7th of May 1777, which marriage did take place. I feel sure that Jane Austin could have written quite a fascinating novel around such events.

From William's marriage were born two daughters, Sarah Ann who did not marry and Esther Maria who did marry but had no children, and William (1790 – 1833) who would succeed his father as a partner. Sarah, William's wife, died in 1797 and William married a second time to Mrs. Ann Hayes at Preston, Lancashire in 1800.

William's father George Hartley died in 1791 and by his will,[37](made 23rd of February 1791) proved and passed at York on the 14th of September, he left, among other bequests, his copyhold estates, via the Manor Court of Colne and Ightenhill, to his son William, £500 to his daughter Betty, and his freehold estate at Earby, parish of Thornton, Yorkshire, to his son Richard. Unfortunately when William, as executor, produced a 'Declaration instead of an Inventory' of his father's possessions he stated that " ... the whole personal estate and effects ... would not amount to the sum of four hundred and fifty pounds" – the will is annotated "*under 300l.*". Thus there were insufficient funds to satisfy the bequests in the will, a deficit which William made good some seventeen years later when he left his sister Betty £500.

On the 25th of April 1793 William Hartley was appointed to the Hunslet Workhouse Committee and on the 20th of June that year the minute book records: "Ordered that Wm. Hartley have an apprentice."[28]

He did not confine his business interests solely to the Leeds Pottery. We find him being involved with many property transactions as recorded in the WYAS (Wakefield) Deeds Registry, for example in a quarry at Idle in partnership with others including John Green. In 1784 he was involved with a cotton-spinning mill at Marsden, Lancashire:- "erected and run by William Hartley of Leeds and Colne" in partnership with his brother Richard and four others.[35]

Further proof of his interest in property in his native county is that on the 19th of January 1795 he insured six tenements under one roof at Colne for a mere £130, together with a stable nearby for £20, a house for £250, a bakehouse and two tenements under one roof for a further £100.[38]

An insurance of a more personal nature was taken out on the 2nd of April 1801:[39]

> "William Hartley of the Pottery at Leeds in the County of York Merchant
> On his Household Goods wearing apparel
> Printed Books & plate in his now Dwelling
> house only situate as aforesaid Brick & Slated
> not exceeding Three Hundred pounds   £300"

This policy may therefore coincide with his move into John Green's former house at the Pottery, adjoining the one occupied by Savile Green.

From the pleadings and evidence taken in the first case before the Court of Chancery, see page 56, it would appear that after John Green's bankruptcy William Hartley and Savile Green, the two most senior partners either assumed or were elected joint managers "subject to the orders and resolutions of the majority". I write "it would appear" deliberately, as the matter is not as clear as one would wish in order to state categorically what the situation was. In the pleadings of George Hanson and Jas. Winter Butterworth, *et al* :

> "... at a meeting holden after the Bankruptcy of the said John Green the said Savile Green and William Hartley
> were appointed by the other partners or a majority of them to act in the place of the said John Green in the
> management of the said business and at another of the said meetings prior to that at which the said Savile Green
> and William Hartley were appointed managers of the said business it had been determined to erect two
> dwellinghouses upon or near to the premises ... for the accommodation of the partners having the management
> thereof..."

The second part of the statement is obviously untrue as the two houses had been built and paid for by Richard Humble when the Pottery was first built, see page 17, and see also the Insurance Policy page 18: "On a building not yet finished near but separate intended for two Dwellings to be Occupied by the said Messrs Green ...". As we see that the second part was partially incorrect how much credence can we attach to the first part? Given that William Hartley undoubtedly did occupy John Green's old house and given that we know that the partners sought and employed a practical potter from Staffordshire to take the place of John Green so far as the practical aspect of his work was concerned then it may have been the case that Savile Green and William Hartley, as resident and senior partners, would merely see to the implementation of the wishes of the other partners in consultation with the advice of the practical potter, who would not have been necessary if they had had all the knowledge, skill and ability of John Green.

Evidence that William Hartley never did hold a managerial position comes from evidence, given under oath, to the Court of Chancery, by Ebenezer Green and Mary Ackroyd, see page 58 :

" ... the said William Hartley being appointed to the situation of corresponding clerk by the express agreement with all the partners at the time he first came into the said concern and the said Savile Green being employed in the said capacity of Book-keeper long previous to his becoming a partner by Richard Humble who had the authority given him by the original Articles [see Articles of Agreement at Appendix I, No. 12] ... AND these Defendants further answering deny that the said William Hartley and Savile Green were to their knowledge and belief appointed by the said partners or a majority of them to act in the place of the said John Green or otherwise in the management of the said business except that they believe they were continued to be one of them Book-keeper and the other corresponding clerk ..."

The above statement was certainly true so far as Savile Green was concerned as we saw earlier, page 17; his signature as a witness was on the Indenture of November 1770, seven years before he became a partner. If we consider the circumstances when William Hartley became a partner, by the 1st of January 1776, here was a young man aged only 24, styling himself 'Gentleman', joining a group of older partners, the youngest of which, John Green at 33 was a Master Potter who had the "Direction and Management of the said Work" – the other partners all very experienced businessmen – Joshua Green aged 56 and Richard Humble aged 61. This would hardly be the scene from which to build a plausible scenario centred around William Hartley as has been done by some previous writers who, without any evidence to support their statements, have given him the credit for not only the " ... increasing prosperity ..." but also " ... the style and manufacture of the wares themselves ...". Leaving aside the question of whether or not William Hartley was 'elected' or 'assumed' the management of the Pottery after John Green's bankruptcy, the most significant point is that neither of the parties to the above quotations gave any hint that, before John Green's bankruptcy, William Hartley had held any managerial status in the Leeds Pottery.

By the 25th of March 1806 William Hartley was very ill. This is born out by three pieces of evidence. The first being that on that date he signed his Will and his signature is very 'shaky'. The second piece of evidence is in a letter from Savile Green, junior, to his Sister of the same date and written from the Leeds Pottery :

"Mr. Hartley who was at Leeds and cheerful on Saturday Evening was on Sunday taken ill and I am this morning told by Mr. Dickinson that his complaint is an inflammation on or about his lungs which he and Dr Walker think will prove mortal in the course of a very short time if a very great and unexpected alteration does not immediately take place."

And in another letter from the same to his sister, written from St. Petersburg and dated the 6th of September 1806 :

"I was really extremely sorry to hear Mr. H was so poorly and begin to think I shall see him no more ...".

William Hartley died on the 30th of January 1808, *The Leeds Intelligencer*, of the 8th of February reported :

"On Saturday week died, at his residence near this town, Wm Hartley, Esq; upwards of 30 years a principal acting partner in the Leeds Pottery, not less distinguished for his honour and integrity as a man of business, than he was esteemed in the circles of social life."

Note that the above described him as "a" not "the" principal acting partner, and "acting" partner, signifying that as a partner he worked at the Pottery and was therefore not an 'otherwise-occupied' shareholder as John Barwick, surgeon, and Henry Ackroyd, fulling miller, had been.

He was buried in his native Lancashire, at Colne Parish Church, the registers recording that he died of "a decline". By his will, passed the 14th of June 1808[37] he left an estate valued at "under £7,500". Some four years after his death, on the 20th of June 1812, *The Leeds Mercury* announced the sale of his furniture etc. :

"To Be Sold by Auction By Messrs LUMB

On the Premises at North-Town-End, on Friday the Twenty-sixth Day of June 1812

THE Neat and Modern HOUSEHOLD FURNITURE of the late WM HARTLEY, Esq.

comprising Mahogany Dining, Card and other Tables; Chairs Chest of Drawers,

Desk and Book-Case, Wash-hand Stands, &c. A set of handsome

Drawing-Room Painted Chairs, with Cushions and

Covers; an excellent Sofa, Pier and Swing Glasses, Floor and Stair Carpets an

Eight Day's Clock, Mangle, and a variety of Kitchen Requisites,

and other useful Articles of Furniture.

Also, A very good GIG and HARNESS; a Capital Three Light Hot Bed Frame, which will be

sold precisely at One o'Clock. Also, a very good Pillion; a Set of Surgical Instruments;

and a good set of Maps, nearly new, with a Mahogany Frame.

The Sale of Furniture to commence at Half-past Ten o'Clock."

Two more partners join the Company

By an Indenture of 13th August 1777, Richard Humble sold a fourteenth share in the Leeds Pottery to Samuel Wainewright, Gentleman, of Ferrybridge for the sum of £450 and, from the deed of the 19th of February 1781 we learn that on the same day, i.e., the 13th of August 1777, Richard Humble sold another fourteenth share to the Company's Book-keeper Savile Green, both shares sold on the terms set out in the Articles of Agreement. The shareholding, divided into fourteen parts or shares, now stood as follows :

Richard Humble – 3	Joshua Green – 2	John Green – 2	Savile Green – 1
Wm. Hartley – 2	Henry Ackroyd – 2	John Barwick – 1	Samuel Wainewright – 1.

Savile Green.

I can well remember the day, sometime in the late 1950s, when I first became interested in local potteries, consulting the entry for Mexborough in the Rev. Joseph Hunter's *South Yorkshire* Vol I, 1828, and finding the following entry in his pedigree of the Savile family :

> "Catherine w of ...Green of Swinton, and mother of Savile Green of Leeds; bap. 26 Apr. 1709."

It was therefore not too difficult to discover the entry in the relevant register of baptisms :

> "12th Sept.1743 – Savile son of John Green of Swinton."

The Savile family with its coat of arms: *Argent, on a bend sable three owls of the field*, was a well known gentry family going back many generations prior to this branch settling in Mexborough sometime in the early seventeenth century. Joseph Hunter introduces the family at Mexborough thus :

> "At what is called the Hall ... flourished for three or four generations a branch of the wide-spread family of Savile. The first who settled here was Samuel Savile whose descent was from that part of the family known as Savile of Hullenedge. His immediate ancestor was of Wakefield, where he practiced as an attorney, ... He

16. SAVILE GREEN, senior. (1743 – 1805). Pastel portrait by John Russell, R.A., (unsigned), see notes to Plate 14. Below his hands on the table is a letter addressed to Hartley Greens & Co., from St. Petersburg. Still in its original frame it is a proud possession of one of the sitter's descendants. The portrait measures: twenty-four and a quarter inches by twenty-nine and a quarter inches.

himself was a student and fellow of King's college, Cambridge, and is described as 'a good philosopher, mathematician, and poet.' He went as secretary to James earl of Carlisle, in his embassy to France, in the reign of James I. After long service and attendance at court, he married and retired into the country, settling at Mexborough.

In the time of the Civil Wars he suffered much for the king, being imprisoned at Hull, and in other ways ..."

In the church at Mexborough are some splendid examples of seventeenth century monuments to the family.

Savile's father *John* and Joshua Green's father *Joshua* were brothers. See the pedigree on page 594.

Apart from his baptism nothing is known about his early life except that when he married his first wife Mary Taylor, by license at Haxey, Lincolnshire, on the 19th of July 1766, Savile described himself on the Marriage Bond and Allegation as a "Mercer and Linen draper". Mary died in "childbed" the 28th of September 1774 and I have not been able to trace any children of the marriage. Savile married the second time – Sarah Parkin, widow, at Sheffield Parish Church on the 4th of June 1775, again by license and with his neighbour John Green acting as both his bondsman and witness to his marriage. From this marriage were born two sons and a daughter, none of whom survived infancy. For his third wife he married Rhoda Green the daughter of his cousin William, by license, at Rothwell on the 13th of September 1784. From this marriage were born two sons and four daughters, one son with the Christian name Savile and all the others with Savile as their second name. Obviously old Savile was very proud of his maternal ancestors.

One of the valuable archive sources from which I am able to add considerable flesh to the bones of the history of the Leeds Pottery is the collection of letters passed down through the descendants of Sarah Savile Green. Most of these are from Savile junior but a few are from Savile senior. From these it is very obvious that he was a very kind and affectionate husband and father as the following will show.

This is the end of a letter to his wife then staying with his cousin William Green's daughter, Lydia Gilpin, at Somerset Place, London. It is undated but is from the early 1790s :

"... with respect to the Dr Bairns, Mary I think gains strength in her paddling and looks better than when you left home – Kate is pretty much the same but frequently when vexed wants me to fetch her Mubby home – Savile and Sarah are very unruly and the Girls make very heavy Complaints of their behaviour to them I believe there are faults on both sides – However, on the whole we are, thank God all in good health and I sincerely wish that this may find you and all friends in the same state to whom my Love, thanks and best Wishes, Pray answer me <u>in your Ladyship's own Scrawl,</u> by return of Post, and say When you will leave Town and by what Coach. I think you will not find a better Conveyance than the Rockingham. Inform me at same time how much I am indebted to Brother Gilpin for his Advances I desire you will furnish yourself while in Town with everything you wish and in so doing you will oblige my Dearest and only Dr Rhoda

Your faithful and affectionate Husband

Savile Green

The aforegoing wrote on Monday morning before ½ past nine o'Clock –

<u>Monday noon. Dinner ended on Cold boiled beef.</u> Savile says I must say Mother come home and bring me a Prayer book. Sarah says Mother I don't like you stay so long I have got Savile's stocking off and have begun of the other, I want a new hat and a Common Prayer book – Savile desires to have added a box of Soldiers such as Miss Roebuck gave him if you have money but if you have not you are not to buy them Kate says "I want to meet my Mother" and sends a kiss – and Old Savile Says Pray God bless you and Preserve you till We meet and see each other with Comfort. ..."

Savile died the 17th of May 1805 followed by his wife in October of the same year. By his will, made the 4th of May 1805, he left an estate valued at under £7,500.[37]

Samuel Wainewright, I

Very little is known about Samuel Wainewright except his relationship to other partners. His son Samuel II, 1792 – 1834, became a partner via his father's will. Samuel I had a sister Eleanor who married George Hanson in 1783 and who was a partner from the 1st of January 1783. By his will he left under £4000.[37] Thomas Wainewright, Postmaster of Ferrybridge, who became a partner in 1781, was brother to Samuel and Eleanor, (see page 596).

Richard Humble Retires from the Partnership

On the 20th of February 1781 *The Leeds Intelligencer* announced the retirement of Richard Humble from the partnership in the Leeds Pottery, which from the 19th of February would trade under the name of Hartley Greens & Co.

If any of the founding partners could claim to be the 'father' of the Leeds Pottery then surely Richard Humble was that person. As the reader will have noted, Richard Humble purchased Rushy Pasture and invested far more capital into the partnership than any one of the other partners, he built the two dwelling houses for messrs Savile Green and John Green and he also had "the appointment of all Stewards Agents Book keepers Managers and other necessary Supervisors". Now, at the age of 64 he had decided to retire and hand over the running of the Pottery to all the other partners who would henceforth exercise those responsibilities by voting, each with a power limited to the number of shares that each held. Thus apart from "the Direction and Management of the Work and the appointment of all Workmen and labourers" which would continue the sole responsibility of John Green, no other partner would have such an influence as Richard Humble had kept to himself.

The Articles of Agreement[5] dated the 19th of February 1781 by which Richard Humble ceased to be a partner do contain some relevant information for the account of the development and history of the Leeds Pottery. They begin by reciting the Indentures of Deeds and Agreements from which it is noted that the first partners had, prior to the Indenture of the 22nd of November 1770, " ... agreed to become copartners together and jointly ... for the term of 99 years" and that articles of co-partnership had been made dated the 5th of November 1771; unfortunately these do not seem to have survived and were possibly destroyed after the articles of the 1st of January 1776 had been drawn up and signed.

The Agreement of the 19th of February 1781 specifies that Richard Humble would transfer the fee simple of the site and buildings of the Leeds Pottery and all its equipment and trade etc., on or before the 24th of December 1781, provided that they, the other partners, had paid him or " ... secured to be paid to the said Richard Humble ..." the sum of £5,403-5-0d.

Included in this sum is the £1000 with interest which Joshua Green, John Barwick, John Green and Henry Ackroyd had by way of a mortgage from Samuel Ellis, see page 20, and which since the death of Samuel Ellis had been vested in Richard Humble his son-in-law. This sum was then paid to Richard Humble with interest amounting to £1,032-10-0d on 28th of February 1781, together with £403-5-0d paid by William Hartley, Joshua Green, John Barwick, Henry Ackroyd, John Green, Savile Green and Samuel Wainewright, at the signing of the agreement. Followed on the 4th of December 1781 by the full remaining partners paying the further sum of £1,036-14-7d (including interest).

The remaining £2000 was secured to Richard Humble by assigning to Nathaniel Clayton of Newcastle-upon-Tyne, Gentleman, "all and singular the said Premises comprised in the said term of 99 years for and during the now residue of such term In trust ... for the further and better securing the said sum of 2000*l* ... agreed to be continued at Interest...".

The paying out of such large sums of money by the partners after the first eleven years of the Pottery is a further indication that it had certainly become a sound financial success by this date.

During the same year, 1781, Thomas Wainewright, Postmaster of Ferrybridge joined the partnership. Once again from the articles of this Agreement[5] dated the 27th of August 1781, we are able to make definitive statements. Thus we learn that the partners, after the withdrawal of Richard Humble, had agreed to reduce the number of shares to twelve, still retaining the same individual proportions as before. Thomas Wainewright came to an agreement for the purchase of one moity or half part of one twelfth share not only in "such Partnership Trade and Business and of the Profits thereof but also of one moity of a Twelfth part of the Freehold and Inheritance of the said close of land called Rushy Pasture ... at the price or sum of nine hundred pounds ...". The partners therefore agreed to the first part of the transaction taking effect from the "1st day of January now last past ...". They also agreed that when they had acquired the freehold of the property that they would convey one half of one twelfth share in this to him. Thomas Wainewright agreed to pay £700 on the 10th of October next and £200 on the 5th of January next.

Thus the balance between the partners was not altered. This Indenture also gives credence to Ron Morley's suggestion[40] that there were separate shares for business and property: for example Henry Ackroyd's two fourteenths meant that he held two fourteenths shares in the trade and business as well as two fourteenths in the property.

Following Richard Humble's withdrawal from the partnership on the 19th of February 1781 he acknowledged the payment of all money due to him by the remaining partners by an indenture of the 24th of December 1781, except for the sum of £2000 which he bargained and sold to William Wrigglesworth of Middleton, Gentleman, on condition that he leased it to the partners for 1000 years. Then, with regard to Richard Humble's three fourteenth shares in the partnership, these he divided into eleven parts and assigned them as follows to the other partners : William Hartley 2, Joshua Green 2, John Barwick 1, Henry Ackroyd 2, John Green 2, Savile Green 1, Samuel Wainewright 1.

The shares, now divided into twelve parts stood as follows :

William Hartley 2, Joshua Green 2, Henry Ackroyd 2, John Green 2, John Barwick 1, Savile Green 1, Samuel Wainewright 1, Thomas Wainewright one half of one twelfth (by now in both the business and the property). One other half of one twelfth share, in abeyance, was sold to George Hanson of Leeds, Linen Draper, for £1,100 by Articles of Agreement dated 28th of April 1783,[5] he agreeing to pay £300 at the time of signing the Agreement but the partners agreed that he would be a partner from the 1st of January 1783 " ... subject to such Clauses, Covenants, restrictions and Agreements as are mentioned and comprised in the ... Articles of Partnership of 1st January 1776 ...", £300 the 13th of May next (1783), and the remaining £300 on or by the 25th of December 1785 with lawful interest.[41] Justus Christian Ruperti witnessed this document.

I have not been able to ascertain a precise date when the partners decided to divide their shares into twenty-four parts but it was most likely around the time that George Hanson joined the company: in that Agreement 'one half of one twelfth share' is mentioned and later on 'one twenty-fourth share' is mentioned which would be a far more logical way of describing them. The share holding now stood as follows, into 24 parts : William Hartley 4, Joshua Green 4. Henry Ackroyd 4, John Green 4, John Barwick 2, Savile Green 2, Samuel Wainewright 2, Thomas Wainewright 1, George Hanson 1. We know that George Hanson paid £1,100 for his one share, (see the previous paragraph), therefore if we multiply this by twenty-four, being the total number of shares in the partnership, we see that in 1783 the total shareholding was worth £26,400, which is equivalent to somewhere in the region of £2,517,504 in 2003. (Source: Jim O'Donoghue, Louise Goulding and Grahame Allen – *Economic Trends*, Office for National Statistics, March 2004, pages 41 and 43 "Table 1. Composite Price Index, 1750 to 2003").

The Thorp Arch Flint Mill

Reference was made earlier, page 20 to the Pottery grinding its flints by means of a windmill on the site of the Pottery and of the problems most likely encountered by this method, also that the partners took a lease, from 1775, of a water driven mill, presumably on the river Aire. As the Pottery increased its production, see the records of its coal consumption in Chapter 7, maintaining a reliable supply of ground flint would be a necessity. It should not come as a surprise, therefore, to learn that the partners would seek to ensure a constant supply entirely under their control.

Preserved in the Leeds Archives, under reference: TA3/2/2, is an agreement made the 1st of June 1782 between Wilmer Gossip of Thorp Arch, Esq., and the partners in "...the Pottery Manufactury at Leeds ..." whereby the partners agreed with the said Wilmer Gossip :

"... that they will erect and build at their own Expense a Dwellinghouse and mill of stone and to be covered with Roundhay Slate upon a piece or parcel of Ground of the said Wilmer Gossip called or known by the name of Whinny Flats ... contiguous with the River Wharfe; and also a Mill Dam of Stone extending from ... Whinny Flats over and cross the ... River from the North to the South side ... upon the lands of Mr John Allen at a place called Lady Head Land in Woodhouse Farm on the South side of the River in the township of Clifford and Parish of Bramham ... and that they will furnish the same with all Wheels Engines Cloughs Floodgates Races Hecks Sluices and other proper Gears Implements Machinery and Materials for the grinding of Flint Stone for Manufacturing Pottery Ware and such other articles only as are hereinafter mentioned according to a plan hereunto annexed [which has not survived] ... and that they will also erect a Bye Clough or Salmon Heck adjoining ... and of catching Salmon and other fish one eighth in weight and value of such ... to be appropriated for the benefit of ... Wilmer Gossip and the other seven eighths thereof for the benefit of the parties ... Wilmer Gossip agrees to pay them ... 700*l* towards defraying the Expenses"... [The partners agree that before 13 February next that the Building is to be completed and that they are to be allowed to get stone and lime from Wilmer Gossip's quarry called Whinny Flat Quarry and all buildings to be covered with Roundhay or Woodhouse slate. The mill to be used for] ..."the grinding Flint Stone or other materials necessary for manufacturing of Pottery Glass and China Wares Mustard or Tobacco or for sawing of Timber or for preparing any Article not being Paper or Oil for the use of the Woollen Manufactury and for no other purpose without the License and Consent in writing of ... Wilmer Gossip" ... [land surrounding etc] ... "For a term of 21 years full and under the yearly rent of 75*l*" ... [To keep in good repair and maintain the premises also stiles and hedges, gates, bridges, fences, drains and ditches ... In times of drought or scarcity of water or dry seasons shall] ... "at two o'clock in a Morning and continue the same so shut or set down until five o'clock in the same morning under the penalty of ten Pounds in any one morning in times of such scarcity" ... [may not allow more than five of their servants to] ... "lodge or inhabit in the Township of Thorp Arch at one and the same time" [Each party binds itself in the penal sum of £1000 for breach of contract.]

Signed by: Wm Hartley   Joshua Green   John Green   Henry Ackroyd
John Barwick   Savile Green   Sam. Wainewright
Thos Wainewright – in the presence of :- J.C. Ruperti, Geo Hobson
Stamped and sealed in the presence of :- Michael Wood, Leeds Pottery
                                          Samuel Milns, Hunslet Lane."

This is the first evidence that I have found of Justus Christian Ruperti being at the Pottery, a man whose presence, ability and contribution to the wellbeing of the Pottery would become evident in the second decade of the nineteenth century

The partners would appear to have negotiated a very good contract, not only the not inconsiderable sum of £700 from Wilmer Gossip but also free stone and lime from his quarry nearby. The restrictive covenants regarding the limited use during night hours in periods of drought was on account of Wilmer Gossip having other water mills further downstream.

The added advantage of fresh salmon from the river is referred to in one of Savile Green junior's letters of the 26th of March 1806. It was written from the Leeds Pottery and addressed to his sister Sarah, then staying at Thorp Arch :

" ... I should like to taste a bit of Salmon but when I come shall play the D...L if Mother Mason does not suit my guts and advise you to do the same ..."

From this and other correspondence which I have examined it would appear that the partners and their families used the Flint Mill Grange as a healthy place to retreat to from the less salubrious areas in and around Leeds.

17. THE WATER-POWERED FLINT MILL AT THORP ARCH. From Plate 4 of the Kidsons' account of the Leeds Pottery, published in 1892. The building still stands looking very much as it did when this photograph was taken. It has been converted, fairly recently, into a private residence with very little in the way of alterations to its external appearance.

18. END ELEVATION OF THE FLINT MILL, as published by the Kidsons. It was built very close to the rock face and just out of sight, behind the tree branches to the right, is the entrance to a wide tunnel which gave access to the other end of the building for horses and carts etc. The fenestration on the end of the building remains virtually as seen here.

19. VIEW ACROSS THE FLINT-MILL WEIR. – " ... a Mill Dam of Stone extending from ... Whinny Flats over and cross the ... River from the North to the South side ..." (see p. 35).
This photograph was taken in the summer of 2003 and shows the mill still in the rural setting in which it was built in the early 1780s. *Photographed by kind permission of Mrs. A. Everett.*

We must now turn to Llewellynn Jewitt for some more information regarding this outpost of the Pottery. On page 470 of Volume I of his *Ceramic Art* he recounts how a team of four horses was kept employed solely in taking the raw flints to the mill at Thorp Arch, approximately ten miles distant from the Pottery, and returning with the ground flint. Jewitt was however wrong in stating that when at Thorp Arch, the same horses worked the mill, for as we have seen, the mill was water-powered. Jewitt continues his account by informing us that the Leeds Pottery continued using this mill until 1814 after which the old windmill at the Pottery, which had been converted to a corn mill, was converted to a steam driven flintmill by the Leeds firm of Fenton, Murray & Company, and that such mill was still in use at the time he was writing, c.1865.

If the date of 1814 as given by Jewitt is correct it would mean that the partners' original twenty-one year lease had been extended by a further ten years. Corroborative evidence for this date being fairly reliable is that *The Leeds Mercury* of the 10th of February 1816 carried the following notice :

"Flint-Mill-Grange, near Wetherby
To be SOLD, by AUCTION,
At Flint-Mill-Grange, near Wetherby, on Monday and Tuesday, the 26th and 27th of February, 1816,
ALL the HOUSEHOLD FURNITURE there the Property of Messrs, Hartley Greens, and co. consisting of Four-Post and Camp Bedsteads, excellent Feather Beds and Bedding; Pier and Swing Glasses; Mahogany and other Chests of Drawers; Mahogany Wash-Hand Stands, and Night Tables; Mahogany and Elm Chairs; Floor, Stair, and Bedside Carpeting; and Eight Days' Clock; an Excellent Mangle; Brewing and Dairy Utensils; Kitchen requisites; Table and Bed Linen; Glass and Earthenware. Also, all the FARMING IMPLEMENTS, consisting of Carts, Waggons, Ploughs, Harrow, Horse Gears, &c. &c. – likewise Two good Black Colts and a Milch Cow. N.B. The Household Furniture will be sold on Monday the 26th, and the Farming Implements on Tuesday the 27th. The Sale to Commence each Day at Ten o'Clock."

20. FLINT MILL GRANGE stands on higher ground behind the mill. It was built by Hartley Greens & Company and used by the partners and their families as a holiday residence with a resident housekeeper. The well-proportioned symmetrical Georgian house with its two wings has an extensive range of farm buildings at its rear. It is still a private house situated in a delightful secluded rural setting which cannot have changed materially since it was first built and when the partners rented 200 acres of farm land around it.

After the Leeds Pottery vacated the Mill and other premises the mill was converted to a corn mill and let on a fourteen-year lease from 1st of January 1819. A notice in *The Leeds Intelligencer* of Monday the 12th of May 1817 announced :

"To be let, and Entered to Immediately

A very Comfortable and well built

DWELLING HOUSE

with extensive Domestic and Farm Offices called

FLINT MILL GRANGE, most delightfully situate

on the Banks of the River Wharfe;

together with a compact FARM

of 200 Acres or thereabouts and a

Capital Water Corn Mill, ..."

The references to the sale of farming implements etc., and two horses and a cow together with the letting of a farm of 200 acres would suggest that the Leeds Pottery had run this farm in conjunction with the Flint Mill. Most probably this would have been used for supplying them with fodder for their horses; the Pottery had stabling for twenty, hay would have been needed and oats for the fodder and the straw from the oats used for packing the wares. It would also appear that there was a resident housekeeper at the Grange in the person of "Mother Mason"

Both the Flint Mill and the Flint Mill Grange are still standing. The Flint Mill Grange was advertised for letting in the *Yorkshire Post* of the 26th of January 2002 at an asking rent of £1,250 per calendar month. The Flint Mill has been converted into a splendid residence which still retains some of the original gearing and shafts in the property as well a water wheel though probably not the original one. Externally both properties are still very much as when they were built, the Grange still retaining quite an extensive range of farm buildings at the rear. See Plates 17 to 20.

Design Books

In 1783 the first recorded Design Book was published in German followed by the same in French in 1785 and in English in 1786, all with the same designs of 184 articles, only the title page and explanatory notes being in the languages mentioned. Another impression of the same designs, with none added and in the same three languages, was published in 1794, (see pages 115-133). The Leeds Partners were following the example set by Josiah Wedgwood who had published a smaller catalogue in 1774 – *A Catalogue of the Different Articles of Queen's Ware* ... .

Bricks

In the same year that the first *Design Book* was published, 1783, the Partnership was also producing and selling bricks. The accounts of the Middleton Colliery (MC 44) record: "18 June, pd. Messrs Hartley Greens & Co Viz ... For 2110 fire bricks to the engine at 1d pr brick £8-15-10." See also the reference under Stephen Chappel in Chapter 6, page 76.

Financial Success

Evidence that the Pottery was financially sound and paying handsome dividends to its partners may be deduced from the activities of two of its senior partners, William Hartley and John Green.

In 1784 William Hartley invested, with partners, in the building and running of a cotton-spinning mill in his native Marsden in Lancashire, (see page 30). John Green, in 1785, commenced with partners the building of two Ale and Porter Breweries, one in Hunslet and one in Rotherham, together with a new Mansion House for himself in Hunslet which, together with its contents he insured for £2,400. See page 25 and my book *The Don Pottery 1801 - 1893*, pages 21 - 22. Both William Hartley and John Green had therefore built up enough capital to embark on these ventures and both must also have had enough confidence in the continuing success and progress of the Pottery. It also follows that the Leeds Pottery was not in want of working capital or surely such money would have been channelled there.

Llewellynn Jewitt records[42] that he had noted from an examination of the factory's accounts that in 1791 the "yearly balance then struck amounted to over £51,500."

Further evidence is to be found in the transcript of the journals of John Platt, mason architect of Rotherham and sometime a partner with William Fenny in the Rotherham Pottery.[43]

In 1791 we find the following entries :

"19 Jan. At Leeds Pottery measuring & valuing Buildings &c for Messrs Hartley & Greens. To Feb 27 at ye Pottery, flint mills & other works there Valuing, 24 days.

10 Oct. Finished ye Valuation of the Leeds Pottery to Mr Calvert amounting to £53,860-14-8¾ my bill & part Expenses £51-19-6."

The above valuation would be equivalent to £5,136,159 in 2003. (Source: O'Donoghue, Goulding & Allen). The reader will see that the partners, in 1778, had insured all their property in Hunslet for a mere £4,600, (see page 40).

The Swinton Pottery

Linking with the previous section and adding yet more evidence to what has been written there is the event which took place in 1785, namely the coming together of the Swinton Pottery and the Leeds Pottery. The Swinton Pottery was founded in 1745 and as we have seen on page 25, John Green had worked there in the 1760s and may have held a managerial or book-keeping position as he signed an invoice to Wentworth House dated c.1768.[22] Until 1785 The Swinton Pottery had traded under the firm of Bingley Wood & Co; by May 1787 it was trading under the firm of 'Greens Bingley & Co.'.[44] Strangely although there are several entries in the Wentworth Woodhouse accounts to this firm, all the payments of rent for the Pottery are recorded as being from "Bingley Mr Thos & Co", that is from 1785 up to 1806–07 (Wentworth Estate's Rent Book: WWM A302).

It is a great pity that correspondence regarding the reasons for and origins of this joint partnership, together with any legal documents, including the Articles of Agreement, do not appear to have survived in the Wentworth Woodhouse Muniments. That they did exist in 1806 is shown by their being mentioned in a letter from Charles Bowns, of the 16th of March, addressed to Earl Fitzwilliam, Grosvenor Square, London.[45] What has survived are various entries in the Annual Rent Books of the estate from WWM A273 (1785-86) through to A304 (1807-08). From an earlier Rent Book for 1784 (WWM A272) we see that the rent being then paid was as follows:

"Bingley Thos & Co, for late Butler	£10
- do - for liberty of getting Clay	10
- do - for the Tile yard	10
- do - for the Pot Houses	11"

Thus making a total of £41 per year. From the first entry for the joint partnership a modest increase was noted, WWM A274 :

"Alterations in Tenants & Rents since the last year on the Wentworth Estate ... Swinton ...

Bingley Thos. & Co. advanced from Whitsuntide 1785 for the pottery &c

on their Contracting for a Lease thereof for 21 Years   £3-12-6"

By the end of the lease, in 1806, the rent had risen to £69-16-0d., still a very modest amount when we see how the old rent of £41 was broken down and where only £11 per year was paid in rent for the "Pot Houses".

We know who the Leeds partners were in 1785 but we have to turn to Jewitt's *Ceramic Art*, page 496 for some help regarding who constituted the "Thos. Bingley & Co". "In 1778 Mr Thomas Bingley became a principal proprietor of the Swinton works, and had for partners ... John and William Brameld, and a person named Sharpe." Thomas Bingley was a member of an old Swinton family of farmers and in 1801 was a butcher.[46] In 1778, however, William Brameld would only have been six years of age. The "person named Sharpe" was almost certainly John Sharpe, potter, and cousin of John Green.[47] It is not known exactly when John Brameld became a partner but the most likely date would be at the same time as his brother-in-law, Thomas Bingley, in 1778.

My researches have shown that when John Brameld applied to the Archbishop of York's Surrogate for a license to marry Hannah Bingley at Mexborough in August 1771, that "being Sworn on the Holy Evangelists" he gave his occupation as "Blacksmith" – the same occupation which he gave again when acting as Bondsman when Thomas Bingley applied in the same manner for a license to marry in 1780. The Rev. H.W. Quarrell, sometime vicar of Swinton, published the same occupation against John Brameld's name, which he stated to have obtained from Parish records, in the census list for 1801[46]. During research in the Wentworth Woodhouse Muniments I have discovered two other corroborative pieces of evidence to support this:

WWM A289:- "18 May 1798, Paid John Brameld for Ironwork for the

Haggerens Gate . . .   6s 1d."

WWM A291:- "Nov. 1800, Paid John Brameld for Iron Work . . .   £1-15-8d"

The second payment was for work then being undertaken on the Swinton School. Against this it must also be stated that in the Swinton parochial archives there is a list of men liable for Militia Service and who paid 6/- for a substitute in 1779[48]. In this list John Brameld's name appears and stands out, as it has his 'occupation' given – 'Potter'. The vast majority of names on this list are not given any occupation or trade. The fact that an obviously well-known Swinton man needed his occupation listing may indicate that he was now, in 1779, involved with the Pottery in some capacity, this being different from what most Swintonians would have described him as. Seeing that his father George Brameld had been a blacksmith, it is therefore feasible that John had learned his trade from his father and had become a partner in the Swinton Pottery as an investment and was working there in some managerial, non-practical-potting capacity. Thus the Brameld "Potter" dynasty started with John's son William and in due time was followed by his other sons, who would raise the Pottery to heights of excellence, through the Rockingham Works and its porcelain, which would have been unimagined by their father in the 1780s.

John Green, born 1742 and John Brameld, born 1741, emerge from the few scant records which have survived as fairly obviously on quite friendly and close terms with one another. An Indenture in the Wentworth Woodhouse Muniments dated the 23rd of September 1809 whereby John Brameld mortgaged his house and croft to Earl Fitzwilliam for £5000, shows that this property had been transferred from Jonathan Gawtress in 1793 with John Green as Trustee[49]. Some other land, acquired in 1802, had also involved John Green and which John Brameld had settled " ... to the use of the said John Green ... his heirs and assigns during the said life of the said John Brameld ...". John Brameld, with his son William, entered into partnership with John Green and others in 1801/2 when John Green founded his Don Pottery in Swinton, in the same venture the Bramelds were also shareholders in the Don Pottery's Flint Mill at Sprotbrough.[50] Lastly an extract from a letter from John Green to John Brameld, quoted by Llewellynn Jewitt in his *Ceramic Art*, Vol I, page 469, footnote. Dated the 15th of April 1788 the letter concerns John Green informing John Brameld of the death of the Leeds partner, Henry Ackroyd. The letter is couched in terms which could only have been written to a close friend with whom one could share such intimate expressions of a strong Christian faith :

> "Our worthy friend Ackroyd is dead, and I doubt not but is alive again. It was a pleasant reflection to me, being one of the pall-bearers, to think I was bearing the Cover over a dead Carkess whose soul I had not the least doubt was in heaven. He left this world with as great Composer and Confidence in his future state as was posable for a man to do; and I sincerely wish that you and me may be as well prepared as friend Ad for a future state."

We must now turn our attention to an extract from another letter which Jewitt possessed from John Green to John Brameld, dated between April and June 1788; it is quoted in his above-mentioned work at page 497:

> "Should be glad you and Mr. Bingley will look over the partnership-deeds, and if there be anything that do not meet your ideas, please point it out. When you have done this you may send them in a small box directed to me; they never was in my mind when at Swinton, or should have done the needful then. I have writt Charles with some sponges and ... informing him I expect 4 C^m kills per week exclusive of china, which I hope he will be able to manage without increasing the wages ... Hope your buisket kill turns out well. You have room now if you will but make neat goods and be observing to get money; but it will require a strict attention to keep every wheelband in the nick."

This extract has been quoted and dismissed without much analysis or comment by other writers, including Jewitt, yet when it is considered along with such other facts that we know, it does give us more than hints which go some way to answering questions regarding this merger of the two Potteries.

i. It confirms that formal partnership deeds did exist and that the Swinton partners were given an opportunity to comment on them and to suggest changes before they signed them.

ii. That John Green was obviously the Leeds Partner responsible for overseeing and liaising with the Swinton Pottery thus confirming Jewitt's statement;- "Mr John Green became the acting manager of the Swinton Works." John Green was therefore acting in the same capacity that he held in the Leeds Pottery.

iii. It would appear that the only Swinton partners at this time were Thos. Bingley and John Brameld.

iv. Someone with the name Charles was, what in modern parlance we would call, the Works Manager, i.e., the one with practical potting experience to whom John Green had written separately, sending sponges to be used in the Pottery and specifying the 'through-put' of work expected thereby implying that such matters were not the primary concern of John Brameld.

v. "Hope your buisket kill turns out well" seems to imply that a new kiln may recently have been built. See the details below.

vi. "You have room now if you ... to get money;". The last sentence contains so much : "You have room now". After the amalgamation it is obvious from a perusal of the Wentworth Woodhouse Muniments that building work was being carried out at the Swinton Pottery. :

> WWM A273: 1785/6 "Paid Mr Richard Moxon for Deal Timber for an additional
> Building at Swinton Pottery   £17-11- 6"
> WWM A275: 1787/8 "Paid Mr Ellison for Timber used at Swinton Pottery in
> October 1786   £12-13-11"
> WWM A280:1792/3 "Paid Messrs Green Bingley & Co for bearing Timber used
> in the different Buildings at Swinton Pottery   £83-11-00"

Also, preserved in the Swinton Parish records at Doncaster Archives under ref:: P59/6/A4/3, is the following document, : "The Dimensions of the Ground Plan of the Pottery taken the 30th Jan^{ry} 1788", in which are listed the range of such buildings.

vii. Apart from the obvious interpretation of "You have room now" the expression also has connotations implying a 'breathing space' – an immediate freedom from possible financial worries. The amalgamation with the much larger Pottery at Hunslet had therefore enabled the Swinton Pottery to be enlarged thereby making the 'production-line' more efficient and more productive of wares, therefore making more profits for all the shareholders.

viii. Next comes the punch line " ... if you will but make neat goods and be observing to get money;". There is to be observed in many books on the history of the applied arts, by authors who have not themselves worked in a trade or craft, a strange misguided attitude that beautiful objects could only have been produced by people who were allowed to work in a way which was not constrained by any thoughts of profit and certainly not by time. Nothing could be more removed from reality, then or now. Profit, and therefore income enough for the shareholders as well as pay for the individual craftsmen, only occurs when the goods are made well and fast enough for all costs to be covered and enabling them to be sold at a price which will attract enough customers to make the concern profitable and therefore viable. The great Josiah Wedgwood, whose Pottery produced some of the most sublime examples of both useful and decorative wares, commented in a letter to his partner Thos Bentley, dated the 23rd of August 1772, " ... making the greatest quantity possible in a given time ..."[51] Wedgwood also had commented, in 1769 :" ... to make such *Machines* of the *Men* as cannot err ...".[52]

ix. John Green's comment - "and be observing to get money" may well have been a deliberate and stern warning to John Brameld. Those readers who are *au fait* with the subsequent history of the Swinton Pottery/Rockingham Works under the Bramelds will, apart from appreciating the excellence of their products, be aware that the Bramelds were the most inept family when it came to financial concerns – perhaps John Green knew of this unfortunate trait in his friend John Brameld?

The advice comes right at the end: "but it will require a strict attention to keep every Wheelband in the nick." – in other words, attention to detail, orderliness in the pottery workshops, and above all sound maintenance of all machinery and equipment. A wheelband was the rope or belt which went round one wheel to another transferring the power and increasing the speed from a large diameter wheel to a smaller one, the nick being the groove in the circumference of each wheel. It was a variant of a well-known saying in the West Riding woollen mills: "Keep band in t'nick" – where "t' band" had to be kept "in t'nick", otherwise the work would stop thus costing time and therefore money.

Jewitt comments further:- "In the same letter he speaks of consignments of flint by Mr. Brearey to Selby and Tadcaster. He also offers Brameld from himself and partners a commission of 5 per cent. on all 'wearing apparell sould to your works'."

At the time of writing only one presumed reason for the joining together of the Leeds and Swinton Potteries has been put forward. Both A.A. Eaglestone and T.A. Lockett,[53] and A. and A. Cox[54] have assumed that the Leeds Pottery 'took over' the Swinton Pottery in order to control it and thereby prevent it becoming a rival. I now venture to put forward another hypothesis.

It is clear that John Green and John Brameld were on quite friendly and trusting terms with one another, and that John Green had worked at the Swinton Pottery in the 1760s, also that his cousin John Sharpe, a practical potter, had most probably been a partner in the 1770s and who had, it would appear, left by 1785. We are now looking back at a situation where the Swinton Pottery was without a partner who was a practising potter, and obviously quite a small concern, when we consider the very meagre annual rent that was being paid. Although the Wentworth Estate would, as we have seen, pay most of the cost of new buildings, empty buildings require equipment and materials to work with and these the landlord would not provide. However, by the 16th of October 1786, Richard Fenton, Earl Fitzwilliam's agent, was obviously impressed with what he saw of the pottery under its new management as he commented in a letter to the Earl: " ... Swinton Pottery goes on well ...".[55]

The one clear picture which therefore emerges is that if Thos. Bingley and his partner had wanted to enlarge they could have done so themselves without the intervention of the Leeds Pottery, only two important factors would have prevented them. The first being the absence of a partner with practical experience not only of the manufacturing side but also with a knowledge of the wider markets in which to sell an increased quantity of wares, and secondly the necessary capital to carry such plans to fruition. John Brameld would have been very much aware of the success which the Leeds Pottery had become under the management and direction of his friend John Green. Therefore, who better to turn to for advice and help than his friend. Moreover the Bramelds, if nothing else, were never backwards in coming forward when it came to appealing for financial help. The Leeds Pottery, as we have seen was a very profitable concern at this period and it would have capital to spare; it was large, financially secure with good markets, mainly abroad but also at home. Such a concern would surely not be afraid of a comparatively small concern in Swinton. Moreover if the sole purpose of the Leeds Partners had been to control the Swinton Pottery, would they have bothered to expend capital on enlarging it?

The reader must bear in mind that we have been looking at the scenario in 1785 and not at the troubles at the end of the lease in 1806, which was the year after John Green had died and five years after he had left the Leeds Pottery and therefore no longer able to have any influence on its actions. The final point to remember is that the shares in the Swinton Pottery were not 'floating' therefore the Leeds Pottery could only have got involved with the consent of the Swinton partners. The separation of the two potteries will be dealt with in Chapter 2, pages 47-50.

Insurance, Hazards and Accidents

An insurance policy, dated the 10th of November 1778, apart from some obvious errors on the part of the copy clerk, gives us some further information[56] :

> "Richard Humble, William Hartley, Joshua Green, John Barwick and Henry Ackroyd
> Manufacturers of Earthenware on their Buildings adjoining each other used as a
> Manufactory of said Wares not exceeding One Thousand Pounds   1000
> Utensils and Stock therein only not exceeding Two Thousand Pounds   2000
> Eight Cottages under One Roof near in the Tenure of their Servants
> not exceeding Twenty five Pounds on each   200
> House near in the Tenure of said John Green and Others not exceeding
> Four Hundred Pounds   400
> Wind Mill with Going Gears near Brick and covered with Timber
> not exceeding One Thousand Pounds   1000
>   £4600
> All Brick Stone and Slated except as otherwise mentioned and situate at Huntley in the Parish of
> Leeds & County of York."

From the above we see that the valuation of the Pottery's buildings and cottages had not altered since the earlier policy of 1771, (see page 18). The Stock and Utensils had increased from £500 to £2000. The house occupied by John Green was then finished and the Windmill was given the same value as all the other pottery buildings.

The need for pottery premises to be insured is confirmed by reports of fires at the Pottery – a natural hazard in the days when lighting was by lamps and candles, and when wares were packed for transport in crates and casks with straw.

The Leeds Intelligencer, the 14th of November 1780:

"Yesterday se'night in the evening, the windmill at the Pottery near this town, by some accident took fire, but being immediately discovered it was extinguished without doing any material damage."

The Leeds Intelligencer, the 12th of February 1788 :

"Last Tuesday morning the Leeds Pottery, belonging to Messrs Hartley Greens & Co., accidentally took fire, and before it was got under, several warehouses full of earthenware, and the Workshop, utensils, and sundry articles, were destroyed; the loss in property is supposed to be above 2000*l*. We are informed that the above said proprietors are insured, both in goods and buildings, yet will be considerable sufferers on account of the loss of time during the rebuilding and refitting up of their works &c."

The Leeds Intelligencer, the 27th of May 1799 :

"On Wednesday morning a stable belonging to the Pottery in this town, was set on fire by carelessness of a servant using a naked candle, which entirely consumed the same. A number of horses that were in the stable, were fortunately removed without receiving any injury."

By 1789 it has been claimed that the workforce at the Pottery was 150.[57] In an age before nationally agreed and enforceable safety regulations had been enacted it is not surprising that accidents did happen. We have earlier, (page 16) recorded such an event when one of the hovels collapsed while under construction. The following report emphasises the dangers of unguarded machinery coupled with the hazards of employing children as was then the usual practice.

The Leeds Intelligencer, the 11th of May 1779 :

"Last Saturday evening betwixt five and six o'clock as one Jos. Cocker, a boy about twelve years of age belonging to the Pottery near this town who was amusing himself on the upright part of the Pottery Wind-Mill, his head was unfortunately caught betwixt the cogs of a wheel whereby he was instantly crushed to death."

Another custom, with possible inherent problems, must have been the system of binding apprentices both from independent families, and from the Parish, some of whom may well have been orphans, and where there was no choice, see page 27. The following notice, which appeared in *The Leeds Intelligencer* of Tuesday the 13th of August 1776, highlights such a problem.

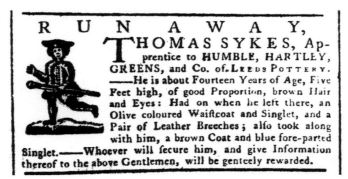

RUNAWAY, THOMAS SYKES, Apprentice to HUMBLE, HARTLEY, GREENS, and Co. of Leeds Pottery.——He is about Fourteen Years of Age, Five Feet high, of good Proportion, brown Hair and Eyes: Had on when he left there, an Olive coloured Waistcoat and Singlet, and a Pair of Leather Breeches; also took along with him, a brown Coat and blue fore-parted Singlet.——Whoever will secure him, and give Information thereof to the above Gentlemen, will be genteely rewarded.

The system of apprentices being bound, usually for a period of seven years from the age of fourteen, placed considerable responsibilities on the part of the person to whom the apprentice was bound as well as the constraints placed thereby on the apprentice. The literature and social history books dealing with the subject abound with depressing and sometimes harrowing accounts of ill treatment. Such stories should, however, not be taken to mean that every apprentice was so treated. As for Thomas Sykes we just do not know what circumstances prompted his departure from Hunslet nor indeed whether he ever returned. See also Appendix VII regarding the employment of children.

The Fear of Invasion and Civil Unrest

Towards the end of the eighteenth century the country was very agitated with fear of an invasion by Napoleon. From 1761 the raising of that old English institution, the Militia, was enforced by law against a penalty fine. The fear of Napoleon must therefore have given a boost to recruitment and the raising of voluntary contributions over and above the money raised by virtue of a compulsory parish assessment. The Militia could also be used to augment regular troops in case of any civil unrest. The reports from France following the events surrounding the early years of the Revolution of 1789 must have caused great anxiety on all those who had property. Thus *The Leeds Intelligencer* in April 1794 reported a meeting following an earlier notice in the same newspaper :

" ... request that a meeting of the Inhabitants of this Borough may be called for the purpose of taking into Consideration the Measure of Raising a Corps of Volunteers for the express Purpose of the Internal Defence of the Borough against Insurrection or any sudden Commotion."

Alexander Turner, see page 45 and Plate 21, Mayor, said to have been one of the foremost inhabitants, called a meeting of the "Gentlemen, Clergy, Merchants, Traders and principle Inhabitants on Thursday 17th April." A Subscription was opened and the following were among the contributors :

C.J. Brandling	£100	[Middleton Colliery owner & Joint Lord of the manor of Hunslet.]
Richard Humble	£50	
John Plowes	£100	[A future partner with David Dunderdale in the Castleford Pottery.]
Alexander Turner	£100	
David Dunderdale	£100	
Hartley Greens & Co.	£75	
Richard Clark	£10-10s.	[Rope Maker and Warfinger of Leeds and a future partner with John Green in the Don Pottery.]

Four years later *The Leeds Intelligencer* of the 14th of May 1798 reported :

"Upwards of one hundred and fifty of the workmen of Messrs Hartley Greens & Co., of the Pottery near this town, have offered their services to government, to march in case of actual invasion, to any part of the country; which loyal example has been followed by the workmen of Swinton, Castleford, Knottingly, and Swillington Potteries; the whole consisting of upwards of five hundred, are to be formed into one regiment, provided the plan meets with the approbation of the Lord Lieutenant, to whom the offer has been forwarded."

The outcome of the above offer is not known but the above two reports do show that anxiety was not confined to any one strata of society and that potters, whether masters or servants were equally involved.

Towards the Close of the Century – Further Partnership Matters

The partners had lost the services and counsel of the Pottery's founding father, Richard Humble, in 1781. In 1798 on the 1st of July he departed this life aged 81, leaving a substantial estate to his surviving family. Three other partners died before the century was out. Henry Ackroyd in April 1788, (see page 23). His four twenty-fourths shares being then divided between his legal representatives – Sarah, his widow, Mary Ackroyd his unmarried daughter, and the Rev. Ed. Parsons the former husband of his deceased daughter Sarah. Thomas Wainewright died on the 28th of April 1798, intestate. Letters of administration were therefore granted to his only child, Jane, the wife of James Winter Butterworth of Leeds, Kerseymere Printer, who thereby became a partner. The other aged founding partner, Joshua Green died in June 1799 aged 79, leaving his shares in both Hartley Greens & Co., and in Greens Bingley & Co., together with confirmation of his earlier sale to his cousin Savile Green of a one twenty-fourth share and the remaining three twenty-fourths to his nephew Ebenezer Green, Brandy Merchant of Leeds, who he appointed sole executor. I have included a full transcript of Joshua's Will at Appendix III as it is very informative regarding many of the off-shoots of his family. He left an estate of under £5000.

As stated earlier, John Green, with other eminent businessmen as partners, had built two ale and porter breweries, one at Hunslet and the other at Rotherham. He had invested considerable amounts of capital in them from 1785 up to 1794. This investment and further capital, borrowed from the Armitage family, on whose land the Hunslet Brewery was built, committed him to paying rent and interest amounting to £612 per year on a 42 year lease. Such a venture would undoubtedly have proved very profitable had it not been for one factor beyond anyone's control, namely the English climate.

The year 1794 witnessed appalling weather conditions resulting in a disastrous harvest followed by an equally bad winter and another dreadful year of adverse weather in 1795 with yet another very poor harvest. Brewers need grain as potters need clay. The two successive very meagre harvests resulted in a state of depression in trade generally and especially so in the West Riding of Yorkshire. Grain was, as it is now, an essential ingredient in the diet and well-being of all people. Prices recorded at Pontefract show the panic situation which must have been felt by all sections of society.[58]

Wheat Prices at Pontefract :-	Nov. 1794	£2.60 per quarter.
	Apr. 1795	£3
	Jun. -do-	£4
	25th Jul. -do-	£5.25p
	Mid. Aug. -do-	£7.55p and up to £9.

Dairy products and meat also doubled in price. This caused all available incomes in the working population to be spent wholly on subsistence with the inevitable slump in the purchasing of clothing and other goods not essential for subsistence.

In such a situation flour millers constantly outbid the brewers for any available grain and brewing production fell to an all-time low.[59] Unfortunately a similar situation was recorded in 1799–1801. As a result of this the Hunslet Brewery was declared bankrupt in May 1797 and John Green's personal bankruptcy was first announced in the *London Gazette* in January 1800.

A number of legal documents in the same collection as before quoted (WYAS, Leeds, DB 214/29) give us a clearer picture than previous writers have been able to do.

John Green and his son John by a bond dated the 22nd of August 1795 became bound to Mary Wrigglesworth in the penal sum of £2080 for the loan to them of the Principal sum of £1000 which sum they did not repay. John Green, the elder, then conveyed to Mary Wrigglesworth a half part of one twenty-fourth share in the Leeds Pottery and its Trade and Business as security for the loan.

By an Indenture of the 22nd of May 1798 John Green asked his fellow partners, William Hartley, Savile Green and John Barwick to lend him £500 and to accept one of his 24ths shares as a security. The agreement was that if John Green paid back the loan with interest at 5% before the 22nd of November next, then the one twenty-fourth share would be returned to him.

Richard Humble, as we have seen, died in July 1798 without having been paid the £2000 still outstanding to him from the partners. By an Indenture of the 8th of August 1799 the partners, in proportion to the shares they held, paid Richard Humble's sons, Joseph, John and Thomas, the £2000, thus securing to themselves the freehold of Rushy Pasture. By the same Indenture the partners conveyed the "Tenements, Hereditaments and Premises" of the Leeds Pottery to Alexander Turner upon trust for the term of 1000 years to and for the interests and purposes of the partners and at the same time Nathaniel Clayton yielded up his trusteeship of the premises to Alexander Turner for the nominal sum of ten shillings. Elisha Perigo was one of the witnesses to the signing of this document.

1. Robin Reilly – *Wedgwood The New Illustrated Dictionary*, pp. 122–23, & 358.
2. P. Mathias – *The First Industrial Nation*, p. 87.
3. Gordon Jackson – *Hull in the Eighteenth Century*, pp. 20, 66 & 337.
4. WYAS (Leeds) – DB 214/48.
5. WYAS (Leeds) – DB 214/29.
6. Guildhall Ms – 11936/202/293213.
7. Guildhall Ms – 11936/208/302865.
8. This information has been conveyed to me by John Goodchild.
9. *The Ceramic Art of Great Britain*, Vol. 1, p.467.
10. UY BIHR – PCY. 5th Dec. 1798.
11. WYAS (Leeds) – MC 40.
12. Barbara C May – *Waggonways and Staiths: The Impact of the Middleton Colliery on the Township of Hunslet*. Thoresby Society, Second Series, Vol 3, 1992.
13. *Diary of Thos. Butler of Kirkstall Forge Yorkshire 1796 – 1799*, London 1906, printed privately. I am grateful to John Goodchild for drawing my attention to this.
14. WWM – D.1753.
15. The John Goodchild Collection.
16. Sheffield Archives – CM 218.
17. I am indebted to Geoffrey Forster, Librarian of the Leeds Library for allowing me to examine the Library's original Members' Register.
18. Sheffield Archives, CM 217.
19. For information see p. 595 & his entry in the DNB.
20. WYAS (Leeds). LO/HU/1.
21. Baptism registers, Parish Church of All Saints, Rotherham.
22. WWM – Stewards papers, Bills 1764 – 1768.
23. *ECC Transactions, Vol 11, part 3, 1983* – Plate 128 (d).
24. WWM G47/16a – Quoted in *The Don Pottery 1801 – 1893*, p.219.
25. *Ceramic Art*, Vol.I, p.497.
26. YAS – MD. 279B6/31,32,33,34 & 35.
27. *The Leeds Intelligencer*, 31st of March & 7th of April 1800.
28. WYAS (Leeds) – LO/HU/1 – Chas. Brandling and Joseph Bilton, Lords of the Manor of Hunslet had granted the land and the bricks for its building free.
29. Under the same date Samuel Rainforth was "putt out apprentice" to Mr. Savile Green. So far as I am aware this is the first documentary evidence that the Rainforths, particularly Samuel, had served their apprenticeships at the Leeds Pottery. Heather Lawrence records Samuel as working at Swillington Bridge Pottery 1797/9 before establishing the Hunslet Hall Pottery in 1800; see also p.18 in her book.
30. WYAS (Wakefield) Quarter Sessions Records, July 1796.
31. Arthur Young – *A Six Month Tour Through the North of England*, Quoted by A.F. Scott in *Every One a Witness, The Georgian Age*, Martins, London, 1970, p.181.
32. A.F.Scott – *Every One a Witness, The Georgian Age*, Martins, London, 1970, p.171.
33. John Thomas – *The Rise of the Staffordshire Potteries*, Adams & Dart, 1971, p.178.
34. *Ceramic Art*, p. 469.
35. W. Bennett – *The History of Marsden and Nelson*, 1957.
36. UYBIHR – Marriage Bonds & Allegations.
37. UYBIHR – PCY records.
38. Guildhall Ms. – 11937/7/636627.
39. Guildhall Ms. – 11937/40/716938.
40. Ron. Morley – *Journal of the Northern Ceramic Society*, Vol. 6, 1987, p.29.
41. By law this could not exceed 5% at this date, – See J.H.Baker, *An Introduction to English Legal History*, 4th Ed. 2002, p. 311. fn. 83: " ... in 1545 parliament set an upper limit of 10% on lawful interest ...(the limit was later reduced to 5% where it remained until the repeal of the usuary laws in 1854.)"
42. *Ceramic Art*, – pp. 469-470.
43. A transcript of the journals of John Platt, on microfilm, is in the keeping of the Rotherham Archives and Local Studies Library,
44. Sheffield Archives, WWM A275, see under "Dr. Spring Woods – To cash recd. of Messrs Green Bingley & Co. for 22 Owlers [Alders]...".
45. D.G. Rice – *Rockingham Pottery and Porcelain*, p.145.
46. H.W. Quarrell – *A History of Swinton*, p. 18.
47. J.D. Griffin – *The Don Pottery 1801-1893*, pp. 16 – 19.
48. Doncaster Archives – P59/6/C3/4/1.
49. WWM – (Add) Box 65, bundle 12.
50. J.D.Griffin – *The Don Pottery 1801-1893*, pp. 30,32,213 & 214.
51. Finer & Savage, editors – *The Selected Letters of Josiah Wedgwood*, p.131.
52. Letter from Josiah Wedgwood to Thos. Bentley post-dated 9th October 1769. – Wedgwood Archives ref.– E 18265-25. Quotation identification supplied by Gaye Blake Roberts and reproduced by courtesy of the Wedgwood Museum Trust, Ltd.
53. A.A. Eaglestone and T.A. Lockett – *The Rockingham Pottery*.
54. A. and A. Cox – *The Rockingham Works; Rockingham Pottery & Porcelain; Rockingham 1745–1842*.
55. WWM – F 106/141.
56. Guildhall MS – 11936/268/405366.
57. John Goodchild – *Aspects of Leeds 2*, – Hunslet in the Eighteenth Century, p. 69.
58. Roger A.E. Wells – UYBIHR *Paper No. 52*, Dearth & Distress in Yorkshire 1793–1802.
59. P Mathias – *The Brewing Industry in England, 1700–1830*.

CHAPTER TWO

A New Century
and
"The Old Order Changeth"

THE PARTNERS in the Leeds Pottery must have moved into the 19th century with heavy hearts. Not only had they lost several of their senior partners through death, now they had to soldier on without the support and guidance of John Green who, on their behalf, had shouldered "... the Direction and Management of the ... work and appointment of the Workmen and labourers..." for the last thirty years. John Green's personal bankruptcy automatically set in motion the implementation of clause 17 and the second part of clause 16 of their Articles of Agreement, (see page 575).

However, as soon as his bankruptcy was announced in the *London Gazette* in 1800, certain legal formalities were instigated, one of which was the appointment of assignees who would act as 'officers of the court', usually local businessmen, and the following were duly appointed :

John Brooke of Hunslet, Esq.

John Hinchcliffe of Leeds, Coachmaker.

Robert Gray of Leeds, Glass Merchant.

It was the responsibility of these gentlemen to call meetings of the creditors and to assess and gather in the assets of the bankrupt party and then to distribute to the creditors according to and in proportion to the sums owing to them.

With regard to John Green's shareholding in the Leeds Pottery, the Swinton Pottery and the property at Thorp Arch, this had to be valued in order that it could be purchased by the other partners from the assignees and shared between the other partners in proportion to the shares that each already held. The Original Award, dated the 26th of July 1802, details the carrying out of this procedure as laid down in the Partnership Articles of Agreement of the 1st of January 1776.[1] Thus we learn that the assignees, together with John Green and the other partners: William Hartley, Ebenezer Green, Sarah Ackroyd, Mary Ackroyd, Edward Parsons, Savile Green, Samuel Wainewright, James Winter Butterworth and George Hanson, could not come to an agreement regarding the value of John Green's shareholding.

Following the Rules two arbitrators were then duly appointed, namely :

John Hebblethwaite of Leeds, Merchant

Elihu Dickinson of High Flatts, Yorkshire, Tanner.

After the stipulated period of 30 days, as laid down in the Articles of Agreement, they stated :

" ... but on Account of the extensive Trade and Affairs of the ... Pottery Concern, the time limited by the ... Articles for making the Award of the ... Arbitrators ... was not sufficient ... and that the ... Partners ... and the ... Assignees had mutually agreed to extend the same ... [and had agreed to deliver their findings] ... on or before the first ... of July then next ... [an agreement was still not achieved therefore the two arbitrators, in accordance with the Articles of Agreement, had nominated Alexander Turner of Leeds, Esq., to act as] ... the Umpire or third Person ..."

The three arbitrators delivered their Award on the 26th of July 1802 as follows :

"That the Shares Right and Interest of the said John Brooke, John Hinchcliffe and Robert Gray (as Assignees of the Estate and Effects of ... John Green) of in and to the Freehold Leasehold and personal property and Effects of the Leeds Pottery, the Swinton Pottery and the Flint Mill and Farm at Thorp Arch are worth or of the value of the Sum of Ten Thousand Two Hundred and Thirty Pounds Ten Shillings and Threepence [Worth approx. £630,763 in 2003. Source: O'Donoghue, Goulding & Allen.] after deducting and making allowance for the Sum of One Thousand Four Hundred and Twenty Nine Pounds Nine Shillings and Ninepence which ... John Green stands indebted to the ... Partnership concern which ... Sum of Ten Thousand Two Hundred and Thirty Pounds Ten Shillings and Threepence is subject to a Mortgage Claim of Messrs William Hartley, Savile Green and the Executors of the late John Barwick of Five Hundred and Eighty one Pounds Eighteen Shillings and Ninepence and also to a Mortgage claim of Mrs Mary Wrigglesworth for the Sum of One Thousand One Hundred and fifty one Pounds Four Shillings and Eightpence."

The Award further stated that the remaining partners:

"Shall and will on the first day of September next [1802] at the House of John Greaves the Hotel in Leeds aforesaid between the Hours of three and five of the Clock in the afternoon, well and truly pay or cause to be paid ..."

– to the assignees the sum of £8,497-6-10d, and to Wm. Hartley and Savile Green and the executors of the late John Barwick, the sum of £581-18-9d. and to Mary Wrigglesworth the sum of £1,151-4-8d. Upon payment of which they, the partners, would secure to themselves :

> "All the Share and Shares Right and Interest whatsoever of them the ... [assignees of John Green] and of ... John Green of and in [Rushy Pasture] with all the Messuages or Dwellinghouses Cottages Workshops Warehouses Buildings and Improvements made or erected thereon and called the Leeds Pottery Also of and in All that Leasehold Farm or parcels of Ground with the Dwellinghouses Workshops Warehouses Buildings and Erections situated near Swinton ... called Swinton Pottery and also of and in All that Farm of Lands Messuage Buildings Mill and Premises situated in the Town of Thorp Arch ... called Flint Mill Grange And also of and in all the Stock in Trade Goods Chattels and Effects whatsoever and wheresoever of or in anywise belonging or appertaining to the ... several Concerns of the Leeds Pottery and Swinton Pottery and the said Mill and Farm called Flint Mill Grange or any of them ..."

Finally the costs of the prolonged arbitration were to be born equally between the Assignees and the remaining partners; the fees were not specified.

An Indenture made on the 1st of September 1802[1] informs us further that John Green's four twenty-fourths shares in the Leeds Pottery were, by the assignees, John Green, William Hartley and Savile Green as trustees for William Barwick, and Mary Wrigglesworth,

> " ... bargained released and confirmed unto Alexander Turner ... to have and to hold ... to the only proper use and behoof of ... Alexander Turner in trust nevertheless for the said ... William Hartley, Ebenezer Green, Savile Green, Mary Ackroyd, Sarah Ackroyd, Edward Parsons, Samuel Wainewright, James Winter Butterworth and George Hanson ."

John Green's shares, in the Swinton Pottery and the Thorpe Arch property, were similarly dealt with. The quantity is unspecified, but it may confidently be presumed that they would have been in the same proportion as those he held in the Leeds Pottery,

Thus the remaining partners had now conveyed all their shares in the Leeds Pottery to Alexander Turner to hold in trust on their behalf, (see page 44).

21. ALEXANDER TURNER, an oil painting by John Russell, RA. Alexander Turner was twice elected Mayor of Leeds: in September 1793 and again in September 1810. After the personal bankruptcy of John Green, Alexander Turner held the shares of all the partners in trust for their benefit until his death in 1816 at the age of 64. In his obituary, which appeared in *The Leeds Intelligencer* of the 29th of July, it was remarked: "He was a man of such amiable disposition, so mild, so good, so conciliating, so humane, that ALL loved and honoured him."– traits which seem to have been captured by the artist in this portrait. For information regarding John Russell, see the caption to Plate 14. *Leeds Museums & Galleries.*

At some time between the 1st of September 1802 and the 4th of May 1805 the partners had agreed to divide their shares into 20 parts as follows :-

William Hartley	4	
Ebenezer Green	3	
Sarah Ackroyd		
Mary Ackroyd	} 4	– The legal representatives of the late Henry Ackroyd.
Edward Parsons		
Savile Green	3	
Samuel Wainewright	2	
James Winter Butterworth	1	
George Hanson	1	
The said William Hartley	} 2	– Trustees holding the late John Barwick's shares in trust.
The said Savile Green		

Before we continue the history of the Leeds Pottery we must pause for a while to consider some facts regarding the events concerning John Green prior to his departure from Hunslet. The Hunslet Brewery, trading as it had under the firm of 'John Green & Company' had been declared bankrupt as a company and a final dividend paid on the 4th of April 1800[2], Mary Wrigglesworth being one of the partners in this concern. John Green's personal bankruptcy, for which a commission of bankruptcy was originally issued on the 20th of January 1800 but which was superseded by another dated the 24th of February,[3] described him as a "Maltster, Common Brewer, Dealer and Chapman." It should be explained that until 1841 the legal status of being a bankrupt was confined to *traders* owing more than £100 – hence the term "Dealer & Chapman" was usually used for most bankrupts thereby signifying that such a person was a trader. In the case of a potter – he bought clay and sold pots.

John Green's Certificate of Conformity was announced in the *London Gazette* in 1800 :

"to be allowed and confirmed as the said Act directs, unless Cause be shewn to be contrary on or before the 17th Day of June Next. [i.e. 1800]".

After which date he would be discharged and at liberty to commence in business again. Unfortunately only five per cent. of bankruptcy case files have survived for this period and John Green's is not one of them. Two dividends were paid, amounts unknown, on the 13th of November 1802, and on the 3rd of March 1803, both being announced in both the *London Gazette* and the Leeds newspapers.

Before leaving the subject of John Green's bankruptcy and his departure from the Leeds Pottery it is worth mentioning one document which links his brewing interests with the Leeds Pottery. I refer to a Memorial of an Indenture in the West Riding Registry of Deeds at Wakefield (Ref: EH 86/98). Dated the 1/2 September 1800 it records the sale, by John Green's Assignees, of the White Cloth Hall – " ... situate and standing on the south side of and adjoining to the Coal Staith in Leeds part of which Building is used as a warehouse and now in the tenure or occupation of Messrs Hartley Green and Company the other part thereof is used as a Wool Warehouse and in the occupation of Henry Close and Messrs Acklom and Payton ... and other part thereof ... is now used as a school and the remainder thereof was lately used as a porter warehouse but is now unoccupied and also a cottage dwellinghouse or tenement ..". Readers will recall that mention was made in Chapter One that this building was one of John Green's properties. The above quotation shows that it was made use of by different bodies including the brewery, which had been the cause of its owner's financial downfall, and the Leeds Pottery. Unfortunately most of the indentures recorded at Wakefield are very vague so far as the actual transaction is concerned to which they refer. All we know is that it was presumably being sold to Joseph Humble of Middleton, one of the late Richards Humble's sons. The building was the second White Cloth Hall which was opened in 1756 in Meadow Lane and which was superseded in 1776 by a new Hall, north of the river Aire, between the Calls and Kirkgate. The building in question was quite an imposing structure being seventy yards long, ten wide and three stories high.

When I wrote my book on the Don Pottery I could not, from contemporary archive sources, account for the one year's gap between the date of John Green's bankruptcy and his founding of the Don Pottery;[4] I am now able to clarify this situation. From evidence given in the first Court of Chancery case, (see page 56), we learn that the remaining partners had agreed to employ him for a period of about a year, after which it was necessary to employ someone with practical potting experience and skills to take his place, thus proving that none of the other partners was capable of taking over from him.

As noted earlier John Green died on the 2nd of January 1805 and although this event did not affect the running of the Leeds Pottery, the death of Savile Green in May of the same year must have been a considerable loss to the business. Savile's widow, Rhoda, died just five months later. Savile Green, junior, the only son and heir at law being only 18 could not inherit his father's shares and estate until February 1808, they being left in trust for him and his sisters in the hands of his friend Edward Brooke together with William Hartley and James Winter Butterworth until he reached his majority. Meanwhile in 1806, William Hartley became seriously ill and died on the 30th of January 1808 leaving William Hartley, junior, his only son and heir at law who would not attain his majority until August 1811. William, senior, had left his estate and shares in trust for the benefit of his son and two daughters to his brother Richard, and his friends: Thomas Clayton, Edward Brooke, James Ridehalgh and James Winter Butterworth.

We now have the very unsatisfactory situation of only two of the shareholders, Samuel Wainewright holding two twentieths and George Hanson with but one twentieth, being the sole remaining partners who had been sold shares by the original founding partners. All the remaining seventeen twentieths being held by people who had either inherited or, by virtue of Savile Green's and William Hartley's wills, were holding shares in trust for minors. A situation which augured ill for the future 'direction' of the Leeds Pottery.

22. THE EARLIEST KNOWN BILL HEAD from the Leeds Pottery (1804). The engravers, Butterworth of Leeds, show a classical urn within a rococo frame! The signature is that of Elisha Perigo who was a book-keeper at the Pottery. *Leeds Museums & Galleries.*

Before proceeding to follow the train of events which ensued it is necessary to deal with another problem which arose in 1805/6, namely the end of the twenty-one year lease of and partnership in the Swinton Pottery.

The Swinton Pottery

Some interesting archive material has survived in the Wentworth Woodhouse Muniments relating to the situation when the twenty-one year lease and partnership came to an end on the 1st of May 1806. Fortunately a transcript of these documents has been published by Dr. D.G.Rice in his *The Illustrated Guide to Rockingham Pottery and Porcelain*, 1971, pages 139-152. Being chiefly from the Bramelds and Charles Bowns, Earl Fitzwilliam's agent, they inevitably but perhaps quite naturally, give a somewhat biased account. Another document is published in Llewellynn Jewitt's *The Ceramic Art of Great Britain*, Vol I, page 500, this being from the Leeds Pottery. The above archives have formed the basis from which A. and A. Cox, A.A. Eaglestone and T.A. Lockett have constructed their accounts of the break-up of this partnership and which I believe has led to a rather biased account in favour of the Bramelds. Now with the aid of archive material not available to previous writers it is, I believe, possible for the first time to put forward a somewhat different interpretation of these events.

Charles Bowns, Earl Fitzwilliam's agent, started the ball rolling rather brusquely in August 1805 when he issued all the partners with a notice to quit the premises of the Swinton Pottery at the end of their current lease. In a letter to the Earl of the 16th of March 1806[5] he reported from a conversation that he had had with a certain Mr Prince, one of the Leeds Pottery's agents, which set forth the attitude of the Leeds partners :

" ... 'that the Leeds Gentlemen thought themselves extremely ill and disrespectfully treated, by my giving them so rigid a Notice to quit, that I should have written a civil letter to them as Gentlemen; but they were determined to obey the Notice and apply to your Lordship for a compensation towards the loss they would sustain by being turned out. – that they conceived any application to take the premises again, would be fruitless on account of the partiality which your Lordship and I have shewn Messrs. Brameld, by whom they had been told that unless they, Messrs. Brameld, were reinstated to the management of the pottery, again, the Leeds Gentlemen would not be treated with, therefore they thought it high time to give up, if your Lordship and I were to dictate to them who should manage their Concerns' ... that the Leeds Gentlemen after receiving 'such a Notice to quit would never submit to go Cap in hand to apply for the premises again' ...".

Obviously Charles Bowns quite rightly regarded his first duty was to his employer and his employer's local tenants, but it is surely easy to appreciate such feelings of resentment and hurt as expressed by the Leeds Partners. Surely a letter reminding them that their lease was nearing its completion and seeking to know if they would be likely to seek and negotiate a renewal of it would have been both more civil and diplomatic however legally correct his actual letter had been? To his credit, however, Charles Bowns did write to the 'Leeds Gentlemen'[6] informing them that the information which they had been given by Messrs Brameld regarding their being given preferential treatment, for any renewal of the tenancy, was not entirely correct :

" ... I think it necessary to say that if Messrs. Brameld have given you such information, <u>they have not my authority for it</u>; I told them that the pottery would not be let to a company, of whom some of the partners were interested in different connections in the same Trade, ... "

Had the Bramelds been somewhat mischievous in planting such a story in the minds of the Leeds Partners? One also wonders when the Bramelds first knew of the Agent's stipulation and if this is what made them withdraw *their* partnership from the Don Pottery and the Sprotbrough Flint Mill so soon after investing in them.

Following the above mentioned letter of August 1805 a meeting took place at the Swinton Pottery on the 30th of December 1805 at which William Hartley and James Winter Butterworth, on behalf of the Leeds Partners, together with Thomas Bingley, offered John and William Brameld terms for purchasing their shares in the Swinton Partnership. It is interesting to note that Thomas Bingley, John Brameld's brother-in-law, was on the side of the Leeds Partners. The following is a *précis* of the terms:[7]

"1st. They are willing to sell unto the said John and William Brameld and their Friends their Interest in the Swinton Pottery ... upon the following terms ... [that the Pottery be valued by] two indifferent persons one chosen by each party ... [by 1st of March 1806 and if they cannot agree then a third to be chosen and then to report on or before the 1st of April 1806].

2. That the value of the respective Shares of Mr. Thos. Bingley and the Leeds Pottery Company, shall be paid for in the following manner

One fourth on 1st May 1806
One fourth on 1st January 1807
One fourth on 1st January 1808
One fourth on 1st January 1809

the three last installments to bear Interest after the rate of 5 Pounds pr.Ct: p. Ann: from the 1st day of May 1806, until the time the respective principals shall be paid ...

3. [The Leeds Pottery to be] refunded the Monies that they are in advance (or may be hereafter in advance during or after the Existence of the present Copartnership) out of the outstanding Debts, and that the remaining outstanding Debts shall be placed in the hands of

Thos. Bingley
Wm. Hartley
Jas. Winter Butterworth."

Thus it is quite clear that the partners in the Leeds Pottery were desirous of quitting the partnership and were offering quite business-like and reasonable terms for so doing. We must remember that the 'old order' had changed since the launch of the Swinton partnership in 1785. In particular John Green, who I believe was a friend of John Brameld, had left the Leeds Pottery in 1801 and established his Don Pottery in the same year, with none other than John and William Brameld as partners who had each paid £600 for their shares in the Don Pottery and the Sprotbrough Flint Mill.[8]

If we now turn to the long letter from John Brameld to Earl Fitzwilliam of the 1st of January 1806[9] we learn that in the same year in which the Don Pottery was established, 1801, John and William Brameld had offered to sell their shares in the Swinton partnership, through the Earl's agent Mr. Bowns, to the Leeds Pottery for £600 each. This offer was rejected. A plausible explanation for this rejection being that the Leeds partners knew that they would have to find considerable sums of money in the not too distant future in order to purchase John Green's shares from his assignees, (see pages 44/5). They may also have decided that as John Green had been the manager of the Swinton Pottery on their behalf, now that he was leaving the Leeds Pottery they would not want the added problem of overseeing another pottery so distant from the one in Hunslet.

Assessing the information in the previous two paragraphs it is obvious that the Bramelds, in 1801, had tried to withdraw from the Swinton Pottery partnership and 'change horses' by joining John Green at his new Don Pottery. (The cost of their buying the two shares in the Don Pottery being balanced by their hoped-for income from the sale of their shares in the Swinton Pottery.) This is yet another piece of evidence to support the argument that John Green and John Brameld were on very friendly terms and that they trusted one another. Perhaps John Green could see the way things were developing at the Leeds Pottery and had confided his feelings to his friend.

However, what was of more topical interest is the fact that on the 16th of January 1805, (note the year), just two weeks after the death of John Green, John and William Brameld withdrew from the partnership of the Don Pottery and the Sprotbrough Flint Mill. Curiously in the Agreement whereby they took this action[8] they agreed to their two shares of £600 apiece, together with other sums owing to them amounting to a further £600, amounting in total to the sum of £1,800, remaining with the Don partners until their repayment, with interest at 5% on the 31st of Jan. 1811(one third), 31st of Jan. 1812 (one third) and the final third on the 31st of Jan. 1813. Bearing this in mind the statement in the above-quoted letter from John Brameld to Earl Fitzwilliam of the 1st of January 1806: " ... we have now no funds at all ...", was somewhat misleading to say the least. John Brameld goes on to state that he had approached "... some Gentlemen of Property and Respectability ..." seeking finance to purchase the 18 shares held by the Leeds partners in the Swinton Pottery and which he estimated could amount to between £12,000 and £18,000, but without success.

The whole purpose of John Brameld's letter was to seek support, in the way of finance, from the Earl to enable the Swinton Pottery to continue under the Bramelds, including a hope that extra funds would also be forthcoming to provide a Flint Mill, perhaps even a steam-driven one. One wonders if the Earl or his agent knew that the Bramelds had been partners in both the Don Pottery and the Sprotbrough Flint Mill and that the Bramelds had decided to tie up some capital in these concerns for another five to seven years when John Brameld wrote : " ... It is only support we want, it is only Money, ...".

Returning to the Leeds Pottery and its partners who, as we have seen, were very different from those in 1785 and, as we shall see under the first Chancery case, were in all probability keen to sell up and realise their assets – hardly a frame of mind which would countenance negotiating a further lease of the Swinton Pottery.

In the midst of the period when the various letters and statements, from and to the Swinton Pottery, the Leeds Pottery and the Wentworth Estate, were flying backwards and forwards, an event of great significance took place at the Leeds Pottery on or about the 23rd of March 1806, William Hartley was taken seriously ill, (see page 31). By this date he was the only surviving partner who had actually worked at the Pottery as "corresponding clerk". All the other partners being merely shareholders by virtue of inheritance or were holding shares in trust for minors. Savile Green, the other active partner had died in 1805. Thus the Leeds Pottery was now approaching an almost rudderless period, to be dealt with below and in Chapter 3, and from which one cannot imagine that any objective decisions could be readily forthcoming.

However is seems obvious that, in spite of these circumstances, if the main objective of the Leeds Pottery had been to prevent the Swinton Pottery becoming a rival, then surely the safest and easiest method of achieving this would have been to control and use it by continuing in it as its majority shareholders. In 1806 John and William Brameld held one share each, the Leeds Partners plus Thomas Bingley held between them eighteen shares.[9] This being so, once the decision had been taken by the 18 'Leeds Pottery' shareholders not to seek a new lease and when it became known to them that the Bramelds could not purchase their 18 shares, then the Leeds Partners had every right to begin to close down the Swinton Pottery and to reclaim any equipment and materials, in proportion to their shareholding, that had been purchased over the previous twenty-one years. The following notice appeared in *The Leeds Mercury* of the 6th of February 1808 :

PARTNERSHIP DISSOLVED

Notice is hereby give, That the Partnership
carried on by Messrs HARTLEY GREENS and Co and
THOMAS BINGLEY, JOHN BRAMELD, and WILLIAM
BRAMELD, as Manufacturers of Earthen Ware, at
Swinton, near Rotherham, in the County of York,
under the Firm of Greens Bingley and Co., was
dissolved by mutual Consent, on the First Day
of May, 1806, and that all Debts due to, or arising
from the said late Partnership, will be received and
paid by the said Messrs Hartley Greens and
Co., at Leeds Pottery – Witness our Hands this
Thirteenth Day of September, 1807.

HARTLEY GREENS AND CO.

THOMAS BINGLEY.

JOHN BRAMELD.

WILLIAM BRAMELD.

Interestingly when William Barwick sold his two inherited shares in the Leeds Pottery, in 1813, the Indentures by which they were conveyed to their new owners stated that they were entitled to " ... any Goods debts and Effects belonging or appertaining to the said Pottery at Swinton."

In summing up this episode of the Leeds Pottery's history one can appreciate the natural feelings of the Bramelds, father and son, at the prospect of losing their livelihood. It can also be presumed that John Brameld had, in 1785, entered into the partnership of his own volition. Now, twenty-one years later, the Bramelds were out-voted by 90% of the partnership votes. It was undoubtedly a great disappointment but it was democratic. The Bramelds could be said to have had 'some neck' in writing to and expecting their landlord to make good the deficiency after the 'Leeds Gentlemen' had withdrawn. That their landlord did step in and rescue them owes more to his altruistic nature than to any legal or even moral claims which the Bramelds had in this affair. What is certain, however, is that the Swinton Pottery, later the Rockingham Works, did go on to achieve a degree of excellence in its productions under the Bramelds, but at a cost in financial terms to the Fitzwilliam family which, time and time again in the next four decades, would respond to pleadings for financial assistance from the Bramelds until, in 1842, the fifth Earl, seeing no hope of ever recouping the money which his father and he had poured into the gaping coffers of the Bramelds' commercial and financial mismanagement, finally refused any more help. Thus was brought to an end a ceramic adventure unparalleled in the annals of English ceramic history.

Back in Hunslet

The illness which William Hartley contracted and which became evident about the 23rd of March 1806 may well have precluded him from continuing in any capacity in the affairs of the Leeds Pottery. His doctor commented that it " ... will prove mortal in the course of a very short time if a great and very unexpected alteration does not immediately take place ..."[10] From another letter from the same hand and to the same addressee, from St. Petersburg, dated the 6th of September, 1806: "I was really extremely sorry to hear Mr. Hartley was so poorly & begin to think I shall see him no more ...". Certainly the words of his doctor were taken seriously as his will is dated the 25th of March 1806 and is signed in a very shaky hand. Relative to this matter, Ebenezer Green and Mary Ackroyd, in the answer they gave to the pleadings in the first Chancery suit[12] stated : " ...the business ... was carried on with considerable success and advantage ... but the same was not carried to any profit or advantage for the last year of the life of ... William Hartley ...". John Green had left the concern in 1801, Savile Green had died in 1805 and Wm. Hartley, the last of the old partners to have worked in the business died the 30th of January 1808 of "a decline"[11] and was buried at Colne, Lancashire.

The second, third and fourth decades of the nineteenth century were overshadowed by two lengthy and expensive suits which were pursued and contested through the High Court of Chancery and which are dealt with separately in Chapters 3 and 5.

Preserved in the Wedgwood archives at the University of Keele are a few letters to and from Etruria and the Leeds Pottery. The first is from the Leeds Pottery and is dated the 19th of December 1804 and is addressed to Messrs Josiah Wedgwood and Byerly :[13]

> "Gentlemen
> The petition of which you handed us a Copy by your esteemed favor of the 12th instance we have got signed by the principal Exporters in our neighbourhood and this post hand the same to your Mr John Wedgwood in hand on requesting he would have the goodness to present the same, we shall indeed be happy to learn that our representations are likely to produce a good effect.
>
> I Remain Gentlemen
> Your most obedient Servant
> Hartley Greens and Co."

It is interesting to see that the Leeds Pottery was acting as some sort of coordinator among the Yorkshire businesses and is therefore indicative of the good standing which the firm was held in in this respect. Unfortunately I have been unable to discover the subject of the petition.

At the Great Election of 1807 it is interesting to note that George Hanson was by this date residing in Leeds and styling himself "potter". He recorded a plumper for the young Whig candidate, Viscount Milton, as did the Rev. Edward Parsons, Dissenting Minister, and Samuel Wainewright who by now was also styling himself "potter".[14]

After the departure of John Green the partners appointed Sampson Daniel, a potter from Staffordshire and a member of a well-known family of potters in that county, to take his place in the management of the Pottery. Just how long he stayed in Hunslet is not known, certainly he would have left when the workforce was dismissed *circa* August 1808 but I have not found any material which indicates whether or not he returned after the dispute had ended.

The effects of the closure, just alluded to, and which is referred to in some detail in Chapter 3, must have delivered a near fatal blow to the well-being of the firm of Hartley Greens and Company. Not only on account of the dispersal of the workforce built up over many years and which would be extremely difficult to replicate once the works started up again but also the disruption of the regular supply of wares to customers both at home and overseas, some of whom would no doubt find other sources for their needs.

As well as the 'home-made' problems of the disagreements among the partners there were other events and conditions way beyond the control of a mere Yorkshire pottery but which must have given many partners in countless other businesses considerable cause for anxiety and concern. The chance survival of the following in the Gott Papers[15] dated 8th of October 1807 refers to one such event :

> " ... Messrs Hartley Greens & C[o] Pottery have just sent up that M[r] Wulff of Copenhagen has wished them to inform us that he has suffered nothing from the military operations. We have known some time ago they have a Clerk or Traveller in Copenhagen of the name of Perigo at the time the Siege was going."

Elisha Perigo was the Book-keeper at the Pottery, most likely the one who took over from Savile Green and who was probably succeeded by Robert Nicholson. William Hartley had, in his Will, left: " ... to Elisha Perigo the Book keeper at the Leeds Pottery the sum of ten pounds".

The military operations referred to were carried out by the Germans on land and the British by sea in order to prevent Napoleon seizing the Danish fleet and also thereby closing an important gateway into the Continent. The British captured eighteen Danish ships-of-the-line plus fifteen frigates and brigs which they packed with all available naval stores and sailed them back to England, having bombarded and set alight a considerable part of Copenhagen during an action of the 2nd to the 5th of September 1807. It was an action which was reported to have been much more violent than that carried out by Nelson in 1801[16]. These were very dangerous circumstances for the Pottery's agent to find himself in the midst of and, one would imagine, not at all conducive to good trade. See Appendix V for a detailed account of the consequences of this military action, the confiscation of goods from the Leeds Pottery and the eventual compensation paid by the Danish Government.

Such documents which have survived relating to the Leeds Pottery tell us that the Pottery had a very extensive trade with Russia. Savile Green, junior, journeyed to St. Petersburg in 1806 where William Barwick, the nephew of John Barwick was an agent and merchant for the Pottery. Fortunately a fascinating archive of letters has survived in the family, mainly from Savile junior, to his sister Sarah Savile Green (Sal). The following extract paints in vivid colours the problems which he met shortly after his arrival. Unfortunately the complete letter has not survived but from a reference in the letter it is possible to state that it was written in the last week of June 1807 :

" ... that this Party, prompted by their desire to diminish the Consequence of the British in Russia & seconded by a set of blackguard German Merchants, envious of their Priviledges, as well as by the intrigues of a set of Russian Brutes have had sufficient influence in the Cabinet to produce that most abominable of all compositions called "the <u>MANIFEST</u>. The <u>professed</u> Design of this said MANIFEST is the Encouragement of Russian Merchants by introducing them to the Foreign Trade; to promote this scheme they have taken advantage of the Expiration of the British Treaty of Commerce to throw such obstacles (by new regulations) in the way of Foreigners as must tend to drive all those away who will not become Russian Subjects. –

The English by their Treaty have hitherto had the right of trading with every description of native Merchants in the Empire, have been protected by their Government, subject to their own Laws and free from all those taxes and impositions to which the subjects of this Country are liable. –

If the British wish for ye free and open exercise of commerce they can obtain it <u>now</u> only on condition of renouncing, for the time of their residence here their priviledges & the protection of their Country as <u>British</u> Subjects. – They must become temporary <u>Russian Subjects</u> – liable to the capricious imposition of unknown, unsettled & unequal Taxes and subject to indefinite <u>Laws</u> & Regulations the interpretation and execution of which are committed to corrupted Magistrates ever ready either to be influenced in their decisions by those superiors whom it may be their <u>Interest</u> to please, or to receive the bribes and listen to the lies of your opponents, their own <u>rascally countrymen.</u> – A charming Situation this, is it not, lass? –

The lower Class of Russian Tradesmen, by far the best fellows in the Empire & with whom the English Merchants have traded are not all pleased with the Idea of their own Countrymen being the Merchants through whose hands they are to receive foreign commodities knowing as they do that the few <u>great</u> Merchants among them are great rascals. Indeed, the only classes of people <u>engaged in commerce</u> that are pleased with this vile thing are either a set of German smugglers who have no Country of their own or a few of the first Russian Houses that have made rapid fortunes by contraband Trade, a set of Brutes just 'got upon their <u>hind</u> Legs', with just enough reason to be rogues but who have not yet learnt how to use their fore paws, two out of three of them not being able to write their own Names – this is fact by Jingo.

We hope however that the political consequence of Great Britain to this Country will be able to crush the faction & destroy this confounded scrawl; but should it prove otherwise & these people persist in their endeavours to drive the English from this Country, however injurious it may be for a time to our Merchants & Manufacturers I wish they may refuse to let them have either a yard of Cloth or a royal Plate so that the Beasts may return to their Sheep Skins and eat again out of troughs. If you were as great a politician as our poor dear Mother you might I think find out some Place or other <u>else</u> from whence we could get our Hemp for the Navy & then let these chaps hang themselves in their own twine. I have treated this Subject at length because it does not seem to be well understood on your side of ye Water & because on account of this uncertain State of things the presence of Perigo is immediately necessary here; for Mr. Barwick will become no '<u>foreign</u> Guest' so that after next Monday the 1st July, the day the Manifest begins to operate & on or before which the Merchants are required to declare whether they will become '<u>Guests</u>' or not, Mr. Barwick cannot possibly according to the new Law, take upon himself any transactions relative either to our E–Ware Business or his own; consequently ye sales of all our Goods that may arrive before E. Perigo, cannot be made 'till the said EP be properly qualified <u>here</u> to clear the Goods at the Custom House & dispose of them – he will receive every Assistance from Mr. B. – when he gets here, but the Pots cannot be disposed of without the <u>Name</u> of somebody <u>qualified</u> to sell them. –

NB. The term '<u>Guest</u>' I have made use of above is the name given by the Manifest to the'<u>Temporary Russian Subjects</u>' before-mentd who when once entered and declared as such, cannot leave the Country without paying three years' Taxes to be calculated upon an average at the discretion of a Magistrate. –

After having so fully explained the State of things you will naturally ask one question viz. 'Well then Savile, what dost thou intend to do with thyself?', I'll tell thee directly Sarah. – In the first place I think that the Manifest is founded on such absurd <u>principles</u> that these People will find it their Interest to repeal it in a short time <u>even</u> <u>without</u> the interference of the Government on your side. In the 2nd place I think that the Leeds Pottery administration can never seriously think of Mr. Perigo's <u>remaining</u> here as Agent for any long time for who in their present divid State must look after their Affairs at Home! Besides I think E. Perigo is already too far advanced in life to begin a new career in a foreign inhospitable Country.[17] – Should these conjectures prove to have any foundation in them a road will still be left open for my Proposal. When Mr. Perigo arrives I shall learn more and will immediately let you know the result by Post. ... "

It is interesting to note that, in the last paragraph, Savile refers to the divided state of affairs in the Leeds Pottery which ultimately took the company into the first Chancery suit with all the ill blood and upheaval which ensued from that action.

1. WYAS (Leeds) – DB 214/29. – See Appx. I.
2. *The Leeds Intelligencer,* 31st of March 1800.
3. PRO. B4.
4. See John D. Griffin – *The Don Pottery 1801–1893,* Ch.2.
5. WWM – F 106/41.
6. WWM – F 106/39.
7. WWM – F 106/37.
8. John D. Griffin – *The Don Pottery 1801–1893,* Appx. I, p.213.
9. WWM – F 106/40.
10. Letter from Savile Green, junior, to his sister Sarah, dated 25th March 1806.
11. Burial register of Colne Parish Church.
12. PRO – C13/1642/33, dated the 28th of April 1812.
13. Wedgwood Archives, Keele University – L11/2025.
14 *The Poll for the Knights of the Shire,* York, 1807.
15. W.B. Crump – *The Leeds Woollen Industry, 1780 –1820,* The Thoresby Society, 1931, p.247.
16. J. Steven Watson – *The Reign of George III,* Oxford, 1960, pp. 455 – 457.
17. Because of this statement he must be referring to Elisha Perigo senior, who was baptised at Headingley on the 4th of March 1739 and therefore would have been 68 at the time of this letter. Elisha junior would have been 36 in 1807.

CHAPTER THREE

Into the High Court of Chancery

"I think ... there is likely to be some
disagreeable work at LP."
Savile Green, junior, Sept. 1806.

THAT the Leeds Pottery was involved in the Court of Chancery has been alluded to by other writers, but without giving any inkling of either the causes or results of so doing. Having spent many days trawling through the several indexes and extant archives of this class of documents in the Public Record Office and then untying the knotted cords which bind the large rolls of grimy parchment documents and volumes, relating to the cases, I can state quite positively that I do not believe them to have been disturbed since the day they were, shortly after the two cases, consigned to some dusty recess of the Court's store room.

Anyone who wishes to get a feel for the atmosphere and proceedings of the High Court of Chancery at this period is strongly advised to read the first chapter of Charles Dickens' *Bleak House*. If having read that first chapter they think that it is an over-exaggeration then perhaps the following extract from page 111 of the fourth edition of J.H. Baker's *An Introduction to English Legal History*, published in 2002, should dispel such thoughts :[1]

" ... the word 'Chancery' had become synonymous with expense, delay and despair. That the Court survived at all owed something to the vested interests of its officials but still more to the curious fact that expense and delay do not extinguish hope. Those landed families, if any there were, who escaped the throes of Chancery litigation were fortunate indeed."

In the previous chapter I referred to the fact that the Pottery had lost all its founding partners by the early years of the nineteenth century and that those who had inherited their shares seemed to have a different 'agenda' from their predecessors. I also stated that I felt that this was probably the reason why the Leeds partners did not take steps to renew their lease, in partnership with the Bramelds, in the Swinton Pottery in 1806. I feel sure that this explanation will become more readily obvious as the chapter proceeds.

Of considerable importance for our understanding of this phase of the Pottery's history is the fascinating and valuable collection of letters which have survived through a branch of the descendants of Savile Green. These give a commentary on the events and add a welcome human perspective to the otherwise very factual and somewhat dry account to be gleaned from the legal documents.[2] I will begin by quoting in full a letter written by William Barwick, the nephew and heir at law of John Barwick one of the founding partners. William's letter is addressed from St. Petersburg to Savile Green, senior. It is dated the 8th of November 1804 and is the earliest evidence so far discovered which indicates an unpleasantness among the partners at the Leeds Pottery :

"Dear Sir,

In answer to your favour of 10 October, received only last Wednesday I have left the sale of my shares in the Leeds Pottery entirely to the management of my friend Mr. Jno Schneider and as he had proposed to you to fix the sale on the 15 or 16 November and meant personally to attend that Business the whole will be settled before this reaches you. Your recommending my old fellow Labourer Mr. Ruperti as a Buyer woud I am sure entitle him to a preference with Mr. Schneider and as you know I do not now want the whole Purchase Price in money Mr. Rs funds falling short would not prove an insurmountable bar to his buying. All I wanted from the time of my late Uncle's Decease was you know to realise that Property by turning it into available Securities thereby ending my responsibility in a concern out of which I expected no advantage to myself and in which it was pretty evident I had not controul that I was entitled to & whatever the Partners may think of this and my conduct in the course of our long correspondence in this Business I do not hesitate to say again and again that I have met with such treatment at their hands as I had not deserved. I expect in the last stage of the Business to go out at an apparent heavy loss, but I am Determined to have an end of the affair without further loss of time, and increase of trouble to you & Mr. H [Hartley] and my friend Mr. S. who can ill spare so much time from his Business and home as this affair has taken. Coud I have foreseen what time, trouble, anxiety, ill-blood and expense this work has caused I should, I assure you have gone very differently to work in the years 1800 and 1801.

However tis now coming to a finish and if possible I will forget the past. I should wish to offer something to Mr. E. Brooke and Mr. A Furniss in the way of thanks for their trouble. What would you and Mr. H. recommend?

I am glad to receive such pleasant news of my Mother and Ann S Green. I wrote them both by the Walrus, Capt. Gatecliff.

Our young Folks are all very well and Mrs. B - saving her hardness of hearing has nothing to complain of. She is now almost as Lusty as Mrs. E. Green was when we were last at Leeds.

Best wishes to yourself, Mrs. G and family,

William Barwick."

The sentiments so strongly expressed indicate a disturbing state of affairs some eleven months before the death of Savile Green and over three years before the death of William Hartley, but after 1800 when John Green had ceased to be a partner. Turning to the instructions in the letter, the shares were advertised for sale[3] but were not sold until the 15th of May 1813, (see p. 61).

The quotation at the head of this chapter by Savile Green junior is from a letter to his sister 'Sal' (Sarah), dated the 6th of September 1806, from St. Petersburg :

" ... I must confess I think with you that there is likely to be some disagreeable work at LP after which I think that weary with snarling that they GH, JWB, SW will for the good of the concern go to sleep convinced that it can manage itself without them."

Thus we learn who Savile considered the trouble makers to be, namely: George Hanson, James Winter Butterworth and Samuel Wainewright who, it would appear, were interfering in the running of the Pottery, but with what knowledge or expertise in the business? –

– Samuel Wainewright who had joined the partnership in 1777 with one share and who styled himself then as 'Gentleman of Ferrybridge".

– George Hanson of Manchester, Linen Draper, with one share when he became a partner in 1783 and still "of Manchester, merchant" in September 1802.

– Jas. W. Butterworth, Kerseymere Printer who had inherited one share from his father-in-law, Thos. Wainewright, Postmaster of Ferrybridge.

George Hanson had married Samuel Wainewright's sister Eleonor and, if Ebenezer Green's evidence is correct (see page 58), they were brother and sister of the above Thomas Wainewright. Thus we have three partners, all related. Were they plotting to take over the pottery or possibly to close it down in order to realise its assets?

Returning now to extracts from other letters from Savile Green, jnr., to his sister Sarah, which give further proof of the unhappy state of affairs at Hunslet :

From the Isle of Wight, en route to Brazil, dated the 3rd of August 1808.

" ... The conduct of the mad Brutes &c., &c., at LP is too disgusting to speak about – I am affraid it will injure the Credit of the Concern ... as to his [uncle Ebenezer Green's] sneak wife she may go to the d ... l as soon as she likes ..."

From Madeira, en route to Brazil, dated the 7th of September 1808.

" ... If you all go to the Dogs at LP ..."

From Rio de Janeiro, dated the 22nd of October 1808.

" ... I hope they have long ere this settled their ridiculous disputes at LP ... But respects to the House and every one that cares a straw whether I'm kicking or not ...".

From Rio de Janeiro, dated the 28th of November 1808.

" ... and as I was literally forced from England for want of a Situation of any kind ...".

From Rio de Janeiro, dated the 28th of February 1809. He had not received a letter from his sister Sarah since the 31st of July 1808.

" ... what a dreary time it has been since I last heard from you and particularly considering the critical period at which I left you all – I have been kept in a continual fever by hints from every quarter that there has been the devil to do amongst the fools and mad-men at LP (for I can call them no better) and am yet unable to quash these reports for want of information – from what I have heard I have more than once concluded the Concern is completely dish'd. and have often construed your Silence into confirmation of this idea."

From Rio de Janeiro, dated the 3rd of June 1809.

" ... I feared but did not altogether expect that the LP Business would end in a shut-up and yet perhaps it won't turn out much worse for it – for my part the Actors had lost my confidence long before I left England and if we save one half from the muck I think we shall be no great losers by the Stoppage – I don't know how the deuce you'll be able to jog on till the Concern be wound up – we are all in a Cage, we can none of us get out – I wish to God I could squeeze through the Wires and open the Door a bit – but [?] a bit do I see the chance of it just now so we must sing for better times."

From Rio de Janeiro, dated the 23rd of January 1810.

"I consider our Property at LP as a dead loss and shall like to hear of its paying the Debts – pray will the Legacies under Nuncle Joshua Green's Will be paid? – it would help you now ... If we get through all these bad black times we'll have a laugh then – but they make me confounded gloomy now and then. Is WH [William Hartley] almost of age – if he and EG [Ebenezer Green], convinced of no good being done by squabbling – should lay their heads together – I think they might make LP pay our Debts at least. ... How dost thou think LP will turn out? – dost think it will be a Bankruptcy altogether – ...".

From Rio de Janeiro, dated the 31st of August 1811.

"By the by this Pot Shop Story goes on very comically – My good friend William [Hartley] gave me but a black Acct I can't form a correct idea of what this Nuncle of ours would be after – time will shew and in the meantime I don't feel inclined to add my kick at him – I wish he would give this Pottery Tale up, it would be more to the Satisfaction of every one. – I will write to you more about this when I have more time."

It is always frustrating only having one side of a correspondence; if only the letters from Sarah Savile Green had also come down to us then the interpretation of the events would be so much clearer. However, we do have Savile's comments on the situation and a knowledge of these will help to interpret the material which is preserved in the High Court of Chancery's archives in the Public Record Office. Before passing on to the legal proceedings it is worth noting that Savile's sentiments, expressed in his letter of 28th of November 1808, would seem to reflect those of William Barwick in his above quoted letter.

I opened this chapter by referring the reader to the writings of both Charles Dickens and J.H. Baker from which I will now give two further quotations, one from each, by way of an introduction to the actual cause papers from which the ensuing account is taken. Firstly from J.H. Baker :

"Since every step in litigation attracted more fees, there was no incentive to expedition ... One typical innovation was that which enabled Masters' reports to be lengthened by reciting the whole of the previous proceedings verbatim in a 'whereas' clause before starting on the substance of the report. ... The documentation produced in most Chancery suits was elephantine, and by Lord Eldon's time the work seemed to be grinding to a halt. Eldon was Lord Chancellor from 1801 to 1827."

Now from Charles Dickens :

"The raw afternoon is rawest, and the dense fog is densest, and the muddy streets are muddiest, near that leaden-headed old obstruction, appropriate ornament for the threshold of a leaden-headed old corporation: Temple Bar. And hard by Temple Bar, in Lincoln's Inn Hall, at the very heart of the fog, sits the Lord High Chancellor in his High Court of Chancery.

Never can there come fog too thick, never can there come mud and mire too deep, to assort with the groping and floundering condition which this High Court of Chancery, most pestilent of hoary sinners, holds, this day, in the sight of heaven and earth."

COURT OF CHANCERY,
LINCOLN'S INN HALL.

23. THE COURT OF CHANCERY. This print was first published in 1808 so is contemporary with the first Chancery Suit with which the partners were involved. It is from a painting by Rowlandson and Pugin, the latter being the father of the famous Victorian architect.

Chancery suits are listed under two surnames, the first being that of the principal orator for the plaintiffs and the second the principle orator for the defendants. Only the plaintiffs are arranged alphabetically and by the first letter only. The suite under consideration is listed under :

Hanson v Green

There are many references to this case in the various indexes from 1811 up to 1819.

The following quotations and notes are taken from the pleadings of the plaintiffs, dated the 18th of June 1811, under PRO Ref. C13/1642/33, and addressed to : "To the Right Honourable John Lord Eldon Baron Eldon in the County of Durham Lord High Chancellor of Great Britain."

George Hanson of Leeds

James Winter Butterworth of Chapel Allerton, Merchant

Samuel Wainewright of Thornton, Gentleman

Justus Ruperti of Leeds Gentleman

Edward Parsons of Leeds Dissenting Minister – Your Orators.

The said James Winter Butterworth and Edward Brooke of Leeds Merchant the surviving executors of the last Will and Testament of Savile Green late of Leeds Potter Deceased.

Savile Green of Leeds Gentleman and your Orators –

Richard Hartley of Bradley in the County of Lancaster, Thomas Clayton of Carrhill in the County of Lancaster, Esquire, the said Edward Brooke, the said James Winter Butterworth and James Ridehalgh of Schofield in the township of Colne Executors of the last Will and Testament of William Hartley late of the Parish of Leeds deceased.

The pleadings of the above, written as one continuous pleading, and not as separate ones from each of the above persons, is on parchment membranes measuring approximately 33inches (840mm) wide and, being sewn together, measures approximately 7 feet 4 inches (2m 213mm) in length.

They open with a lengthy statement and recital of documents outlining the origins of the Pottery in 1770 and stating that everything had been done according to the Articles of Partnership Agreement of the 1st of January 1776 until John Green's bankruptcy in 1800. We then learn that John Green had been employed by the partners for about another year :

"and it having then become necessary to appoint some other person to succeed him there-in one Sampson Daniel was appointed and agreed with for that purpose".

Sampson Daniel was from Staffordshire, (see page 46, 62).

It was then stated that after the bankruptcy of John Green that the partners, or a majority of them, elected William Hartley and Savile Green to:

"act in the place of ... John Green in the management of the ... Business and at another of the ... meetings prior to that at which ... Savile Green and William Hartley were appointed managers ... it had been determined to erect two Dwellinghouses ... for the accommodation of the partners having the management thereof ... and were occupied by ... Savile Green and William Hartley".

This is very misleading as the two houses in question were built at the instigation and sole expense of Richard Humble at a cost of £460: "for the convenience of the said John Green and others."[4] The pleadings then go on to explain that the deaths of Savile Green and William Hartley happened within a short space of time which then leads to the following which is one of the two main contentious issues of their cause :

" ... after the deaths of William Hartley and Savile Green a meeting of the persons then Interested as Partners in the ... Business was called for the purpose of appointing two other ... partners to succeed ... in the management ... and that your Orators James Winter Butterworth and George Hanson were appointed by a majority of all the partners to be the managers ... and as such to reside in the houses ... and ... the votes of the ... partners were taken as it had always been ... but ... Ebenezer Green acting together with ... Mary Ackroyd ... against the wishes and consent of all the other partners except the said Mary Ackroyd [&]took possession of the House lately occupied by ... William Hartley and he not only refused to permit ... James Winter Butterworth ... to reside therein but forcibly retained the possession thereof ... and still continues to reside ... And your orators further shew ... that ... Mary Ackroyd at the instigation and by the advice of ... Ebenezer Green executed a power of Attorney by which she appointed ... William Taylor who is cousin to ... Ebenezer Green[5] and who had been ... employed as a Salesman in the Warehouse ... and had only a few weeks before been discharged from and had actually left his situation ... to act as her agent or Attorney in all the concerns of the ... Business and thereupon ... William Taylor took upon himself to act and has ever since acted as if he were a principle partner ... and in particular ... of his own authority and in defiance of and in opposition to all the other partners except Ebenezer Green and Mary Ackroyd who supported and encouraged him in so doing took upon himself to act in the superintendence and management of the whole concern" ... [without reference to the other partners or paying any attention to their remonstrances repeatedly expressed and that Wm. Taylor sold and disposed of all or a good deal of the goods which had been manufactured and refused to go to arbitration or to discuss and come to any agreement so that the plaintiffs]... "entered into a resolution to discontinue the ... Business and in pursuance of that resolution the several workmen employed therein were discharged and the premises ... were shut up and the whole capital employed therein from that time has been rendered completely unproductive except that ... Ebenezer Green and William Taylor have carried on the ... Business to some extent upon the premises and with the Capital of the ... copartnership and since that time without the consent or interference of your Orators And your Orators" ... [further show that they have communicated with the defendants to see if they could come to some agreement or settlement but Ebenezer Green, backed by Mary Ackroyd refused to discuss anything which would not recognise Ebenezer Green as being in control of the Business] ... "the ... Business has been discontinued except as aforesaid nearly two years ... since the month of December 1808" ... [the plaintiffs also maintained that the concern was quite profitable until the defendants took over and who pretend that the loss was] ... "occasioned by a change of some political relations of this Country which was prejudicial ... by preventing or diminishing the exportation of their goods to foreign Countries and more especially to Russia ... your Orators charge that the defendant made use of the right of interference which he claimed in all concerns of the ... Copartnership for the purpose of harassing and oppressing the other partners and of preventing your Orators James Winter Butterworth and George Hanson from managing and conducting the same at all or at least in such manner as they and the majority of the said Partners judged to be expedient and he upon no occasion (or at least very few) concurred or acted with any other ... partners or submitted to any of the resolutions adopted by them since the decease of ... Savile Green and William Hartley but on the contrary took upon himself to interfere in and direct the management of the ... Business without attending to or consulting the wishes of the other partners ... William Taylor took upon himself the situation of manager or superintendent not only of the Warehouse but generally in all the concerns of the ... Business ..."

The following allegations were also made by the plaintiffs :

That they had offered to go to arbitration. This had been rejected.

That they had offered to purchase the defendants' shares or, to sell theirs' to the defendants.

That the Defendants had refused access to the books and papers belonging to the Business which were kept in locked iron chests in the Counting House.

That the Defendants should be required to pay a "proper and fair rent" for the house that they were occupying.

Lastly the following extract from these pleadings seems very relevant :

"And whether it is not therefore expedient that the Copartnership subsisting in the ... Business should be dissolved and the Capital Stock Monies Debts Effects Estates Property belonging thereto should be sold and disposed of or collected in and recouped and the clear produce of the same divided amongst the partners according to their respective shares in the said Business or if not why not. And whether it is not also expedient that in any event the necessary accounts of all the concerns relating to the ... business should be taken and finally closed up to the present time or if not why not ... And whether the ... Defendants have not refused to comply with such requests and for what reason."

The next relevant document is dated the 29th of July 1811 and is filed under PRO reference - C33/581/952. The opening words, which follow, bear out the earlier quotations from Baker and Dickens regarding the 'fog' surrounding the records of the High Court of Chancery at this period :

"Upon Opening of the matter this present matter this present day unto the Rt. Honble ye Lord High Chancellor by Sir Saml Romilly Mr Mell & Mr Wetherill of Counsel for the Plaintiffs It was alleged that the Plaintiffs have exhibited their Bill in the Court against the Defendants setting forth among other things ..." [There then follows a long recital of the Plaintiffs' Bill from the foundation of the Leeds Pottery and making reference to and quotations from its subsequent legal documents, including the Articles of Agreement. Eventually we reach the following]:

"His Lordship doth Order that it be referred to Mr Steele one of the Masters of this Court to appoint a proper person or persons to take and have the possession and management of the partnership premises stock and effects and to take and have the superintendence of the carrying on the partnership trade in question and to call and get in the outstanding debts and Effects owing and belonging to the ... partnership and the Plaintiffs and Defendants are to be at liberty to propose themselves or any other person or persons to be such Manager and Receiver or Managers and Receivers ... "

It would occupy far too much space if I were to publish in full all the pleadings and orders of the suit. The rest of the Lord High Chancellor's orders on this day are summarised as follows :

The plaintiffs and defendants are to hand over to the Receiver & Manager all books, accounts and papers in their possession.

The Receiver and Manager are to take all necessary action to get in debts due to the business and to be indemnified against all costs of so doing.

Receiver and Manager to pay out all debts due from the partnership.

Receiver and Manager to pass all accounts and books before the Master of this Court and to pay all balances into the Bank ['of England'] "with the privity of the Accountant General of this Court to be then placed to the credit of this cause subject to further orders of this Court"

William Taylor to be restrained from "intermeddling" with the copartnership and the defendants Ebenezer Green and Mary Ackroyd to be also "in like manner restrained ... until the further order of this Court".

The suit is mentioned several times in the Order Books but without much of any relevance. On two occasions it recorded pleas from the defendants to allow them extra time to prepare their defence, such time was granted. The defendants' pleadings, when completed and submitted, were contained on three parchment sheets each measuring approximately 31 inches (790mm) wide by 25 inches (635mm) - in all about 8,000 words. It is filed with the plaintiffs' pleadings under PRO reference C13/1642/33, and is dated the 20th of April 1812.

The defendants begin, as did the plaintiffs, with a recital of material concerning the early history of the Pottery up to the time when John Green became bankrupt and then :

"And these Defendants further answering say they believe that William Hartley and Savile Green in the ... bill named did also during the ... period [i.e. before John Green's bankruptcy] act in and about the ... business ... the one acting as a Book keeper and the other as a corresponding clerk ... but not otherwise William Hartley being appointed to the situation of corresponding clerk by express agreement with all the partners at the time he first came into the ... Concern and ... Savile Green having been employed in the ... capacity of Book keeper long previous to his becoming partner by Richard Humble who had that authority given him by the original Articles" ... [They agree that after John Green became a bankrupt that he was employed by all the partners for about a year after which Sampson Daniel was appointed "to succeed him as Overlooker of the Works"] ... "And these Defendants ... deny that ... William Hartley and Savile Green were to their knowledge and belief appointed by the ... partners or a majority of them to act in the place of ... John Green or other wise in the management of the ... business except that they believe they were continued to be one of them Book keeper and the other corresponding clerk of the concern" ... [They assert that the two dwelling houses were built long before Savile Green became a partner or William Hartley joined the concern.] ... "And these Defendants further answering deny that after the deaths of William Hartley and Savile Green any meeting of the several persons then interested as partners in the ... business was duly called according to the terms and provisions of the ... Articles for the purpose of appointing two other of the partners to succeed ... Savile Green and William Hartley in the management of the ... business and that at such meeting James Winter Butterworth and George Hanson were duly appointed by a majority of all the partners to be the managers or acting partners And these defendants deny that any such meeting was or could be duly had for that purpose But ... believe that some kind of meeting though not duly called or convened pursuant to the terms of the ... Articles but in direct violation thereof did take place about the time... mentioned and that the same was called by the complainants or some of them for such purpose as they believe as is mentioned in the Complainants' bill but deny that the same was duly called and they say that for anything they know to the contrary the majority of the persons present may have taken upon themselves to appoint James Winter Butterworth and George Hanson to be managers and as such to reside in the Houses which had ... been occupied by William Hartley and Savile Green but say that such meeting not being as they insist properly convened and there not being as they also insist any power reserved by the original Articles of appointing such managers ... these Defendants did not attend at the ... meeting and cannot therefore set forth as to their belief or otherwise what passed thereat except as appears by the ... Complainants bill And these Defendants further say that the only persons present at the ... meeting were the Complainants Samuel Wainewright George Hanson and James Winter Butterworth and that they possessed among them only five out of the twenty shares into which the ... partnership was divided and that Samuel Wainewright and George Hanson were nearly related to ... James Winter Butterworth being his uncles in law ... And these Defendants say that George Hanson and James Winter Butterworth not being duly appointed had no right to reside in the ... Dwellinghouses ... And these Defendants further say that not being present they do not know how the votes were taken at the ... pretended meeting ... George Hanson and James Winter Butterworth were willing to take upon themselves the management of the ... business as is mentioned and that their object hath always been to engross the whole of the business to themselves but these Defendants deny that George Hanson and James Winter Butterworth were competent to conduct and manage the ... business for the ... benefit of all the partners ... for these Defendants say that no person can be competent so to do unless he has served an apprenticeship to the business which was not the case with either [of them] ... And these Defendants say that this defendant Ebenezer Green did take possession of the ... House ... mentioned without any consent from the Complainants because ... George Hanson had previously thereto improperly and against the consent of these Defendants who are two of the principal shareholders in the said partnership [occupied it] ... this Defendant Ebenezer Green did at the time he took possession of the... house offer to pay a fair and proper rent as he hath often since done on condition that George Hanson would also pay a proper rent for the house so improperly possessed and occupied by him... they admit it to be true that ... Mary Ackroyd did execute a power of Attorney by which she appointed William Taylor ... he having for many years been a faithful servant of the ... partnership" ... [they agree that Wm. Taylor did sell goods for retail as had always been the custom of the partners and they further deny that they] ... "did not in all respects take upon themselves or himself the management of the business ... but they say that in order to prevent the concern being totally ruined by the abandonment of the ... complainants they carried on the work partially by manufacturing only such articles as could be sold for ready money and that they did not even do so until they had given some months notice of their intention so to do to the Complainants and that they were obliged so to do in consequence of the Complainants having previously put a total stop to the works in direct violation of the Articles of Partnership" ... [they did not stop any of the partners entering the works, some of them] ... "selling and receiving money for considerable quantities of the ware so manufactured by these Defendants" ... [They agree that offers have been made to them to go to arbitration but as these have been of a general nature and not a specific point of contention, they have never agreed to cooperate in such action] ... "they believe it to be true that the ... Complainants did enter into a resolution to discontinue the ... business ... and that in pursuance of such resolution the ... Workmen were discharged and the ... premises shut up and that the whole capital employed in the ... business has since that time and by reason of the ... conduct of the ... Complainants been rendered completely unproductive except as in the ... bill mentioned but these Defendants say that such resolution to discontinue the ... business was not as they believe entered into after these Defendants had refused to refer the ... differences on the contrary they say they believe that it was a purpose which the ... Complainants had resolved on long before and that in fact it formed one great objection to these Defendants going to a general reference [to arbitration]" ... [They agree that they have carried on the work against the consent of the complainants but without their interference, being compelled to do so] ... "in order to prevent all the Trade of the ... concern from being lost by reason of the ... Complainants having shut up the same and discharged the workmen ... Ebenezer Green ... says that he has not refused to acquiesce in any proposal which would preclude him from exercising an absolute controul over the ... business but on the contrary thereof he says that he ever has been and still is ready and willing to accept of fair terms of accommodation agreeable to the true intent and meaning of the original Articles of Copartnership as shall secure the future management of the business for the benefit of all the parties interested" ... [Eb. Green stated that accounts had been kept and money regularly paid to the Book keeper up to the time when the Book-keeper was ordered by George Hanson not to accept any more payments, this being at the time the works were shut. Since then they, the defendants, have kept accounts of money paid in and out. He further stated that he denied that the complainants had 'frequently asked and been refused' access to the books and accounts except to those relating to the period after the closure of the Pottery, which he regarded as not being their concern] ... "The Complainants have actually sold a considerable quantity of the ware manufactured by these Defendants and received the money for the same and they have also received a considerable sum of money from Russia and a further sum amounting to nearly three thousand pounds for Goods which lay at Hull and had been originally intended for the Russian market and which ... Ebenezer Green had been fortunate enough to sell to a person who paid for them with the greatest punctuality ... And ... further say that the business of the said Copartnership was carried on with considerable success and advantage during some part of the lives of the said Savile Green and William Hartley but ... that the same was not carried on to any profit or advantage during the last year of the life of William Hartley although the export trade was not at that time entirely stopped And these Defendants admit that since that time and until the discontinuance thereof by the said Complainants the ... Business may have been so conducted that the outgoings and expenses of the ... concern in some degree but in what degree ... are unable to state may have exceeded the returns ... but they say that the same was owing merely to a temporary pressure upon the trade arising from the state of public affairs and the interruption of the trade with Russia and elsewhere abroad ... And these Defendants further say that no offer of sale or purchase of the ... shares as ... is mentioned were ever made to these Defendants or either of them agreeable to the Articles of Partnership ...

This Answer was taken and the above named
Defendants Ebenezer Green and Mary Ackroyd
were duly sworn to the truth thereof upon the
Holy Evangelists at Leeds ... "

The Leeds Intelligencer of Monday the 15th and 22nd of June 1812 carried the following notice :

The **LEEDS POTTERY**

The Public are respectfully informed that the RIGHT HON. the LORD CHANCELLOR has appointed Mr.
J.C.RUPERTI and Mr. ROBERT NICHOLSON Receivers and Managers of the LEEDS POTTERY.
All monies, therefore, due and owing to Messrs Hartley, Greens and Co. must be paid into their Hands, and to no one else.
And all Persons having Demands on the said Messrs Hartley, Greens and Co. are requested to send a Statement thereof to
them at the Counting House. N.B. The Warehouse will open for Sale on Monday the Twenty-ninth of June.

The suit was again brought before the Court on the 10th of August 1812, under PRO reference C33/589/1247. As usual the report recites at length the previous report of the 29th of July 1811. The following is a *resumé* of the relevant points :

The Master, Mr. Steele, had approved the appointment of Justus Christian Ruperti and Robert Nicholson as Receiver and Manager in his report of the 25th of April 1812 and had also approved of Edward Brooke of Chapel Allerton in the parish of Leeds and William Hartley of Leeds, Esq., to be Securities for J.C. Ruperti and R. Nicholson :

> "truly and duly managing the ... Copartnership ... the ... Master had settled and allowed a Recognizance wherein ... J.C. Ruperti, Robt. Nicholson, Ed. Brooke and Wm Hartley were severally to be bound to the Rt. Honbl. Sir Wm Grant, Bt., Master of the Rolls and Nicholas Smith Esq., the senior Master of this Court in the penal sum of £30,000 ... and that ... Edward Brooke and William Hartley having made oath that they are severally worth the sum of £15,000 ... "

That the defendants Ebenezer Green and Mary Ackroyd had been served with a writ of Injunction requiring them to hand over the Stock, Goods, Effects, Books, and Accounts to the Receiver and Manager who, at the appointed date and time (25th of May 1812 at 11 o'clock) visited the Counting House at the Pottery but the Defendants did not hand over anything in compliance with the notice. On the afternoon of the same day J.C. Ruperti met Ebenezer Green in ... Leeds when he demanded from him what was required, whereupon Ebenezer Green said "I have nothing but the keys to give you I shall give you nothing else." On the 27th of May Messrs Ruperti and Nicholson went to Ebenezer Green's house and received the keys but not the books. Mr. Richards and Mr. Horne, counsel for the Defendants, confirmed that Ebenezer Green had handed over the keys, which gave access to all the buildings, but he had not handed over the Books and Accounts relating to the period in which the Defendants were carrying on the concern after it had been shut up by the Complainants, until the same shall have been examined by and approved by the Court.

Ebenezer Green was reported to be willing to pay a fair rent for the house provided George Hanson was required to do the same for the other house that he occupied. Finally :

> "His Lordship doth Order that the Defendants Ebenezer Green and Mary Ackroyd do within a month deliver up to Justus Christian Ruperti and Robert Nicholson all Books and Accounts and that Ebenezer Green before the 1st day of next Michaelmas Term deliver up to Justus Christian Ruperti and Robert Nicholson the possession of the Dwelling House now in his possession belonging to the Copartnership."

The Complainants, via their solicitors, issued some 'Interrogatories' to the defendants. The following is a summary of the answers dated the 15th of December 1812. They are filed under PRO C13/1642/33. The gist of the questions should be fairly obvious from the tenor of the answers:

Ebenezer Green had occupied the house until the 6th of December 1812.

Ebenezer Green was at a meeting when going to arbitration was discussed but he regarded the subject to be too general a matter for arbitration. He was always willing to go to arbitration to determine a specific point, but the others would not assent to this.

A suggested subject had been sent by the Complainants' solicitors to the Defendants' solicitors which had been rejected as being too general. The Complainants persisted in refusing to point out any particular causes or charges as the grounds of such reference to arbitration.

The Complainants did suggest to the Defendants the dissolution of the partnership or to sell their shares to the Defendants or for the Defendants to sell their shares to the Complainants but as the value had fallen the Defendants would only sell at the old value before such falling off.

Ebenezer Green always believed that the Complainants looked for and pretended differences between them in order to violate the Articles of Copartnership with a view to their own prejudices.

If the Complainants had acted fairly and been willing to conduct the business according to the Articles of Partnership "as they ought to have done" the concern could have been carried on to the advantage of all concerned.

Reiterated that the Complainants have no right to demand the dissolution of the partnership and that he, Ebenezer Green, would not consent thereto. Nevertheless he would be willing to sell his shares, as would Mary Ackroyd, for the price that the last shares were sold for, but the Complainants have rejected the offer.

Before continuing with the account of the suit I must insert here that on the 15th of May 1813 William Barwick's two inherited shares were finally sold.[6] One share was sold to James Winter Butterworth who was by this date living, presumably as an agent or merchant, somewhere in the kingdom of Portugal; the other was conveyed to John Edward Brooke to be held on trust for the use and benefit of Justus Christian Ruperti. This was because J.C. Ruperti, who was born at Ottersberg, near Bremen in Germany, on the 2nd of November 1757,[7] was an alien and was not, therefore, allowed to hold freehold property. The price paid for each share was £3,150. The shares, of one twentieth each, included a one twentieth share not only in the Leeds Pottery but also in the property at Thorp Arch and also " ... of and in any goods debts and effects belonging or appertaining to the said Pottery at Swinton ...". It is interesting to note that seven years after the Leeds partners had withdrawn from the 'Greens Bingley' partnership, that they still had expectation of some funds from this pre. 1806 partnership.

To return to the main subject of this chapter, the following are summaries of written statements made to the Court, all were for the Complainants excepting that of William Taylor. They were made in Leeds, at the house of Sarah Greave, the Hotel, the 29th of September 1813 and are filed under PRO Reference C13/1989/31 :

WILLIAM HARTLEY, of Bradley, Gent., aged 23.

Does not know if George Hanson and James Winter Butterworth were competent to the Management of the Business but may be with the aid of overlookers and has known them for six years and upwards. Does not know whether Ebenezer Green and Mary Ackroyd had notice of the meeting but does know that they do not acquiesce in the management of George Hanson and J.W. Butterworth. Ebenezer Green took possession of the late William Hartley's house before all goods and furniture were removed and only gave it up to J.C.Ruperti after an Order of the Court. Sometime in June 1808 he was in one of the warehouses with J.W. Butterworth and G. Hanson who had ordered Wm. Taylor not to sell some goods to a person then present, whereupon Ebenezer Green instructed William Taylor to carry on with the sale and that if J.W. Butterfield and G. Hanson interfered he was to "knock them down". On the same occasion J.W.Butterfield instructed the purchaser not to purchase the goods in question and not to pay William Taylor for them but Ebenezer Green encouraged the person to proceed with the purchase, to pay William Taylor, and to take away the goods. "And the said goods were taken away by force ...".

JOHN PARKINSON, of Hunslet, Overlooker at the Leeds Pottery, aged 37.

He knows all the parties except Thomas Clayton and James Ridehalgh. He knows that Ebenezer Green did assume the management of the Leeds Pottery against the wishes of all the other partners and that orders were given to the workmen by Ebenezer Green and William Taylor against the wishes of the other partners and that they procured "many of the men ... to attend to their orders and to disobey the orders of the said other partners". He stated that Ebenezer Green did not obtain possession of the house with the consent of the Plaintiffs but he saw him take forcible possession by " ... breaking open the Locks and Bolts of the door with an Iron Crow at the time the said James Winter Butterworth and Samuel Wainewright were in the House."

JOHN THIRHILL, late Porter at the Pottery, aged 52.

" ... And this Deponent saith that the wife of the Defendant Ebenezer Green desired this Deponent but when he doth not remember to get the key of the House lately occupied by the said William Hartley as she said she wanted to see the Rooms of the said House And this Deponent got the key which had been left at the House of the Complainant George Hanson of Mrs. Hanson but he did not tell her what he wanted the Key for nor did Mrs. Hanson ask him and he delivered it to the said Ebenezer Green and by that means this Deponent believes the Said Ebenezer Green took Possession of the said House and afterwards and when the said Ebenezer Green was absent from the said House at Leeds as this Deponent believes the said James Winter Butterworth took possession thereof and the said Ebenezer Green upon his return finding the said James Winter Butterworth in possession of the said House with the doors fastened proceeded and did enter the same by force and a Disturbance took place between the said James Winter Butterworth and Ebenezer Green concerning which of them had the right to the possession of the said House ...".[Ebenezer Green had advertised his own house in St. Peter's Square, Leeds, for letting in *The Leeds Mercury* of the 28th of November, 1808.]

PEARSON BRIGGS, late Assistant in the Warehouse, aged 50.

Stated that Ebenezer Green and Mary Ackroyd did assume the management of the concern. After the bankruptcy of John Green Savile Green and William Hartley did manage the business:- " ... according to their own judgment and discretion subject to the orders and resolutions of the majority of the said partners and that Ebenezer Green did not interfere against the orders and resolutions ...".

JOB WRIGHT, Overlooker of the Copartnership, aged 41.

Virtually word for word the same as the evidence given by Pearson Briggs.

ROBERT NICHOLSON, late Cashier and Book keeper, now of Leeds, Wharfinger, aged 34.

[Having been employed in the Counting House of the Pottery for some time before the legal proceedings started and then again as one of the Receivers and Managers appointed by the Court, it would be reasonable to assume that he would have had his 'ear to the ground' and should have been well and fairly accurately informed regarding the background to the troubles etc. His statement is quite a lengthy one of which the following is a summary] :

After the deaths of Savile Green and William Hartley a meeting was called in the usual way which was by sending either a verbal or written notice but he did not know whether in accordance with the Articles for the appointment of two other partners to succeed them he does not know nor whether J.W.Butterworth and G. Hanson were appointed to be managers and to reside in the houses or whether the votes were taken. But at a meeting held the 20th of April 1808 "at which only attended J.W. Butterworth, S. Wainewright, G. Hanson and Ed. Brooke they delivered to him a paper marked with the letter D and now produced" – the resolution respecting J.W. Butterworth and G. Hanson being appointed to reside in the houses lately occupied by S. Green and Wm. Hartley, part of which notice was in the writing of E. Brooke and part in that of G. Hanson. Ebenezer Green and Mary Ackroyd did not attend this meeting – Mary Ackroyd had no notice of this meeting as Ebenezer Green usually acted on her behalf. He reported that in the Letter Book there is a copy of a notice of this meeting "purporting to be such and which he believed was sent to Ebenezer Green but which did not state the purpose of the meeting. ... but by whom or how or in what manner it was sent ... or whether he received it" That Ebenezer Green and Mary Ackroyd "did by their general conduct refuse to acquiesce in the appointment (if any) of the said James Winter Butterworth and George Hanson as managers" William Taylor was discharged about the 2nd of June 1808 because he refused or neglected to enter in a book given to him by J.W. Butterworth and G. Hanson, particulars of items sold and the money taken. William Taylor did interfere in the management by re-employing discharged workmen and paying their wages.

Sometime in or about July 1808 J.W. Butterwoth in conversation with Ebenezer Green offered on the part of himself and the other Complainants "to refer the settlement of the said concerns to the Arbitration of any two Aldermen of the Borough of Leeds as the said Ebenezer Green should name or appoint with which he refused to comply saying 'we have nothing to refer' or words to that effect". He further stated that in consequence of the refusal of Ebenezer Green to refer to arbitration it was resolved by the Complainants gradually to stop the works but in consequence of the insubordination of the workmen it was by another resolution, made by the Complainants, Edward Brooke, J.W.Butterworth, S. Wainewright and Geo. Hanson, resolved to stop the works forthwith and the workmen were discharged about August 1808. Ebenezer Green and William Taylor did in about six months after the stoppage go on with the business without the consent or interference of the Complainants. Ebenezer Green and William Taylor did receive several sums of money belonging to the business amounting to £13,185-16-2½d. as appears in a book marked A. He stated that to the best of his knowledge that Savile Green and William Hartley did manage subject to the orders and resolutions of the partners and that Ebenezer Green, during their lives, did not interfere against the resolutions of the majority or assume any managerial or control positions in the business – except once in refusing to execute a power of Attorney and again to execute a Deed of Dissolution of certain Articles of Copartnership in which the other partners were interested. Commented on the political state of Europe affecting business, and after examining the books he concluded that the business had been injured to a considerable degree, but to what he could not fully state. But, from the books he found a deficiency in the Stock of Earthenware, Materials and Farming Stock from the 31st of December 1808 (when the Leeds Pottery had been shut for about three months) up to June last, about 3 weeks after Ebenezer Green had left the works, of about £4,407-19-8d. which cannot be explained or accounted for. Ebenezer Green had entered in the books cash paid to himself of £745-1-6d. and to Mary Ackroyd £75-10-0d. and a balance in hand of £195-18-1½. and debts acknowledged in the books by Ebenezer Green of £605-13-05d. In the cash books kept by William Taylor about 50 instances for the period the 22nd of May 1809 to the 15th of September 1810 in which the daily accounts of cash received and paid are equal on each side, without showing any surplus cash, although such daily entries for the most part consist of several sums paid and received in pounds shillings and pence.

SAMPSON DANIEL, late Manager of the Works, now of Hanley in Stafford, China Manufacturer, aged 52.

He had known the Complainants, except Thomas Clayton and James Ridehalgh for 16 years past. " ... does not know that ... James Winter Butterworth and George Hanson consented and agreed to take upon themselves the management of the ... Business ... otherwise than by their taking upon themselves the management and their informing this Deponent that they had agreed to take the management thereof And this Deponent saith that the said James Winter Butterworth and George Hanson in the opinion of this Deponent with the assistance of the Clerks and Managers that were then employed in the ... concern were competent to the management thereof properly for the Advantage of the Partnership. ... this Deponent saith that ... Savile Green and William Hartley did during their lives manage the ... Business according to their own Judgment and Discretion Subject as this Deponent believes to the orders and Resolutions of a majority of the ... Partners And this Deponent saith that ... Ebenezer Green did not to this Deponent's knowledge and belief during the lives of ... Savile Green and William Hartley interfere against the Orders and Resolutions of the majority or assume the individual Management and Control of the ... Business."

TIMOTHY BELL, late a Salesman in the Warehouse, now a Warehouse man, aged 58.

Stated that Wm. Taylor must have caused considerable loss, injury and detriment to the copartnership in consequence of his selling goods in an improper manner – in large quantities "by the Lump" or in large lots without knowing or ascertaining the quantities but the extent of such loss he was not able to state. He also stated that he did not know whether the conduct of EbenezerGreen and Mary Ackroyd had resulted in any loss to the concern.

RICHARD CRAVEN, late a Packer in the Warehouse, now a Sorter of Pots, aged 66.

Had known the parties for sixteen years except Thomas Clayton and James Ridehalgh. Stated that William Taylor had been dismissed by George Hanson for not complying with an order which he, George Hanson had given him, William Taylor replying – "I shall not for thee." He did not know whether the conduct of Ebenezer Green and Mary Ackroyd had produced any adverse effect on the business. But, he knew that William Taylor must certainly have done so – he had witnessed him selling – "Bowls of a description called twenty-four to the Dozen for Bowls of a description called thirty to the dozen and also Eighteens for twenty-fours and twelves for eighteens ... and also at various times sold plates and cups and saucers in the same way by giving greater quantities or selling them at lower prices than he ought to have done whereby a considerable loss was produced to the said copartnership but to what extent this Deponent cannot set forth."

The following is a summary of the statement given by William Taylor who, being a Quaker, did not swear an oath but made a public affirmation to tell the truth. It is filed with the main pleadings under PRO reference C13/1642/33 :

WILLIAM TAYLOR stated that he was given power of Attorney by Mary Ackroyd and therefore acted to his best ability to carry out this function. He sold goods and handed over the money daily to Robert Nicholson who accepted the same for about 10 or 11 months until, as he believed, George Hanson instructed Robert Nicholson to not accept any more... he handed all the money thereafter to Ebenezer Green. He believed that Ebenezer Green and Mary Ackroyd took over the business to prevent it being closed down by the Plaintiffs George Hanson and James Winter Butterworth. He believed they would have done so. He did refuse George Hanson access to his books on the orders of Ebenezer Green. He believed that it was not the wish of Ebenezer Green and Mary Ackroyd to take over the concern – only to keep it going – "in order to prevent the ruin of the concern by the total loss of its business and connections".

By the 25th of May 1815 the Court was able to make some orders which are recorded under PRO reference C33/614/1731. The entry begins thus :- "This Cause coming on the 8th, 9th, 13th & 14th of December 1814 and heard and debated before this Court in the presence of Counsel learned on both sides the substance of the Plaintiffs Bill appeared to be that . . ." We then have further vindication of the previously quoted extracts from the writings of Baker and Dickens – no less than nine and a half pages amounting to approximately fourteen and a half thousand words of which only the last half page contains any orders, the rest being a recital of both pleadings, and other documents from the partnership and other evidence. From this ocean of words we do learn that the Complainants had offered to sell their shares to the Defendants for £1,700 each and to purchase from the Defendants at £2,000 each, which offer was rejected, and that the business had been stopped for about two years. We then come to the following: "The Proofs taken in this Cause read and what was alleged by the Counsel on both sides This Court did order that this Cause should stand for Judgment and this Cause Standing for Judgment this present day accordingly in the presence of Counsel learned on both sides and :

This Court doth Order that so much of the plaintiffs Bill as seeks to have the Copartnership in the pleadings mentioned dissolved be dismissed out of this Court with Costs to be taxed by Mr. Alexander one of the Masters of this Court ..."

Round one to the defendants! The Court then went on to pronounce as follows :

"And this Court doth declare that the power of appointment of all Stewards Agents and Book keepers Managers and other necessary supervisors to be employed in the partnership Trade and Business ... is by the 12th Article of the Copartnerships Agreement vested in the partners or the major part of them according to their respective interests in the said Partnership ... but in all matters wherein such articles are silent the same is to be conducted in such manner as the said partners voting in the same manner at their meetings directed by the articles to be held or any other meeting duly convoked for that purpose ... The Master to decide a fair rent for the Houses ...

All Books to be made available to this Court ... It is ordered that the Receivers and Manager be discharged and pass their Accounts before the Master and pay the balance which shall be reported due from them into the Bank with the privity of the Accountant General of this Court to be then placed to the Credit of this Cause subject to the further order of this Court and thereupon it is ordered that the said Receiver and Manager be at liberty to apply to this Court to have the Recognisance entered into by them and their securities upon their being appointed Receivers and Managers vacated ... And this Court doth reserve the consideration of all future directions of the rest of the costs of this suit until after the Master shall have made his report and any of the Parties are to be at liberty to apply to this Court as there shall be occasion ...”

The first judgement regarding the plaintiffs' plea to have the partnership dissolved is clear enough. The declaration which merely states what is written in the 12th Article seems rather unsatisfactory for surely the nub of the matter was whether or not: (a) the meeting had been properly convened, that is, were ALL the partners given proper and adequate notice of such a meeting and (b) were the votes of the partners taken and recorded and (c) was a record of the meeting ever entered in a minute book and was such a book ever requested by the Court? These are questions which do not seem to have been answered or pronounced upon in the judgment.

We left the Savile Green correspondence in August 1811. We will now resume this somewhat distant yet telling commentary on this turbulent phase of the Leeds Pottery's history just over a year later. Such a long gap is accounted for in a letter of the 29th of July 1812 in which he refers to a letter which his sister had written to him having never been received in Rio de Janeiro. Savile accounts for this: “I conclude your letter must have been lost in the Wellwood, which Ship was lost on the coast of Ireland in her passage for this Place.” This brings home very clearly the problems with communications encountered by merchants working so distant from home.

Letter from Rio de Janeiro, dated the 9th of November 1812.

“ ... I shall be glad to hear from you with some pottery news as soon as possible, for I really think this is a favourable time for bringing the affairs of that concern to a conclusion and God grant they may turn out better than we have had reason to expect ...”

From Rio de Janeiro, dated the 25th of February 1813.

“ ... I received a letter from W. Hartley of Eleven pages! – with a Long History of LP affairs, he says they have got some money from Russia & Hemp & Flax, which would put some Cash into the Hands of the Managers, – God grant after this long gloomy time we may be able to pay our Debts & have a trifle to spare; ... W's letter to me is very friendly he talks of settling in London & hopes we may be able to do business together, ...”

From Savile, back in England writing to his sister Sarah, from the Leeds Pottery, she being then a teacher at a Boarding School at Hall Cross, Doncaster. It is dated the 8th of December 1813.

“Disappointed – crossed – & nearly gone mad with all my arrangements frittered away and a most serious change in my prospects effected by the change of Politics &c., &c., you will not when I see you be surprised at my not having written you 'ere this I am this morning just recovering from the Stupor occas[d] by the wreck of my Hopes – and looking round on the prospect before me it it a very poor one ... I am in Company with Mr. Nicholson now getting at the exact State of all our affairs and shall be able to let us all know the exact Way in which stand – horrid badly I forsee it will be but still the best foundation for Building & laying plans for the future – the real & true knowledge of our affairs be what they may – ...”

From Portsmouth, en route to Rio de Janeiro, dated the 10th of May 1814.

“ The signal for sailing is just made I shall be off in an hour ... W Hartley has taken a very good House in Great Coram Street Brunswick Square but not yet got into it. He has come down with me to Portsmouth – he has on every occasion behaved to me in the most cordial & brotherly manner ... Should anything happen William will be your friend ... send your ltr to Ruperti he will forward it ... Our ship is under sail – I must jump on board immedy ...”

From Rio de Janeiro, dated the 20th of November 1814.

“I am sending home Accts to LP ... both Wm [Hartley] and Ruperti say you have been in London ... Ruperti's last letter he informs me they go on very well at LP – God be thanked for it – the horrid tide of Interest is stopped by it & I am rather sanguine our dear-earned paternal bit may yet turn out well ... Ruperti will be continually writing me & can always send your Lrs. ...”

From Rio de Janeiro, dated the 12th of March 1815.

“... I've written William [Hartley] frequently since I had it in my power – I hear from Ruperti & write him by every conveyance ... LP goes on very nicely – they have not dissolved the Partnership and hush Sarah 'tell it not in Gath'[8] I am glad they have not, ...”

From Rio de Janeiro, dated the 26th of December 1815.

“ ... Pottery Affairs have ended just as they aught to do for our Interest, they have turned out as I hinted to you long since & have turned out for the best. ...”

From Rio de Janeiro, dated the 26th of May 1817.

> After a long letter describing how ill he has been – "Six months out of the last Twelve I have been confined to my bed & chamber ... I don't between ourselves half like LP now and don't care how soon we've all done with it ..."

From Rio de Janeiro, an extract from a letter which he sent to Edward Brooke, dated the 5th of December 1817, a copy of which he enclosed for his sister Sarah in a letter to her dated December 1818,

> "... I have no wish at present to sell my Share and hope the concern will do well & repay for some of the miseries of its Ten Years War."

The following extract is from the copy of another letter, this one to J.C.Ruperti, which Savile sent to his sister under cover of the same above mentioned letter of December 1818, this one being of the same date as the covering letter.

> " ... I want to secure to my Sisters their Share of good times at Leeds Pottery – they have gone through the bad ones – and their Shares must not be sold for Debt if I can help it – I feel no fear about the Pottery doing well so long as you and friend Hartley are in it and while you stop in the Concern I have not the least intention of selling & will therefore thank you to say a word or two on this subject at your leisure. ... No man can be more highly sensible than myself of the favors our family have recd. from Mr. E. Brooke – he kept my Sisters afloat when I could not help them – he has behaved with the greatest kindness to me when I could not help myself – But the shortest line betwixt any two points is a direct one – I am certain that you & I can best understand each other on LP Affairs."

The following is from the covering letter to his sister :-

> " ... Your discretion my dear Sarah I have no doubt about ... and now then dearest Sister cheer up! my Plan shall be carried on with Spirit and prudence – my Arm (a very thin one God knows!) shall protect you while there is life in it – write me all you hear and see on this Subject an invaluable Epistle from you gave rise to my [letter] to Mr. Brooke – I have come to close action with the Monster Debt – I'm his Match and I know it – and a D . . . l of a thrashing he shall have . . . it is now near One o'Clock in the morning – I shall write you again very soon about our family chat – In the meantime give my best love to all our Sisters & if ever there was a happy man in this World of care it was your Brother... This crisis will have an excellent effect on my future Spirits & Correspondence and praying God Almighty to protect & bless you all I remain for the first time these 12 Years
> Your happy Brother
> Savile Green."

Savile Green died, a bachelor, at Rio de Janeiro just three years later on the 14th of July 1820 having made his Will on the 7th of July 1808, shortly after attaining his majority. By his will he left all to his sisters with a bequest of his books in French, Latin, German, Italian and Russian, to his cousin George Gilpin of Somerset House, London. The Will was passed at York on the 15th of December 1820 showing that the value of his estate was "under £800". On the 12th of December 1821 his personal possessions, with an inventory, were sent to his friend Edward Brooke, executor of his Will, on board the ship *Ninus*.

Summing up

In presenting the account of this case I have tried, as far as possible, to let the documents and my summaries of them, tell the story. Certain points are, however, worth stressing. It is obvious from all the evidence presented that Ebenezer Green had not interfered in the running of the Pottery before the deaths of William Hartley and Savile Green, senior. It is also very clear that sometime after 1800 and certainly before their deaths that there was an undercurrent of unpleasantness among the partners, as evidenced by the letter from William Barwick, (see page 53). and the extract from Savile Green, junior's letter of the 28th of November 1808, (page 54). From Savile Green, junior's letter of 6th of Sept, 1806, (see page 54). the unrest seems to have been centred around the three related partners: George Hanson, James Winter Butterworth and Samuel Wainewright, "snarling" – "mad brutes" to quote Savile Green. These three and perhaps others who they may have persuaded to their point of view would appear to have wanted to change some aspect of the Articles of Agreement, *this* is what Ebenezer Green objected to. It is equally obvious that he, Ebenezer Green, believed that they wanted to close down the Pottery and realise its assets. With this belief in mind he dug his heals in and was prepared to resist any such course of action at whatever cost such action would necessitate. If this was the main bone of contention between the Complainants and Defendants, then Ebenezer Green, by the judgement of the Court had won the day.

Let us now survey the fall-out from the case which had ensured that the Pottery would continue, albeit somewhat injured. By May 1813 James Winter Butterworth was living in Portugal, possibly as an agent or merchant, this is known from the Indenture by which he purchased one of William Barwick's shares. He had obviously left the fight to his two other partners. He died in Lisbon on the 13th of February 1816. However the case dragged on until the final reference to it appears as late as 24th of March 1819.[9] Then in *The Leeds Mercury* of the 26th of February 1820 was announced the death of Ann the wife of Ebenezer Green[10] and in the same newspaper of the 17th of June 1820 we read the notice of the bankruptcy of both Ebenezer Green and his sister-in-law Mary Ackroyd. Exit the defendants and thus the case and, no doubt, the appearance of some long faces in the legal profession as, one may presume, their full legal fees would not now be recoverable! At this juncture it must be emphasised that it was only these two who were declared bankrupt and *not* the Leeds Pottery as has erroneously been claimed by some previous writers. Ebenezer Green died the 7th of July 1827, aged 69.

Another of the three "snarlers", Samuel Wainewright died in April 1824 to be followed by George Hanson on the 12th of June 1829 and whose assets, declared when his will was proved, had dwindled to "under £100".[11] Robert Nicholson, the erstwhile Book-keeper and Cashier at the Pottery and one of its Receivers and Managers and also an executor of the will of James Winter Butterworth, was declared a bankrupt on the 28th of November 1829. He was described as "Earthenware Manufacturer of Bradford" on account of him holding, as a trustee, the shares in the Leeds Pottery of the late James Winter Butterworth and being at that date resident in Bradford. Finally another of the partners the Rev. Edward Parsons who had inherited a share from his first wife Sarah, one of the daughters of Henry Ackroyd a founding partner of the Leeds Pottery, was declared bankrupt in December 1829,[12] yet another of the parties in the costly Court of Chancery proceedings. Fortunately his Certificate of Conformity is recorded in the Bankruptcy Archives in the Public Record Office.[13] It shows that of the eleven creditors who signed his Certificate, four were solicitors, two were bankers, three merchants, one ran an academy, and the remaining two were most likely solicitors as their names were linked with known solicitors in Leeds.

Thus it would appear that the case had bankrupted several of the players in this drama, in which the legal actors had exacted their fees till some of the coffers were bare. The only good thing to come forth being that Ebenezer Green's dogged, and at times 'dog-like' tenacity had ensured the survival and continuance of the 99 year term of the original Partnership Agreement. This achievement was however at a considerable cost in stress and money to so many of his fellow partners and their families, not to mention the team of skilled and faithful workmen which John Green had put together and which had been scattered. Some no doubt found work at other Yorkshire potteries, we know that some went to the Swinton Pottery[14] and no doubt some to the Don Pottery, but with others more than likely trudging back to Staffordshire.

To end the chapter may I remind the reader that on the 15th of May 1813 Justus Christian Ruperti had purchased a one-twentieth share in both the property and trade of the Leeds Pottery from William Barwick for the sum of £3,150.[15] It is quite evident that for some time he had played an important role in the affairs of the Pottery and would continue to do so into the fourth decade of the century.

1. J.H.Baker, Q.C., L.L.D., F.B.A., is Downing Professor of the Laws of England and Fellow of St. Catherine's College, Cambridge, and Hon. Bencher of the Inner Temple.
2. All these documents will be referred to as the Savile Green Archive (SGA).
3. *The Leeds Intelligencer* of the 8th of October 1804, and – *The Hull Advertizer* of the 6th of October 1804.
4. See Indenture of 26 Nov. 1770 at p. 17 & Insurance Policy dated 12 Oct. 1771 at p. 18.
5. Wm. Taylor was a son of Jonas & Elizabeth Taylor, Elizabeth being a sister of both Joshua Green and William Green who was Ebenezer's father. Mary Ackroyd was a spinster sister of Ebenezer's wife Ann, both of whom were the daughters of Henry Ackroyd one of the founding partners. See the Green family pedigree at pp. 594 and also Joshua Green's Will at Appx. II.
6. WYAS (Leeds) - DB 214/29.
7. IGI.
8. A Biblical quotation from Samuel II., Ch.1, v.20. Savile was here confiding to his sister that he was secretly pleased that the Defendants had won! "v.19 – How are the mighty fallen! v.20 – Tell it not in Gath, publish it not in the streets of Askelon; lest the daughters of the Philistines rejoice ...".
9. PRO, C33/655/672.
10. *The Leeds Mercury* of Saturday the 14th of February 1820 – "On Monday evening last, in the 54th year of her age, Ann, the faithful and affectionate wife of Ebenezer Green, one of the proprietors of the Leeds Pottery, who, after she had suffered many years under the most grievous afflictions, which she bore with the greatest magnanimity, calmly resigned her spirit into the hands of her Lord and Saviour Jesus Christ, with hopes full of immortality, without a struggle or sigh. Her temper was open, generous, and friendly, and her talents of the domestic kind were equalled by few and exceeded by none."
11. UYBIHR – PCY, George Hanson, 10th of March 1830.
12. *The Leeds Intelligencer* – 24th of December 1829.
13. PRO – B5/29.
14. WWM – F.106/12
15. WYAS (Leeds) – DB 214/48.

CHAPTER FOUR

Interlude

A GLIMPSE at the annual coal consumption in Chapter 7 and Appendix VIII will show the periods when the works were virtually closed down (10th of August to the 23rd of September 1808 and 1810 and 1811) followed by the resumption of work in 1812 after the appointment, by the Lord Chancellor, of Messrs Ruperti and Nicholson as Receivers and Managers in June of that year. Before the recommencement of the Works workmen would have to be sought, interviewed and set to work. No doubt a certain amount of maintenance of machinery and equipment as well as the preparation of materials etc., would all be necessary before things could be brought back to normal on Rushy Pasture. Agents would have to be informed also that work had begun again and that wares would shortly be available for sale. Interestingly the quantities of coal purchased in each year show a steady increase following the resumption of work until, in 1819, no less than 9,308 tons were purchased, this being the highest amount since the pottery opened in 1770. However, in 1820 only 85 tons were recorded as having been purchased from the Middleton Colliery, see Chapter 7, page 88, for a possible explanation.

From Baines' Directory of 1817 we learn that a certain John Braim was then Manager to Hartley Greens and Co. It is recorded that from 1818[1] the famous Thomas Lakin was either Manager, or a Manager of some departments, at the Pottery until his death in 1821. He was succeeded by his son Thomas who tragically died in 1824 and who was described in his obituary notice as "superintendent of the Leeds Pottery" (see Chapter 9 for a more detailed account of the Lakins at Leeds). Two Hunslet Valuation Books for the years 1823/4 and 1826 supply further information regarding who was living in properties on the site of the Pottery.[2] It would appear that there were four houses on the site, two being those built by Richard Humble, one for the manager John Green and the other for Savile Green. These are shown as being occupied by George Hanson and a certain Mr. Bedford – could he have been another Manager of the Pottery? Another house described as "House Brewhouse and Coal House, Garden" etc., was occupied by "Mr. Rupertee". The fourth house was occupied by Mr. Wainewright. Workmen's cottages were occupied by John Wild, William Inman, John Coope and Timothy Bell. The latter gave evidence to the Court of Chancery (see page 63) when his occupation was "late Salesman in the Warehouse now Warehouseman, aged 58."

Two other important persons in the story of the Leeds Pottery must now be mentioned. First, Alexander Turner who held the shares in the Pottery in trust for the benefit of the Partners, (see page 45). A fine portrait in oils by the renowned portrait artist John Russell, R.A., is shown at Plate 21. Alexander Turner was one of the leading citizens of Leeds being twice Mayor, in 1793 and again in 1810. He died on the 24th of July 1816, aged 63, after which his trusteeship of the Leeds shares passed to his only daughter and heir at law, Mary, the wife of the Rev. James Armitage Rhodes. The other person who played a significant role during this period was William Hartley son and heir at law of the former partner of the same name. He is mentioned in the Savile Green Correspondence, (see Chapter 3, page 64); from reading this correspondence it is obvious that Savile Green confided in William and trusted him. We also learn from one of the letters that in 1814 William had a house in Great Coram Street, Brunswick Square, London which fits very nicely with the date, quoted below, when he was in business in London with George Green, one of John Green's sons. The following dates and addresses have been extracted from various London directories :

1814. Green & Hartley, Merchants, 28 St. Swithen Lane.
    1820. Green & Hartley, Brazil Merchants, 28 St. Swithen Lane.
    1821. Green & Hartley, Merchants, 9 Pancras Lane.
    1821. Green & Hartley, Merchants, 12 Pancras Lane.
    1826-7. Green & Hartley, Merchants, 38 Old Broad St.

The following announcements are taken from the *London Gazette* :
    LG. 1829, Vol.II p. 2167: "Notice is hereby given that the Partnership business subsisting since the year 1819 between George Green, William Hartley and Joseph Tulley, and carried on in the city of Rio de Janeiro, under the firm of Green Hartley & Tulley has been dissolved by mutual consent from the 30th September 1829.

                        George Green
                        William Hartley

Joseph Tulley."

LG. 1833 Vol I. p. 202: "The Firm of Green & Hartley, Merchants in the City of London is dissolved from the 31st of December 1829.   George Green
                                                                                        William Hartley
                                                                                        Frederick Favarger."

The reference to one of William Hartley's partnerships, described as being in Rio de Janeiro, is very interesting as it shows that, after the death of Savile Green junior in 1820, the Pottery had continued to maintain the presence of a merchant in that city. The Don Pottery also maintained a merchant in the same city and shipped large quantities of its wares to that area. A letter from a ship owner, William Rooth, is quoted in my Don Pottery book at page 38. In that letter is the following : " ...Mr. Hartley the merchant of Rio and Mr. Potter's son of this place as Clerk to him ..." were passengers on board one of his ships, the *Falcon*, sailing to Rio in July 1828. Whilst in London, William formed a close friendship with a certain Miss Sarah Jones, alias Sarah Browne, about whom more will be found in Chapter 5. William Hartley died on the 24th of May 1833 after playing a not insignificant part in the instigation of the second Chancery suite, see Chapter 5.

Sometime in 1814, or shortly after that year, Hartley Greens & Co. published another edition of their enlarged Design Book, which had first been published in the early 1800s in an edition in Spanish and English and with extra illustrations which increased the first section from 152 to 221 designs and the Tea-Ware section from 32 to 48 designs. The paper is watermarked for 1814, which date has been traditionally given to this edition. See page 116 *et seq.* "Leeds Pottery" was also printed on each page of engravings.

At the Pottery another fire was reported in *The Leeds Mercury* of Saturday the 29th of September 1817 :

"About midnight on Tuesday last an alarming fire broke out in the workshop under the warehouses at the Pottery of Messrs Hartley Greens and Co., of this place, but by the prompt and rigorous exertions of the inhabitants, aided by the military, the fire was got under about three o'clock, and before four it was completely extinguished – The Pottery engine being upon the spot, was got to work almost as soon as the flames were discovered, and three other engines were soon after brought to afford their co-operation. The premises we learn, were fully insured in the Norwich Union Office."

The partners placed the following notice in the same newspaper :

"Hartley Greens & Co., beg Leave to return their sincere Thanks to their Neighbours and the Public, for the Spirited Assistance they received from them, at the FIRE which broke out upon their Premises on Wednesday Morning last. They also feel particularly indebted to Lieut. HAMMEL of the Kings Dragoon Guards, and the Men under his Command, who kindly hastening to the Spot, and preserving good Order, were materially instrumental in arresting the Progress of the Flames:

Leeds Pottery, 27th Nov. 1817."

By an Indenture dated the 19th of February 1820,[3] William Hartley purchased a parcel of land adjoining the Leeds Pottery known as the "Dowbridge or Dowbrigg" close, otherwise known as part of Windmill Close, containing 1a.2r.4p. from a John Pearson of Leeds, for the sum of £480-7-0d., which close was duly "conveyed and assured" unto John Edward Brooke in trust for William Hartley who had purchased it at his sole expense for the co-partnership. From the long 'Abstract of the Title of Mr. Richard Britton and his Mortgage to the Leeds Pottery'[3] it would appear that this close of land had formed part of the entirety of the Leeds Pottery and had been included in the Indentures of the 7th and 8th of August 1799. This was therefore an altruistic gesture on the part of William Hartley who thereby made the Pottery site more complete.

As we move further into the nineteenth century it is to be expected that a manufactory the size of the Leeds Pottery would not escape being affected by the increasing agitation and unrest, coupled with the emergence of the Union Movement, which sought to improve the hours of work, as well as the conditions and pay of the employees. Workers were prohibited from joining together to form 'unions' by the Combination Acts of 1799 and 1800. Following the repeal of these acts in 1824 the pressure was released and craftsmen and other workers in many trades did form their own 'Unions'. That there was a growing agitation for reform generally at this period is well documented and most will be aware of the infamous 'Peterloo Massacre' which occurred in August 1819. Reverberations of this event were felt all over the country and especially in the industrial regions, Leeds being no exception. Preserved in the British Library is an interesting pamphlet entitled *Reform and the Manchester Outrage* which describes a Reform Meeting held on Hunslet Moor on the 20th of September 1819.[4] The Manchester event had mainly concerned handloom weavers; therefore it would obviously have been of particular concern to the woollen weavers of the Leeds area. The pamphlet describes how an estimated crowd of between thirty and forty thousand had assembled, led by a band, which after the speeches had led the crowd in singing "Rule Britannia". Such an event must have been the talk of all in the area for some time and surely the potters of Hunslet would not have been immune from such a highly emotive issue and meeting; in all probability many would have attended it.

It is not therefore surprising to find that there was a strike at the Leeds Pottery in December 1825. Fortunately Llewellynn Jewitt has reproduced a handbill which outlined the reasons for this, otherwise we may never have known that it took place as I have been unable to discover any information or notice regarding it elsewhere.[5] It was printed for the men by Mr. Edward

Baines (1774-1848) who later became the MP for Leeds, 1834–41.

"*An Appeal to the Public from the Journeymen Potters of Leeds and its Neighbourhood.* It is with painful feelings that we are under the necessity of laying before a discerning public the following brief statement of Facts relative to those differences now existing between us and our Employers.

At a time like the present, it is very strange that our Employers should attempt an unparalleled Reduction of our Wages, amounting from 20 to 30 per cent. upon the prices we have received, when those prices were barely sufficient to support a Man and his Family, and at the same time raise the price of his goods to the Public at least 50 per cent.

We feel confident the above Statement of Facts will at once convince every thinking individual that our conduct in standing out to oppose such uncalled-for proceedings is just and right. We should have exposed ourselves to the censure of every reasonable Man, and all who have alive in their bosom a spark of honest indignation, had we tamely submitted to the fiat of our Employers, and not made every effort in our power to preserve that which is every man's natural right – a fair remuneration for his labour.

We respectfully solicit the aid of a generous Public, to enable us to withstand the unjust proceedings of those who have driven us to this alternative, by their unceasing endeavours to reduce us to a state of misery and degradation from which we hope to be preserved by your kind assistance, and enabled to withstand those encroachments which would inevitably plunge ourselves, our families, and our successors into inevitable ruin. –Dec. 13, 1825."

The outcome of the above action and its duration are, unfortunately, unknown. The wording of the above notice does indicate a very unsatisfactory state of affairs *vis à vis* the relationship between the partners and their workforce. This in turn would engender feelings of desperation on the part of the workers who had been driven to taking such action and an equally strong feeling amongst the partners of frustration and despair at the effort needed to keep such a large concern constantly fully employed by a never ending stream of orders thereby ensuring full production and sale of the wares produced.

One piece of information, however, may be of relevance although it does not refer to a strike. I refer to a letter, preserved in the Doncaster Archives, from Anthony Fisher the Overseer of Hunslet to the Overseers of Swinton. It is dated the 3rd of April 1826[6] :

"Gentlemen Josh Bullough residing here but belonging to Swinton has been out of employment for the last ten weeks he has a wife and three children under 7 years of age – he is a potter by trade but we well know that the Leeds Pottery has been set down a long time which throws a great weight upon our town & we have asked them if any prospect of beginning again presents itself – but they cannot tell when – he will not be able to do with less that 6/- per week – we allow ours in like situation more – your answer will oblige."

By the middle of the third decade of the nineteenth century only J.C. Ruperti and George Hanson were left as partners who had actually purchased their shares, all the others had inherited theirs and who may not have had a liking for or interest in the potting trade and may well have wanted to get out of it. This may therefore have been the cause of the Leeds Pottery being advertised for sale by auction which appeared in *The Leeds Intelligencer* of the 30th of April 1826 :

"LEEDS POTTERY - TO BE SOLD

by AUCTION, in the Month of May next, either together or
in Lots, unless previously disposed of by Private Contract, of
which due Notice will be given; all that old-established and
well-known EARTHENWARE MANUFACTORY, called the LEEDS
POTTERY, consisting of Four Biscuit Ware Kilns, Eight
Glazing Kilns, a corresponding Number of Hardening and
Enamelling Kilns, spacious and commodious Counting
Houses, Warehouses, Workshops, Slip Houses, Drying
Houses, Sorting and Packing Rooms, Sheds for Straw, and
other convenient Buildings surrounding inclosed Yards."

The notice went on to list two Dwelling Houses and workmen's cottages, stabling for twenty-four horses, Blacksmiths', Joiners', Coopers', and Crate Makers, Shops. Also a Flint Mill powered by a thirty-six horsepower steam engine, lately erected, and the whole occupying seven acres of ground: "... comprising every requisite Convenience for continuing the Foreign and Home Trade, which has been extensively carried on for upwards of Fifty Years." Also the following explanation for its sale: "The Managing Partners of this Important Establishment being desirous to retire from it ...".

Nothing else is presently known about this proposed sale save one fact, it was not sold, but the omens for what would follow

1. Harold Blakey – "Thomas Lakin, Staffordshire Potter 1769–1821", *NCS Journal Vol. 5*, 1984.
2. WYAS (Leeds) – LO/HU/5.
3. WYAS (Leeds) – DB 214/48, pp. 29, 30.
4. BL. Shelf mark – 10347.ee.(18)2.
5. Llewellynn Jewitt – *Ceramic Art of Great Britain, Vol. 1*, pp. 472/3.
6. Doncaster Archives – P59/6/B/7/3.

CHAPTER FIVE

Once More into
The High Court of Chancery

ICOMMENTED in Chapter 1 that clause 15 of the Partnership Agreement of 1776 would eventually create considerable problems for the partners. This chapter, and the Chancery suit which it deals with, will justify that comment, namely the way that shares, held by the original partners, became divided through inheritance, trusteeships, the assignees of partners who became bankrupt, and mortgagees. From the original five partners the fourteen shares which they held between them in 1770 had, by 1842, no fewer than forty-five persons who claimed some interest in them, but this was not all. If we add to the confusion caused by the increased number of shareholders the fact that several partners died intestate some of whom had not administered the wills of earlier partners, then the reader will get some idea of the legal knots which had to be unravelled by the various lawyers involved.

The account which I will now give is as succinct as is deemed necessary in order to deal clearly with the history and progress of the Pottery and at the same time give a flavour of the complexities involved.

By 1830 it is obvious, from reading the papers associated with the Chancery proceedings, that the firm was owing several debts which it was then unable to discharge. It is also clear that although there were, by that date, many partners and others with an interest in the Pottery, that there were only three partners with sufficient interest or ability to play a meaningful part in the running of the Pottery, namely Samuel Wainewright and William Hartley, both the sons of former partners and Justus Christian Ruperti who was the only one who had actually purchased his share. These three, describing themselves as the "continuing and surviving partners", executed an Indenture[1] dated the 1st of May 1830 between themselves and James Hargreave of Leeds, Merchant and Edmund Dawson of Rothwell Haigh, Coal Agent, of the second part and an unlisted number of persons being the creditors of the firm of Hartley Greens and Company of the third part. The implementation of this Indenture resulted in the Leeds Pottery, its land, property and equipment being conveyed and assigned by the partners to messrs Hargreave and Dawson upon trust "to make sale and dispose of the same either by public sale or private contract". The money so raised was then to be used, first, to pay all the creditors and then to hand over the remainder to Thomas Everard Upton the elder of Leeds, Solicitor, in trust for the "several parties entitled to the same". Messrs Hartley, Wainewright and Ruperti had also agreed that if the money realised proved insufficient to pay all the creditors then they would make good the deficiency out of their own "private Estates and Effects". From the evidence in the recital of documents in the Chancery suit under PRO C13/1874/1/3 we further learn that "the trade or business had been lately discontinued" :

> "In or about the month of May 1827 the persons interested in the ... partnership came to an agreement that William Samuel Gibson and Robert Nicholson should examine the books and accounts ... and that the partnership of the Leeds Pottery or firm of Hartley Greens and Company has not been carried on since the 25th of June 1827."

24. BILL HEAD OF 1827. Apart from the one illustrated at Plate 22 this is the only other one presently known. 1827 was the year in which the Hartley Greens & Co's partnership ended. It shows a view of the Pottery from the west and was engraved by the same firm of Leeds engravers as the previous one. *The John Goodchild Collection, Wakefield.*

From the second half of 1828 the Middleton Colliery Journals show that coal was being sold to S. Wainewright.[2] Also in the PRO C13/2390/99458 we see that Sam. Wainewright was paying rent to Messrs Hargreave and Dawson, as trustees of the Leeds Pottery, of £493 per year from the second half of 1830, (see page 74).

The Leeds Intelligencer of the 29th of July 1830 carried an announcement that the Leeds Pottery would be offered for sale by auction on the 25th of August; again it was not sold.

In March 1831 the deeds and papers relating to the title of the land, Rushy Pasture and its buildings, were deposited with John Dodgson Charlesworth as an equitable lien for securing the sum of £1609 and interest owing to him by the partnership.

One problem which had to be addressed in order that any sale could proceed, and which may have been the cause of previous sales not being completed, was to establish the vendors' full legal title to the property and thereby the shareholders to their shares. Thus, on the 23rd of February 1832, Samuel Wainewright successfully applied to the Exchequer Court of the Diocese of York for authority to administer the "goods and chattels" of :

Joshua Green, left unadministered by Ebenezer Green, his sole executor, who had died intestate.

Henry Ackroyd, and those of his wife Sarah, and his daughters: Sarah Parsons, Mary and Ann, the wife of

Ebenezer Green and, on the 26th of May 1832, those of Catherine Savile Horsfall.

Such administration being limited only so far as to enable Samuel Wainewright to make a good title to the Leeds Pottery property and no further – and in order to enable him to file a Bill in the Court of Chancery against James Hargreave and Edmund Dawson. It having became very clear to Messrs Hartley, Wainewright and Ruperti that not all of those people who had shares or other interests in the Pottery agreed with the actions being taken and thus the cause was taken to the High Court of Chancery, the first Bill being presented on the 23rd of June 1832 under :

Ruperti v Wilson

and subsequently under

Ruperti v Hargreave.

The following being the Plaintiffs :

James Ridehalge

John Boulcock Hayes and Esther Maria his wife

William Hartley

Justus Christian Ruperti

Samuel Wainewright of Leeds

Thomas Clayton

Sarah Ann Hartley

John Hindle and Jane his wife

Elizabeth Butterworth

Winter Butterworth

Ann Butterworth

Thomas Pilkington and Jane his wife

James Butterworth

Thomas Butterworth

Sarah Butterworth

Maria Butterworth

Thomas Kendall

John Kendall

William Hardwick

James Hanson

Benjamin Hardwick and Mary his wife

The Defendants were :

James Hargreave

Edmund Dawson

Thomas Everard Upton the elder

William Morley Heginbotham

Charles Turkington

Richard Bramley

Thomas Mawson

John Ed. Brooke

James Armitage Rhodes and Mary his wife

John Dodgson Charlesworth

Robert Nicholson, Robert Atkinson the elder and

Sarah Savile his wife

Mary Savile Green

Henry Broomhead and Ann Savile his wife

By their Bill the plaintiffs petitioned that the Indenture of the 1st of May 1830 might be established and executed. Unfortunately Sarah Ann Hartley died on the 14th of September 1832 followed by her brother William Hartley on the 24th of May 1833, after which William Hartley's "dearly loved and valued friend Sarah Jones commonly known by the name of Sarah Brown" who was the sole executor of William's Will, by which she inherited not only Willaim's estate but also that of his sister Sarah Ann, joined the list of plaintiffs. Following any such change in the '*dramatis personæ*', the Bill had to be presented again to the Court; this was known as a 'Revivor'.

The Revivor was presented in Court on the 1st of March 1834. Following this the Court declared that the Co-partnership under the name of Hartley Greens and Company was to be taken as being dissolved on the 2nd of June 1827 and that by direction of the Master of the Court, Sir Giffin Wilson, the Leeds Pottery was advertised for sale.

In pursuance of the above order the Leeds Pottery was offered for sale by auction on the 15th of October 1834 and Samuel Wainewright agreed to become the purchaser for the sum of £9,000. However, only four days after the sale Samuel Wainewright died intestate, leaving Harriett Wilson and Charlotte Clementson, his sisters, co-heiresses at law and sole next of kin.[3] When Samuel Wainewright's personal estate and effects were valued they were found to be "wholly insufficient to carry into effect the said purchase". His two co-heiresses disclaimed all interest in their late brother's offer to purchase the Pottery whereupon the Court decreed, on the 23rd of December 1835, that the contract should be rescinded and that Messrs

Hargreave and Dawson should be at liberty to accept another offer, presumably made at the time of the auction, by a certain John Waddingham, who on being approached, "absolutely refused to complete the same".

Following the death of Samuel Wainewright it was further discovered that he had not implemented his authority for the limited administration of the previously mentioned unadministered estates. In order to execute what Samuel Wainewright had failed to carry out, Stephen Chappel, on the 3rd of April 1835, likewise applied to the Prerogative Court of the Diocese of York and was granted powers for limited administration of the estates and possessions of the following, again only so far as to enable him to obtain legal title to the Leeds Pottery property and the shares involved :

The estates of: Henry Ackroyd, who had died in 1788, his wife and three daughters.
                   Joshua Green who had died in 1799.
                   George Hanson who had died in 1829.
                   Catherine Savile Horsfall who had died in 1832.

The proceedings of the suit were thus abated for the second time until a Bill of Revivor was exhibited on the 2nd of June 1835 followed by the necessary Order of the Court of the 26th of June.

Another stumbling stone encountered along the way by both the plaintiffs and the defendants occurred in April 1836 with the death of Justus Christian Ruperti, who died intestate. Letters of Administration were granted to James Hargreave and Edmund Dawson, limited to his interest and share in the estate and effects of the co-partnership, by the Prerogative Court of York. However searching in the archives at York reveals nothing of any interest save a meagre £20. This represents nothing like the full story. Justus Christian Ruperti, as has been stated earlier, was born in Germany and therefore classed as an alien. Thus although he had purchased one full share in the Leeds Pottery and its partnership from William Barwick in 1813 for the sum of £3,150, this had had to be held in trust for him as, being an alien, he could not hold the 'fee simple' of any freehold property; moreover at his death such freehold property would 'escheat', i.e. revert to the Crown. The outcome of this was made good by virtue of a Royal Warrant of Queen Victoria dated the 22nd of December 1837 whereby Her Majesty, at the recommendation and with the advice of the Commissioners of Her Treasury, granted to James Hargreave and Edmund Dawson the shares and interest which Justus Christian Ruperti had held in the Leeds Pottery.

There then followed two more deaths: Thomas Everard Upton the elder of Leeds, solicitor, and Samuel Wainewright of Pontefract. Once more the Cause was abated and once more a Bill of Revivor had to be exhibited. This was done in Trinity Term 1838, after which more deaths occurred :

James Hanson, brother of the late George Hanson, died and letters of administration were granted to Stephen Chappel on the 23rd of May 1839, only as to enable him to revive the Suit in order to make a good title to the estate of the co-partnership. The next of kin of James Hanson having been cited but failed to appear.
Thomas Clayton.
John Hindle.
Mary Hardwick, and
Sarah Savile Atkinson.

The proceedings having yet again been abated, a Revivor was again exhibited and the Cause was duly revived by an Order of the Court of the 6th of July 1839.

On the 28th of July 1840 Stephen Chappel who, since at least 1837,[4] had been the manager of the Leeds Pottery, did consent and agree with Messrs Hargreave and Dawson, subject to the agreement of all the parties concerned as well as the approval of the Court, to purchase the Pottery, its lands, buildings and equipment and machinery for the sum of £9,000. The matter was referred to the Master of the Court who made his report, dated the 23rd of December 1840, that the contract was a proper one for the benefit of all parties and that it should be executed.

Mary Savile Green, the spinster daughter of the late Savile Green senior, died on the 7th of February 1841 and, by her will, bequeathed all to her sole surviving sister Ann Savile Broomhead, thus her estate was passed quite smoothly and on the 25th of January 1842 an Indenture of that date conveyed the Leeds Pottery to Mr. Stephen Chappel.[5] The Indenture is written on sixteen parchment membranes and signed by 40 persons with another six not signing. Of the six who did not sign, four were minors: Savile Atkinson, Robert Atkinson, Mary A. Wainewright and Thompson Wainewright; James Butterworth was in Buenos Aires in South America, and the sixth was William Hardwick. R. Upton attested for all six, which was allowed by Sir Giffin Wilson, Master of the Court.

Stephen Chappel paid the £9,000 plus £226-16-11d for interest into the Bank of England, "with the privity of the Accountant General of the High Court of Chancery to the credit of the said Cause", on the 4th of March. The Court also certified that the sum of £1,609 owing to John Dodgson Charlesworth on Mortgage had been "fully satisfied and paid", (see page 74).

A further sum of £1,107-10-0d., being the amount received by Messrs Hargreave and Dawson for a plot of land at the NE end of Windmill Close which they had sold to the North Midland Railway Co., was handed over to Stephen Chappel.

It had taken almost ten years to pass this second Cause through the Court of Chancery with eleven deaths along the way including all three of the "continuing and surviving partners" who had instigated the Cause: William Hartley, Samuel

Wainewright and Justus Christian Ruperti. The following were the final parties to this Cause and to the final episode of the greatly enlarged co-partnership which had begun in 1770 with just five partners :

The Rev. James Armitage Rhodes of Horsforth, Clerk and Mary his wife of the 1st part.
John Edward Brooke late of Leeds Esq., but now of Crayke in Co. Durham of the 2nd part.
James Hargreave of Leeds, Merchant, and –
Edmund Dawson of Rothwell Haigh, Coal Agent of the 3rd part.
James Ridehalgh of Schofield, near Colne, Lancashire, Gentleman of the 4th part.
John Boulcock Hayes of Lytham, Lancashire, Gent. and Maria his wife of the 5th part.
Sarah Browne otherwise Sarah Jones now or late of Regent Street in the County of Middlesex, spinster of the 6th part.
William Morley Heginbotham of Heaton Cottage nr. Didsbury, Cheshire, and –
Charles Turkington of Leeds, Gentleman of the 7th part.
Henry Broomhead of Brighouse, Yorkshire, Schoolmaster and Ann Savile his wife of the 8th part.
John Burnley of Wetherby, Yorkshire, Farmer of the 9th part.
Robert Atkinson the elder of Liverpool, Surgeon of the 10th part.
Savile Atkinson of Liverpool a minor and Robert Atkinson the younger a minor of the 11th part.
Richard Bramley of Leeds Merchant and the said Edmund Dawson of the 12th part.
John Wilson of Thornton, Yorkshire, Farmer and Harriett his wife, and –
The Rev. John Clementson of Wolve in Co. of Warwick, Clerk and Charlotte his wife of 13th part.
John Kendall of Leeds, Upholsterer of the 14th part.
Robert Nicholson of Bradford, Yorkshire, Book-keeper of the 15th part.
Jane Hindle of Stamford, Co. Lincoln, widow of the 16th part.
Elizabeth Butterworth of Stamford, Spinster, Ann Butterworth of Sunderland, Co. Durham, Spinster, Thomas Pilkinton of Stamford Architect, and Jane his wife, James Butterworth of Buenos Aires in South America, Merchant, Thomas Butterworth of Liverpool, Sailor, Sarah
Butterworth of Stamford, Spinster, Maria Butterworth of Sunderland, Spinster – all of the 17th part.
William Hardwick of Huddersfield, Colliery Agent of the 18th part.
John Jackson of Liverpool, Merchant of the 19th part.
Elizabeth Wainewright the elder of Pontefract, Spinster of the 20th part.
Thomas Jackson Wainewright of Pontefract, Druggist, Elizabeth Wainewright the younger of Pontefract, Spinster, James Wainewright of Pontefract, Gentleman, Mary Ann Wainewright of Pontefract, Spinster, Thompson Wainewright of Pontefract, a minor – all of the 21st part.
John Upton of Leeds Gentleman, Thomas Everard Upton of Leeds Gentleman and the Rev. Robert Upton of Morton Say, Co. Salop, Clerk, of the 22nd part.
John Dodgson Charlesworth of Chapelthorpe Hall in the parish of Sandal Magna, Co. York, Esq., of the 23rd part.
Stephen Chappel of Leeds, Potter, of the 24th part.

As stated earlier the foregoing account of the lengthy somewhat difficult ten years' journey through the High Court of Chancery will, I feel sure, have given the reader a sense of the problems and frustrations which must have been experienced by the parties striving to get the Pottery's ownership and its legal affairs sorted out and in order. Now, in 1842, the Leeds Pottery had its new owner, not a group of partners but an owner who was quite young, aged nearly 32, who had managed the Pottery for at least five years. Stephen Chappel was joined by one partner, his younger brother James who had been the Book-keeper at the Pottery.

Fortunately, among the documents relating to the Court of Chancery Case, there is one set which does contain some very valuable information regarding the debts owing to the Pottery as well as some of the receipts and payments made by Messrs Hargreave and Dawson. These occur in the answers given by the Defendants, Hargreave and Dawson to some Interrogatories exhibited by the Claimants.[6]

The first list is – "... a list of various Debts due to the said firm of Hartley Greens and Company." At this juncture I am only going to give the total value of the debts as the list will be found on pages 92/3 where it will prove more appropriate when considering the firm's customers and markets. The total value of the debts listed came to £10,456-2-2d.

Under Receipts :

"<u>1st Part – In respect of the real Estate.</u>

1830 Dec 30 These Examinants received of the late Plaintiff Samuel
Wainewright for half a Years Rent of the
Leeds Pottery and Premises held therewith   £250 - 00 - 00
Less half a years Rent of Railroad agreed
to be provided for the use of the Tenant   3 -10 - 00 [7]

	Net rent	£246 - 10 - 00

[There then follows payments entered for every 30th of June and 31st of December,
from June 1831 to June 1840 showing the full half year's rent of £246-10-00d   £4,683 - 10 - 00]
1840 Aug 31 ... received of the said Samuel Wainewright's Representatives one
quarters rent of the said Pottery and Premises up to this time when possession
thereof was delivered to Mr Stephen Chappel the purchaser pursuant to the Contract   123 - 5 - 0

	£5053 - 5 - 00

<u>2nd Part - Personal Estate.</u>

1832 Jul 13 These Examinants received Cash for Earthenware sent by the said firm of
Hartley Greens & Co the 25th of June 1825 on Consignment to Zante[8]   86 - 16 - 10
1833 Mar 1 These Examinants received for Earthenware sent by the said
firm the 25th June 1825 on Consignment to Zante the further Sum of   68 - 17 - 2

	155 - 14 - 00

1836 Mar 1 ... from the Commissioners apptd by the British Government to
Adjudicate on Claims for Compensation in respect of Property Confiscated by the
Danish Government the Sum of   299 - 17 - 00
... from the said Commissioners further and in full of such Claims the further sum of   914 - 8 - 3

	£1369 - 19 - 3

[Earlier in the same document] Certain Claims on the British
Government for compensation in respect of the Confiscation of certain property of the
Said firm of Hartley Greens & Company being in the Kingdom of Denmark and Confiscated by order of the
Danish Government upon the Declaration of War between the British Government and that of Denmark in the
year one thousand eight hundred and seven. [See Appx. V].

Under Payments :

<u>... payments and allowances for the said Defendants the Trustees on Account of the Aforesaid Estate and Effects.</u>
[Legal fees. Under this heading most of the payments were to the firm of T.E. Upton
& Son of Leeds, later Messrs Upton & Son, and finally Messrs Upton & Clapham.
In addition to these there was one payment to William Jones and one to Messrs Moore
& Snowden, in total]   £2,122 - 10 - 0
[For fire insurance with the Sun Fire Office, nine annual payments of £11 - 16.]   106 - 4 - 0
[To Samuel Wainewright interest was being paid half yearly on "the Sum of £1800 lent by
Samuel Wainewright the Father of the Said late plaintiff to the said Partnership firm" –
eight payments of £45 and one of £46]   406 - 00 - 0
[Annual interest payments were also being made on the mortgage from John Dodgson
Charlesworth – six of £80-9s.]   482 - 14 - 0
1831 Jun 11 pd Miss Carmichael for Silk lawns[9]   1 - 16 - 0
        25 pd for a stamp[10]   2 - 6
    Dec 31 pd for Sundry Stamps[10]   1 - 14 - 0
          pd Wm Hartley the expence of his Journey to London to have an interview
          with several of the Creditors and prevail upon them to accept the provisions of the
          Trust Deed   20 - 00 - 0
1832 Jul 31 pd John Bell the sd Partnership acceptance due to Timothy Bell   110 - 00 - 0
    Oct 1 pd J & R Gothard for Iron Work   4 - 14 - 6
1833 Apr 14 pd Union Cos Account for freight of Goods to Liverpool   27 - 5 - 6
    Dec 18 pd The Revd J Williams the amount of Acceptance in his hands & Expences   40 - 2 - 0
1837 Mar 21 pd John Dodgson Charlesworth the Amount of the Principal Monies due
          to him upon and by virtue of his said Mortgage   1609 - 0 - 0

	£4985 - 2 - 7

... paid the following Creditors of the said firm on Bills of Exchange the
Sum of 10s/ in the £ on the amount of their Debts.

1832.		Amount of Bill	
Apr 20	W & D Melville	£425 - 3 - 6	£212 - 11 - 11
"	Smith Payne & Co.	798 - 4 - 10	399 - 2 - 5
"	Prescott Grote & Co.	299 - 18 - 9	149 - 19 - 5
21	W R Vigers	250	125
"	Peter Dixon	300	150
22	J H Schroeder & Co.	174 - 2 - 11	87 - 1 - 6
"	John Gae & Co.	200	100
25	H Blakelock	385 - 1 - 4	192 - 10 - 11
"	Perfect & Co.	145 - 6 - 8	72 - 13 - 4
"	Chas. Shearman	300	150
Jun 28	Barrandon & Co.	200	100
Apr 26	J Linnelor	27 - 15 - 9	14 - 17 - 11
Jan 25	Lindus or Wm Hartley in full with charges	30	34 - 11
Jan 10	Althorpe & Co.	190 4	95 2
Jul 5	Hirst Bramley & Co.	350	175
			£7043 - 11 - 2 "

1. Contents from the following sources: recital in the "Abstract of the Title of Mr. Richard Britton ..." WYAS (Leeds) – DB 214/48. And also from PRO – C13/1874/1/3.
2. WYAS (Leeds) – MC, – 70, 71, 72 and 73.
3. I have not been able to discover any contemporary evidence that Samuel Wainewright died of Cholera, as has been stated by some writers.
4. White's *Directory and Gazetteer of the West Riding*, 1837. Llewellynn Jewitt, in the *Art Journal* of 1865, p. 306, claimed that Samuel Wainewright, presumably the younger, had: "... employed as his confidential cashier Stephen Chappel...". If this is correct it would mean that Stephen Chappel had worked at the Leeds Pottery since at least 1834. See also p. 588.
5. WYAS (Leeds) – DB 214/48.
6. PRO – C13/2390/99458.
7. See p. 17. When the Leeds Pottery was first built in Hunslet this amount of rent was paid to the owner of the land, then Richard Humble, who deducted this amount from the rent which he charged the other partners. £7 per year being the amount of "wayleave rent" then paid by Charles Brandling for the right to cross that land with his railroad from the Middleton Colliery to the Leeds Coal Staith.
8. The name and capital of one of the Ionian islands off the west coast of Greece.
9. Before the introduction of fine phosphor-bronze wire mesh, sieves were constructed using a fine material called 'Lawn' for separating unwanted coarse particles from slip, glaze or colours in the liquid state.
10. Not postage stamps before 1840! These would be the tools used to impress a number, letter, workman's mark or the factory mark in the body of the pot before it became too hard. They would have been made of either brass, bronze or a fine stoneware, see Chapter 8, p. 109.

CHAPTER SIX

Of Clerks, Chemists and Cashiers
Until Final Closure

WHEN the Leeds Pottery was founded in 1770 the Chapelry of Hunslet had somewhere in the region of three and a half thousand souls. By the Census of 1841 there were fifteen thousand eight hundred and fifty two. By the time Stephen Chappel, in partnership with his brother James, had taken the Pottery, the former rural nature of Hunslet had become a hive of industrial activity, interspersed with many small houses for the people employed there. Not only had the aspect of the area changed dramatically over the seventy years but the Pottery itself had, as the account so far given has shown, also changed. Humble Greens & Company had given way to Hartley Greens & Company which in turn had ceased to exist in 1827. Then, as the Leeds Pottery Company, it had been let to Samuel Wainewright. The Pottery continued under the same trusteeship and with Stephen Chappel as manager until he himself purchased it and, with his brother, traded as Stephen and James Chappel.

Stephen and James were the sons of Stephen and Ann Chappel of Batley, Yorkshire, where they were both baptised – Stephen on the 22nd of April 1810 and James on the 26th of March 1815. Their father was a shopkeeper who had married Ann Watson at Batley in 1803. Later the family moved to Leeds where, in a directory of 1822,[1] Stephen senior is listed with a shop in Mill Street and where, in another directory of 1837, he was described as "Grocery, Flour &c., Dealer"[2] and Stephen junior was described as "Manager, Leeds Pottery."

In the same year, 1837, Edmund Dawson of Rothwell Haigh, coal agent, bought the Leathley Lane Pottery which occupied part of Windmill Close and was therefore adjacent to the Leeds Pottery. Stephen Chappel junior was a partner with Edmund Dawson in this enterprise.[3]

In Chapter 5 it is recorded that Stephen Chappel paid £9,000, plus some interest, for the Leeds Pottery. The payment of such a large sum of money by a grocer's son aged only 32 and the manager of the Pottery, would seem a very large sum for a man of his apparent station. The simple answer of course is that he and his brother raised £6,000 by a mortgage of the machinery, steam engine and other effects and hereditaments to Sir William Pilkinton, Bart., of Chevet Hall, Yorkshire and Charles Dawson, Esq., of Edwardstone Hall, Suffolk. Then by an Attornment of Tenancy, Stephen and James Chappel agreed to pay a yearly rent of £300. Samuel Fozard Harrison of Wakefield, Gentleman, and Henry Brown of Wakefield, Gentleman and Solicitor, were also parties to this transaction.[4]

By another Indenture of the 22nd of October 1842 John Dodgson Charlesworth and Joseph Charlesworth lent Stephen Chappel £1,610 on the Pottery Lands, subject to the above mortgage.[4] The Charlesworths were a wealthy coal owning family, (see *Studies in the Yorkshire Coal Industry*, page 55, *et seq*).

The life of Stephen Chappel presents a picture of alternating periods of great joy and excitement punctuated by others of profound sadness and misfortune. On the 3rd of April 1834 Stephen, styling himself "Office Clerk" had married Margaret Jane Haigh of Hunslet, spinster, by license at St. Peter's Church, Leeds. On the 24th of June 1836 his bride of but two years, aged 22, was buried at St. Peter's Church. However, on the 1st of March 1837, he married Theresa Pointon at the same church, again by license. At Appendix VII it will be seen that he served as a Guardian at the Hunslet Workhouse; he also served as Churchwarden, with Samuel Warburton, at St. Mary's Church, Hunslet, from 1843 – 46.

Pigot & Co's *National and Commercial Directory of Leeds*, 1841, listed "Stephen and John (*sic*, James) Chappel" as Earthenware Manufacturers at the Leeds Pottery. It also listed Stephen Chappel under "Brickmakers". (In April 1844 the Middleton Colliery's accounts record a payment to St. & J. Chappel of £24 for 8,000 bricks). Dawson and Chappel were also entered as Earthenware Manufacturers at Leather (*sic*, Leathley) Lane. This period, when the Chappel brothers had achieved the proprietorship of the Leeds Pottery proved to be a very difficult, unsettling and anxious time in our country's history, coinciding as it did with the civil unrest surrounding the activities of the Chartists. The newspapers of the period carry accounts of unrest, marches and rioting in many areas of the country, Yorkshire being no exception. *The Leeds Mercury* of the 20th of August 1842 carried a lengthy account of the Magistrates' response. All seemed to come to a head during the "Sacred Month" of August, the month so called by the Union leaders for a stoppage of work to enable meetings and demonstrations to take place. In Leeds the Magistrates, fearing great civil unrest, appealed to the Home Secretary for some military assistance and :

> "Major General Bretherton was sent down to Leeds ... to take command of the district ... 635 men and officers
> of the 32nd regt. of Infantry from Portsmouth arrived in Leeds, where they would remain till further orders. ...

accommodated partially in the Assembly rooms, partly in a new warehouse in Trinity St., and partly billeted on the innkeepers ... three troops of the Yorkshire Hussars ... have been stationed in the town and have rendered every possible assistance to the magistracy ... 60 men of the Royal Irish Fusiliers ... came to Leeds by railway from Hull at the request of the Leeds Magistrates ... two troops of horse artillery at our barracks with two guns ... ample for the defence of the town against much more serious danger than has ever existed – About 1,700 Special Constables have been sworn in, and they have displayed spirit and activity ... of course business has been almost at a stand during the week."

The same newspaper reported some very serious happenings in the Pottery areas of Staffordshire, the report stating that the troops had opened fire in Burslem and that "three men have been killed ... and five or six others wounded."

Such an atmosphere, with rumour and stories being passed by word of mouth, must have fuelled the more extreme elements on both sides and it would be hard to imagine that the workforce at the Leeds Pottery would have been unaffected by such events. However I have to state that I have not found any reference to any of the Leeds potters being involved, either singly or in groups.

The first effective Factories Act (1833), enforced by a salaried inspectorate, was limited to the textile industry except for the lace section of that industry. However the momentum which had been set going by this Act was, quite rightly, unstoppable. In 1840 a Parliamentary Commission of Inquiry was established to look into the workings of the 1833 Act and also to look into the employment of Children in industries not covered by that Act. The Commissioners published their findings, together with recorded evidence taken from children, adults and employers in May 1842.[5] Evidence from the Leeds Pottery and potteries in south Yorkshire gives, to our enlightened and sensitive consciences, a very harrowing picture and the accounts given were by no means peculiar to Yorkshire.

It is always easy to condemn a system which to our present-day thinking seems somewhat barbaric but we must remember that before legislation provided compulsory free education for all children up to the age of ten years in 1891, most children had formed part of the nation's workforce. Traditionally from a very early age and when capable, children had worked within family units, e.g., on farms and in small family trades and businesses. This custom had been absorbed into the factory system which thereafter locked them into a system from which only Parliamentary Legislation could eventually set them free. Moreover they had become 'essential' components in the industries in which they worked, not only for the owners of those industries but also as 'assistant bread winners' for their own families. The previous sentence does not in any way justify the system – it merely accounts for its existence.

I have reproduced all the evidence from the above Inquiry which related to the Leeds Pottery at Appendix VII. From this we get the only presently known authentic glimpse of what life must have been like in the Pottery at this period.

In Stephen Chappel's evidence to the Inquiry he stated that he believed that he was "the largest producer of earthenware out of Staffordshire". We also learn that the children working in his pottery were doing so at two levels; this practice would apply throughout the pottery trade generally. In the first category were children who he employed directly, of these some would go on to become bound apprentices in due course. All those so employed were therefore subject to his control and regulations respecting their work and hours of work. The second category were employed directly by the men and women on his workforce who needed extra help, they were paid by the men and women employing them and were not therefore under Stephen Chappel's control and, *ipso facto*, not his responsibility. He also implied that as this 'sub-contracted' workforce was constantly changing that he neither knew who they were nor how many there were. The hours of work were from six to six in summer and from seven to seven in winter. These hours were usually extended to eight o'clock in the evening in summer when necessary. He expressed himself quite strongly against any legislation which would change the *status quo* with regard to the employment of children, stating: "I object to all legislation on the subject, because, first, I cannot see the right of interfering with property in that way ... It would half ruin the trade to prevent children under 13 from working more than 8 hours a day...".

Two years later Stephen and James Chappel had, by October 1844, introduced the "Jolly", a machine invented by George Wall for the rapid production of flatware and which therefore reduced the number of hands required to produce the same ware by traditional methods. The Unions viewed it as a means of making many of their members redundant and therefore unable to support their families. I dealt at some length with a similar dispute which arose at the Don Pottery, under Samuel Barker, in my book on the Don Pottery. The following quotations are from the newspaper of "The United Branches of Operative Potters" and will show the strength of feeling on the part of the journeymen potters which in turn provided another problem for the Chappel brothers. The newspaper was *The Potters' Examiner and Workman's Advocate*:

Saturday 4th of January 1845.

"JOLLY, JOLLY AT LEEDS. Friends, Brothers, and Fellow-Workmen. – It will be seen, from the heading of this epistle, that your mortal enemy is now at Leeds. It has commenced working at the Messrs. Chapel's Manufactury, and is proceeding with all the success, that the worst enemies of Labour can possibly desire. It is capable of making SIX HUNDRED DOZEN OF PLATES PER DAY. Here is a prospect for the Flat-branch of the Potting Trade! Read the following letter, addressed to the Executive of your society, and let its contents sink deep into your heart.

'GENTLEMEN, – I am instructed, by the Central Executive of the Leeds Society of United Potters, to call your attention to a subject, which is of vast importance to all working Potters; – namely, MACHINERY. I have to inform you, that one of Mr. Wall's patented machines, for the making of Flat-ware, is now in active operation at the works of Messrs S. and J. Chapel, Leeds. I have also to inform you, that it is certain to succeed as far as manufacture is concerned. It has been in operation between two and three months; and every time it is altered, it is improved. I can assure you, it is making, at the present time, good Plates. SIX HUNDRED DOZEN went into the last kiln; the whole of which were made in three, or four days. It is capable of making, when in full operation, SIX HUNDRED DOZEN PER DAY. Gentlemen, we are of opinion, that the sooner it is legally obstructed, the better. All branches are ready, at any minute, to strike work, until it is removed out of the yard. We wish you to take this into your most serious consideration, for if it be allowed to succeed at Leeds, it must extend throughout all the potting districts of this empire. – *Yours very respectfully,'*

Now comes the question. – 'What shall be done?' We have driven it from the Potteries; we must also drive it from Leeds. We must legally and constitutionally stop the works of the Messrs Chapel; and NEVER allow them the *opportunity* of doing an injury to working potters *any more!* Our motto has heretofore been, and must continue to be, 'CLOSED FOR EVER!' "

Saturday, 8th of March 1845.

"THE DEATH OF THE LEEDS 'JOLLY'! Leeds Feb. 21st,1845.

Mr. Editor, – Some time ago, you were informed of the birth of the Leeds 'Jolly.' I rejoice now, to have to inform you of its *Death*. I believe, he gave up the ghost on Tuesday, Feb. 11th, 1845; and I hope he will soon be confined and sent off to the place of his birth, the famous town of Manchester; to be buried there, and to repose in breathless silence, until the arrival of that day when the conflicting elements of wild and tiger-like competition that have settled down into the serene sunshine of co-operative prosperity; a time when no real argument can be raised against a resurrection of 'Jolly'. No! not if he should come forth with his powers increased a hundred fold; for then, it will not be 'iron against flesh and steam against blood,' but iron and steam will work that men may enjoy ease and pleasure; not as now, be made to suffer poverty and pain. ... I understand that Messrs Chappel promised to put away their machine on condition, that they should be supplied with sufficient hands to make flat-ware.

I hope that the men, who are working at the Leeds Pottery, and all other potteries, will not spend their money and precious time at the ale-house, when their employers want them at their work. A great deal of harm has been done to working men by such conduct.

A Leeds 'Loiner'."

Saturday, 13th of December 1845.

The Leeds Pottery was mentioned in verse nine of an eleven-verse poem entitled "Jolly" – *Mr. George Wall's Patented Flat-Pressing Machine.:-*

"But this would not do
For the Cent-making crew,
So they stopp'd me, at once, for to try something new.
Off they posted to Leeds,
To enquire my needs,
But the Chappels were sick of my wonderful deeds,
And vow'd that I robb'd all their moulds of their beads."

Affairs could not have been going at all well for Stephen and James Chappel for, on the 25th of March 1847 a Fiat of Bankruptcy was issued against them. Shortly afterwards George William Freeman of Leeds, Gentleman, Samuel Warburton of Hunslet, Manufacturing Chemist and Thomas Smith of Shelton, Staffordshire, Lawn Manufacturer, were appointed the Assignees. Thus came to an end a very short-lived partnership which must have seemed so exciting to the two brothers when it started just a few years earlier.

The bankruptcy proceedings took their appointed course with *The Leeds Intelligencer* of Saturday the 15th of July 1848 announcing that a dividend would be made in the bankruptcy of S & J Chappel on the 11th of August, unfortunately, but as usual in these notices, no inkling of the size of the dividend was mentioned. However an item of news in the same edition of this newspaper carried a much sadder announcement :

"Hunslet – Saturday last, of consumption,
after a long and tedious illness, born with
the most exemplary fortitude, in the 38th
year of his age,
Mr Stephen Chappel, of the Leeds Pottery."

The protracted and very debilitating illness which had afflicted Stephen Chappel must have been a considerable factor in the failure of the partnership. James Chappel would obviously have had to oversee both the Leeds Pottery and the Leathley Lane Pottery; the latter was advertised for sale in June and July 1849.[6] A directory for 1848 had listed: "Chappel, James (Salt & Fine Ware) Leathley Lane Pottery, Hunslet.". Another directory for 1849-50 showed "Chappels' Assignees" at the Leeds Pottery.

One can only begin to imagine how Stephen Chappel must have struggled to keep the Pottery going while at the same time trying to cope with an advancing medical condition for which he would know there was no hope of a cure. This brings home to us just how cruel life must have been before the advent of modern medical knowledge and treatments which we all take so much for granted.

Another frightening scourge was taking its toll in the area in the second half of 1849, namely Cholera. *The Leeds Intelligencer* of the 6th of October reported that, although the epidemic was then on the wane, the previous week had witnessed 159 deaths in Leeds township and 32 in Hunslet.

Meanwhile, during the same month the Leeds Pottery was being advertised, both locally and in Staffordshire, for sale by auction to take place on the 14th of November 1849. The notice stating that: "It is now in full work. The Trade connected with it is of the first order, and may be considerably increased ...". It also reported that "It is capable of Manufacturing Nine Gloss Kilns per week." However tempting the advertisement may have been it did not succeed in persuading anyone to offer an acceptable bid for its purchase. The day after the sale Samuel Warburton reported to the Wakefield Solicitor, Henry Brown: " ... we had but one <u>Bid</u> for this Estate last night – and that from Joshua Bower of this place – who offered £5000." Joshua Bower's name appears in Slater's *Royal National Commercial Directory* of 1848, as a Glass Manufacturer (Crown and Window) of Hunslet. It is also evident from another letter from Samuel Warburton, to the same solicitor, dated the 30th of October 1849, that he was then contemplating purchasing the Pottery and also that a certain "Mr. Barker" had also shown an interest; could this have been Samuel Barker of the Don Pottery? See Appendix IV, letter No. 4.

Another notice appeared in *The Leeds Intelligencer* of the 19th of January 1850 :

LEEDS POTTERY.

TO EARTHENWARE MANUFACTURERS, DEALERS AND OTHERS. LARGE AND IMPORTANT

SALE OF EARTHENWARE, WORKING TOOLS AND UTENSILS USED IN THE

MANUFACTURE THEREOF.

MR. JOHN HEPPER begs to announce to Earthenware Manufacturers and

Dealers that he has received instructions from the Assignees of Messrs S. and J.

Chappel, of the Leeds Pottery, to SELL BY AUCTION, on the Premises, on

Wednesday NEXT, the 23rd Day of January, 1850, and Seven Following Days of

Business,

ALL THE VERY EXTENSIVE AND VALUABLE MANUFACTURED STOCK;

Including

15,000 TO **20,000** DOZENS OF MANUFACTURED EARTHENWARE,

Consisting of Printed, Blue Edged, White, and Yellow Ware of very superior

Patterns and Quality.

50 Dozen of Ware not Fired, and a great Quantity of other Articles, which will be

fully enumerated in Catalogues.

ALSO

On Monday, Tuesday and Wednesday, the 4th, 5th, and 6th Days of

February, 1850,

THE SUPERIOR WORKING TOOLS AND UTENSILS,

Comprising 20 Tons of Blue Clay, 10 Tons of China do., 20 Tons of Cornish

Stone and Flints, 15 Tons of prepared Clay, 6 Tons of Shavings do., 2700 Pecks

of Ground Flint and Stone, 4 Tons of dried Ground Stone, and a Quantity of

Cream Colour Glaze, Soda, Pearl Ashes, Under Glaze and Enamel Colours,

Printing Paper, Working, and Block Moulds.

9000 GLOSS AND BISCUIT SEGGARS.

1680 Boards, 100 Stools, Ton of Crate Wood, 10 Tons of Raw Ochre, a Quantity

of Manganese, White Lead, 90 Gross Serge, 1840 Middle and Small Cockspurs.

17 PRINTING PRESSES,

A large Quantity of Engravings of various Patterns, with a variety of other

Utensils connected with the Trade. Also the Counting House and Warehouse

Fixtures;

5 USEFUL HORSES, 2 WAGGONS, 5 CARTS,

1 Wherry, Shaft and Trace Gears, &c., &c., Descriptive Catalogues are now ready,

and may be had at the Pottery, and of the Auctioneer.

The whole will be Sold in Lots to suit Manufacturers and Dealers, and without

the LEAST RESERVE.

Sale to commence each Day at Eleven o'Clock in the Forenoon."

Unfortunately I have not been able to ascertain whether or not all or any of the above products and equipment etc., were sold but the notice does give us a glimpse of the range and capabilities of the Leeds Pottery at this period.

We must now introduce another name into the history and development of the Leeds Pottery; I refer to Richard Britton

who would remain the main proprietor until almost the end of the story. Richard Britton was baptised in St. Peter's Church in Leeds on the 10th of August 1817 along with William, both the sons of Samuel and Elizabeth Britton; from this it is reasonable to assume that Richard and William might have been twins. Samuel was a plumber and glazier in Leeds. Richard was working at the Leeds Pottery by 1842 when he witnessed an Indenture for Stephen Chappel dated the 25th of January and signed himself " ... of Leeds Clerk to the said Stephen Chappel".[7] In the 1841 Census Richard had given his occupation as "Book-keeper", and William as "Cloth Warehouseman". Following the bankruptcy and death of Stephen Chappel it would appear that Richard Britton 'changed horses' for a short period as the following advertisement, which is taken from Charlton and Archdeacon's *Leeds Directory Advertiser* of 1848, shows :

Slade & Roebuck's *Directory of Leeds* for 1851 shows William Britton, China and Ornament Dealer at Saddle Yard. This information fits very neatly with the fact that an Indenture of the 5th of June 1851[4] states that: "Richard Britton has contracted with ... George William Freeman, Samuel Warburton and Thomas Smith [the assignees of the late Stephen Chappel and James Chappel for the purchase of the] Leeds Pottery Tenements and Hereditaments and the Steam Engine Machinery and fixtures belonging to the Freehold thereof for the sum of 7,610,*l.*" This indenture was

RICHARD BRITTON'S
WHOLESALE
China, Glass, and Figure Warehouse,
AND
GENERAL COMMISSION AGENT,
Collector of Rents, Accounts, &c.
SADDLE YARD, BRIGGATE, LEEDS.
RESIDENCE, 4, HUNSLET LANE.

witnessed by: Thomas Smith, one of the assignees, Robert Martin, a partner in a Cornish China Clay pit,[8] and Charles Edward Keeling, of Shelton, Staffordshire Potteries. A later Indenture of the 18th of November 1863 informs us that Richard Britton and Samuel Warburton, Manufacturing Chemist, had agreed to become partners for a term of 15 years from the 1st of March 1850.[4]

In the 1851 Census, Samuel Warburton, aged 53, stated that he was born in Sheffield and that his wife Deborah, aged 54, came from Sand Hutton; they had two teenage daughters and two female servants and were residing at 'White House' Hunslet, Samuel described himself as: "Potter employing 400 hands/22 apprentices, Manufacturing Chemist employing 19 men & Town Councillor for Hunslet Ward." In the same Census, Richard Britton was residing in Jack Lane with his wife Ann, two young sons, Alfred and Walter and two female servants; he described himself as "Earthenware Manufacturer".

From an indenture dated the 28th of July 1852[4] we learn that Charles Dawson of Edwardstone Hall, Suffolk, had 'called-in' the £4,500 still owing to him from the mortgage which Stephen Chappel had secured from Sir William Pilkinton of £6,000. Richard Britton was unable to pay this sum of money and requested John Kenton Dawson to advance him £4000 – which he agreed to do, Richard Britton paying him 5% interest and also agreeing to insure the Pottery in Dawson's name. This indenture further informs us that Richard Britton and Samuel Warburton had agreed to become tenants from year to year of John K. Dawson in order to secure the payments to him, paying the annual rent in two instalments of £200.

The 1861 Census shows a reduction in the workforce of 25%, down to 300 hands. Richard Britton, Earthenware Manufacturer, was now residing at the Pottery House with his wife, Ann, and a growing family: Alfred, Arthur, Richard, Hannah and Matilda. It is also interesting to see that not all those who lived in the 'Pottery Yard' were employed at the Pottery, e.g. – a Coal Agent, a Master Tool Maker, a Bricklayer and a Forgeman. There were, however, two "Timekeepers – Pottery", and the Pottery Manager - John Myers, aged 45, born in Rotherham, with his wife Mary, born in Swinton, a daughter, Mary A, aged 18, a Pottery hand, born in North Hylton, Durham and a son, Arthur, aged 15, a potter born in Swinton. This indicates that John Myers had previously worked in other pottery areas.

Richard Britton's partner, Samuel Warburton died in the same year as the Census on either the 20th or 21st of September, aged 73, followed, sadly, by his eldest daughter the following day. By his Will, Samuel had appointed both his wife and his son William Henry as his executors. Deborah, Samuel's wife had, however, predeceased him thereby making William Henry Warburton, chemist, a partner with Richard Britton - (the earlier-mentioned indenture of the 18th of November 1863 stated that when Richard Britton and Samuel Warburton became partners, in 1850, they had agreed that if one of them were to die before the fifteen-year term of their partnership ended that the executor(s) of the partner so dying could become partner(s) with the remaining partner). William Henry Warburton had no desire to become a partner in the Pottery so he and Richard Britton came to an agreement that the partnership should be dissolved as from the 1st of July 1863. Richard agreed to purchase the share from his former partner for £4000, by executing a mortgage of the Pottery premises etc., – " ... and also of all additions thereto ..." paying 5% interest in two annual payments. William Henry Warburton agreed that if payments were made regularly and within 30 days of the 1st of January and the 1st of July that he would not require repayment of the principal sum of £4000 before the 1st of January 1867. The same indenture also witnessed that Richard Britton " ... doth attorn and become tenant from year to year of ... William Henry Warburton ...".[4]

Preserved within the archive, in which most of the documents quoted in this account of the Pottery's history belong,[4] are two valuations of the Pottery. One by C. L Dresser, which is not dated and which gives a total valuation of £16,414. The other, dated the 6th of January 1866 by James Fox, Architect and Valuer, of 22a Albion Street, Leeds, is as follows :

"VALUATION OF THE LEEDS POTTERY ESTATE in Jack Lane in the
Parish of Leeds and West Riding of the County of York the property of Mr Richd Britton

----

I have measured and valued these premises occupying a site of 6a. 2r, & 8¾p. and comprising the several Dwellinghouses Cottages Grinding Mills, Engine and Boiler houses Smiths Shops, Stables, Cowhouses, Coachhouse Moulding places, Cupolas, Workshops, Packing places Warehouses, Offices, Sheds, Painting houses Saggerhouses, Claypits, Grinding Sheds, Reservoir, piggeries, Out offices, yards, spoilheaps, site of Brandling's Railway Gardens and Waste Land as shown on the plan hereto attached [unfortunately missing] and thereon edged with a red line all which said premises I have valued as a working concern as at present occupied (exclusive of Engines, Boiler & Machinery) at the sum of	£15,000
The engines, Boilers Shafting Rollers and all other Machinery I have had Scheduled and valued at the sum of	2,134
Add for Wood work in racks shelves Tables, Counters and other fittings in Warehouses, Offices, Counting houses, Sale Rooms &c., &c.	1,000
TOTAL VALUE	£18,134"

This valuation would be equivalent to £1,365,203. in 2003 (Source: O"Donoghue, Goulding & Allen).

By August 1868 Richard Britton, who banked at Messrs William Williams Brown & Co., Leeds, had become "greatly overdrawn". In order to extricate himself from this situation and at the request of the Bank he had agreed, on the 21st of August, to mortgage the "Leeds Old Pottery" to the Bank for securing advances not exceeding £3,500. By this agreement or rather the necessity for it, it may be presumed that the financial status of the Pottery was not at all healthy. The Census of 1871 does not help too much as there is no reference to the number of hands at the Pottery but six years earlier Llewellynn Jewitt, when writing his article for the *Art Journal* of 1865, had commented that the Leeds Pottery " ... at the present time gives employment to about two hundred and fifty persons ...". However we do learn, from the Census, that Richard's son, Alfred was then married and living in a property in the Pottery Yard as "Cashier (Pottery)". Richard Britton's other son, John Broadbent,[9] by now aged 26 styled himself "Earthenware Manufacturer" in the same Census, a possible indication that he was already a partner with his father at this date.

The reader may recall that Stephen Chappel was able to purchase the Leeds Pottery with the aid of a loan from Sir William Pilkinton and Charles Dawson and that in 1852 Charles Dawson had 'called-in' £4,500 which was still owing – this problem being overcome by John Kenton Dawson agreeing to advance £4000 to Richard Britton at 5% interest. On the 5th of October 1857, John Kenton Dawson died. By his Will he left his real and personal estate to Henry Dawson and a 'Charles Kenney of Portsmouth' – "Upon trusts inconsistent with an intention to pass trust and mortgage estate". He also appointed Henry Dawson and 'Charles Kenney' executors and the will was duly proved at the Prerogative Court of York on the 7th of January 1858 by Henry Dawson alone. There then followed yet another Suit in the High Court of Chancery which lasted from 1871 until May 1874 :

Kenney v Dawson

in which it was alleged that the testator John Kenton Dawson had no relation of the name of 'Charles Kenney' and that the person thus named should have been Edward Herbert Kenney. The Court eventually declared that Edward Herbert Kenney should be substituted for 'Charles Kenney and that the trust property formerly held by the late John Kenton Dawson should be assured and transferred "so as to vest the same in the said Henry Dawson and Edward Herbert Kenney".[10]

The remaining story is of a continual decline towards bankruptcy throughout the 1870s. In 1874 The Middleton Estate and Colliery Company Limited took over the existing mortgages, amounting to £13,503-5-0d. recorded in an Indenture of the 1st of October.[4] By another Indenture of the 17th of February 1876 Richard Britton and Sons 'secured a sum of £4,500' by mortgaging Rushy Pasture, Windmill Close and the Machinery to Robert Addyman, Esq., subject to the earlier mortgage to the Middleton Estate and Colliery Company Limited. This agreement was to enable Robert Addyman to stand surety for the firm of Richard Britton and Sons to the Leeds and County Bank Ltd., Leeds, for all sums of money which may become owing and due to that bank up to the above-mentioned sum.

Thus, by 1876, Richard Britton had taken his two sons, Alfred and John Broadbent into partnership with him.

Unfortunately the Britton partnership did not last very long for on the 15th of June 1878 Richard Britton and his two sons filed a Petition under the Bankruptcy Act of 1869 in the County Court of Yorkshire, Leeds, for the Liquidation of their affairs by arrangement or composition, with their creditors. Simultaneously the two sons: "John Broadbent Britton and Alfred Britton also carrying on business at the same place as Earthenware Manufacturers in copartnership under the firm of J.B. & A. Britton", filed their petition. Following this a statutory majority of the creditors of the partnership assembled at the General Meeting on the 5th of July 1878 and in accordance with the Act, it was resolved that the firm should be liquidated by arrangement and not in bankruptcy and that John Routh of Leeds, Accountant, should be appointed Trustee. John Routh then agreed to release and convey to the Middleton Estate and Colliery Company Limited, all the property relating to and comprised in the mortgage agreement of the 1st of October 1874. In consideration of which the Middleton Estate Co. Ltd., relinquished all claims to the repayment of the sum of £13,503-5-0d. together with interest amounting to £978-3-0d. thereon or for rent under the attornment then owing. John Routh also undertook to realise funds for the benefit of the creditors within six weeks, from the firm's stock in trade, plant, chattels and effects not comprised in the above mortgage "but being in or about the said Leeds Old Pottery Estate". Under the same agreement the Middleton Estate Co. Ltd., paid Robert Addyman the sum of £1,000 in respect of his mortgage agreement dated the 17th of February 1876 whereupon he granted and released the property concerned to that Company.[11]

Thus the Leeds Pottery now, somewhat ignominiously, called 'The Leeds *Old* Pottery' did, to all intents and purposes, come to an end. However a mere twitch of further life is indicated by three scraps of information. First, preserved in the Leeds Archives from which most of the archival information so far quoted has emanated, are two Draft Agreements dated the 24th of December 1878. By the first Draft, Marshall Nicholson, as secretary of the M.E & C. Co. Ltd., and one of its directors, was proposing to let to James, Joseph and Charles Taylor, all of Hunslet, Potters and brothers, the premises of the Leeds Pottery, together with the Steam Engine, Boilers and all necessary machinery and equipment for 10 years at an annual rent of £375. Draft number two was for letting the Flint Mill and engine etc., and its land including the reservoir, for one year and then from year to year at an annual rent of £125 – again to the Taylor brothers. Secondly, the 1881 Census return shows "Charles Taylor, aged 49, Master Potter (imploying 250 Men & Women)" living in "Pottery Yard" with his wife and eight children and one female servant. Two of his sons, James aged 18 and Herbert aged 16, were each described as 'Clerk & Cashier'. At another house in 'Pottery Yard' we find Grace A. Taylor, single, aged 18, an Earthenware Painter, living with her brother George aged 13 described as 'Potter'.Thirdly, in *Kelly's Directory of Leeds* for 1881, Taylor Brothers, Earthenware Manufacturers, are listed at 99 Jack Lane, Hunslet. This was the same address at which "Britton R. & Son, Leeds Pottery" were listed in a directory of 1876. *The Post Office Directory* of 1882 lists "Taylor Brothers, potters, Hillidge Rd.,[12]" Hunslet – the Leeds Pottery not being listed.

The 1881 Census shows Richard Britton, by now sadly a widower, living at 107 Jack Lane and describing himself as a "Commission Agent" the same occupation which he had included in his advertisement of 1848, (see page 80) the two sons who had been his erstwhile partners were living with him – John Broadbent now a "Municipal Market Collector" and Arthur, a "Clerk"; his daughter Matilda, aged twenty-one was also at the same address, namely the Leeds Pottery House. In *The Post Office Directory* of 1882 Richard had moved to 9, Green Mount Terrace, a Commercial Traveller, with his son John Broadbent. Alfred, now an Insurance and Commission Agent, had his office at 2, Tomlinson St., and was residing at 70a, Samuel St.

26. COPPER PLATE FOR PRINTING UNION MEMBERSHIP CARDS. The image is here reversed to show the lettering as it would appear on the printed cards. The earlier Union, "The National Union of Operative Potters" was, by c.1843, superseded by fragmented District Union Branches. From c.1883 there was a movement to reunite the districts and different branches of the trade. *(I am grateful to Phillip Wheeler of Stoke-on-Trent Archives for supplying me with this information). The copper plate is in the collection of The Leeds Museums & Galleries.*

25. THE END OF THE HISTORY OF THE LEEDS POTTERY. In this photograph, taken by Alf. Mattison in 1904, we see the sorry remains of a once thriving pottery which gave employment to over four hundred workers in 1851 and at times was burning over nine thousand tons of coal a year. From this scene of dereliction it is hard to visualise the vast quantities, range and quality of the wares which were dispatched to many very distant countries and climates. Equally difficult would it have been for those early partners to have contemplated their wares being so avidly sought after, collected, valued and researched some two centuries after they were made. *The Thoresby Society, Leeds.*

1. Baines – *Directory & Gazetteer of the County of York*, 1822.
2. White – *Gazetteer and Directory of the West Riding of Yorkshire*,1837.
3. Heather Lawrence – *Yorkshire Pots and Potteries*, p. 55.
4. WYAS (Leeds) – DB 214/48.
5. *Children's Employment Commission, Appendix to the Second Report of the Commissioners. Trade and Manufacturers, Part I, Reports and Evidence from Sub-Commissioners*, London, HMSO, 1842.
6. *The Leeds Intelligencer* of Saturday the 16th of June & 14th of July, 1849.
7. WYAS (Leeds) – DB 214/48 & WYAS (Wakefield) – OL 686/567.

8. R.H. Barton – *A History of the Cornish China Clay Industry*, 1966.
9. Richard Britton, Book-keeper, had married Ann Broadbent at Leeds Parish Church on the 20th of September 1843.
10. WYAS (Leeds) – DB 214/157, Typewritten abstract of title of the Middleton Estate and Colliery Co. Ltd., pp. 18/4 & 19/5.
11. WYAS (Wakefield) – Registry of Deeds, 805/334; WYAS (Leeds) – DB 214/157 (as fn. No 10) pp. 33/19;34/20;35/21.
12. The site of the 'Hunslet New Pottery' – See Slater's Directory for 1887.

CHAPTER SEVEN

Manufacturing and Marketing

THE LEEDS POTTERY was a large pottery producing considerable quantities of fine earthenware. The three Cs – coal, clay and canals (including of course navigable rivers), were the necessary components for success. It requires a much greater weight of coal to fire a given weight of clay; the exact ratio cannot be given as so many variables are involved: the design and size of the kiln, biscuit and glost firings followed perhaps by enamel firings and gilding. Added to these, coal was also needed to calcine the flints and enamels before being ground, which process was carried out by steam power from the second decade of the nineteenth century and which would obviously require yet more coal. It is, therefore, desirable to site a pottery near to a source of coal. In the eighteenth century the generally poor state of the roads and the sheer weight of both the fuel and the clay needed to feed and fuel the Pottery made water-borne transport the only viable and safe method of transport, not only for its raw materials but also for the safe transit of the finished wares to its customers. The Leeds Pottery at Hunslet was approximately half a mile to the south of the river Aire, which had been navigable out into the Humber and the important port of Kingston-upon-Hull for many years. The Aire's course was improved with stretches of canals, e.g., the Selby Canal and the Knottingley Canal. The Leeds-Liverpool Canal became operative from 1816.

Coal

Coal, that essential fuel for the potter, was in abundance to the south of Hunslet from the mines belonging to Charles Brandling, Esq., " ... Lord of the Manor of *Middleton*, and of an undivided Share of the Manor of *Hunslett, ...*"[1] See Plate 3.

The story of Charles Brandling supplying coal to the town of Leeds at a greatly reduced price began in 1757 as outlined by a notice which appeared in *The Leeds Intelligencer* of the 6th of December: "Proposals having been made for reducing the Price of Coals." Meetings were held and considerable support from the inhabitants of Leeds was obviously forthcoming. The scheme involved laying down a waggon-way or railroad from Middleton to a point in Casson Close, a piece of land near the great bridge over the river Aire in Leeds. In order to accomplish this Brandling had to negotiate wayleave over all the land between these two points. He also sought and obtained an Act of Parliament, in 1758, in support of this venture, see Plate 27.

At the Bill's second reading which led to the Act, Joshua Green who, twelve years later would be one of the founding partners in the Leeds Pottery, gave evidence to the House of Commons :

> "Mr *Joshua Green* was examined as to the Price of Coals in the Town of *Leeds:* Who said, That for Five Years last past, Coals had been sold for about 7½d. a Corf; and that Corfs are the same Dimensions as those which Mr *Brandling* proposes to deliver at the Coal Yard aforesaid for 4¾d. each Corfe.
>
> And, being asked as to the Consumption of Coals in the Town of *Leeds*, he said, That he

An ACT *for Establishing Agreements made between* Charles Brandling, *Esquire, and other Persons, Proprietors of Lands, for laying down a Waggon-Way, in order for the better supplying the Town and Neighbourhood of* Leeds, *in the County of* York, *with Coals.*

Whereas *Charles Brandling,* Esquire, Lord of the Manor of *Middleton,* in the County of *York,* is Owner and Proprietor of divers Coal-works, Mines, Veins, and Seams of Coals, lying and being within the said Manor of *Middleton,* and Places adjacent; and hath proposed, and is willing to engage and undertake, to furnish and supply the Inhabitants of the Town of *Leeds* with Coals for their necessary Use and Consumption, at the Rate or Price of Four Pence Three Farthings a Corf, containing in Weight about Two hundred and Ten Pounds, and in Measure Seven thousand Six hundred and Eighty cubical Inches, for the Term of Sixty Years, to commence from the Second Day of *January* One thousand Seven hundred and Fifty-eight, and for such further Term, or longer Time, as the said Mines, or any of them, shall continue to be used and wrought; and, at his own Charge and Expence, to carry and convey, or cause to be carried and conveyed, from

27. PAGE ONE FROM CHARLES BRANDLING'S FIRST ACT OF PARLIAMENT OF 1758.

apprehended the Consumption to be annually about 30,000 Doz. Corfs, such as before described, which are furnished from different Collieries in the Neighbourhood of *Leeds*."

The Act defined the Corf as " ... containing in Weight about Two hundred and Ten Pounds, and in Measure Seven thousand Six hundred and Eighty cubical Inches."[3] The Act further stipulated that Charles Brandling would deliver from his mines yearly and every year 20,000 dozen corfs at least, " ... and deposited upon a certain field or open Place called Casson Close ..." for a term of 60 years from the 2nd of January 1758. In the same year Jeremiah Dixon of Leeds had let Rushy Pasture to Charles Brandling for laying down his waggon-way over the land for an annual rent of £4 and the entire close for an annual rent of £13-2-6d. There was a stable on Rushy Pasture and as Charles Brandling had agreed to attend carefully to the disposal of all horse dung and waste straw and hay from the premises it has been suggested that he may have used Rushy Pasture for stabling and grazing or perhaps as a staging-point where horses could be changed and rested.[4] Of course what we do know about Rushy Pasture is that Richard Humble purchased it from Jeremiah Dixon in 1770 for £600 and that upon it the Leeds Pottery was built.

Charles Brandling's first delivery to Casson Close was recorded in *The Leeds Intelligencer* of Tuesday the 26th of September 1758 to have taken place on the previous Wednesday, the 20th. The newspaper reported :

" ... the Bells were set a ringing, the Cannons of our FORT fired, and a general joy appear'd on every Face."

The waggons, being on rails, enabled heavier loads to be pulled by horses than if they were being hauled on uneven roads. Needless to say the scheme was a resounding success to all concerned and Brandling doubled his output in ten years; the customers were also very satisfied with the 37% reduction in the price of their coals.

In 1779 another Act of Parliament was obtained whereby Charles Brandling increased his deliveries to 40,000 dozen corfs a year and increased the price to 5½d. a corfe. He was also, by this Act, allowed to deliver up to 1,000 dozen corfs to any place, *en route* between his collieries and Casson Close, in any quarter of each year. This Act laid down a table of charges which could be made by independent hauliers for delivering waggons of coal to different parts of Leeds, e.g. - "from the said Repository to Dowbridge or any intermediate Place 1/-"

Another Act of 1793, which increased the price of coal to 13/1d. per waggon of twenty-four corfs, forbade the sale of coal to anyone not being an inhabitant of Leeds. Charles Brandling had to agree to deliver daily, on each and every day of the week except Sunday, sixty-four waggons to Casson Close not more than twelve of which could be delivered *en route*.

In 1803 a fourth Act of Parliament was obtained. This Act increased the price yet again, to 16/- per waggon and Charles John Brandling, the new owner, had to deliver every day of the week except Sunday, Good Friday, Christmas Day and Fast Days by proclamation, eighty waggons of which twelve only could be delivered *en route*.

Before ending this account of the waggon-way I must mention that *The Leeds Intelligencer* of the 29th of June 1812 carried the first account of a steam locomotive being used commercially and which therefore pre-dates George Stephenson's at Killingworth Colliery by approximately two years :

"The machine invented by Mr. Blenkinsop, Agent to C.J. Brandling, Esq; at Middleton, near this town, for the conveyance of coals, or any other article, without horses, was set to work on Wednesday afternoon. It is, in fact, a steam-engine of four horses' power and has been constructed by Messrs. Fenton, Murray, and Wood, of this place: with the assistance of cranks turning a cog-wheel, and iron cogs placed on one side of the rail-way, it is capable of moving, when lightly loaded, at the rate of ten miles an hour. Eight waggons of coals, each weighing three tons and a half, were hooked to the machine, and in 23 minutes ran from Hunslet-Moor, to the coal-staith, about a mile and a half, principally on a dead level, without the slightest accident. This invention will, in Mr. Brandling's concern, supersede the use of 50 horses. It ranks Mr. Blenkinsop high in the world of mechanism."

The Leeds Intelligencer of the 27th of July 1812 carried the first ever illustration of a steam engine to appear in any newspaper, together with an abstract of the Patent specification, dated the 10th of April 1811.[5]

Before I give an account of the coal purchased by the Leeds Pottery from the Middleton Colliery it is essential to deal with two beliefs which, through repetition, have become ingrained in the 'history' of the Leeds Pottery, *viz* :

1.   That because Brandling's wagon-way ran through the Pottery estate it has been assumed that coal was therefore delivered directly into the Pottery from the waggon-way.

2.   On the basis of the fact that Charles Brandling only paid £7 per year for wayleave to run his waggon-way through the Pottery estate it has been 'deduced' that the Leeds Pottery had negotiated a reduction in the prices paid for its coal.

The first assertion I believe to have been assumed without any awareness of the facts or thoughtful assessment of the practicalities involved. It is true that a map in the Leeds Archives, dated 1787 by Jonathan Teal entitled: "A Plan of the Waggon Ways belonging to the Colliery of Middleton in the County of York" does show a spur running off the main line to the north west and which is marked "length 154 yards". One must therefore accept that in 1787 this map showed what existed at that date. However, I submit that this was most likely a left-over spur from the time when Rushy Pasture was rented by Charles

Brandling from Jeremiah Dixon as a staging post for his horses and where he used stabling and from where he had agreed to remove dung, straw and hay from the area. As will be seen from the above Acts of Parliament, until the second Act of 1779 it would have been 'illegal' for Brandling to deliver coals *en route* to Casson Close. I have examined the Account Books and Ledgers of the Middleton Colliery and can find no payments for constructing such a spur had it been constructed specifically for the use of the Pottery. Other maps which I have examined do not show such a spur, *viz* :

1791 -   An Assessment Map of Hunslet shows the waggon-way but without a spur,[6] (see Plate 2).

1815 -   Plan of the Town of Leeds and its Environs – Giles.

1824 -   Henry Teal's "Plan of the Township of Hunslet in the Parish of Leeds".[7]

1850 -   5 ft. to 1 mile OS Map, surveyed in 1847 shows the waggon-way line very clearly with some spurs *en route* but does not show one into the Pottery, (see Plate 31).

1865 -   Lithographed map, contained in a printed Abstract of Title of the Middleton Estate and Colliery Co. , Ltd., shows the waggon-way running straight through the Pottery Estate without any spur from it into the Pottery.[8]

Looking at this from a practical standpoint, anyone who has shovelled coal will appreciate that it is comparatively easy to do when one's shovel can be pushed along a flat surface under the coal but the task is made very difficult if one has to dig into the top of a loaded waggon. Moreover the time that it would take to unload a waggon by this method would be considerable, particularly, as will be seen from the figures quoted below, the Pottery was receiving an average of ten and a half waggons a day in 1807. From 1813 the waggons unloaded over vaulted arches in Kidacre Lane in Leeds near to Casson Close. A Dr. Spiker, in 1815, reported seeing the waggons overturned for unloading into 'coal drops'. From c.1825 the waggons discharged their loads through doors in their bottoms into shoots in the centre of each arch.[9] But supposing that the waggons were, by some means or other, unloaded at the Pottery, the coal would have had to be then loaded into horse-drawn carts, hand carts or wheelbarrows and taken to the end of the Pottery buildings and round to the kilns as required, see Plan at Plate 12. Surely it would have made more sense to build the kilns on the side next to the waggon-way rather than on the opposite side as was the case, if it had been intended to unload at the Pottery. The Pottery's needs of over ten waggon loads each day would have consumed almost the total of that allowed by the Acts of Parliament for Brandling to deliver *en route* to the Leeds Coal Staith.

Finally and to link the above with what Llewellynn Jewitt wrote in *The Art-Journal* of 1865 :

"This tramway passed through the Leeds Pot works, to the proprietors of which a nominal rental of £7 a year was paid, and to whom, as a further consideration for the right of passage, an advantage in the price of coals was allowed."

Thus Llewellynn Jewitt did not claim deliveries into the Pottery. The figure quoted for the annual rent of £7 a year is correct and remained constant throughout the entire history of the Pottery. However I have now to state that Jewitt's statement regarding preferential treatment with regard to the price of coal is completely untrue. I have examined all the extant Account Books and Journals of the Middleton Colliery from 1770 and all payments made by the Pottery were at exactly the same price as those by the other customers. All such payments, apart from a very small proportion, were for: "coals had from Leeds Staith"; occasionally one finds small quantities being purchased from the Hunslet Staith, which was south of the Pottery and at a greater distance from the Pottery than the one in Casson Close.

28. THE [MIDDLETON] COLLIER. One of the original watercolours from which the series of well-known prints entitled "The Costumes of Yorkshire" was engraved. There are forty prints in the series which were first published in 1814. Drawn and painted by George Walker and engraved by R. & D. Havill, the Yorkshire Archaeological Society is privileged to own the bound volume of Walker's original watercolours for this series. Interestingly this volume was formerly in the extensive library of Edward Hailstone, see Plate 30. *The Yorkshire Archaeological Society, Leeds.*

The following table shows, in tons, the annual amount of coal purchased from the Middleton Colliery up to the date when the Ledgers and Journals cease to exist. The tonnage has been converted from the accounts where the sales are entered either in corfs or waggons.

YEAR	TONNAGE	YEAR	TONNAGE	YEAR	TONNAGE
1770	66 (From Sept.)	1801	4470	1832	1262
1771	1284	1802	7231	1833	1753
1772	2098	1803	9250	1834	2005
1773	2500	1804	7861	1835	1037
1774	2639	1805	7416	1836	2596
1775	2733	1806	7342	1837	1791
1776	2675	1807	7274	1838	1064
1777	3326	1808	3204	1839	2061
1778	3575	1809	38 (1st half.)	1840	1129
1779	3155	1810	- - - -	1841	391 (Before May.)
1780	3087	1811	- - - -	1842	596
1781	3399	1812	1111	1843	765
1782	3737	1813	3906	1844	2394
1783	3145	1814	4660	1845	2864
1784	2832	1815	6478	1846	4171
1785	4394	1816	7117	1847	1406
1786	4554	1817	9029	1848	749
1787	4846	1818	8557	1849	2486
1788	4725	1819	9308	1850	540
1789	4835	1820	85 (1st half.)	1851	650
1790	5044	1821	- - - -	1852	47
1791	5068	1822	- - - -	1853	4336
1792	5463	1823	- - - -	1854	3249
1793	6116	1824	- - - -	1855	2088
1794	5204	1825	- - - -	1856	862
1795	5841	1826	- - - -	1857	218
1796	6426	1827	- - - -	1858	1975
1797	5765	1828	29 (2nd half.)	1859	412
1798	5681	1829	1629	1860	4 (Up to end of Apr. when rec'ds end.)
1799	6298	1830	1676		
1800	6462	1831	1584		

The purchases in the first year, 1770, are shown at Plate 29. These indicate a steady and very modest supply for the months of September to December, possibly indicating that moulds and pattern pieces were being produced and also that the kilns were being dried out. Flints would also need burning and any enamel colours would need preparing – all in readiness for the production to start in earnest in 1771.

29. A PAGE FROM THE MIDDLETON COLLIERY'S SALES LEDGER for 1770 showing the first sales of coal to the Leeds Pottery from September of that year. The total weight of coal purchased was only 66 tons for the four months as shown. See above where in the following year, 1771, 1,284 tons were purchased thus indicating that any production of wares in 1770 could only have been on a very small scale indeed, if at all. © WYAS (Leeds) ref. MC 3.

The years 1809, 1810, 1811 and 1812 corroborate the evidence given in Chapter 3 regarding the closure of the Pottery. The absence of purchases during the period 1821 – 1827 does not however indicate another closure of the works for this entire period as the following items of evidence indicate the Pottery being in work :

1822 – Sprig moulds bearing the dates February & December, (see page 238).

1822 – or shortly after, see p. 229 for the reference to a marked bowl made to commemorate/celebrate the independence of Brazil from the Portuguese in 1822.

1824 – The death of Thomas Lakin, "superintendent of the Leeds Pottery".

1823/4 & 1826 – Two Valuation Books for Hunslet show the Pottery houses and cottages being occupied by Pottery personnel.[10]

1825 – A Strike at the Pottery. (See Ch. 4, page 68.)

– Records of consignments of wares being sold abroad, (see pages 74, 92).

1826 – Sale Notice of the Pottery, " ... for continuing the Foreign and Home Trade."

1826 – However, see reference, in Ch. 4, page 69, to a letter from the Hunslet Overseer to the Swinton Overseer.

We must therefore presume that during this period the coal was being purchased from another colliery. The Middleton Colliery Journals show no purchases of coal after the 30th of June 1820 until "Leeds Pottery (Mr. Wainewright)" purchased 13 waggons at 16/- per waggon in the half year ended the 31st of December 1828. The Colliery Ledgers show a small debt of £156-6-5d. being carried forward throughout the 1820s with each year £16 being added to it for "Land & Cottage Rent" and £7 being deducted for Wayleave credits from the Middleton Colliery so that, under "Hartley Greens & Company", a balance owing of £179-6-5d. was carried forward until an entry of the 31st of December 1837 records - "By Bad debt £179-6-5d". Presumably it was then written off, being from the former partnership which had ceased to exist in 1827, (see page 71).

Heather Lawrence recorded that John Goodchild had informed her that in 1850 Warburton and Britton purchased coal from the Altofts Colliery of Pope & Pearson. Unfortunately, despite extensive enquiries and searches it would appear that the archival source of this information, which John Goodchild had examined when in private hands, may not have survived. Certainly the quantities of coal purchased in the 1850s appear somewhat uneven from the Middleton Colliery. We know that production at the Pottery must have been high as the 1851 Census records 400 being employed there. The reason for the small quantities being purchased from the Middleton Colliery may be accounted for by the fact that the Middleton Colliery was obviously in some difficulty at this period as it was advertised for sale three times between October 1850 and October 1853 by order of the High Court of Chancery (Brandling v Plummer)[11] All three attempts failing to attract a purchaser. Such uncertainty regarding the regular supply of coal no doubt prompted the Leeds Pottery to seek supplies from elsewhere.

In 1849 the Pottery purchased the following grades at the prices shown :

April : 36 waggons @ 14/6d.		Up to the 10th of May : 90 waggons @ 14/6d.	
1	-do-	12/-	8	-do-	9/-
4	-do-	9/-	30	-do-	6/-
24	-do-	6/-	18	-do-	4/-
5	-do-	4/-		

Not all the coal would be used in firing the kilns – biscuit, glost and enamel etc., – it would also be needed for the steam engine, and for burning the flints as well as for the drying and heating stoves in some of the workshops. The different grades of coal most likely had different uses within the Pottery.

Some of the Colliery's accounts are more detailed than others. Thus, for some years, the daily sales of coal are shown and which give us a clear picture of the continual production or otherwise of the Pottery; tables for the years 1807 and 1808 may be seen at Appendix VIII.

Clay

The type of fine earthenwares which the Leeds Pottery produced needed considerable quantities of consistently high quality clay. Although it is known that bands of white-firing clay were to be found in the areas of the coal fields near Leeds it is very doubtful whether these were ever tapped by the Leeds Pottery, at least I know of no contemporary archive material which confirms such use. The comparatively small quantities available from such local sources were however being used, by 1714, by the tobacco-pipe makers of Leeds. [12, 13] Ralph Thoresby :

"Here is a good vein of fine clay, that will retain its whiteness after it is burnt (when others turn red), and therefore used for the making of tobacco-pipes, a manufacture but lately begun at Leeds."

However, I feel certain that John Green and his partners would have been keen to emulate Josiah Wedgwood and others already producing fine creamwares and would have realised the desirability of obtaining clay from the same source. Unfortunately no archive material appears to have survived from the areas of Dorset where the best clay was then being dug so we must rely on that monumental and splendid work: *The History and Antiquities of the County of Dorset*, in 2 volumes, by the Rev. John Hutchins (1698-1773) sometime Rector of The Holy Trinity in Wareham, Dorset. The first edition of 1774 contains only a few lines on the clay industry, at page 24 :-

"Good tobacco-pipe clay is dug round this town, at Arne, Hungerhill, Norden &c. It formerly sold for 50/- a ton, but now at fifteen. Great quantities are exported to London, Liverpool, &c., but for want of a proper sand to mingle with it, and proper fuel, no manufacture can be carried on here."

This edition had been written prior to 1762 when his wife rescued the manuscript from a devastating fire which swept through Wareham that year.

The second edition, "corrected, Augmented and Improved in Three Volumes" of 1796 – 1815 with most of the work undertaken by a Mr. Gough, contains the following informative passage in Volume I, 1796, at page 47 :

"Good tobacco-pipe clay is dug round this town, at <u>Arne, Hungerhill, Norden, &c.</u> It formerly sold <u>for 50s. a ton; but now at 14 or 15s.</u> Nearly ten thousand tons are annually exported to London, Hull, Liverpool, Glasgow, &c. but the most considerable part to Liverpool for the supply of the Staffordshire potteries, and to Selby for the use of the Leeds potteries. The principal pits are on Norden and Witch farms; the former belonging to William Morton Pitt, esq. the latter to John Calcraft, esq. and the clay taken from the same is in great repute with the Staffordshire and Yorkshire potters, from its peculiar excellency, and being the principal ingredient in the composition of the ware, commonly called Staffordshire ware, so universally in use in this Kingdom, as well as in many other parts of Europe. For want of proper fuel, the manufacture cannot be carried on here; and the clay is consequently exported.

In the summer season 180 labourers are constantly employed in raising clay from these pits, at the wages of from 6s. to 10s. a week. The cost of a ton of clay to the potters is from 35s. to 37s.6p. the expense of raising the clay, and carrying it from the pits to the water side for shipping, about 13s. inclusive of the ground rent to the owner of the soil; freight to Liverpool about 11s.6d. commission there 1s. average canal freight 9s.9d. porterage, agents commission, and other charges, 2s.3d. Total cost to the potters in Staffordshire 37s.6d."

The third edition of 1861 – corrected, Augmented and Improved by William Shipp and James Whitworth Hodson, Vol. I, pp. 95, 96, unfortunately repeats the above-quoted extract from the second edition and erroneously claims that it was written by John Hutchins before 1760! However the account does state that " ... the average exportation at the present time ... may be ... 75,000 tons ..." to twelve foreign countries and thirty-one English destinations including the following in Yorkshire and the North East: Hull, Leeds, Middlesboro, Newcastle, Stockton, Sunderland and Shields.

The clay from the Furzebrook Estate, between Wareham and Corfe Castle, was noted for its lack of impurities, particularly traces of iron, which gave it the white-firing quality so highly prized by Wedgwood and his contemporaries – the Leeds Pottery being one such pottery. At some date China Clay might have been incorporated into the body, most likely from the St. Austell area of Cornwall.

Flints.

Flints were most likely obtained from some coastal regions south of the Humber – Lincolnshire, Norfolk and Suffolk, as well as from the South Coast regions – Gravesend and Brighton and the Isle of Wight. The South East coast of Ireland was another source of flints.

Cobalt.

Some interesting letters from the Leeds Pottery have survived in the archives of the Hull firm of Merchants – Messrs Wray & Hollingworth[14] see Appendix IV, B. From these we learn that by 1791, Hartley Greens and Company had stopped preparing their own cobalt and were purchasing it, prepared and ready for use, from an un-named source.

Workforce.

In the absence of any factory archives it is impossible to give a comprehensive list of workers at the Pottery. The size of the workforce has been mentioned at different dates as the story has been told; these figures are now drawn together showing the sources of the information, abbreviations used are listed at the end :

1789 – 150, John Goodchild "Hunslet in the Eighteenth Century" *Aspects of Leeds 2.*
1851 – 400 plus 20 apprentices, – Census return, William Warburton, Earthenware Manufacturer.
1857 – 400, Joseph Marryat, *A History of Pottery & Porcelain.*
1861 – 300, Census return, Richard Britton, Earthenware Manufacturer.
1881 – 250, Census return, Charles Taylor, Master Potter.

The following is an alphabetical list of names of people who worked at the Pottery or who are known to have lived in the Pottery's houses and cottages :

1773 – Ball, Jesse, – Pottery Leeds. HL.
1823 – Bedford, Mr. – Possibly the Manager as he occupied one of the managers' houses. Hunslet Valuation book.
1813 – Bell, Timothy (58) – Late Salesman in the Warehouse at the Leeds Pottery. H v G.
1854 – Blackburn, Mr. – Recorded in a letter, see Appx. IV, A., 18 Aug.
1855 – Boywater, Joseph, – Salesman. Jug presented to him.

1817 –   Braim, John, – Manager Leeds Pottery. Baines' Directory of Leeds 1817.

1813 –   Briggs, Pearson (50) – Late Assistant in the Warehouse, Leeds Pottery. H v G.

1842 –   Britton, Richard, – Clerk to Stephen Chappel.

1820 –   Bullough, John, – "of Leeds Pottery". Marriage reported in *TLM*.

1842 –   Butterfield, Sarah (14) – Parliamentary Commission Witness.

1791 –   Calvert, Mr. – "of Leeds Pottery". John Platt's Journal. Also recorded as the father of John Calvert, gunsmith, of Leeds.

1773 –   Cartledge, Ralph, – Pottery Leeds. HL.

1837 –   Chappel, James, – Book keeper, Leeds Pottery.

1837 –   Chappel, Stephen, – Manager, Leeds Pottery.

1779 –   Cocker, Joseph, – Killed in an accident at the Windmill, see page 41.

1823 –   Cooke, John, – Occupant of a "cottage within the Gate". Hunslet Valuation Book.

1771 –   Coope, William, – Pottery Leeds. HL

1772 –   Coup, Jesse, – Pottery Leeds. HL.

1813 –   Craven, Richard (66) – Late Packer & now a sorter of pots. H v G.

1817 –   Craven, Thomas, – Painter, Leeds Pottery. *TLM*.

1834 –   - - - -do - - - -   – Enameller, Hunslet. HL.

1801 –   Daniel, Sampson (39) – Took John Green's place as 'Manager'. H v G.

1881 –   Davis, Maria (40) – Pot Hawker. Census return.

1819/39 – Dean, Peter (47) – Sagger Maker, Parliamentary Commission Witness in 1842.
                    (Worked at Leeds Pottery for 20 years but left there c.1839).

1848 –   Dunwell, Christopher, – Occupied a house at the Pottery. HL

1851 –   Elley, George (30) – Book-Keeper. Census return.

1807 –   Fazackerlay, Wm. – Printer of Earthenware. Poll Book.

1821 –   Fenton, William, --Potter, – Manor Court Rolls, Duchy of Lancaster.

1842 –   Fieldhouse, James, – Thrower, – Parliamentary Commission Witness.

1770 –   Green, Savile, senior, – Book-keeper – Witnessed an Indenture of the 26th of November.
                    He later became a partner and died in 1805.

1861 –   Hanby, Robert (27) – Timekeeper, the Bell House at the Pottery. Census return.

1881 –   Hill, Matilda (19) – Earthenware painter. Census return.

1841 –   Inman, George, – Potter. Census return.

1848 –   Inman, Joseph, – Occupied a house at the Pottery.

1823 –   Inman, Wm. – Occupant of a "cottage within the Gate". Hunslet Valuation Book.
                    Appears in the 1841 Census as a 'potter' & in the 1851 Census, aged 71.

1821 –   Lakin, Thomas, snr, Death of – A Manager at the Leeds Pottery.

1824 –   Lakin, Thomas, jnr, Death of – Superintendent at the Leeds Pottery.

1861 –   Myers, Arthur (15) – Potter. Census return.

1861 –   Myers, John (45) – Manager of the Pottery. Census return.

1861 –   Myers, Mary (18) – Pottery Hand. Census return.

1881 –   Myers, Thomas (62) – Earthenware Turner. Census return.

1854 –   Naylor, Henry – Most likely held a clerical position. Appx. IV, A.

1842 –   Naylor, William (12/13) – Parliamentary Commission Witness.

1813 –   Nicholson, Robert (34) – Late Cashier & Book Keeper at the Leeds Pottery. H v G.

1851 –   Parkin, Anthony (44) – Time Keeper, occupying the "Bell House" at the Pottery.

1813 –   Parkinson, John (37) – Overlooker at Leeds Pottery. H v G.

1841 –   Peover, Frederick, – Occupied a house at the Pottery, engraver. Census return.

1802 –   Perigo, Elisha, – Book-Keeper, mentioned in William Hartley's Will.

1807 –   Pool, Wm, – Potter, Hunslet. Poll Book.

1806 –   Prince, [Charles ?] – Leeds Pottery's Agent at the Swinton Pottery. WWM..

1773 –   Rainforth, Samuel, – Apprenticed to Savile Green (Hunslet overseer of the Poor A/Cs.)

1773 –   Rainforth, Thomas, – Apprenticed to John Green   - - - - do - - - -

1851 –   Rider, George (40) – Potter. Census return.

1814 –   Ruperti, H, – Recorded as a "Rider" in the Danish Claim. See Appx. V.

1782 –   Ruperti, Justus Christian, – Most likely held a clerical position as he witnessed an Indenture of the Thorp Arch
                    Flint Mill. He Later purchased a share in the Pottery. See Index.

1776 –   Schofield, Edward, – Leeds Pottery. HL.

1819 –   Scott, James, – Leeds Pottery. HL.

1865 – Senior, James, – Notes in Leeds Local History Library.

1842 – Senior, Joshua (12) – Parliamentary Commission Witness.

1777 – Smith, Jeremiah, – Leeds Pottery. HL.

1851 – Sykes, Edward (19) – Pottery labourer. Census return.

1776 – Sykes, Thomas, – A runaway apprentice. Notice in a local newspaper, see page 41.

1861 – Taylor, Benjamin (48) – Time Keeper at the Pottery. Census return.

1881 – Taylor, George (13) – Potter. Census return.

1881 – Taylor, Grace A. (18) – Earthenware painter. Census return.

1841 – Taylor, Josiah (12/13) – Potter's-boy, Parliamentary Commission Witness.

1773 – Taylor, William, – Leeds Pottery. HL. Joshua Green's nephew.

1813 – Thirhill, John (52) – Late Porter at the Leeds Pottery. H v G.

1871 – Turnbull, Adam (39) – Thrower at the Pottery. Census return.

1871 – Turnbull, Alfred (14) – Thrower at the Pottery. Census return.

1871 – Turnbull, Prescilla (16) – "Taker off at Pottery". Census return.

1823 – Wild, John, – Occupant of a "cottage within the Gate". Hunslet Valuation Book.

1881 – Wood, George (63) – Pot Burner. Census return.

1782 – Wood, Michael, – possibly a clerk, he witnessed an Indenture of the Thorp Arch Flint Mill.

1823 – Wild, ? – Lived at Leeds Pottery. HL.

1817 – Wilkinson, George, – Earthenware Printer. HL.

1841 – Woodhead, Michael, – Potter. Census return.

1772 – Woolf, John, – Pottery, Leeds. & 1792 – Potter, Hunslet. HL.

1807 – Wright, George, – Death "Of Leeds Pottery". HL.

1813 – Wright, Job.(41) – Overlooker of the Partnership. H v G.

1770 – Wright, Matthew, – Died 1804 after 34 years at Leeds Pottery, aged 56.

1807 – Wright, Matthew, – Death. HL.

1809 – Wright, Thomas, – Potter, Leeds. HL.

> HL – listed by Heather Lawrence in *Yorkshire Pots & Potteries*.
> *TLM – The Leeds Mercury.*
> H v G – The 'Hanson **v** Green' Chancery Suit.
> WWM – Wentworth Woodhouse Muniments.
> A number in brackets denotes the age at the given year.

Markets & Marketing

It is quite obvious that the early partners in the Leeds Pottery must have embarked on a policy to produce and sell the bulk of their wares to foreign markets shortly after they commenced trading. Preserved in the Wedgwood Archives is a series of letters from Otto Setler of St. Petersburg, to Josiah Wedgwood; they date from 1773 to 1785. In 1776 Setler wrote to Wedgwood complaining that he could not sell his wares in Russia and that casks remain unopened and asks Wedgwood to take them back. (E7/30361 and E7/30362). More specifically in a letter dated the 21st of March 1777, he wrote :

> "Your neighbours at Boslom sell their Earthen Ware very cheap and they get large Orders from hence and so does
> Mr. Green of Leeds who was here and affords cheaper in the Common way than anybody else ... ". (E7/5816).

Yet another letter, again from St. Petersburg, dated the 25th of February 1785 (Wedgwood/Mosely, WM 1459), quoted in full at Appendix IV, opens :

> "It is some years ago I hav not had the pleasure to write you since the Pottery estrablished at Leeds we draw all
> our Common Earthen Ware from thence – As I was not sure if you did continue your Pottery ... ".

Thus we have proof that the Leeds Pottery was well established in the export of its wares to Russia by March 1777 and a possible inference may be drawn from the last-quoted letter that such an export trade may have begun soon after its foundation. It is also very interesting to note that Otto Setler reported that the Leeds Pottery appeared to be undercutting most, if not all, other English potters in the sale of common earthenware; at that time this would mean creamware. The closer proximity of the Leeds Pottery to the North Sea, via the port of Kingston-upon-Hull, would ensure cheaper transport costs than the Staffordshire potters would have to bear. Another factor which would have enabled the Leeds Pottery to produce cheaper wares was the reduction in the price of coal as a result of Brandling's rail road which had reduced the price of coal delivered to Leeds by 37% (see page 85). Although the statistics of the export of earthenware from Hull[15] do not show individual manufacturers it is significant to record that in 1768 the number of pieces exported from Hull was 1,624,700; by 1783 this had risen to 13,287,000. Wares from the Leeds Pottery would obviously have formed part of this vastly increased trade but exactly what proportion it may never be possible to determine.

The first known editions of their Design Books were published in German, French and English and with a later Spanish edition, recorded by Llewellynn Jewitt (see page 116). We also know that they had a thriving trade with Russia, Denmark, the

Low Countries, Poland, Portugal and later, in the early nineteenth century, with both South and North America, the islands of Sicily, Zante and with Italy.

Earlier, in Chapter 3, I recorded that William Barwick the nephew and heir-at-law of John Barwick, one of the founding partners, was in St. Petersburg as a merchant and agent for the Pottery. Savile Green junior also ventured to St. Petersburg and eventually traded as a merchant in Rio de Janeiro from 1808 to 1820.[16] William Hartley junior was also in business as a merchant in London from c.1814 to 1829 as recorded in Chapter 4, page 67, and did himself travel to Rio de Janeiro in 1828 where he was in business as a merchant with George Green, a son of John Green.[17] James Winter Butterworth, another of the partners was, by May 1813, living in Portugal as a merchant; he died in Lisbon in 1816.

Many drawings and sketches of wares requested from agents and customers abroad were pasted into old order books; two of these known as "*Original Drawing Books Nos.1 & 2*", are reproduced at Plates 445 to 567. The identities of the customers/agents requesting the wares are unfortunately mainly indicated by a system of code letters for which, unfortunately, no key is given. See pages 100-106 for some records of the size of orders submitted by agents/merchants c.1792.

Two important archive sources have been preserved in the Public Record Office, namely the second Chancery suit of Ruperti v Hargreave and the Danish-Claims File, see Chapter 5. Both these collections list customers, agents and merchants linking their names to their countries and home towns. The list, reproduced below, shows people who were owing money to the former firm of Hartley Greens & Co., in March 1834, from the dates shown.

1818	Elisha Perigo, Leeds	5 - 0 - 6½
1817	Hall Ellah and Co. Hull	3 - 6 - 0
1815	John Matson, Hull	36 - 11 - 10
1818	George Rayson, Leeds	19 - 7 - 8
1823	J.J. de Campose Sr, Lisbon	216 - 1 - 10
1827	George Hanson & others, Leeds	230 - 16 - 8½
1817	Earthenware to Palermo with G Oates & Son	484 - 19 - 7
1821	Swinton Pottery, Swinton	551 - 9 - 6
1818	F.G. Studwell, Norwich	12 - 3 - 4
1829	Andreas Paterson, Russia	3286 - 11 - 5
1819	Adr Vander Klift, Rotterdam	49 - 7 - 2
1815	J.H. Moclec, Leyden	72 - 8 - 2
1828	Augs Lacomblet, Dusseldorff	28 - 11 - 3
1823	J.A. Bley, Bernburg	29 - 3 - 5
1816	J.U. Nebell, Cobleuter	4 - 14 - 7
1820	Thomas Wood, Wortley	3 - - 6
1819	P. Nedelmann, Essen	145 - 9 - 1
1818	Geo Oates & Son, Palermo	295 - 1 - 6
1825	Earthenware with J.B. Hayes	284 - 0 - 10
1818	D.B. Jordening, Elsinore	2 - 16 - 1
1819	Wm Vandon Bos & Co., Groningen	4 - 18 - 11
1820	Robinson & Caley, Hull	450 - 12 - 7
1820	John Braim, Leeds	57 - 16 - 5
1818	Jos Kirkay, Hull	26 - 3 - 6
1822	J.L. Kupffer, Milan	1 - 16 - 3
1822	Bayner Muller & CVo., Santander	9 - 0 - 5
1825	Geo Pohlu, Cadiz	110 - 2 - 3
1828	J de Cavo Cardano & Co., Madrid	303 - 16 - 5
1821	Jn Gualdi, Rome	1 - 9 - 4
1820	Diego Alfairo, Malaga	21 - 9 - 0
1826	Wm Houseman, London	19 - 0 - 4
1830	Earthenware to Palermo with Bentley & Co.	62 - 8 - 5
1822	Thos Lakin, Leeds	98 - 13 - 10
1824	Earthenware to New York with D Hadden	316 - 11 - 8
1825	Thos Lakin Jr, Leeds	36 - 11 - 0
1828	Underwriters for Vrow Webbina	551 - 8 - 11
1830	Robt Hodgson, London	431 - 1 - 6
1826	Wm Fenton, Leeds	5 - 12 - 3
1828	Manl Malute, Madrid	110 - 9 - 10
1817	M Liebmann & Son, Elsinore	85 - 15 - 8

1823	Cante Brothers	909 - 4 - 4
1819	Country Dealers various places	194 - 8 - 9
1828	August Lacomblet, Dusseldorff	4 - 10 - 0
1829	J.B. Hayes, Hull	11 - 10 - 8
1827	Milner & Morris, London	516 - 5 - 4
1828	Earthenware to Rio with Briggs	150 - 0 - 0
1833	Earthenware to Zante, Barff	200 - 0 - 0
		£10,456 - 2 - 2

The total sum is equivalent to approx £859,564 in 2003.[18]

The full list has been given although it is accepted that several of the names may not have been actual customers owing money for pots. Elisha Perigo was a former Book-keeper. John Braim had been the Manager of the Pottery in 1817 and in the 1822 Directory of Leeds a John Braim is listed as "Auctioneer". Wm. Fenton was a Shopkeeper in Leeds and J.B. Hayes of Hull was a Ship and Insurance Broker and General Agent. Messrs Milner & Morris were Potters & Glass Men at 116 Lower Thames Street;[19] Robert Hodgson was a China, Glass &c. Dealer at 120 Cock Hill[20] and Wm. Houseman could have been either William Henry Houseman of 5 Sun Street, Bishopsgate or, of W & H Houseman of 57 Aldermanby, both China etc., Dealers.[21] In 1833 a William Houseman was listed as an "Agent" at 9, Coleman Street Buildings.[22] The inclusion of "George Hanson and others" is interesting since we know that he was a partner in the Pottery, however, in the 1822 Directory he is listed as "Earthenware Merchant" indicating that he must have been dealing in wares produced at the Leeds Pottery and obviously taking and accepting more than his financial state would cover. As stated earlier in this book George Hanson died on the 12th of June 1829 leaving an estate of under £100. Both the Lakins, father and son, had held managerial positions in the Pottery. The comparatively small sum owed by "Country Dealers various places" may or may not indicate only a modest amount of trading with such customers or it could indicate that payments from such customers had been promptly made. Another intriguing inclusion in the list is "Swinton Pottery" shown to have been owing £551-9-6d in January 1821 – the second highest on the list and equivalent to approximately £38,292 when converted to its present-day value.[18] The Bramelds were declared bankrupt in December 1825 and there is no mention in the Leeds Pottery Trustees' accounts, submitted to the Court of Chancery, that any payments or dividends were forthcoming from the Bramelds or their assignees.

Presumably the Leeds Pottery had located its erstwhile Danish Agent, A. Paterson, (alias Peterson) in Russia, the country to which he had fled, see below. I made mention, in Chapter 5, of the 1807 Battle of Copenhagen and the British/Danish war which ensued from it. Reference was also made to a compensation claim which was settled in 1836, some 29 years after the above event, by the British Government in collaboration with the Danish Government in respect of British goods confiscated under the "Decrees of Confiscation issued by the King of Denmark" in 1807. Fortunately a file of papers has survived in the Public Record Office regarding this claim.[23] It is quite detailed and I have given a transcript of the relevant papers at Appendix V. From these papers it appears that Andreas Peterson had been acting for Hartley Greens and Company in Copenhagen and that a total of £3,142-16-7d. was owing to the Pottery for "sundry goods sent". However A. Peterson (alias Paterson), after selling the goods, paid into the Danish Treasury, as he was required to do, a sum of £259-1-0d. and gave the King of Denmark a bond for £1000 stirling, which sum of money he held – " ... but sometime after He fled the country without discharging the Bond." To its credit the Danish Government honoured the bond and paid the British Government which enabled the Pottery to be awarded the sum less "the usual deductions i.e good for £978-6-3½d". The papers relating to this Danish Claim show the value of the Pottery's business through one of its agents and lists the names and values of the orders supplied through that agent. The Leeds Pottery's full Danish claim amounted to £3,393-0-7d. stirling. The Don Pottery also submitted five claims amounting to £2,957-1-6d. stirling. I did not discover any other Yorkshire pottery which submitted a claim but a small one was submitted by Wedgwood to the value of £35-5-10d.

Prices

The foundation of the Leeds Pottery took place just as some of the potters in Staffordshire had agreed to combine and fix prices for their wares, thus preventing individual potters undercutting one another. Interestingly among the first list of such potters, dated the 1st of February 1770, was John Platt, one of the partners in the Rotherham Pottery, this indicating that concern about this matter was felt in Yorkshire as well as Staffordshire[24]. The situation was summed up perfectly by Josiah Wedgwood in a letter to Thomas Bentley, dated 21st & 22nd of April 1771 :[25]

" ... it may perhaps be expedient to lower the prices of the Table plates to 4/ Per doz in London, as our people are lowering them to 2/3 or 2s here. Mr Baddeley who makes the best ware perhaps of any of the Potters here, and an ovenfull of it Per Diem, has led the way, and the rest must follow, unless he can be prevailed upon to raise it again, which is not at all probable, though we are to see him tomorrow, about a dozen of us, for that purpose. They (The Potters) called upon me yesterday to consult with me upon this dilemma, and we are to have a meeting at Newcastle tomorrow. ... the *General Trade* seems to be going to ruin on the Gallop ... The Potters seem sensible of their situation, and are quite in a pannick for their trade, and indeed I think with great reason, for *low prices* must beget a *low quality* in the manufacture, which will beget *contempt*, which will beget *neglect* and *disuse*,and there is an end of the trade. ..."

Proof that some form of agreement was reached by a number of the potters but precisely how many we do not know, is shown by Arnold Mountford[24] who published a group of agreed price lists for the years 1783, 1795, 1796 and a list of 1814 which had been revised and enlarged in 1843 and 1846: "in public Meetings of Manufacturers". In the same publication he reproduced a "Chamber of Commerce, Staffordshire Potteries" book of June 1836 which includes, among other items, "A Form of Hiring" agreement as well as "The Minimum Working-Price List", which includes most of the processes then used in the trade, the intention being to standardise the payment to all operatives in the Potteries for any given process. The tenor of this was very much in the same vein, though not so detailed, as the agreements which had existed between the journeymen cabinet-makers and their masters, in London and elsewhere, since the late 1780s.

There is evidence to show that the Leeds Partners had become signatories to such price-fixing agreements, but by what date it is impossible to say, as the following letter from Leeds of the 12th of May 1817 to Josiah Wedgwood, Esq., Etruria, implies[26]:-

"Sir,

Several of our foreign correspondents having informed us that you and some of your neighbours had sent out Lists with prices much below those agreed upon in 1814. We should feel obliged by your having the goodness to hand us one of your present Lists, or in case you have not framed a new one, please note to us such articles as you have made a reduction in, and what that reduction is.

As we have always most cordially joined in any plan for the benefit of the Trade, we have felt a little surprized at not having been advized of the late alteration.

Sir, respectfully, your obt Sets

Hartley Greens & Co"

From the above letter it is reasonable to deduce that Hartley Greens & Co., had at least been in the habit of informing their 'brothers' in Staffordshire of any changes in their lists, and *vice versa*. Other letters in this correspondence are reproduced at Appendix IV,c.

In 1966 a copy of the 1794 edition of the Leeds Pottery's *Design Book* came into the possession of the Print Room and Art Library of the City Art Gallery, Leeds; it is reproduced at pages 118 to 133. This book is of considerable interest and importance not only on account of its date but also because many blank pages were originally bound with it and which contain 46 original drawings of wares not in the published section, together with 11 coloured drawings of teacups. Of particular significance to this stage of the account of the Pottery are the alterations, made in ink, to the contents pages and also the prices, also in ink which, together with a list of sizes, appear alongside the individual wares illustrated in the printed section.

In the course of my research for the present work I discovered the only presently known "New Price Current" published by Messrs Hartley Greens & Co., on the 1st of February 1796 and, as the following transcription of this publication will show, was to replace an earlier list[27]. Of particular interest is the statement that it differed from the previous one in that it was based on " ... a new Method of counting the Dozen." It would appear that the prices inked in the 1794 *Design Book*, now generally known as the "Agent's Book", mentioned above, are either taken from the 1796 "Price Current" list or formed the basis for that list as they do agree with one another. A more detailed account and analysis of this book will be found in Chapter 8.

The Price List is of importance not only to the Leeds Pottery but also for the Swinton Pottery of Greens Bingley and Co. Llewellynn Jewitt records:[28] " ... the same price lists which were printed at Leeds with the Leeds Pottery heading, had that heading cut off, and that of 'Greens Bingley, & Co., Swinton Pottery' written in its place. Later on large fresh price lists were published. They were headed 'Greens, Hartley, & Co. Swinton Pottery make, sell, and export ... [the same list of wares as on the Leeds List below] ... dated Swinton Pottery, 1st February 1796' – announcing an advance in prices and a revised system of counting." It is therefore very fortuitous that the only presently known Leeds price list which has survived is the very one to which Jewitt referred and which bore the same date as the Swinton list which he also recorded. It is however very obvious that any list issued by the Leeds Pottery, during the period when it had the twenty-one year's lease of the Swinton Pottery, would coincide with any such list from the Swinton Pottery.

The Leeds Pottery's Price List is printed on a single sheet of paper measuring 20 by 16¼ inches folded to produce four pages of which only pages 1,2 and 3 carry any text. £1 in 1796 would have a value of £71-52p in 2003.[18]

Page 1 is headed as follows :

"HARTLEY, GREENS, and Co. LEEDS POTTERY,
MAKE, SELL, and EXPORT WHOLESALE,
ALL SORTS of EARTHEN-WARE,
VIZ:
Cream Coloured or Queen's, Nankeen Blue, Tortoise Shell,
Fine Egyptian Black, Brown China, &c.
Also the above Sorts enamelled, printed or ornamented with Gold or Silver."

Running vertically down the left-hand side of page 1 is a 12 inch scale divided into quarter inches and reading from the top when viewed from the left, and with the heading: "A Scale of Twelve Inches English Measure." This was important as many countries used a measure called a foot, the problem was that not all these were of the same length! For example :

The Danish 'Fod' – four different foot lengths from 11.46 ins. to the Rhineland foot of 12.36 ins.

The French 'Pied' varied from 9.78 ins. in Avignon to 13.48 ins (old measure) in Lyons.

The German 'Fuss' varied from 9.25 ins. in Wesel (old measure) to the Surveyor's Fuss in Weimer of 17.76 ins.

The Russian foot varied from the use of the Rhineland Fuss of 12.36 ins. to the one used in Moscow of 13.17 ins.[29]

See also Plate 463 where an order from France included a rule of the French measure requesting goods to be produced to the scale provided.

Page 1

CREAM COLOURED																				
INCHES	4	5	6	7	8	9	10	11	12	13	14	15	16	17	18	19	20	21	22	
Dishes, Oval flat,							3s.	4s.	5s.	6.s	8s.	10s.	12s.	15s.	18s.	22s.	26s.	34s.	42s.	
Ditto, Round ditto,							3s.	4s.	6s.	8s.	10s.	12s.	15s.	18s.	21s.					
Covers to suit Oval Dishes							9s.	12s.	15s.	18s.	24s.	30s.	36s.	45s.	54s.					
Ditto, - - - - - Round Ditto,							9s.	12s.	18s.	24s.	30s.	36s.	45s.	54s.	63s.					
Soup, or Deep Dishes, Oval,							4s.	5s.	6s.	8s.	10s.	12s.	15s.	18s.	22s.					
Ditto,----------ditto, Round							4s.	6s.	8s.	10s.	12s.	15s.	18s.	21s.						
Fish Drainers, to suit Oval Dishes,							4s.	5s.	6s.	8s.	10s.	12s.	15s.	18s.	22s.					P
Ditto ------------------Round ditto,							4s.	6s.	8s.	10s.	12s.	15s.	18s.	21s.						E
Ragou Dishes, with Covers, Round) or Oval)--							12s.	15s.	18s.	21s.	24s.	30s.	36s.	42s.						R
Vegetable Dishes, Oval							42s.	54s.	66s.											
Compotiers or Shallow Salads, Oval,) Round, Square, or Triangular,)--				2s.6d	3s.	4s.	5s.	6s.	8s.	10s.	12s.									D
Baking Dishes, Round or Oval,			1s.9d	2s.	2s.6d	3s.6d	4s.6d	6s.	8s.	10s.	12s.									O
Nappies, plain,			2s.	2s.6d	3s.	4s.	6s.	8s.	10s.	12s.	15s.									Z
Ditto, pierced,			3s.	4s.	5s.	6s.	8s.	10s.	12s.	15s.	18s.									E
Tureens, Oval					18s.	21s.	24s.	30s.	36s.	42s.	54s.	66s.								N
Ditto, Round with Stands,			21s.	27s.	33s.	39s.	48s.	60s	72s.											
Glass Trays						24s.	30s.	36s	42s.	54s.	66s.									O
Sauce Tureens, Stands and Spoons,	14s.	16s.	21s.	26s.																F
Oval Butter Tubs and Stands, plain	7s	9s.	11s.																	
Ditto --------------------------pierced,	9s	11s.	13s.																	T
Plates Breakfast, or Twifler, Common Patterns,)---			1s.	1s.2d	1s.4d	1s.6d														W
Ditto or ditto, Paris, Bath and) Concave Patterns) ---				1s.2d	1s.4d	1s.6d	1s.9d													E
Fruit Plates, pierced,			2s.6d	3s.	3s.6d	4s.	5s.													L
Twisted Fruit Baskets and Stands,) Round or Oval,)---			20s.	22s.	24s.	27s.	30s.	36s.	42s.											V
Pierced ditto and ditto,			15s.	18s.	21s.	24s.	27s.	30s.												E
Ditto covered Oval, ditto and ditto				32s.	36s.	42s.	48s.	54s.												
Ditto, ditto, Round, ditto and ditto,			30s.	36s.	48s.	66s.	90s.	102s.												P
Tea Trays,							10s.	12s.	16s.	20s.	28s.	36s.	44s.	54s.	66s.	78s.				I
Garden Pots and Stands,	3s.	4s.	6s.	9s.	14s.	21s.	30s.	42s.												E
Shaving Basons, Round or Oval,							7s.	9s.	12s.	15s.	18s.	21s.	26s.	30s.						C
Deep Salads, Oval, Round, Square) or Octagon)--			2s.	2s.6d	3s.	4s.	6s.	8s.	10s.	12s.	16s.									E
Escolloped Nappies,		2s.	2s.6d	3s.	4s.	6s.	8s.	10s.	14s.	18s.	22s.	26s.								S

95

	Per Doz. of 12 Pieces		Each
Plates, Table or Soup, Paris, Bath and Concave Patterns	2s.	Ice Cellars,	7s.6d
Ditto, Common Patterns, say Royal, Queen's, Feather or Shell Edge,	1s.9d	Candlesticks,	1s. to 2s.6d
Salts, plain,	1s.	Common Ink Stands,	6d
Ditto, with Legs	1s.6d	Wafer and Sand Boxes,	[?] 6d
Ditto Oval	2s.6d	Fountain Ink Stands	[?]
Common Mustards	1s.6d	Bidets	7s.[?]
Sugar and Pepper Castors, and Oil and Vinegar Cruits	2s.6d	Furnished Castors	5s. to 6s.
Egg Cups, from	1s.6d to 3s.	Tureen Ladles, 1. 2. 3 sizes	1s. 9d. 6d.
Sauce Boats, from	1s.3d to 4s.6d	Oil and Vinegar Stands	2s.6d
Table Spoons,	3s.	Chocolate Stands,	5d to 7d
Tea or Mustard Spoons,	1s.	Quintal Flower Horns,	1s.6d to 1s.9d
Sauce Spoons,	4s.	Radish Dishes	9d to 1s.
Sauce Spoons, pierced	6s.	Ink Stands furnished,	1s.6d to 4s.
Oval Chambers,	10s. to 12s.	Crosses, with Cup for Holy Water	1s.
		Ice Pails 2 Quart, 3 Pint, 2 Pint, and 1 Pint	
		Plain, 2s.6d 1s.6d 1s. 9d	
		Fluted, 3s. 2s. 1s.6d 1s.	

ARTICLES PROPER FOR SERVICES

Made complete in the Paris, Bath, Concave, Royal, Queen's, Feather or Shell Edge
Patterns, printed or enamelled with Coats
of Arms, Crests, Cyphers, Landscapes, &c. - Also Blue Printed Nankeen Patterns.

Page 2

Dia.	Ht.		Nearly the Former Sizes	No.	Price per doz. of 12 Pieces	Dia.	Ht.		Nearly the Former Sizes	No.	Price per doz. of 12 Pieces
	6	Broad Mugs,	4	1	6s.	$10^{1/2}$		Washing Basons,	3	1	10s.
	$5^{1/2}$	Ditto	6	2	4s.	$9^{1/4}$		Ditto	4	2	8s.
	$4^{7/8}$	Ditto	9	3	3s.	$8^{1/4}$		Ditto	6	3	6s.
	$4^{1/8}$	Ditto	12	4	2s.	$7^{1/2}$		Ditto	9	4	4s.
	$3^{5/8}$	Ditto	18	5	1s.6d	$10^{1/4}$		Water Ewers,	3		14s.
	$3^{1/4}$	Ditto	24	6	1s.	$9^{1/4}$		Ditto	4		10s.6d
	3	Ditto	30	7	10d	$8^{1/4}$		Ditto	6		7s.
	6	Ditto covered,	4	1	13s.6d	7		Ditto	9		5s.
	$5^{1/2}$	Ditto	6	2	9s.	6		Ditto	12		3s.6d
	$4^{7/8}$	Ditto	9	3	6s.	12		Ewer Basons, Round	3		14s.
	$4^{1/8}$	Ditto	12	4	4s.6d	11		Ditto	4		10s.6d
	$3^{5/8}$	Ditto	18	5	3s.	10		Ditto	6	3	7s.
	$3^{1/8}$	Ditto	24	6	2s.3d	9		Ditto	9	4	5s.
$12^{3/4}$		Bowls with Covers and Handles		1	54s.	$5^{1/2}$		Milk Ewers	18		2s.6d
$11^{1/2}$		Ditto	2	2	42s.	$4^{7/8}$		Ditto	24	2	2s.
$10^{1/2}$		Ditto	3	3	30s.	$4^{3/8}$		Ditto	30		1s.6d
$9^{1/4}$		Ditto	4	4	21s.	$3^{3/4}$		Ditto	36	4	1s.4d
$8^{1/4}$		Ditto	6	5	15s.	$5^{1/2}$		Spitting Pots	18		3s.
$7^{1/2}$		Ditto	9	6	9s.	$4^{3/4}$		Ditto	24	2	2s.3d
7		Ditto	12	7	6s.	$4^{1/8}$		Ditto	30	3	2s.

Page 2 continued

Dia.		No.	No	Price			No.	No	Price
$6\frac{1}{2}$	Ditto	18	8	4s.	5	Round Butter Tubs and Stands,	12	1	7s.
$5\frac{7}{8}$	Ditto	24	9	3s.	$4\frac{1}{2}$	Ditto	18	2	5s.6d
$5\frac{1}{8}$	Ditto	30	10	3s.	$3\frac{7}{8}$	Ditto	24	3	4s.6d
4	Ditto	36	11	3s.	$3\frac{1}{4}$	Ditto	30		3s.6d
$12\frac{3}{4}$	Bowls with Covers, but not handled,		1	48s.	5	Ditto, fast stands	12	1	10s.
$11\frac{1}{2}$	Ditto	2	2	36s.	$4\frac{1}{2}$	Ditto	18	2	9s.
$10\frac{1}{2}$	Ditto	3	3	24s.	$3\frac{7}{8}$	Ditto	24		8s.
$9\frac{1}{4}$	Ditto	4	4	16s.	$3\frac{1}{4}$	Ditto	30	4	7s.
$8\frac{1}{4}$	Ditto	6	5	10s.	5	Ditto, pierced,	12	1	10s.
$7\frac{1}{2}$	Ditto	9	6	7s.	$4\frac{1}{2}$	Ditto	18	2	9s.
7	Ditto	12	7	5s.	$3\frac{7}{8}$	Ditto	24	3	8s.
$6\frac{1}{2}$	Ditto	18	8	3s.6d	$3\frac{1}{4}$	Ditto	30	4	7s.
$5\frac{7}{8}$	Ditto	24	9	3s.		Jugs, 6 Pints,	2	1	12s.
$5\frac{1}{8}$	Ditto	30	10	2s.6d		Ditto, 4 Pints,	3	2	8s.
4	Ditto	36	11	2s.6d		Ditto, 3 Pints,	4	3	6s.
$8\frac{1}{4}$	Chamber Pots,	2	1	12s.		Ditto, 2 Pints,	6	4	4s.
$7\frac{1}{2}$	Ditto	3	2	9s.		Ditto, $1\frac{1}{2}$ Pints,	9	5	3s.
$6\frac{3}{4}$	Ditto	4	3	6s.		Ditto, 1 Pint,	12	6	2s.8d
6	Ditto	6	4	5s.		Ditto, covered, 6 Pints,	2	1	8s.
$5\frac{1}{2}$	Ditto	9	5	4s.		Ditto, 4 Pints,	3	2	8s.
$4\frac{3}{4}$	Ditto	12		3s.		Ditto, 3 Pints,	4	3	13s.6d
4	Ditto	18	7	2s.		Ditto, 2 Pints,	6	4	9s.
$3\frac{3}{4}$	Ditto	24	8	1s.6d		Ditto, $1\frac{1}{2}$ Pints,	9	5	6s.
						Ditto, 1 Pint,	12	6	4s.6d

Tea and Coffee Ware

Dia.	Ht.		Nearly the Former Sizes	No.	Plain	Flute	Enam'd	Queen's Blue Painted	Nankeen Blue Printed	Tortoise	Brown China	Egyptian Black	
$5\frac{1}{8}$	4	Tea Pots	9	1	6s.	7s.4d	14s.	14s.	16s.		8s.	14s.	P E R D O Z E N O F T W E L V E P I E C E S
$4\frac{5}{8}$	$3\frac{1}{2}$	Ditto	12	2	4s.6d	5s.6d	10s.6d	10s.6d	12s.		6s.	9s.6d	
$4\frac{1}{4}$	$3\frac{3}{4}$	Ditto	18	3	3s.	3s.8d	7s.	7s.	8s.		4s.	7s.	
$3\frac{3}{4}$	$3\frac{1}{4}$	Ditto	24	4	2s.6d	3s	5s.3d	5s.3d	6s.		3s.	6s.6d	
$3\frac{1}{2}$	$2\frac{1}{2}$	Ditto	30	5	2s.3d	2s.8d	4s.6d	4s.6d	5s.6d		2s.6d	5s.	
	$10\frac{1}{4}$	Coffee Pots or Milk Pots	2	1	28s.	34s.	63s.	63s.	72s.		36s.	56s.	
	$9\frac{1}{4}$	Ditto	3	2	18s.	22s.	42s.	42s.	48s.		24s.	42s.	
	$8\frac{3}{8}$	Ditto	4	3	13s.6d	16s.6d	31s.6d	31s.6d	36s.		18s.	28s.	
	$7\frac{1}{2}$	Ditto	6	4	9s.	11s.	21s.	21s.	24s.		12s.	19s.	
	$6\frac{5}{8}$	Ditto	9	5	6s.	7s.4d	14s.	14s.	16s.		8s.	14s.	
	$5\frac{3}{4}$	Ditto	12	6	4s.6d	5s.6d	10s.6d	10s.6d	12s.		6s.	9s.6d	
	$4\frac{5}{8}$	Ditto	18	7	3s.	3s.8d	7s.	7s.	8s.		4s.	7s.	
	$4\frac{1}{4}$	Ditto	24	8	2s.6d	3s.	5s.3d	5s.3d	6s.		3s.	6s.6d	
	$3\frac{5}{8}$	Ditto	30	9	2s.3d	2s.8d	4s.6d	4s.6d	5s.6d		2s.6d		
$4\frac{5}{8}$	$3\frac{1}{8}$	Sugar Pots	12	1	4s.6d	5s.6d	10s.6d	10s.6d	12s.		6s.	9s.6d	
$4\frac{1}{8}$	3	Ditto	18	2	3s.	3s.8d	7s.	7s.	8s.		4s.	7s.	
$3\frac{1}{4}$	$2\frac{5}{8}$	Ditto	24	3	2s.6d	3s.	5s.3d	5s.3d	6s.		3s.	6s.6d	
$3\frac{1}{8}$	$2\frac{1}{4}$	Ditto	30	4	2s.3d	2s.8d	4s.6d	4s.6d	5s.6d		2s.6d	5s.	
		Tea Canisters	12	1	4s.6d	5s.6d	10s.6d	10s.6d	12s.			14s.	
		Ditto	18	2	3s.	3s.8d	7s.	7s.	8s.			9s.6d	
		Ditto	24	3	2s.6d	3s.	5s.3d	5s.3d	6s.			7s.	
		Ditto	30	4	2s.3d	2s.8d	4s.6d	4s.6d	5s.6d			6s.6d	
$12\frac{3}{4}$		Bowls		1	21s.								
$11\frac{1}{2}$		Ditto	2	2	15s.								

Page 2 continued

												PER DOZEN OF TWELVE PAIRS
10½	Ditto	3	3	9s.								
9¼	Ditto	4	4	6s.								
8¼	Ditto	6	5	4s.	6s.	18s.	18s.	16s.				
7½	Ditto	9	6	3s.	4s.4d	12s.	12s.	12s.			14s.	
7	Ditto	12	7	2s,	3s.	9s.	9s.	8s.			9s.6d	
6½	Ditto	18	8	1s.6d	2s.2d	6s.	6s.	6s.			7s.	
5⅞	Ditto	24	9	1s.3d	1s.9d	4s.6d	4s.6d	4s.			6s.6d	
5⅛	Ditto	30	10	1s.	1s.5d	3s.8d	3s.8d	3s.3d			5s.	
4	Ditto	36	11	10d	1s.2d	3s.	3s.	2s.8d			4s.	
	Chocolate Cups			10d	1s.2d	2s.	2s.	2s.	1s.		4s.	
	Ditto and Saucers			1s.4d	2s.	3s.8d	3s.8d	3s.8d	1s.8d		4s.	
	Handled or Coffee Cups and Saucers			1s.4d	2s.	3s.8d	3s.8d	3s.8d			4s.	
	Cups and Saucers, Irish, or 1st Size			1s.	1s.8d	3s.	3s.	3s.8d				
	Ditto — London, or 2nd Size			11d	1s.7d	2s.8d	2s.8d	3s.				
	Ditto — Large Holland, or 3rd Size			10d								
	Ditto — Large Middle, or 4th Size)											
	Ditto — Small Middle, or 5th Size) ---			9d								
	Ditto — Small or 6th Size)											

Terms

5 per cent.	Breakage
5 per cent.	Discount with Liberty to draw on handing Invoice
2½ per cent.	for Liberty to draw at End of Three Months; or ½ per cent per Month for anticipated Payment; or in Lieu of the Discount, 6 Months Credit.

Price of Crates and Hogsheads

Small Crates, ~~Freight to Hull and Shipping~~ 5/6 each[*]

Larger ditto, ~~ditto — and — ditto~~ 6/-

Crates for Plates and Twifflers, ditto ~~and ditto~~ 7/-

Large Crates, ditto ~~and ditto~~ 8/6

Hogsheads, Cooperage, ditto ~~and ditto~~ 15/-

[* The crossing out has been done in ink with the original prices obliterated and the new prices, as given, added in ink.]

Page 3:

"LEEDS POTTERY, 1st February, 1796

Messrs Wray & Hollingworth
Gent } – [added in ink]

ANNEXED we transmit you a New Price Current, which you will observe differs not materially from the Old One, except in Two Points – one of which is an advance of Price on many of the Articles; the other, a new Method of counting the Dozen.

Instead of the old Method, we now count Twelve Pieces to the Dozen of every Article we have been accustomed to count in Dozens, except cups and saucers, of which we count Twelve Pairs to the Dozen.

We have also regulated the Sizes of the different Articles, and affixed to each its appropriate Number, and also its Dimensions, agreeable to a Scale of Twelve Inches English Measure, which you have on the first Page of the Price Current.

The Business of counting the Ware is rendered so much easier by this new System, and its Liability to Error and Confusion, consequently so much less, that we can have no Doubt of its meeting with your Approbation.

With respect to the other Point, viz. the Alteration in Prices – we have so long burdened with the great Advance on the Prices of the Raw Materials, the Difficulty of procuring many of them, together with the great Increase on the Workmen's Wages, that we find it absolutely necessary to join the other Manufacturers in taking this Step. – We therefore trust that these Circumstances, confirmed by the unanimous Consent of the Trade, will be deemed a sufficient Apology for our Conduct on this Head.

The Advance takes Place from the First of February, 1796, notwithstanding which it is our Intention to execute all Orders prior to that Date at the old Prices.

We shall be happy to receive your future Favours, and remain

[hand-written] – Gent.

Your most obedient Servants

[hand-written] – Hartley Greens & Co.

[hand-written] – PS/

In addition to the Terms,
shall allow to the Merchts
in Hull 5 pCent more Commission."

Earlier I mentioned the practical approach adopted by the Leeds Pottery in including an English-foot scale on the first page of its Price List in order to avoid any confusion regarding the sizes specified in the list. Another very practical step was also introduced and in which the Leeds Pottery may well have been a trailblazer (or more likely a lone voice of sanity crying in the wilderness!) – I refer to the rejection of the practice, which must have been confusing to all outside the pottery trade, of counting wares by the 'potter's dozen'. This practice is recorded as having been in use from at least the fifteenth century[30] and which continued as a bone of contention between potters and their unions, and their employers well into the twentieth century. It is not possible to state exactly how many pots of a particular size or capacity made a dozen except that as a general rule the smaller the pot the more there would be to the dozen, and *vice versa*. The Rev. George Malcolm, in 1908, published the following which shows the confusion which this 'system' must have caused outside the world of the potters and their agents :[31]

"... we need to understand the Potter's Arithmetic. Any ordinary person would take it for granted that a dozen means 12, but this is quite contrary to the whole principle of a potter's count.

The Potter's Arithmetic is arranged to simplify the payment of the oven men, or to simplify the calculations with regard to the number of articles placed in the oven.

Every kind of plate is calculated at 12 to the dozen; baking dishes and meat dishes are 12 to the dozen; all Hollow-ware-pressers' work is counted 12 to the dozen. But cups and saucers are 36 to the dozen; other small ware 18, 24, 36, even as far as 72.

The chief 'counts' as they are called, are the 'Oven' count and the Printer's count, but there are others, and all different to each other. The whole system of Potter's Arithmetic is antiquainted and absurd, an anomaly and a nuisance, and altogether unreasonable, but no steps have yet been taken to abolish or supersede it."

From the above quotation it is obvious that the Leeds Pottery's valiant attempt to rationalize the Potter's Dozen had not succeeded. See *Drawing Book No. 4*, (pages 484-495) and Plates 768 to 794 which show the traditional method being used and where plain bowls are illustrated 'Russian Doll' method in the following sizes: 2s, 3s, 4s, 6s, 9s, 12s, 18s, 24s, 30s, and 36s – to the dozen.

However, Diana Edwards in her *Black Basalt Wedgwood and Contemporary Manufacturers*, at Appendix I, quotes the following from notes by George L Miller :

"In 1796 the [Staffordshire] Potters attempted to fix the Potters' dozen sizes in terms of capacity. On that list teapot size capacities were listed as :

12s = 1 1/2 pints
18s = 1 pint
24s = 3/4 pints

In that list, 30s were not listed, but they may have held a half-pint ...".

By cross-referencing the items on the Price List with the published *Design Book* it is possible to understand most of the wares being priced. However one or two items do seem somewhat puzzling e.g., the range of sizes listed for Chamber Pots from eight and a quarter inches down to three and three quarter inches in eight stages. I believe "Pierced sauce spoons" to be a misprint which should have read "Sugar spoons", *vide* No. 130 in the *Design Book*.

The price list for Tea and Coffee Ware is interesting in showing the comparative prices for the varying range of shapes materials and decorations available for each size. 'Nankeen Blue Printed' being the dearest, such decoration adding approximately 166% on top of the same item 'plain'. The inclusion of prices in a column headed "Brown China" takes us back to the information, above quoted from Jewitt, that this 1796 list was identical with the one of the same date from the Swinton Pottery. It is therefore fairly safe to assume that "Brown China" referred to what we now know as 'Rockingham ware/glaze', the use of the word china most likely indicating a finer quality of ware and not porcelain. Such a glaze has been recorded by A. and A. Cox who discovered shards of this ware in one of their excavations.[32] The same authors also record an invoice of 1770 for such ware to Wentworth House.[33] I feel that it is therefore justifiable to assume that as both concerns were joined, at the period of the price lists under consideration, and as we have seen earlier that John Green was managing both potteries, that the transfer of recipes and technology would pass easily from one Pottery to the other. Moreover as the brown glaze was in production as early as 1770 it is quite feasible that it was developed in the 1760s when John Green was working at the Swinton Pottery prior to his move in 1770 to Leeds, and if so then he would most likely have taken the recipe with him.

To return to the Price List. It is interesting and informative to read "Handled or Coffee Cups and Saucers" – thus indicating that tea cups at this date were not handled and were what we now call 'tea bowls'. Lastly the names given to tea cups, *viz:* Irish, London and Holland, refer here to size and not shape. This of course does not imply that the London sized cups were not of the shape which we now call London.

Certain items are included in this list which do not feature in the published Design Books, either the early ones or the '1814' edition, namely :

Covers to suit round dishes.   Plain oval salts with legs.
Nappies, plain or pierced.   Tureen Ladles [other than sauce ladles].
Garden Pots and stands.   Tea & Coffee ware other than plain and fluted.

Some Evidence of the Scale of Production

In the Introduction to this book I record my disappointment that the Ledgers and Day Books have not survived which would have enabled an accurate account to be given of the full range of the wares produced, the quantities and periods when each design was in vogue.

We do however have a brief glimpse at the Order and Stock Books as two of them were used to paste designs in for goods ordered by customers and agents. I refer to *Original Drawing Book No.1* and *Original Drawing Book No.2*, now in the safe keeping of the Victoria and Albert Museum and reproduced here at Plates 445 to 567. Unfortunately, in *Book No.1*, most of the figures and other information have been covered up with the designs which have been pasted in that book. However, we are more fortunate with *Book No. 2* where most of the tables of figures etc., remain uncovered and it is therefore from this volume that I have been able to extract the following information and tentatively to deduce further information regarding the range and popularity of some of the wares. See Plates 520.a., 520.b. and pages 100-106.

The original book had been used, from the front, for keeping an ongoing record of orders, stock and requirements. The entries are dated February 1792. Strangely, for some reason not at present clear, this was abandoned after the 29th of February; perhaps it had been decided to adopt a different method of accounting. Only Royal Oval Dishes and Round Royal Dishes have had their accounts completed. Some have no entries while others have just one or two lines of figures but together these brief accounts do give an accurate if brief insight into one winter month's orders and stock figures. Another section begins at the end of the book and works backwards. This section lists, under specific headings which describe the various wares and their sizes, the quantities ordered by customers/agents – each one being identified by a series of code letters, unfortunately without a key being given to enable us to know either the customer's name or where he was ordering from. This section of the book is not dated but I expect that it would be approximately the same date as the entries at the front.

In perusing both sections of this book it is clear that the pages were ruled and the headings made prior to the orders being entered as some pages which were so prepared contain no entries. We are thus able to see what items were expected to be ordered and which were not – their absence possibly indicating that they were by 1792 passing out of fashion, an obvious example being 'shell edged' wares. The quantities in the columns must refer to potters' 'dozens' as some figures include a fraction, eg "7½" Royal Pattern sauce boats size 2, obviously could not have been ordered if the figures had represented single items. See also the Price Current List on pages 95, 97 where the prices for most items were quoted by the dozen.

No indication is given in either list regarding the wares being either creamware or pearlware, neither is any indication given regarding any surface decoration in the form of enamelling, painting or printing, the one exception being the engine-turned, brown-striped teawares. I find it hard to believe that the Leeds Pottery was not producing pearlwares before 1792 as well as printed and colour-decorated creamwares and pearlwares. It must therefore follow that other order books existed with more specific details for such wares. The two lists presently being considered may therefore refer to either plain, glazed creamware or pearlware which could be enhanced with onglaze decoration, either printed or enamelled, as required. These lists would therefore be a guide to the quantities to be manufactured in the various styles and sizes, the bulk of which may well have been sold after glazing but with some going to the warehouse to be withdrawn and decorated as required.

The lists at the front of the book

A specimen page is reproduced at Plate 520a.

I believe that the purpose of this series was to keep some form of running totals of stock under the various headings thereby indicating the quantities to be produced in order to complete the orders received.

Before considering what the figures mean we must remember that under the Partners' Articles of Agreement of 1776, Clause 7 they had agreed to hold a meeting on the first Wednesday of February " ... yearly ..." to " ... settle accounts of all the said Partnership Stock Trade and Business ...". As these lists bear the dates 25th February 1792 and 29th February they would be the first ones in the new trading year. In 1792 the first Wednesday in February fell on the 1st of the month. The 25th was a Saturday and totals to that date would most likely refer to orders received in the week, or period, ending the 25th. The quantities entered against the 29th would indicate the orders received after the 25th, up to the month ending.

In the transcript below, headed "Royal Oval Dishes", the numbers running from left to right across the top refer to the range of lengths in which this form of dish was made. Reading down the left-hand column we first see the date "25th feb:" this is sometimes followed by the letter 'S' which fortunately elsewhere is extended to "Sunds" which I interpret as meaning 'Sundry Orders', i.e. up to the 25th. Below this we find "Ba", sometimes just "B" or, in Book No. 1, where one of the entries is not covered, it is extended to "Ball" which would seem to indicate the Balance brought forward from the period prior to the one which ended on the 25th. Finally "29th feby" before a double line has been ruled across below which the figures above are added together to give the totals so far. Below this we have the totals in the "Warehouse" which are then subtracted from the previous line leaving the totals required to be made in order to complete the orders received. Finally, below, the "Wanted" list has been written: "Add to Wanted INN" signifying a late order after the books had been made up from a customer with the coded letters "INN". Or it might have been an omission on the part of the clerk from the previous entries. In the section headed "Bowls" the numbers, which run from 36 to 2, refer to the numbers to the dozen.

From the transcripts which I give below for Round Royal Dishes we learn that a total of 14,612 dozen such dishes had been ordered in February 1792. We must not of course be tempted to simply multiply this figure by 12 hoping to arrive at the number of dishes ordered as, prior to 1796, the Leeds Pottery had worked to the time-honoured tradition of the 'potter's dozen' whereby the larger the pot the fewer to the dozen.

The comparisons between table plates of various designs is also revealing, showing the popularity or otherwise of each design :

Royal 4017   Queens 208   Feather 517½   Concave 28

It is interesting to see 'Concave' being ordered but somewhat surprising not to see 'Shell' being listed or ordered; however we must remember that this only refers to orders received in one month of 1792. The "Quite Plain" would refer to what was later known as "Paris or Plain" - see *Design Book* No. 166.

"Total of Articles	page				
Royal Twiffs 8½ Ins	1	Feather dishes	4	Oval Royal Terrines	11
Concave Twiffs	1	Round royal dishes	5	Twiffs Roy:	11
Quite Plain Plates	1	Queens dishes	6	do Feather	12
Roy: Queens & Feather plates	2	Concave do	7	do Queens	12
Concave - do -	2	Quite plain dishes	8	Round Terrs pressd	13
Oval Roy dishes	3	Drainers	9	do Thrown	13
do Soup - do -	3	Bowls	10	Royal Salads	14

1) Royal Twifflers Concave

	Flatt		Soups		In	Flatt		
	8½	p	8½	p	8	p	7	p
25th feb: Sunds	120				4		10	

2)

	Royal			Queens			Feather		
	Tables		Soups	Tables		Soups	Tables		Soups
	o	p							
25th Feb Ba:	4017		1604	208		162	517½		236½
	7700		7800	200		200	140		130

	Concave [covered							]	
	Tables	Soups [covered						]	
25th feb:	28	19							

3) Royal Oval Dishes

	6	7	8	9	10	11	12	13	14	15	16	17	18	19	20
25th feb:	24	24			88	359	410	478	396	225	65	27	39	18	12
Ba:							870	1400	1700	485	1662	305	273	65	60
29th feby				120	120	330	300	300	120	72					
Tot	24	24		120	208	689	1580	2178	2216	782	1727	332	312	83	72
Warehouse	W	W		0	400	280			700	2010	150		600	510	
Wantd				120		409			1516		1577	332		0	72
Add to															
Wantd INN	72	24	24	24	24	36	72	120	144	180	180	144	96	72	24
Soup Dishes	[covered			]	36	36	2		8	6 [covered			]		

4) Feather Oval Dishes

	6	7	8	9	10	11	12	13	14	15	16	17	18	19	20
25th feby					24	18	18								
Soup Dishes															
Round Feather [covered													]		

5) **Round Royal Dishes**

	10	11	12	13	14	15	16	17	18	19					
25th feb: S	128	837	1210	716	380	208	100	30	37						
B		1348	1885	1485	1855	400	783	20	10						
29 feby	300	454	108	48		64	10			1					
Tot	428	2639	3203	2249	2235	672	839	50	47	1					
Ware:	240	134	-	71	160	240	226	58							
Wanted	188	2505	3203	2178	2065	432	667	-	47	1					
Add to	72	144	240	240	180	144	96	48	24						
Round															
Roy. Soup [covered														]	

6) **Queens Oval Dishes**

	6	7	8	9	10	11	12	13	14	15	16	17	18	19	20
25th feby	4		4		4		4		2		2				10
Queens															
Roun [covered															]

7) **Oval Concave Dishes**

	10	11	12	13	14	15	16	17	18	19	20			
25th feby					10									
Round Dishes Concave														

8) **Quite Plain Dishes Oval**

	10	11	12	13	14	15	16	17	18	19	20			
do Round [covered				10										]

9) **Oval Drainers for Dishes**

	10	11	12	13	14	15	16	17	18			
25th feb:			2		7		3					

10) **Bowls**

1792	36	30	24	18	12	9	6	4	3	2				
feby 25th	264	213	33	36	50	53	83	98	71	10				
Ba		75	130	140	70	38	31	15	11	5				
Broth														
Bowls [covered														]

11) **Oval Royal Terrines**

	8	9	10	11	12	13	14							
feby 25th: S		44	44	24	80									
	86	110	130	90	24	2								
B Ware:	34	196	304	259	230	204	29							

Twifflers		*Royal F* [covered											]
o 8	p	o 7	p										
25th Feb S	884		246								7		
Ba:	792	1227									38	[3 or 5 ? -covered	]

12)

	Feather		Twifflers		Flat		Do - Soups					
	8		7		6		8		7		6	
25th Feb 1792	120		2				6		21			
Ba:	67½		47½		17½		57½		27½			

The lists at the back of the book

A specimen page is reproduced at Plate 520b.

Under headings describing the different wares we find columns denoting the sizes in which they were made headed either by numbers referring to a measurement in inches or a number referring to the number to the 'potter's dozen, e.g., under "Milk Potts Plain": 12,18,24,30. Below these on the left we have a vertical column of code letters which would be identifiable within the Pottery's office and for which we do not have the key, suffice it to say that some are also geometric shapes, e.g. a triangle while others are letters from the Cyrillic alphabet; I have not transcribed these but an example can be seen at Plate 520b. The column, under each size, is divided into two sub columns: the one, on the left, headed "o" and the other "p". Quite frequently the numbers in the 'p' column add up, horizontally, to those in the 'o' column on the same line. I feel that it is reasonable to assume that 'o' stands for the size of the order and that 'p' may denote 'paid for', 'processed' or 'packed' . As several numbers often occur in this 'p' column it may indicate that the orders were paid for, processed or packed in stages; I have not transcribed the numbers from the 'p' column.

These tables also add to our knowledge and understanding of the relationship between the Leeds Pottery and the Swinton Pottery as some lists contain orders which are annotated "Ordered at Swinton to be marked &c." or "Ordered at Swinton to come here." The latter annotation being obvious, the former I feel sure does not imply that the wares were required to be impressed LEEDS POTTERY but rather that they should be packed and the crates or casks in which they were packed should be marked with the agent's or customer's code letters. A letter from Savile Green, senior, dated the 25th of August 1794, from Buxton and addressed to his wife Rhoda contains the following :

> " ... tell Mr. Hartley He may tell Billy Scorah to mark of[f] the Thumb pattern plates at Hull under the proper
> Marks and part of Soops to match them will be sent from Swinton Pottery - ."[34]

If the reader has access to my book on the Don Pottery reference may be made to the George Malcom Letters at Appendix IV where there are several letters regarding the shipment of pots; the following is an extract :

> " ... consigned to you from us since October last you have received a crate marked RHN No.8 & a crate marked
> IWE No. 23 ..."

The crates may well have been similarly marked from the Leeds Pottery with the code letters as shown in the tables under discussion. If this assumption is correct then it infers that some pots from Swinton were consigned direct to the customers and did not necessarily all go out through the Leeds Pottery's warehouse.

Although, as stated earlier, it is somewhat frustrating that this set of accounts is not dated I nevertheless feel that it must have been of a similar date to those at the front of the book, namely c.1792, for the following reasons. *Original Drawing Book No. 1.* has designs pasted in it with dates ending in 1792. *Original Drawing Book No. 2*, the one under discussion, has at the front accounts which, as we have seen, are dated February 1792 together with pasted-in designs with dates commencing in January 1792 and extending up to 1804.

The value to our knowledge of the Leeds Pottery of these particular accounts is that they show very clearly the popularity of certain wares and also the popularity of certain sizes within each type of ware listed. The staggering volume of items being ordered over what must have been quite a short span of time is perhaps exemplified by the totals recorded under "Sallads Round Roy[al]" where we find 24 orders totalling 5,077 dozen[35] in which one customer ordered 160 dozen at 6 inch, 160 dozen at 7 inch, 160 dozen at 8 inch, 160 dozen at 10 inch, and 80 dozen at 11 inch.[36] On the same page by contrast only two customers ordered a mere 42, single, 6 inch "Melon Teriens & Spoons" (see the *Design Book* No. 68) interestingly this item was not included in their 1796 Price Current List, but it was still retained in the c.1814 edition of the published *Design Book*.

The inclusion, with quantities, of 'Toy' wares is also of interest as it is not generally recognised that such wares were produced at the Leeds Pottery. It is also significant that no orders were entered under Candlesticks, Ornamental Jars and "Dock Leaves" – could the latter mean "Pickle Leaves" as illustrated at No. 111 in the *Design Book* ?

Headings with the words "Engind" or "Engine" refer to engine-turned wares. The words "Ring" and "Fruit" as sub-headings indicate the form of handle or knop on the lids of such wares, see Plate 795. The description "Coverd & Grated Jugs" informs us that in the 1790s this is how they described what we would now describe as 'Jugs with lids and strainers'. "Slipper" would be synonymous with Bourdalou, Coach-Pot or Oval Chamber Pot.

In the following extracts I have retained the spellings used by the Pottery but have added up and quoted the total number ordered under each size. In italics below each total I have given the number of customers/agents placing such orders.

Covered Mugs					[sizes are not given but the quantities are in columns]
15	15	13	5	4	[doz.]
3	*4*	*3*	*1*	*1*	

[There are three other columns of orders on this page totaling 65 doz. being ordered by 8 buyers – the items are, however, not named thus indicating that one or more pages are missing.]

Chambers				
3	4	6	9	12
37	128	157	41	7
6	*11*	*13*	*6*	*2*

Coffee Pots				
4	6	9	12	[to the doz.]
	11	14	8	[doz.]
		4	*5*	*3*

Mustards Low & Spoons	
3 doz. no spoons	8 doz. spoons wanted.
1	*1*

Ewer Basons Round		
E - 4	E - 6	E - 9
B - 2	B - 3	B - 4
114pr	334pr	124pr
8	*16*	*8*

[these letters and numbers indicate the number to the dozen of the ewers and basons, thus: one 4 to-the-doz. ewer is paired with one 2 to-the-doz bason.]

Milk Pots Plain				
12	18	24	30	[to the doz.]
5	98	221½	177	[doz.]
3	*11*	*14*	*14*	

Covered & Grated Jug				
2	3	4	6	[to the doz.]
5	15	15	15	[doz.]
1	*2*	*2*	*2*	

Milk Ewers	
35 doz.	[no size given]
1	

Sugars Plain Dou: Hands				
12	18	24	30	[to the doz.]
9	42½	33½	5	[doz.]
3	*9*	*8*	*1*	

Pails & hands Double	Do Single
[No entries].	

Round Terreins & Stands										
Rings					Fruit					
8	9	10	11	12	8	9	10	11	12	[inches]
36	559	904	1064	145	38	500	993	893	174	[doz.]
4	*18*	*19*	*20*	*14*	*4*	*19*	*20*	*20*	*14*	

Ice Cellars
36 [singles]
3

Teapots Plain							
Round				Square			
12	18	24	30	12	18	24	30
40	37	190½	222	9	14	22½	28
		10		21	40	71	95
7	*8*	*12*	*13*	*5*	*6*	*9*	*11*

[to the doz]
[doz.]
["Ordered at Swinton to be marked"]

Handᵈ			Toys			
Cups & Saucers	Teapots	Coffee Potts	Sugar Cups	Milk Pots	Bowls	Cannisters
190	115	95	95	105	15	80
5	*6*	*5*	*4*	*6*	*2*	*2*

[doz.]

Pressed Bakers Round										
7	8	9	10	11	12	13	14	15	16	[inches]
1000	925	840	615	260	115	50	30			[doz.]
8	*9*	*9*	*9*	*6*	*3*	*2*	*1*			

Butter Tubbs & Stands Oval Roy		
4	5	6
80		
1		

[inches]

Candlesticks		Compotiers	Ornamented	Dock
Corenthian	Composite	Square	Jarrs	Leaves
[No entries under any of these headings]				

Round Covered Dishes										
Ring					Fruit					
10	11	12	13	14	10	11	12	13	14	[Inches]
550	1164	1291	122	5	309	1135	1150	182	5	[doz.]
72	189	202	74		157	555	572	230		["Ordered at Swinton to
10	*14*	*16*	*8*	*1*	*14*	*19*	*20*	*12*	*1*	be marked &c."]

Triangler Compotiers		
9	10	12
50	250	80
1	*3*	*1*

Oval Cover'd Dishes

Rings					Fruit					
10	11	12	13	14	10	11	12	13	14	[Inches]
15	101	256	32		15	81	266	52	105	["Ordered at Swinton to be marked &c."]
	15	40	52			20	55	102	20	["Ordered at Swinton tocome here"]
1	*5*	*7*	*4*		*1*	*4*	*8*	*6*	*4*	

Ewars & Basons

Oval	Plain		
1	2	3	[sizes]
40	30	30	[doz.]
2	*1*	*1*	

Glass Trays

11 In.	
6 [doz.]	
1	

Slippers / Salts Oval

Slippers			Salts Oval	
Size 1st	,, 2nd	,, 3rd	Roy	Fer
10	30 [doz.]		15 doz.	
1	*3*		*4*	

Sallads Oval Roy

6	7	8	9	10	11	12	13	14	[inches]
	285	392	230	762	442	137	20		[doz.]
	5	*9*	*4*	*14*	*9*	*6*	*1*		

Sauce Boats Roy

1	2	3	4	[Size]
111½	132½	55½	3	[doz.]
8	*20*	*7*	*1*	

Sallads Round Roy

6	7	8	9	10	11	12	[inches]
310	720	1032	1069	1441	415	90	[doz.]
3	*11*	*18*	*19*	*14*	*13*	*5*	

Melon Teriens & Spoons

4	5	6	7	[Inches]
		42		[singles]
		2		

Oval Roy Terriens

Rings					Fruit						
9	10	11	12	13	9	10	11	12	13	14	[inches]
45	115	259	259	197	50	188	425	285	180	35	[doz.]
3	*8*	*11*	*12*	*8*	*4*	*14*	*16*	*15*	*13*	*3*	

Royl Sauce Terrines Spoons and Stands

5	[inches]
30	[doz.]
2	

Glass Trays

10	11	12	[inches]
10	21		[doz.]
1	*3*		

Engined Bowls

6	9	12	18	24	30	[To the doz.]
9		18	15	40	5	[doz.]
2		*4*	*3*	*4*	*1*	

Engine Ice Pails / Milk Pots / Sugar Cups

Engine Ice Pails	Milk Pots			Sugar Cups			
[Singles]	18	24	30	18	24	30	[To the doz.]
455	33	22	41	13	4		
10	*2*	*4*	*5*	*4*	*2*		

Engine Teapots

Round				Square				
12	18	24	30	12	18	24	30	[to the doz]
5	9	39	34	2	72	27	37	[doz.]
		50	50					["Ordered at Swinton to be marked &c."]
2	*2*	*5*	*5*	*1*	*2*	*5*	*5*	

Engine Handled Cups & Sauces [No sizes indicated]

190 [doz.]
4

Pierced Roy Deserts

Tables	Twifflers			
	8	7	6	[inches]
9	160	80	50	[doz.]
1	*8*	*5*	*3*	

Furnished Casters

Small	Large

Oval Twig Baskets & Stands						
7	8	9	10	11	12	[Inches]
[?]			16	30	12	[Singles]
			2	1	1	

Sand Boxes

Eng^d Brown Strip'd Teapots												
Round				Do Square				Inlet or Scalop^d Tops				
12	18	24	30	12	18	24	30	12	18	24	30	[To the doz.]
4	6	60	54		5	24	25		10	32	28	[doz.]
2	2	7	7		2	7	6		2	5	5	

Engine^d Brown Stripd										
Milk Pots			Bowls				Sugar Cups			Cups & Saucers Hand
18	24	30	12	18	24	30	18	24	30	
22	31	31	13	25	31	37	17	16	13	300*
7	7	8	3	7	8	3	5	5	1	5

[To the doz.]
[doz.]

* The 300 doz. cups and saucers have been given the same code as was used elsewhere to indicate "Ordered from Swinton ..." The corner of the page is missing but the word "Ordered" is visible.

1. *Journals of the House of Commons* – Vol. XXVIII, 1758, p. 57.
2. *ibid*, p. 104.
3. 1 waggon contained 24 corfs = 2 1/4 tons.
4. *A History of the Middleton Railway, Leeds*, 7th ed., The Middleton Railway Trust Ltd., p. 9.
5. See also E. Kilburn Scott – *Matthew Murray, Pioneer Engineer*, Leeds, 1928.
6. WYAS (Leeds) – Acc 1849.
7. Leeds Local Studies Library – DD 196/1.
8. WYAS (Leeds) – DB 214/uncatalogued.
9. *A History of the Middleton Railway, Leeds*, 7th Ed., The Middleton Railway Trust Ltd., pp. 18 and 27.
10. WYAS (Leeds) – LO/HU/5.
11. *A History of the Middleton Railway*, op cit., p.35.
12. Ralph Thoresby – *Ducatus Leodiensis*, 1714.
13. Simon Lawrence – "Clay tobacco Pipe Makers in West Yorkshire", *Yorkshire Archaeological Journal*, Vol. 45,1973, pp. 189 – 193.
14. Hull Local Studies Library – L 651.7, (2 Vols.).
15. Gordon Jackson – *Hull in the Eighteenth Century*, 1972, p. 337.
16. See – Ch. 2, p. 51 & Ch. 3, pp. 53, 54, 55, 64 & 65.
17. John D. Griffin – *The Don Pottery 1801 –1893*, pp. 24, 38.
18. Calculated on figures produced by: O'Donoghue, Goulding & Allen, *Economic Trends*, Office for National Statistics, 2004, pp. 41 & 43 – "Composite Price Index 1750 to 2003".
19. Pigot & Co's – *Metropolitan New Alphabetical Directory for 1827*.
20. *The Post Office London Directory*, 1826.
21. Pigot & Co's – *London & Provincial New Commercial Directory*, 1823 – 4.
22. Robson's – *London Directory*, 1833.
23. PRO –T.78/252. T.78/385 & T.78/386.
24. Arnold Mountford – "Documents relating to English Ceramics in the 18th & 19th centuries" *Journal of Ceramic History*, No. 8, pp. 3 – 41.
25. Finer & Savage – *The Selected Letters of Josiah Wedgwood*, 1965, p.106.
26. Wedgwood Archives on temporary deposit at the University of Keele, ref: 17587-20. Reproduced by courtesy of the Trustees of the Wedgwood Museum, Barlaston, Stoke-on-Trent, Staffordshire, England.
27. Hull Local Studies Library – Wray & Hollingworth Letters 1795–1796, Vol. II, No. 544, Ref: L651.7.
28. Llewellynn Jewitt – *Ceramic Art*, Vol I, pp. 497/8.
29. Taken from a listing of European, pre-metric system, units of length kindly supplied by the University of Sheffield, Hawley Collection, with the kind assistance of Mr. K.W. Hawley. It was compiled from the following works :
Harris, J. – *Lexicon Technicum: or an Universal English Dictionary of Arts and Sciences*, vol I, 1725.
Bion, Nicholas – *The Construction and Principal Uses of Mathematical Instruments*, 2nd ed. 1758.
Kelly, Patrick – *The Universal Cambist and Commercial Instructor*, vols 1 & 2, 2nd ed. 1821.
Haswell, Chas. H. – *Engineers' and Mechanics' Pocket Book*, New York, Harper & Bros., 1844.
Alexander, John H. – *Universal Dictionary of Weights & Measures, Ancient & Modern*, Baltimore, 1850.
Grier, Wm. – *The Mechanic's Pocket Dictionary*, 11th ed. Glasgow, 1851.
-----do ---- Weights and Measures, *The Encyclopedia Britannica*, 9th ed., vol. 24, New York, 1888.
Haswell, Chas. H. – *Mechanic's and Engineer's Pocket Book of Tables*, 74th ed. New York, 1909.
-----do------- Weights and Measures, *Encyclopedia Britannica*, 11th ed., vol. 27, New York, 1911.
30. Lionel Burman – *NCS Newsletter*, No.86, p. 17.
31. The Rev. Malcolm Graham – *Cup and Saucer Land*, first pub. 1908, re-published without alteration, 2000, by Staffordshire and Stoke-on-Trent Archive Service.
32. A & A Cox – *Rockingham Pottery & Porcelain 1745 – 1842*, p. 108.
33. A & A Cox – *Rockingham*, p. 117.
34. This is the only reference in the Savile Green letters to the Swinton Pottery.
35. The value of this quantity, priced with the 1796 price list would be approximately £1,133. and at 2003 values £81,032.
36. The value of this single order would have been approximately £140, priced with the 1796 price list. At 2003 values this would be equivalent to £10,012. (See Footnote No. 18, above).

CHAPTER EIGHT

The Wares
Their Attribution and Identification

THE great Llewellynn Jewitt, writing in *The Art Journal* of 1865 at page 305, stated:

"However much was known, years ago, about the productions of this manufactury, nearly all knowledge, even of its very existence, has been lost, and scarcely one collector in a dozen at the present day knows of what its specialities consisted."

Further on he asserts that the Leeds Pottery was in existence in the middle of the eighteenth century; this we know to be inaccurate. Based on this dating he then, quite naturally, assumed that both delft ware and salt-glazed ware would have been among the early products.

J.R. and F. Kidson, writing some twenty-seven years later[1] had little to add, mentioning that prior to 1774 the firm traded under "Humble Green & Co" and going on to state :

"...but nothing is with certainty known of the character of the ware produced"

Later, in the same chapter we find the following very telling sentence:

"As, however, before stated, the earlier years of the Pottery and its productions are but things to conjecture about, and all statements without documentary evidence are but wild guesses."

If only succeeding writers had read, learned and inwardly digested this last statement then not only would the history of the Pottery have been written with less romanticism but many unmarked wares would not have been wrongly ascribed to the Leeds Pottery. In short, 'Leeds Pottery' has become a generic label which has been given to large quantities of unmarked late eighteenth and early nineteenth century creamware.

The late Donald Towner started off his research with high principles :[2]

"The field was open and discarding the bigoted statements of most books on the subject, I began at the beginning by using my eyes and distrusting everything that had been said or written about English pottery till I had thoroughly tested it."

Unfortunately he became obsessed with his belief that the Leeds Pottery was established *circa* 1758 and went to great lengths in his attempts to prove this belief in his *The Leeds Pottery* of 1963. Even when Heather Lawrence had established the correct date of its foundation as being 1770 and had informed him of this information he still was not convinced :[3]

"Your 1770 theory also means that all the early Leeds Pottery must have been made during 5 years only 1770 – 1775 which is very hard to believe and then there are dated pieces – clearly Leeds – prior to 1770. I think when you have still more knowledge of the Pottery and particullarly of the wares you will discard your 1770 theory."

However, some three years later, in another letter to Heather Lawrence dated the 4th of January 1975, he wrote :

"I am sorry I was so reluctant to give up my old theories but you prepared the ground for my doing so – and then the positive information of the Insurances completed my conversion. I think it is probable that there were early potteries in the area that are not yet discovered, particularly as I have groups of early deep cream ware that don't fit in with any known pottery ".

In his *Creamware*, published in 1978, Donald Towner somewhat reluctantly acknowledged the date 1770 as the foundation date of the Leeds Pottery but still reiterated a possibility of a precursor dating from 1758. Sadly, nowhere in that book did he acknowledge the research and information supplied to him by Heather Lawrence and which "prepared the ground" for his reluctant "conversion".

At this juncture I feel it is appropriate to subject Donald Towner's *The Leeds Pottery* to some analysis :

1. Number of pieces illustrated: 129 of which 94 are creamware. Of the remaining 35 pieces, 3 are redware one of which is silver lustre overall, 3 are black basalt, 12 are pearlware figures and the remaining 17 are other pieces of pearlware.
2. 36 pieces are factory marked.
3. 22 of the remaining 93 unmarked pieces have moulded details which appear on the illustrated marked examples.
4. 2 other pieces have moulded details which do not appear on (2) but do appear on (3).
5. 19 pieces he dated as having been made before 1770 of which two pieces carry dates prior to 1770.

In fairness, however, it has to be said that since 1963, the year in which Donald Towner's book was published, a great deal of research has been carried out and published about other potteries working contemporaneously with the Leeds Pottery. As a result, serious collectors and students of the wares produced are now much less likely to be so dogmatic regarding the attribution of unmarked wares as was Donald Towner's generation. The Leeds Pottery was a very convenient 'box' in which to consign large quantities of unmarked creamware, particularly if it had pierced decoration, flower and leaf terminals to crossed strap handles and tilted flower knop handles on lids.

The excellent volume on William Greatbatch by David Barker, published in 1991[4] re-claimed several of Towner's 'Leeds' pieces back to Staffordshire and stated in no uncertain terms, page 277 :

> "... Something of the romance of looking at pottery may have been lost and the imaginations of over-enthusiastic individuals will have less scope to run wild, but this is no bad thing. Objectivity in any research is important, and a proper use of the available evidence is essential if ceramic history is to be taken seriously by a wider public. ...
> It is ironic that many of Greatbatch's most characteristic wares have for many years been hailed as 'typical' of the Leeds Pottery, and that Greatbatch's involvement in their manufacture could only be seen in a Leeds context, so that some writers would have him working at Leeds, or else importing Leeds wares to Lower Lane for decoration. Not only are these hypotheses nonsense, and have been proven so, but, more importantly, they are quite simply not founded upon a single shred of evidence. This confusion is a situation from which ceramic history must be rescued."

A similarly well-written work, albeit dealing with a smaller and less well-known pottery was published in 2001 by Peter Francis – *A Pottery by the Lagen*. Shards excavated from the site of this Irish pottery show very similar, but not identical, moulded details as have been attributed to the Leeds Pottery.

In Yorkshire the several excavations on the site and in the vicinity of the Swinton Pottery by A. and A. Cox show, as is to be expected, identical and very similar products to those from the Leeds Pottery during the period 1785 to 1806. The Don Pottery, founded by John Green in 1801, issued a Design Book, most likely towards the end of 1803, which contains 172 designs identical with designs in the Leeds published Design Books, see pages 115-133 & 139-149. Thus many of the products of the last three mentioned potteries all of which had, at some time, John Green as manager or joint owner of them, would be producing identical wares which, in all probability, were manufactured using the same recipes for both bodies and glazes. It is also inconceivable to imagine that, when John Green left the Swinton Pottery to become one of the founding partners of the Leeds Pottery where he was entrusted with "... the direction and management of the ... work", he would have taken up his new position with a *tabula rasa*. It is, therefore, quite reasonable to assume that the characteristics of the early Leeds wares <u>might</u> have been similar to or even exact copies of what he had been familiar with at Swinton.

The collector should also be aware that not only are some details on creamware products from different British manufacturers sometimes very similar but also that they often bear very close similarity with some products from Continental potteries. In this respect the reader's attention is drawn to the illustrations in the book *European Creamware* by Jana Kybalová; a book which should be essential reading for any would-be or established student or collector in this field of ceramics.

The truth of the matter is that any branch of the applied or decorative arts shows us that at any period most objects were being produced in the style then in demand, *i.e.* in fashion at that period. The field of ceramics is no exception in this regard.

Bearing all the above in mind I have determined to use the present work to establish a sure foundation upon which collectors, students, and anyone else involved or interested in the Leeds Pottery may be able to build their collections and knowledge with attributions completely devoid of such expressions as – 'possibly', 'maybe' or 'similar to', indeed the maxim "similar to also means different from" should be engraved in the minds of all collectors.

How then can we identify unmarked wares from the Leeds Pottery? The simple answer to this question is that it is not always easy with any certainty so to do. As this work, as stated above, is intended to be a base from and upon which to build further knowledge I have decided, as far as possible, only to illustrate :

– Factory marked examples.
– Some shards which are believed to be from the Pottery.
– Some sprig moulds from the Pottery.
– Some block moulds from the Pottery.
– The published Design Books.
– The extant manuscript, drawing and design books.
– The extant pattern books.

I will also draw the reader's attention to factory-marked examples illustrated elsewhere which it has not been possible to include in this work, together with any other evidence which I am able to provide.

Even some of the above categories should carry a warning. Reference to pages 118-149, where the Leeds *Design Book* is illustrated, will show that by no means all the designs were unique to the Leeds Pottery, even when compared only with those Design Books from the Don Pottery, the Castleford Pottery, Sewell's Pottery, Whitehead's Pottery and Wedgwood's 'Useful Wares' Catalogues. We do not know how many other potteries, contemporary with the Leeds Pottery, published design books which have not survived or have not yet been discovered. Furthermore how many other potteries made creamware in the same style and maybe with the same or very similar moulded details and who may not have marked their wares or published design books?

An analysis of the body and glaze of an unmarked pot may seem conclusive if it matched that of a marked example, but only if it could be shown that the compositions of the Leeds Pottery's body and glaze were peculiar to that pottery. This is something which we could only be one hundred percent sure about if it ever became possible to know the analysis for every pottery working at the period in question. The country's pottery workforce was not static; a significant proportion was mobile, as reference to the 19th century census returns show and although an individual pottery owner may have tried to keep secret his recipes for his bodies and glazes some of these pottery workers would be able to convey information to their new employers. Every new Pottery which was established would recruit workers from other potteries, and of all levels of ability.

In short, the attribution of unmarked, particularly creamwares, is up to the person making that attribution to state his or her reasons for so doing, with full references back to proven source material. If all writers, collectors and dealers had adopted this approach it would have prevented most of the wishful thinking and romantic attributions with which the literature and public collections devoted to this subject have been liberally encumbered over the years.

Marking and Marks

It would be quite logical to make out a case that marks were used from shortly after the beginning of the factory in 1770. They are certainly found on pieces illustrated in the Pottery's published Design Book of 1783 and which could, purely on stylistic grounds, show wares which could have been in production since the early 1770s, see remarks on p. 172. See also remarks under Marks 3a and c, below. So far as I am aware there is no archive or other material to show that wares were not impressed LEEDS POTTERY "to any extent before about 1790".[5] None of the nineteenth or early twentieth century writers ventured such a starting date for marking. It is also worth reminding ourselves that Josiah Wedgwood had marked only spasmodically up to 1769 but from that date virtually all his useful wares had been marked.[6]

I mentioned in Chapter 7 the claim by Jewitt that both the Leeds Pottery and the Swinton Pottery had the same Price Lists of wares. In the same chapter I also reproduce lists showing wares being ordered from Swinton by the Leeds Pottery. This being so I feel that it is inconceivable to expect that the Leeds Partners would have countenanced wares consigned under an invoice from the Leeds Pottery, being marked 'Swinton Pottery'. Hence the apparent total absence of any pots having a Swinton mark during the Greens Bingley partnership, 1785 – 1806.

Possible reasons for not marking all pieces

Once again in the absence of factory records it is fully appreciated that the following remarks are my suggestions for possible reasons – all of which could be wrong but they are given to show that very good reasons did exist for not marking :

1. Wares solely for export about which Jewitt claimed :[7]

"The great bulk of the pottery, whether in Queen's ware or otherwise, was made for foreign markets ... and as a rule the goods were sent off unmarked."

However I am not aware of any contemporary evidence to support Jewitt's claim but I do know of several fine pieces of marked Leeds Pottery which have been bought by both dealers and collectors in countries to which the Leeds Pottery in known to have exported its wares.

2. We do know that, in the early nineteenth century, Mintons were instructed not to mark their wares by one of the London retailers who presumably would find it inconvenient if customers came asking for a particular maker's goods as this could reduce the sales of similar stock from other potters.[8]

3. Marking, although a brief operation, was nevertheless another procedure in the manufacturing process. Moreover such a process of impressing a mark was certainly not without a risk of damage to the piece being marked. Flatware, made over a mould, e.g. a plate or dish was in an ideal state for marking as before the mould was 'run' into the drying room a potter would be able to easily impress the stamp into the clay before it had begun to harden. This was not the case with wares which had been thrown on the wheel and which then had to dry to the leather-hard state before being turned on a lathe in order to finish them off including the important task of turning the recess under the base to form the foot ring. On such a pot the thickness of the bottom could be very thin indeed. The same was also true of slip-cast objects. Once these had dried away from the mould they had hardened somewhat and again could be quite thin. Both the above examples could be broken if a stamp with the words LEEDS POTTERY were to be pressed too hard against the underside of such a pot. The Leeds Pottery overcame this problem in various ways :

The stamp used had the words LEEDS POTTERY, or HARTLEY GREENS & CO./ LEEDS POTTERY on a curved surface[9] thus enabling the operative to role the words onto the pot causing only a few letters to be in contact with the pot at any one time therefore much less pressure was necessary. Think of the Fakir's bed of nails – the more nails the less likely that they would either pierce the skin or cause any discomfort. Moreover this method accounts for the marks on the pots being, more often than not, slightly curved or even 'S' shaped. Also, quite often only either the tops or lower parts of the words are impressed indicating that the tool was not held vertical to the surface being marked, perhaps this may have been another deliberate act if the pot being marked was quite hard, (see examples on page 110). Another technique was to impress the mark on the bottom edge of the foot ring where more force could be applied than on the bottom of the pot. A third method was to impress the mark on the vertical side of the base of the pot below the spout on tea and coffee pots for example. Finally the mark is often seen on the inside edge of the foot ring, particularly on black basalt wares where the base has been turned out presenting a surface which slopes upwards and away from the outer edge. Such a situation was ideal, as the workman could support the outer edge of the foot against a finger whilst he rolled the stamp against the concave inner surface. A stamp with a straight, flat surface could not have been used on a concave surface.

The Marks used up to the end of the Hartley Greens & Co's period in 1827

These marks were, as Llewellynn Jewitt stated : "not numerous and are easily distinguished." They fall into four categories: impressed, inscribed, painted (i.e. hand written in an enamel colour) and over-glaze printed and incorporated in the overglaze print. No transfer printed backstamps have so far been recorded for either the factory name or a pattern name in this period.

1. LEEDS POTTERY - impressed. All marks shown actual size and enlarged (x 2).

a.i

a.ii

a.iii

a.iv

a.v

a.vi

a.vii

b.

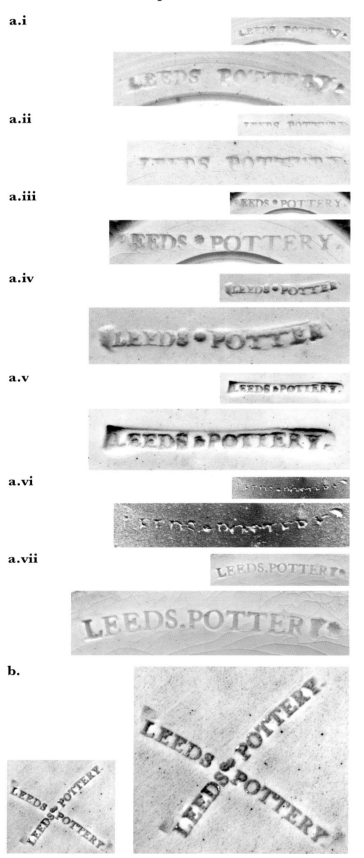

a and **b.** As will be seen by the examples, this mark takes roughly two forms, either impressed once as shown at (a.i) to (a.vii) or impressed twice or three times, either *saltire*, as shown at (b), or impressed again some short distance from the first impression. The reason for impressing more than once is unknown. At the time of writing I know of no significance which can be attributed to the inclusion of asterisks and dots which appear in different positions in this mark. They can certainly not have had any relevance so far as the factory was concerned because the manner in which the stamps were applied, i.e. rolling the mark, often at an angle, would not show a full stop after 'POTTERY' if only the top half of the letters were impressed as at (a.ii) and (a.vi) neither would either a full stop or an asterisk show after 'POTTERY' if the end of the stamp was not impressed as at (a.iv). Any attempt to try to formulate a hypothesis for using the variations for dating the wares can also be dismissed as the three variations shown at (a.ii, a.iii and a.vii), all appear on the coffee pot, teapot and milk jug illustrated at Plates 264, 265 and 266, and which are all *en suite*. The mark at (b) is impressed three times, quite indistinctly, on the plate at Plate 145; another plate from the same service is impressed only twice with the same mark.

The curvature of the mark at (a.vi) and (a.vii) and the almost long 'flat' 'S' shape at (a.iv) illustrate very clearly the resultant effects of rolling the mark. Similarly mark (a.v) shows the effect of firmer pressure at the beginning and end of the 'roll' in the comparatively soft clay on the underside of a plate which would just have been formed over a plaster mould and therefore fully supported and able to bear such pressure without damage. The very clear mark at (a.vii) is on the underside of the foot ring of the teapot at Plate 265, again a situation where the area being impressed had plenty of support. Compare the last two examples with (a.ii) on the turned-out recess on the underside of the coffee pot at Plate 264, and at (a.vi) again on the underside of a turned out base on the milk jug shown at Plate 398. In both examples the base would be quite thin and in the leather-hard state which was necessary before they could have been turned on the potter's lathe. I believe that this mark continued in use after the introduction of Marks 2a and 2b as one frequently finds it used on wares produced *circa* 1820, for example – blue transfer printed "Scene after Claud Lorraine", see Plates 229 and 230.

c. In script found in association with onglaze printed decoration. - Actual size and enlarged (x 2)

d. Enamelled in Roman leters. Actual size

LEEDS.POTTERY,

c. This mark is found in conjunction with over glaze printed decoration – usually at the base of the print but sometimes half way up the side where it may be split with the "Leeds" being at one side of the print and "Pottery" at the other. See Plates 109,115 and 117/118.

d. This mark I have only recorded on one example, the jug at Plates 270 – 272.

---

2. HARTLEY GREENS & CO./LEEDS POTTERY.

It seems very strange that the Leeds Pottery had traded under the name Hartley Greens & Co., since 1781 but did not mark its wares with this title until a much later date. An analysis of the marks which incorporate this title, on the Black Basalt wares illustrated in this work, has revealed some interesting findings pertinent to the dating of such pieces. The pieces which are marked with Mark No. 1 (see Plates 378–386 and Plates 398–410) all match, or are similar to, designs in the first section of the *Drawing Book for Blackware 1806*, design numbers 1–76. All pieces which are marked with Mark No. 2.a (see Plates 388–397) match designs in the later section of the book where the paper is watermarked 1812, design numbers 77–91. The only anomaly being the milk jug at Plate 387 which is marked with Mark No. 1 but which corresponds to design No. 77. As design No. 77 is the first design in the 1812 section of the book it may therefore be termed a transitional piece presumably made before the new marking stamps were available or possibly this design was in production before the new designs were entered in the *Drawing Book*. If I am correct in deducing that the HARTLEY GREENS & CO. mark was not introduced until c.1812 then may I also suggest that this was most likely done at the instigation of William Hartley, junior. William Hartley, senior, had died in January 1808 and his heir at law, William was then under age and whose inheritance had therefore had to be held in trust for him; he came of age in August 1811 when the Leeds Pottery was closed down. It will be remembered that business commenced again from the 29th of June 1812 (see page 60). William, junior, now of age and a partner, through inheritance, did begin to take an active part in the Pottery's affairs and no doubt considered it to be high time that the wares should henceforth bear a mark with the same wording as the partnership traded under. The marking stamp would, however, have an extra 133% additional area to impress than the former simple LEEDS POTTERY stamp. Before leaving this topic it is worth looking at Plate 499. Here we have a drawing sent from an Italian customer, dated 27 August 1791, and where the instructions have been translated: "the whole marked underneath ~~Hartley Green & Co~~". As will be seen the "Hartley Green & Co" has been crossed out and LEEDS POTTERY added. The logical explanation being that the customer in Italy knew the company he was ordering from and presumed that its name would be the Pottery's mark. As stated earlier I believe that the impressed LEEDS POTTERY mark continued to be used after the introduction of the straight HARTLEY GREENS & CO/LEEDS POTTERY mark.

With regard to "HARTLEY GREENS & CO. LEEDS POTTERY" stamped in a horseshoe shape as illustrated at Mark No. 2.d., I feel sure that this was introduced about 1820. It was certainly in use by July 1821 (see Plate 121) as it is found on the plates commemorating the Coronation of George IV. It is the mark also found on the drabware pieces, illustrated at Plates 338–346, which I believe were introduced by Thomas Lakin. I do not, however, claim or suggest that Mark 2.a., was replaced by this mark as it may well have continued to be used in tandem with it until 1827 when the Hartley Greens & Co's., partnership ceased to exist. (See page 71).

HARTLEY GREENS & CO/LEEDS POTTERY - impressed. - All marks shown actual size and enlarged (x 2).

a.i. Impressed in a straight line

This mark, with its two lines of letters on the marking stamp, presented an even greater area to impress into the pots and with a much greater chance of damage than the marks illustrated at 1, above. Any attempt to angle the stamp as it was being rolled onto the pot would result in only one line of letters being clearly marked and with a strong possibility that the other line would be missed altogether. This most likely accounts for the mark recorded by Donald Towner in his *The Leeds Pottery*, at Fig. 5, No. 17, page 144. Here he shows just the first line, i.e. "HARTLEY GREENS & CO." Justification for my statement is to be found in the marks on the saucers belonging to the tea and coffee service illustrated in the present work at Plates 196–198. On some only the top half, i.e., HARTLEY GREENS & CO is clearly impressed and on others only the lower half i.e., LEEDS POTTERY is clearly impressed. However a very careful examination does reveal traces of the beginning and/or ending of the letters of the missing line.

a.ii

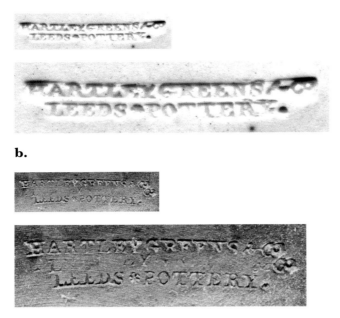

This is a slight variation of 2.a.i.,to which I believe no significance can be attached so far as dating the wares is concerned. This mark, which is here impressed very clearly, should not be confused with the example at 2.b.

b.

This mark is an interesting example of the point made under (a.) above. The person marking this pot, a slip moulded milk jug, being aware that he or she would most likely shatter the leather-hard body of the jug, if any attempt was made to press the two lines simultaneously into the base of the jug, had obviously rolled the top line at an angle and then had rolled the bottom line at an angle. Between these two lines can be seen the faint lettering of the bottom line which had engaged with the surface of the clay when HARTLEY GREENS & CO was being impressed – and also the "CO" was caught when the lower line LEEDS POTTERY was impressed.

c. A. Hurst, in his *A Catalogue of the Boynton Collection of Yorkshire Pottery*, illustrates, at page 10. No. 20, the mark at (2.a.i) impressed *saltire*, as at mark (l.b.). Again I am unaware of any significance which can be attached to this mark.

d. impressed in a horseshoe shape

Because of the shape of the stamp needed to make this impression it is presumed that its surface would not be curved. The mark therefore tends to be found only on flatware which has been made over a mould and which could be easily impressed while the clay was reasonably soft and fully supported on the mould. An exception being the pink-lustre salt at Plate 324; here the area underneath could easily have been supported by the hand/fingers of the person applying the marking stamp. See paragraph two of the introduction to (2) above for a suggested date for the introduction of this mark.

---

3. LP
a. Impressed. - Actual size and enlarged (x 2).

Often found impressed twice and some distance apart. I believe this to have been perhaps the earliest impressed mark used and which carried on being used after the introduction of the full-name stamps at (1) above.

b. inscribed as a monogram. (recorded by D. Towner)
Size of mark not known

This was recorded by Donald Towner on the base of a vase candlestick in the Victoria & Albert Museum which he illustrated in his Leeds Pottery book at Plate 23.

c. In raised Roman Letters. - Shown actual size and enlarged (x 3).

The letters cut **intaglio** into the face of the stamp. This produces **raised** letters on the pot. I am only aware of this mark being presently recorded on one piece, namely the redware coffee pot at Plate 64. This is a rare mark which, because of the absence of any information regarding another pottery with these initials, is ascribed to the Leeds Pottery. It has not been discovered on any shards nor on any other pieces of pottery which, from other criteria, could be ascribed to the Leeds Pottery. See plate 43 where it is recorded that some unmarked shards of redware have been discovered on the site of the Pottery. If, however, irrefutable evidence is subsequently discovered proving it to be a Leeds Pottery mark then its existence would be proof that the Pottery was marking its wares from the early years of its production and would be added support for my belief that the LP impressed mark at (3.a) above was an early mark.

Returning to the mark and the method of its application. The appearance of this mark, seen clearer where I have enlarged it, looks for all the world as though it has been made with a seal used for stamping sealing wax which was used to seal letters of the period, notice the rope twist decoration of the surround on the right-hand side and the finely cut Roman capitals. However, whatever the origins of the stamp used to produce this mark, it should be clear from my statements above that it would need substantial pressure to produce the mark with the consequent possible damage to the pot being marked. This would therefore account for it being discarded soon after its introduction and substituted by a stamp which produced an intaglio mark.

d. - enamelled

See the horse at Plate 322, where these letters are enamelled in the bottom left-hand corner of its saddle cloth.

---

4. Painter's and/or Decorator's marks. Actual size and enlarged (x 2).

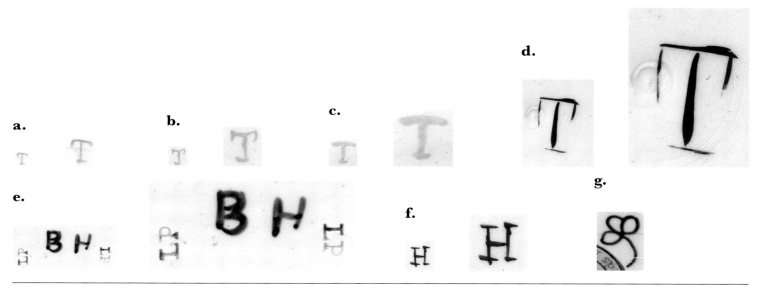

---

5. Pattern Numbers. Actual size and enlarged (x 2).

---

6. Crystal Ware. I believe that this mark was used for a short period c.1820 (see pages 233, 235). Actual size and enlarged (x 2).

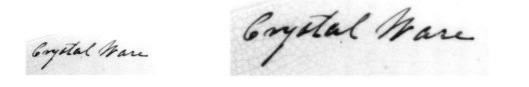

The Marking of Wares after 1827

I do not know of any marks which relate specifically to Samuel Wainewright's tenancy of the Pottery, and only two marks used by Stephen and James Chappel, (see below). I feel, however, that wares were marked with the old LEEDS POTTERY stamp in the years after 1827 – see Plates 422 & 425. It is recorded in Chapter 5, page 74, that new stamps were purchased in 1831 which would replace the Hartley Greens & Co. stamps. So far I have not recorded any wares with an impressed mark peculiar to this period.

7. Backstamps used by Stephen and James Chappel

a. - with "S & J C". Actual size.

b. - with "C". Actual size.

So far recorded only on shards. Some pots are known with a gothic 'C' printed below the backstamp on blue-printed wares. Shards with such a mark have been recovered from a workmen's trench in Leathley Road and may, therefore, have come from the Leathley Lane Pottery under Stephen and James Chappel.

c. - without any initial letters. Actual size.

The Period 1850 to 1878 & c.1881

Very little is known in detail about the wares, let alone the marks used in this period. Llewellynn Jewitt in his article published in the *The Art Journal* of 1865 gave us a contemporary account of its products and stated :

" ... is principally confined to the supplying of the home markets, where, not being marked, the ware usually passes for that of Staffordshire."

This statement would have been formed from information then available from the Pottery itself and he would not have had to rely on the fading memory of some aged workman. If we consider that in the 1851 Census Return, it is recorded that over four hundred were employed at the Leeds Pottery, therefore vast quantities of ware must have been produced. If this fact is placed alongside the fact that only a handful of wares are presently recognised from the Leeds Pottery at the same period, then Jewitt's statement would seem to be valid.

However one mark is recorded. It is clearly illustrated on the last pattern to be registered, on the 17th of September 1874 and would appear to be of a printed backstamp, see Plate 444. The Kidsons in their work on the Leeds Pottery of 1892 stated, p. 110 :

"Richard Britton & Son, however, used within recent years the letters 'R.B,& S.' within an ornamented circle, which also gave the name of the pattern. This was printed in blue or other colours ... ".

Another mark which has been recorded by both the Kidsons and A. Hurst,[10] as having been used by Richard Britton, was a Gothic or Old English letter 'L' within a quatrefoil circle.

8. Marks used during the Richard Britton Period, up to 1878

a. - impressed Mark recorded by the Kidsons and illustrated by A. Hurst. Actual size and enlarged (x 2).

b. - printed registration or 'Kite' Mark for Design No. 79588, registered on the 10th of July 1851. Actual size and enlarged (x 2).

c. - later Mark used by Richard Britton & Sons. Taken from Reg. Pattern No. 285322. See Plate 444. Actual size and enlarged (x 2).

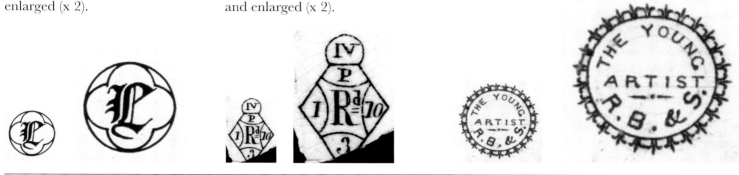

I am not aware of any marks used during the 1878 to 1881 period.
Marks relating to the revivalists, J. & G.W. Senior and J.T. Morton, can be seen in Appendix IX

The Published Design Books

The reader's attention has been drawn to the existence of these books as and when they were published by the Pottery; we must now collate these shorter notices and complete the information presently known about them. Just one point needs to be stressed before we embark upon the account of them and that is they are not <u>Pattern</u> books as they are frequently and erroneously called by most writers; they are <u>Design</u> books as is quite boldly proclaimed on their title pages : "Designs of Sundry Articles of Queen's or Cream-colour'd Earthen-ware ...". Pattern books contain patterns – to wit, surface decoration in the form of painted, enamelled and gilded patterns which the decorators could copy onto the wares.

The earliest known publication was in German and dated 1783, this was followed by a French edition of 1785 and an English edition of 1786, see page 118 where the title pages are reproduced. So far as I am aware there is no reference in any published work to there having been an earlier edition. The Pottery would need its riders[11] to have some form of illustrated material to show to prospective customers. This first edition contained 152 general articles and 32 items of tea-ware. Josiah Wedgwood had printed an illustrated catalogue of 'useful' wares in 1774 and which contained but 35 items. A comparison with its contents and those in the Leeds book shows that only two designs seem to match in each book: a twig basket and stand and a Queen's-pattern sauce boat and stand, both ubiquitous items and designs which must have been produced by virtually every creamware manufacturer of the period. The Leeds Pottery had not, therefore, copied wholesale Wedgwood's designs.

Such design books could only show the shapes of the items and could not give any impression of the quality and 'feel' of any given pot; the only solution being for the riders and merchants to have actual examples of the products for inspection by prospective customers. A letter from Josiah Wedgwood to Thomas Bentley dated the 21st of November 1773 confirms this practice :[12]

> " ... We shall want some hundreds of small dishes to send abroad as patterns the next spring. We shall pack a 10 inch dish of a pattern, about 8 patterns in oval boxes, and these the Merchants will put into their packages without any trouble to them, ...
>
> The patterns I have thought of are: Royal pattern and new feather edge plain. Royal pattern with purple edge; D° with flowers (not too dear); D° with Vine border; D° Red printed; D° Black. new feather edge colour'd with, and without, a flower in the middle; which will be nine different patterns for Table services, and along with each must be sent a printed Catalogue in French of the articles for Table services &c. But this will not be complete without some copper plates of the principal vessels which will give a much better idea of them than the names only. These may be slight etchings, provided the drawings and perspective are good. ..."

The above quotation outlines what would seem a very obvious action for any manufacturer to adopt who was anxious to proclaim both the range and quality of his products. Even if no other potter had done anything similar prior to Wedgwood then I feel certain that after Wedgwood had introduced this method of advertising others would have quickly followed his example. There is evidence that the Leeds Pottery was asked to supply decorated plates as samples in 1791, (see Plate 480). The above quotation, from Wedgwood, is also very valuable in that it gives us a precise date (1773) when the shapes and decorations listed were in production.

By referring to the Pottery's annual coal consumption, page 87, we can see a steady rise in this, indicating an increase in production levels being maintained up to and including 1778, then a period of slight stagnation until 1785 when a rising coal consumption begins again, possibly indicating that the issue of the design books in 1783, 1785 and 1786 had, in all probability, paid handsomely for their production by advertising the range of articles available, and that increased sales had resulted.

30. EDWARD HAILSTONE, of Horton Hall, Bradford and later of Walton Hall near Wakefield, at the entrance portico of which this photograph was taken, succeeded to his father's legal practice and took a leading and active part in many Yorkshire business and philanthropic activities. He amassed a large and very important collection of books and ceramics and, as I have noted elsewhere, contributed information to Joseph Marryat's *A History of Pottery and Porcelain* on the Leeds Pottery, see pp. 163 & 262/3. *The portrait is reproduced by kind permission of Alan Hitchcock.*

The first edition, in German, French and English, was reissued in 1794 without any additions or alterations and in the same three languages, (see page 118 bottom right). Llewellynn Jewitt records that another edition was issued within a "few years" in English and in Spanish and quotes the Spanish title page in full. He further tells us : "Instead of 152 general articles, as enumerated in the previous editions, 221 appear in this; and instead of 32 in tea-ware, 48 appear." The copy just described was in the possession of Edward Hailstone, FSA., a prodigious collector of both ceramics and books, (see Plate 30). Unfortunately I am not aware of a copy of this new enlarged edition published, according to Jewitt, sometime in the late 1790s. What would appear to be a reprint of this edition and which Jewitt dated 1814, was issued in or shortly after that year. Copies of this are known, they are undated on the title pages, unlike previous editions, but the paper is watermarked 1814 and "Leeds Pottery", usually within an outline, is printed between the designs on each page. I am not aware of any foreign editions of this issue but I expect that some would have been published. No further reprints or revised editions are presently known during the Hartley Greens & Co's partnership.

We must now interpret Jewitt's information regarding the time when he claimed that the new, enlarged edition was first published – "within a few years" of the 1794 reprint. With the information now published in Chapter 11 regarding the manuscript Drawing Books, etc., together with other evidence I feel that it is now possible to draw all this evidence together and put forward the following facts and conclusions :

1. In 1783, 1785 and 1786 the Leeds Pottery issued its first known book of designs which numbered 1 to 152 for General Wares and 1 to 32 for Tea Wares.

2. This book was reprinted, without any additions, in 1794, still in the three original languages of German, French and English, see pages 118-133.

3. Sometime between 1794 and c.1814 a new, enlarged edition was issued in Spanish and English in which the General Section was extended to 221 and the Tea Ware Section extended to 48.

4. The manuscript *Drawing Books, 1 to 4*, see Chapter 11, contain numbered designs starting in *Drawing Book No.1* at No. 153, i.e. they follow on after the last number in the first published book of 1783.

5. In *Drawing Book No.1* and *Drawing Book No. 2*, twenty seven drawings of General Wares and eleven of Tea Wares are annotated with another number indicating that they are in the new, enlarged edition of the published book and at the numbers quoted. The last such entry is in *Drawing Book No. 2*, where No. 304 (the book opens at No.274) becomes No. 221 in the new, published edition. Many of the designs in both *Drawing Book No. 1* and *No. 2* are taken from the sketches sent from customers and agents and which are pasted in the *Original Drawing Books* numbers *1* and *2*, see pages 280-406.

6. *Drawing Book No. 1* has its paper watermarked with the years 1781 and 1782 together with the dates 1786, 1788 and 1790 written against three designs. *Drawing Book No. 2* has its paper watermarked with the year 1803 this being the only date associated with this book. What is of interest is that *Drawing Book No. 2* contains some designs which were received as sketches in the 1790s, – e.g. No. 290 is from an order sent from Germany dated the 13th of July 1795 and the original sketch for No. 301 was pasted in between the last quoted order and another dated 23rd of April 1796, thus indicating that they were not copied into the Drawing Books immediately after they had been received.

7. Another fascinating factor comes from the *Design Book* published by the Don Pottery where 48 designs for General Wares and 5 for Tea Wares were taken from the *additions* to the Leeds Pottery's enlarged published *Design Book*.

Bearing all the above in mind I venture to suggest that *Drawing Book No.2* had its designs entered up to and possibly beyond No. 304, shortly after the book was purchased in 1803. Soon after this, most probably later in 1803 or early 1804, a decision was made to up-date the original published book. *Drawing Books Nos. 1 & 2* were then searched for designs which had proved to be popular and with these and others the enlarged version was compiled and published both in Spanish and English as Jewitt has stated but a little later than his "a few years" but certainly before the Don Pottery issued its *Design Book*. In my Don Pottery book, at page 54, I have reasoned that the Don *Design Book* could have been published by late 1803 and most likely before the end of 1804.

With regard to the original publication of 1783, I further suggest that the contents of this publication represent the styles and range of wares being produced by the Leeds Pottery up to that date and quite possibly since its foundation; on stylistic grounds alone this is quite feasible.

No design books or catalogues are known to have been published during any of the remaining period up to the final closure c.1881. It would however be very surprising if it could ever be proved that none had been published.

To return to the edition of 1794, an interesting and very informative copy of this edition is preserved in the Leeds Local Studies Library. Its chief significance is not so much its date and title pages but the fact that someone has written against all the items a table showing the range and individual price of each article, usually per dozen, see page 131. Because of these annotations it is now generally referred to as "The Agent's Book". It is reproduced here at pages 118 to 133, and I have extended its contents with the addition of the extra items included in the enlarged published edition of c.1814. The Agent's Book has two other sections which were obviously bound with it at an early date :-

i. Forty-six pen and wash drawings on twenty-one pages – Nos. 156 to 278 with a total of seventy-seven numbered designs not included, thus only forty-six designs had been selected from this overall sequence for illustrating by hand in this book.

ii. Eleven tea-bowls in pen outline with watercolour patterns, illustrating pattern Nos. 149, 210 – 212, 214 – 219 and 220.

iii. Fourteen blank pages.

One of the most fascinating features of the Leeds Design Books is the fact that items which were in the first edition of 1783 were obviously still desirable and therefore saleable and worth repeating in the c.1814 edition, some thirty years later. – See Plate 100 where the chestnut basket bears Mark No. 2a., which I have dated as being introduced c.1812 (see page 111). The design is No. 137 in the 1783 *Design Book,* also the Ink Stand at Plate 72 which bears Mark No. 2.d., which I date to c.1820, is No. 147 in the 1783 *Design Book* As stated earlier some of the designs in the first edition could well have been in production since the early 1770s, for example, "feather edge', "Royal" and "Queens", all of which Wedgwood had been producing since the mid 1760s. I would also expect that melon tureens, shell and leaf dishes and twig baskets would also have been in production since the early 1770s.

As the prices quoted in both the Agent's Book and the price list of 1796 are the same it may be presumed that the annotations in the Agent's book were either taken from the price list or were done in preparation for its publication. It will also be noticed that the pages from the c.1814 edition all carry the words "Leeds Pottery" which was not the case with the earlier editions of the 1780s and 1794.

In the reproduction of the Agent's Book which follows, I have supplied information which indicates which of the designs are the same as, or similar to, those in the published design books of :

> The Don Pottery, c.1803/04
> The Castleford Pottery, 1796
> Joseph Sewell's Shape Book of c.1815
> James and Charles Whitehead's Catalogue of 1798
> Josiah Wedgwood's Catalogues of 1774 and 1790

The first number in **bold** type refers to the Leeds design; this is followed by the names of the other potters listed above – if in ordinary type the design is the same as the Leeds version and if in *italics* it implies that such a design is similar to the Leeds version.

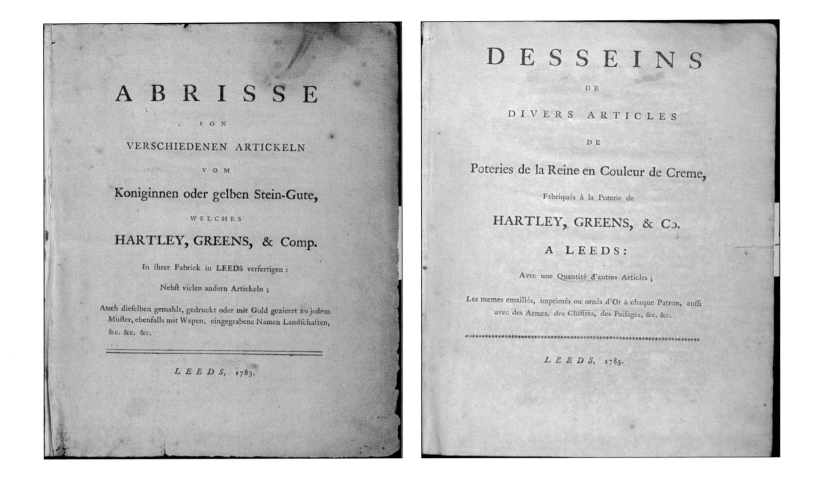

ABRISSE

VON

VERSCHIEDENEN ARTICKELN

VOM

Koniginnen oder gelben Stein-Gute,

WELCHES

HARTLEY, GREENS, & Comp.

In ihrer Fabrick in LEEDS verfertigen:

Nebft vielen andern Artickeln;

Auch diefelben gemahlt, gedruckt oder mit Gold gezieret zu jedem
Mufter, ebenfalls mit Wapen, eingegrabene Namen Landfchaften,
&c. &c. &c.

_____

LEEDS, 1783.

DESSEINS

DE

DIVERS ARTICLES

DE

Poteries de la Reine en Couleur de Creme,

Fabriqués à la Poterie de

HARTLEY, GREENS, & Co.

A LEEDS:

Avec une Quantité d'autres Articles;

Les memes emaillés, imprimés ou ornés d'Or à chaque Patron, auffi
avec des Armes, des Chiffres, des Paifages, &c. &c.

LEEDS, 1785.

The date 1794 has been crossed out on this title page.

DESIGNS

OF

SUNDRY ARTICLES

OF

Queen's or Cream-colour'd Earthen-Ware,

MANUFACTURED BY

HARTLEY, GREENS, and Co.

AT

LEEDS-POTTERY:

WITH

A great VARIETY of other ARTICLES.

The fame Enamel'd, Printed or Ornamented with Gold to any Pattern;
alfo with Coats of Arms, Cyphers, Landfcapes, &c. &c.

_____

LEEDS, 1786.

DESIGNS

OF

SUNDRY ARTICLES

OF

Queen's or Cream-colour'd Earthen-Ware,

MANUFACTURED BY

HARTLEY, GREENS, and Co.

AT

LEEDS POTTERY:

WITH

A great VARIETY of other ARTICLES.

The fame Enamel'd, Printed or Ornamented with Gold to any Pattern;
alfo with Coats of Arms, Cyphers, Landfcapes, &c. &c.

LEEDS,

EXPLANATION of the PLATES.

Reference to each.
No.

1 Oval Feather, 2 Royal, 3 Queen's, 4 Shell Edge — Terrines, from ~~Eight~~ 4 to Fourteen Inches

5 Oval Feather, 6 Royal, 7 Shell Edge, 8 Queen's — Sauce Terrines, Spoons, and Stands, from Four to Seven Inches

9 Feather, 10 Royal — Ditto Ditto with fast Stands, Five and Six Inches

11 Pickle Leaf, ~~from Four to Eight Inches~~
12 Sea Shell, ~~from Six to Nine Inches~~
13 Escollop Shell, ~~from Four to Seven Inches~~
} from 4 to 9 In.

14 Queen's, 15 Feather, 16 Shell Edge, 17 Royal — Sauce Boats, from Four to Seven Inches and a Half

18 Oval Royal, 19 Feather, 20 Queen's, 21 Shell Edge — Dishes, from Six to ~~Twenty~~ 20 Inches
Round Dishes of the same Patterns, from Ten to ~~Twenty~~ 19 Inches

Also Soup Dishes, each Pattern, round or oval, from Ten to Eighteen Inches

22 Queen's, 23 Feather, 24 Shell Edge, 25 Royal — Table Plates, Nine Inches and a Half
Soup Ditto same Size
Smaller Ditto called Twiflers, Six, Seven, ~~and~~ Eight Inches 8 9

26 Oval Queen's, 27 Feather, 28 Shell Edge, 29 Royal — Cover'd or Ragou Dishes, from ~~Ten to Fifteen~~ ~~9 to 15~~ 10 to 15 Inches
Round Ditto from ~~Ten to Fourteen~~ ~~9 to 14~~ 10 to 14 Inches

30 Queen's, 31 Feather, 32 Shell Edge, 33 Royal — Sallads, from Six to Fourteen Inches
Round Ditto the same

[4]

34 Square Royal Sallad, from ~~Nine~~ 6 to Fourteen Inches
35 Turtle Dish, from ~~Twelve to Fourteen~~ 8 to 13 Inches

36 Royal, 37 Feather, 38 Triangular Royal, 39 Feather — Compotiers, from ~~Nine to Twelve~~ 4 to 12 Inches

40 Round Feather, 41 Queen's, 42 Royal, 43 Shell Edge, 44 Royal deep — Pierced Desert Plates, from Six to ~~Eight~~ 10 Inches

45 Oval, 46 Round — Feather Pierced Desert Dishes, from Eight to Eleven Inches

47 Round, 48 Oval — Fish Drainers for Dishes, from Ten to Twenty Inches

49 Oval Royal, 50 Pierced, 51 Queen's, 52 Pierced, 53 Feather, 54 Pierced — Salts, Three Inches
The same without Covers

55 Plain, 56 Engined Pierced, 57 Pierced — Egg Cups

58 Pierced double Salts
59 Ditto with Covers
60 Plain Jug, from Half Pint to Twelve Pints
61 Engin'd Ditto, Ditto Ditto
62 Round Plain Salt
63 Ditto, with Feet

64 Engin'd Cover'd, 65 Plain Cover'd — Mugs, from Half Pints to Four Pints,

66 Engin'd, 67 Plain — Mugs from Half Pints to Four Pints

68 Melon Terrine and Spoon, from Four to ~~Nine~~ 12 In. Inches
69 Round Terrine and Stand, from Six to Twelve Inches
70 Handled Cover'd Bowl, from Half Pints to Eight Pints

71 Cover'd Bowl, without Handles, from Half Pint to Eight Pints
72 Cover'd Ditto, from Six to *12* Inches
73 Ditto, with Partitions, Ten Inches—A. The Cover
74 Oval Queen's
75 Oval Feather } Butter Tubs and Stands, from Four to Six Inches
76 Oval Royal
    The fame, with pierced Covers
77 Hexagon
78 Round Engine'd } Butter Tubs and Stands, from Five to Three and a Half Inches
79 Round Plain
80 Pepper or Sugar
81 Mustard } Castors
82 Oil or Vinegar
83 Round Engine'd } Mustards
84 Round Plain
85 Square
86 Round Strawberry Dish and Stand, Eight to Ten Inches
87 Oval Ditto   Ditto   Eight to *12* Inches
88 Platt Menage, Twelve Inches high
89 Water Bottle and Bafon, from Two Pints to Six Pints each
90 Ice Cellar
91 Oval } Bakers, from Six to *16* Inches
92 Round
93 Plain } Ice Pails for One, Two, Three, and Four Pint Bottles
94 Engine'd
95 Glafs Tray for Ten or Twelve Glaffes *from 9 to 14 A.*
96 Double Pail and Ladle
97 Single   Ditto
98 Oval Water Difh for Difhes of all Sizes
99 Afparagus Shell
100 Efcolop'd Nappy, from Six to *16* Inches
101 Oval Octagon Sallad, from *10 to 13* Inches
102 Large Furnifh'd Caftor
103 Small   Ditto
104 Oil and Vinegar Stand
105 Grand Platt Menage, Seventeen Inches high

B

106 Grand Platt Menage, Twenty-five Inches high
107 Small Compofite Candleftick, Eight Inches high
108 Dolphin   Ditto   Ten Inches high
109 Toilet   Ditto   Six Inches and a Half high
110 Ditto   Ditto   Six Inches and a Half high
111 Ditto   Ditto   Six Inches and a Half high
112 Ornamented   Ditto   Eleven Inches high
113 Griffin   Ditto   Ten Inches high
114 Square Fluted   Ditto   Ten Inches and a Half high
115 Corinthian Candleftick, Ten Inches high
116 Vafe Candleftick, Twelve Inches high
117 Large Compofite Candleftick, Twelve Inches and a Half high
118 Flatt   Ditto
119 Water Ewer, with Round or Oval Bafon
120 Shell Edged Oval Ewer and Bafon
121 Oval Chamber Pot, Four Sizes
122 Round Chamber Pot, from One Pint to Six Pints
123 Spitting Pot without Handle
124 Ditto   Handled
125 Oval Shell Edged Shaving Bafon, from Nine to *16* Inches
126 Round Plain Ditto, from Nine to Twelve Inches
127 Table Spoon
128 Sauce Ladle
129 Tea or Mustard Spoon
130 Pierced Sugar Spoon
131 Pierced Fifh Trowel
132 Pierced Fruit Bafket and Stand, from Five to *12* Inches
133 Ditto   Ditto   Ditto another Pattern
134 Twig Fruit Bafket and Stand, from *6* to Twelve Inches
135 Pierced Cover'd Fruit Bafket and Stand, from *7* to Eleven Inches
136 Pierced Fruit Bafket and Stand, from Five to Eleven Inches
137 Chefnut Bafket and Stand, from *6* to Eleven Inches
138 Ornamented Jarr or Potpourri, from Six to Fourteen Inches

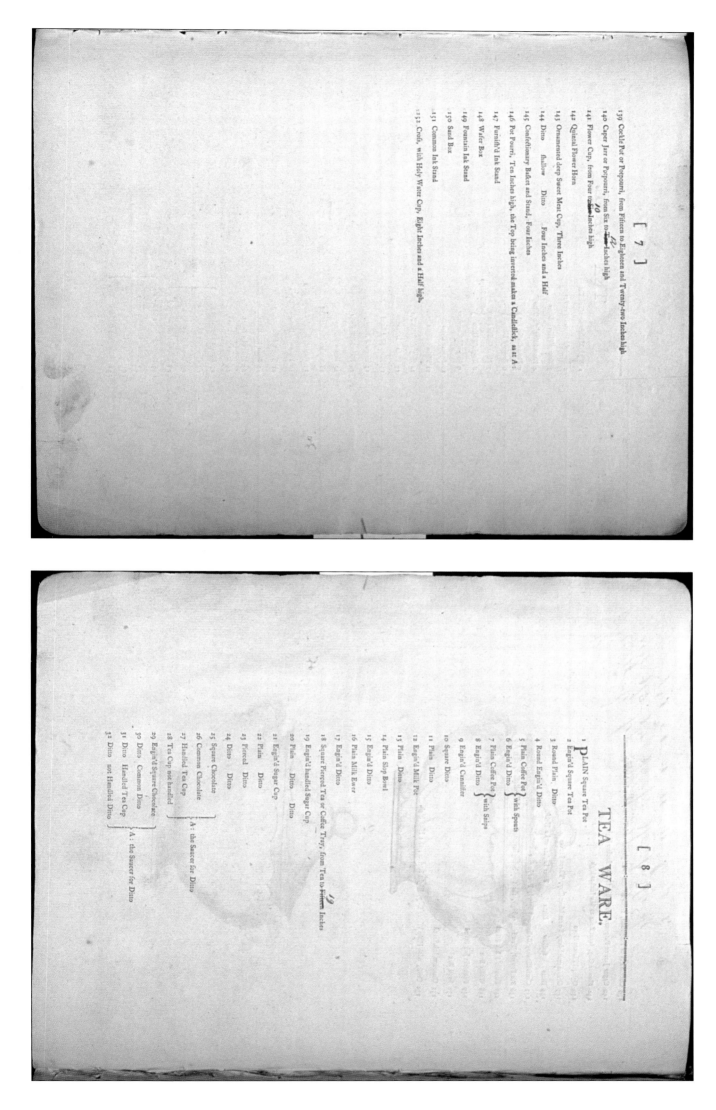

7

139 Cockle Pot or Potpourri, from Fifteen to Eighteen and Twenty-two Inches high
140 Caper Jarr or Potpourri, from Six to Twelve Inches high
141 Flower Cup, from Four to ___ Inches high
142 Quintal Flower Horn
143 Ornamented deep Sweet Meat Cup, Three Inches
144 Ditto   shallow   Ditto   Four Inches and a Half
145 Confectionary Basket and Stand, Four Inches
146 Pot Pourri, Ten Inches high, the Top being inverted makes a Candlestick, as at A:
147 Furnish'd Ink Stand
148 Wafer Box
149 Fountain Ink Stand
150 Sand Box
151 Common Ink Stand
152 Croft, with Holy Water Cup, Eight Inches and a Half high.

TEA WARE.

1 PLAIN Square Tea Pot
2 Engin'd Square Tea Pot
3 Round Plain, Ditto
4 Round Engin'd Ditto
5 Plain Coffee Pot
6 Engin'd Ditto } with Spouts
7 Plain Coffee Pot
8 Engin'd Ditto } with Snips
9 Engin'd Cannister
10 Square Ditto
11 Plain Ditto
12 Engin'd Milk Pot
13 Plain Ditto
14 Plain Slop Bowl
15 Engin'd Ditto
16 Plain Milk Ewer
17 Engin'd Ditto
18 Square Pierced Tea or Coffee Tray, from Ten to Fifteen Inches
19 Engin'd handled Sugar Cup
20 Plain Ditto Ditto
21 Engin'd Sugar Cup
22 Plain Ditto
23 Pierced Ditto
24 Ditto Ditto
25 Square Chocolate
26 Common Chocolate
27 Handled Tea Cup
28 Tea Cup not handled } A: the Saucer for Ditto
29 Engin'd Square Chocolate
30 Ditto Common Ditto
31 Ditto Handled Tea Cup } A: the Saucer for Ditto
32 Ditto not Handled Ditto

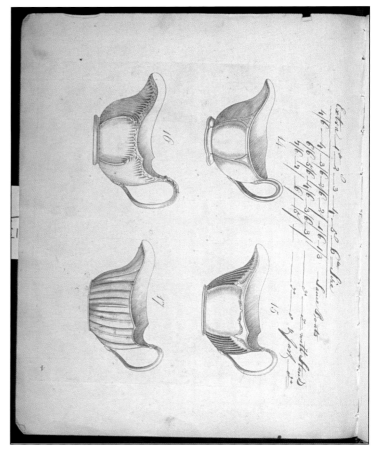

No. 11 - *Castleford 118.* **No. 12** *- Castleford 121.* **No. 13** *- Castleford 119, Whitehead 109.*

No. 14 - Wedgwood (1774) 12, **No.16** *- Castleford 62.*

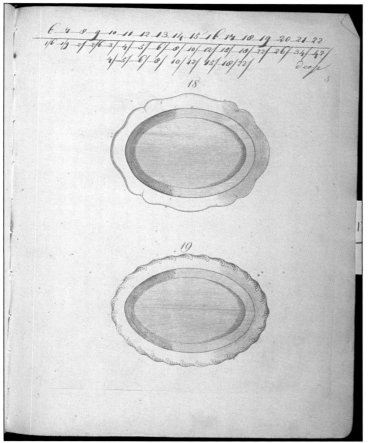

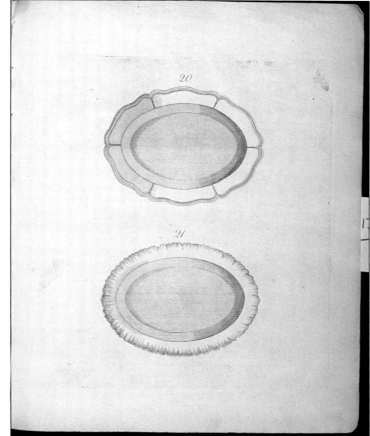

No. 18 - Don 36, Whitehead 28. **No. 19** - Don 37, Whitehead 27.

No. 20 - Don 35, Whitehead 29. **No. 21** - Don 34.

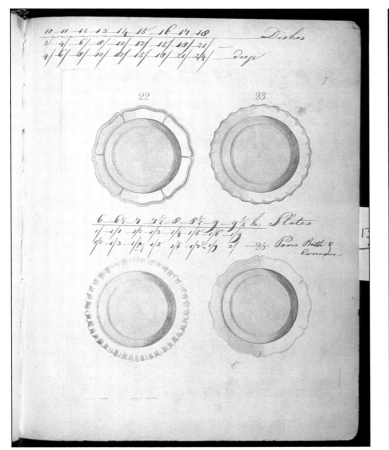

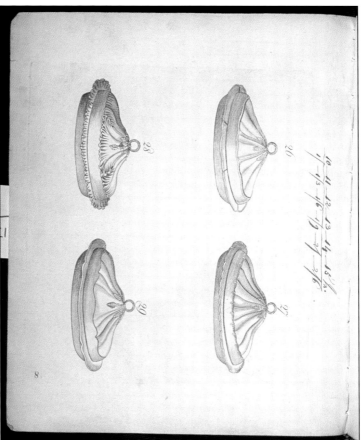

No. 22 - Don 44, Whitehead 25. **No. 23** - Don 39, Whitehead 26. **No. 24** - Don 42, *Castleford 55*. **No. 25** - Don 45, Whitehead 23.

No. 26 - Don 16, Whitehead 33. **No. 27** - *Don 15, Whitehead 34*. **No. 28** - Don 18. **No. 29** - *Don 13*.

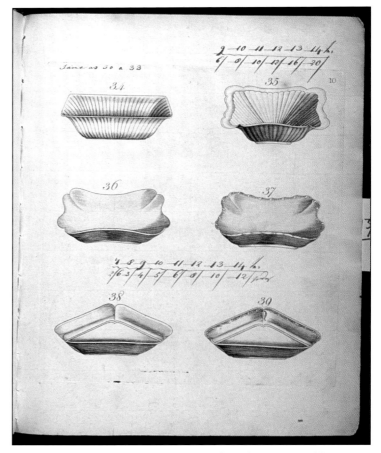

No. 30 - *Don 52.* **No. 32** - Don 54.

No. 34 - Don 57, *Castleford 132.* **No. 35** - Castleford 48. **No. 36 -**
Castleford 124, *Sewell 17B..*
No. 38 - Sewell 17D.

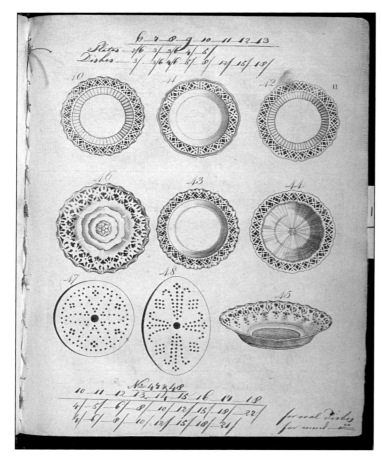

No. 41 - Don 80. **No. 42** - Don 81, *Castleford 128.* **No. 43** - Don 79. **No.**
45 - Don 83. **No. 47** - Castleford 129. **No. 48** - Don 48, *Castleford 127.*

No. 49 - Don 103. **No. 51** - Don 102.

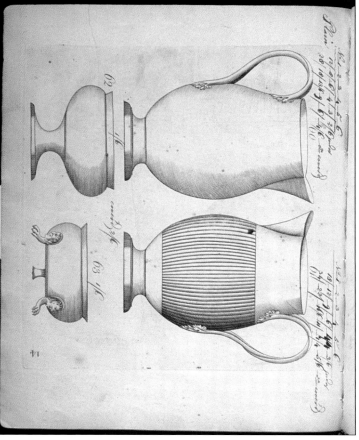

No. 55 - Don 113, Sewell 71. **No. 56** Don 114, *Castleford 225*.. **No. 57** - Don 115. **No. 58** - Don 105.

No. 60 - Don 144. **No. 61** - Don 145. **No. 62** - Don 100. **No. 63** - Don 101.

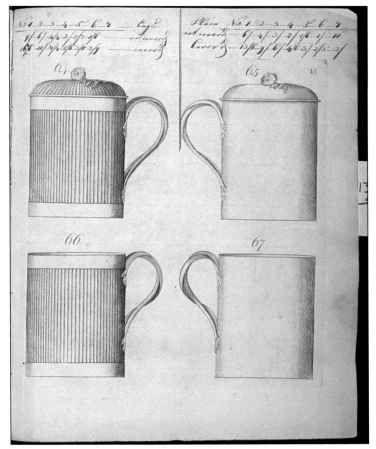

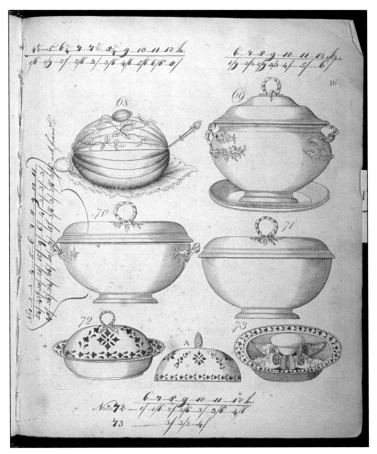

No. 64 - Don 140. **No. 65** - Don 141, *Castleford 180*, Whitehead 136. **No. 66** - Don 142. **No. 67** - Don 143, Whitehead 137.

No. 68 - Don 111, *Castleford 27*. **No. 70** - Don 97. **No. 71** - Don 98.

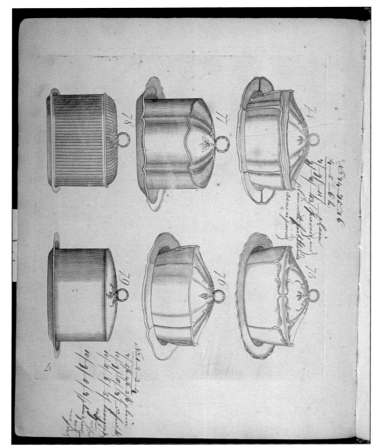

No. 74 - *Don 91.* **No. 75** - Don 88. **No. 77** - Don 85. **No. 78** - Don 84. **No. 79** - Don 86.

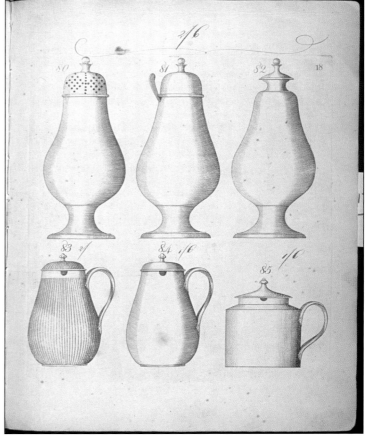

No. 80 - Don 118. **No. 81** - Don 119. **No. 82** - Don 120. **No. 83** - Don 121. **No. 84** - Don 122. **No. 85** - Don 123.

No. 89 - Don 189. **No. 90** - Don 112.

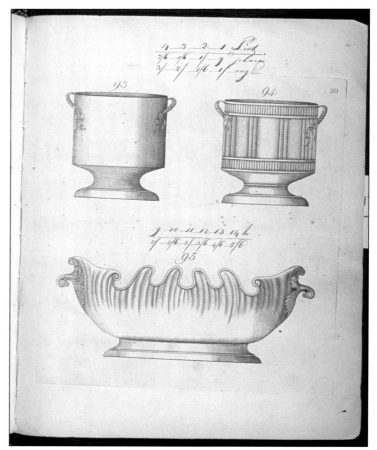

No. 93 - Don 163. **No. 94** - Don 162. **No. 95** - Don 164.

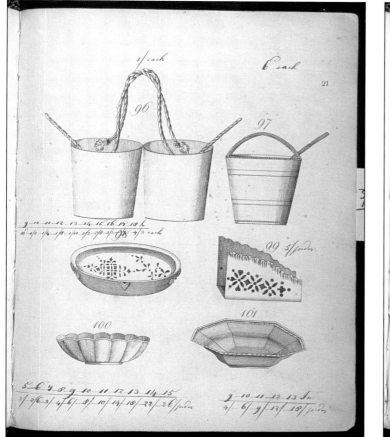

No. 96 - Don 172, Castleford 168. **No. 97** - Don 173, *Castleford 169*. **No. 98** - Don 82. **No. 99** - Don 131. **No. 100** - Don 65, Whitehead 39, Wedgwood (1790) 18.

No. 102 - *Castleford 21.*

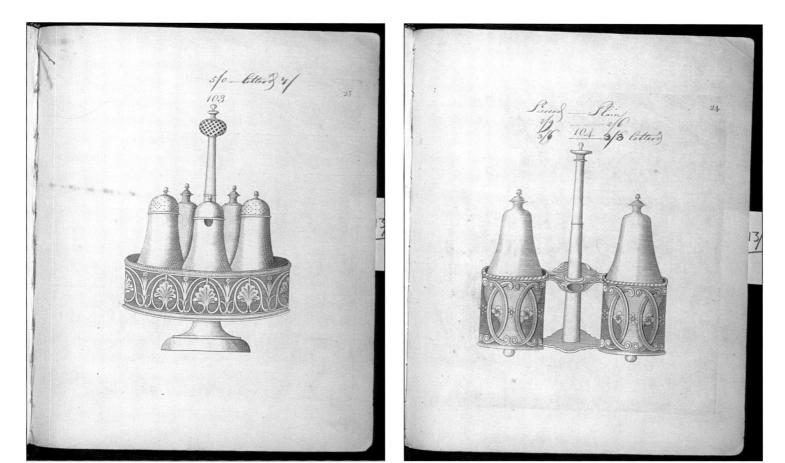

No.103 - *Castleford 23.*

No. 104 - Don 127, *Castleford 22.*

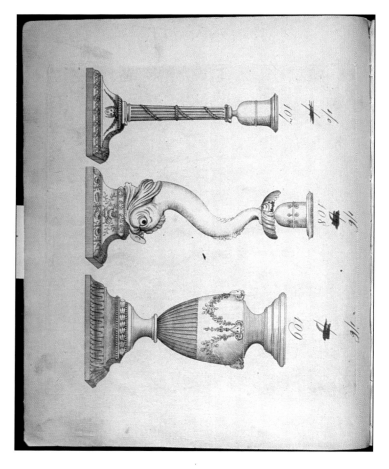

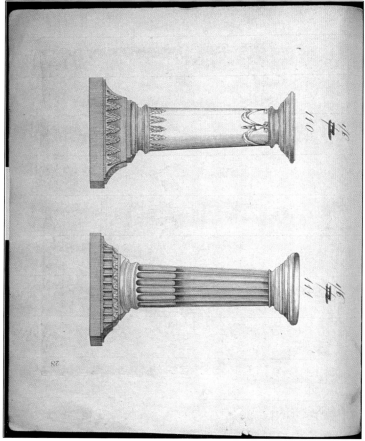

No. 110 - Castleford 259. **No. 111** - Castleford 258.

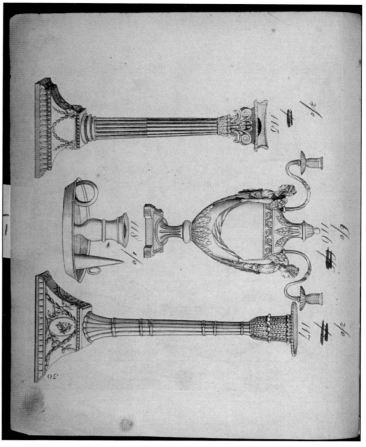

No. 113 - *Castleford 5.*

No. 115 - Castleford 254. No. 116 - *Castleford 6.* No. 118 - Don 212, Castleford 257.

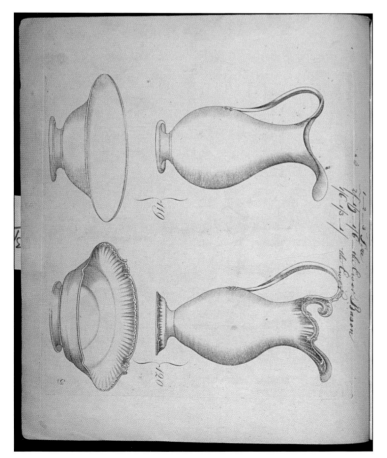

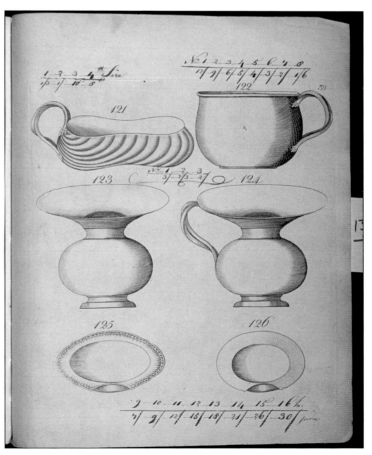

No. 119 - Don 190. No. 120 - Castleford 230, 233.

No. 121 - Don 201, Castleford 248. No. 122 - Don 202, *Castleford 241, Whitehead 125.* No. 123 - Don 175, Whitehead 126. No. 124 - Castleford 249. No. 125 - Don 197. No. 126 - Don 200.

No. 127 - Don 92, Whitehead 140. **No. 128** - *Don 94,* Castleford 142.
No. 129 - Don 93, Castleford 212, Whitehead 138. **No. 130** - *Don 95.*
No. 131 - *Don 96.*

No. 132 - Don 72, Castleford 114, Whitehead 87. **No. 134** - Don 74,
Castleford 116, Sewell 35, Whitehead 80/81, Wedgwood (1774) 28/29 &
(1790) 43/44, **No. 135** - Don 73. **No. 136** - Don 75. **No. 137** - Don 77.

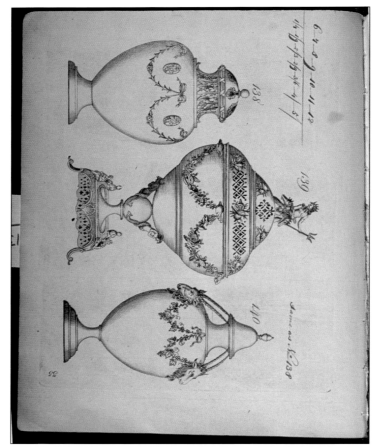

No. 138 - Don 218, *Castleford 11.* **No. 139** - *Castleford 3.* **No. 140** - Don
219, *Castleford 10.*

No. 141 - Don 207, Castleford 28. **No. 142** - Castleford 29, Whitehead
111. **No. 143** - Don 208. **No. 144** - Don 209. **No. 145** - Castleford 112.
No. 146 - Castleford 9

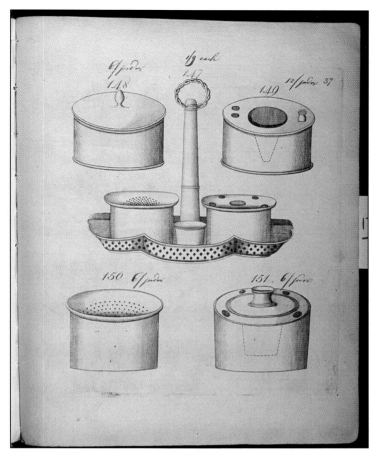

No. 147 - Don 179. **No.148** - Don 177, *Castleford 30, Sewell 89*. **No. 149** - Don 178, *Castleford 31*. **No. 150** - Don 181, *Castleford 32*. **No. 151** - Don 180, Castleford 253.

No. 152 - Don 228, Castleford 47.

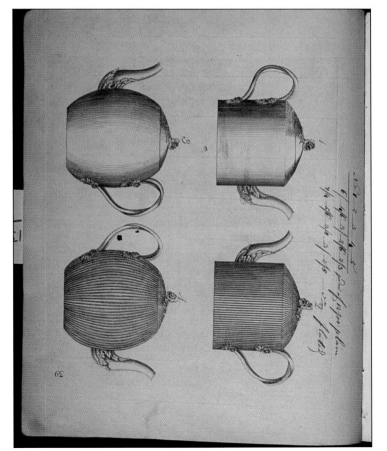

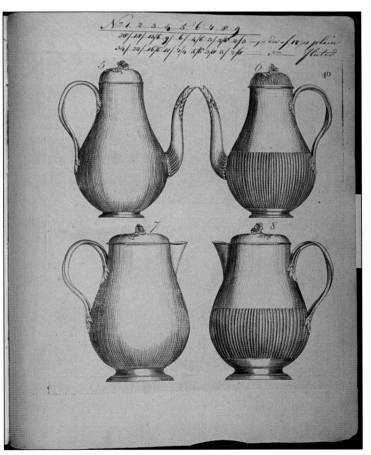

No. 1 - Don 1. **No. 2** - Don 2. **No. 3** - Don 3. **No. 4** - Don 4, *Whitehead 48*.

No. 5 - Don 5, *Whitehead 5*. **No. 6** - Don 6, Whitehead 22. **No. 7** - Don 7, *Whitehead 1*. **No. 8** - Don 8.

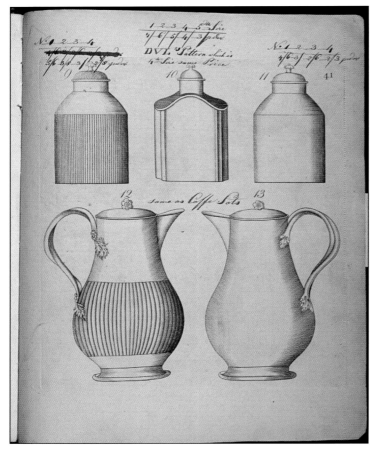

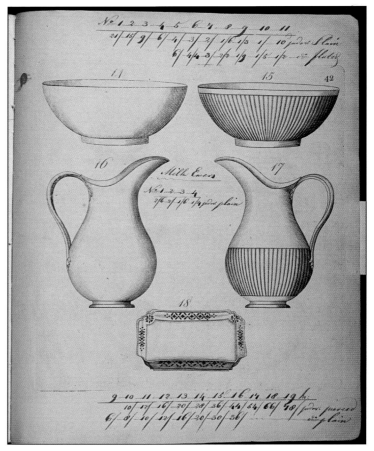

No. 9 - Don 26, Whitehead 21. No. 10 - Don 24, *Sewell 117A*. No. 11 - Don 25, Whitehead 6. No. 12 - Whitehead 20.

No. 14 - Don 21, Castleford 170. No. 15 - Don 22, Whitehead 19. No. 16 - Don 18, Castleford 178. No. 17 - Don 19, Castleford 188. No. 18 - Don 20.

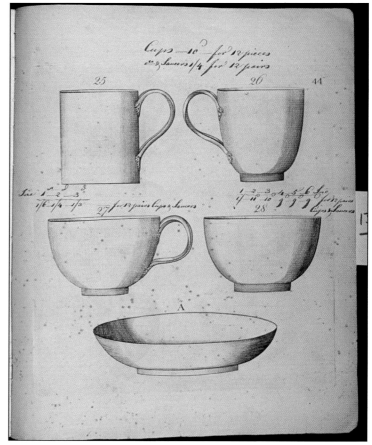

No. 19 - Don 10, Whitehead 17. No. 20 - Don 9, *Castleford 160*. No. 21 - Don 12, *Castleford 204*. No. 22 - Don 11. No. 23 - Don 13. No. 24 - *Castleford 163*.

No. 25 - Don 27, Castleford 175, Whitehead 13. No. 26 - Don 28, Castleford 165, *Castleford 37,* Whitehead 12. No. 27 - Don 29, Castleford 174, *Castleford 35,* Whitehead 15. No. 28 - Don 30, Castleford 176,

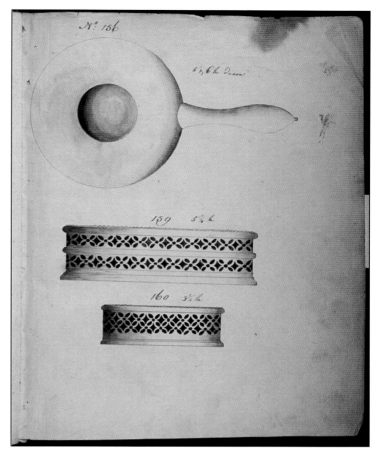

No. 29 - Don 32, Castleford 205. **No. 30** - Don 33, Castleford 199. **No. 31** - Don 34, *Castleford 201*. **No. 32** - Don 35, Castleford 195. **A** - Don 36, Castleford 198.

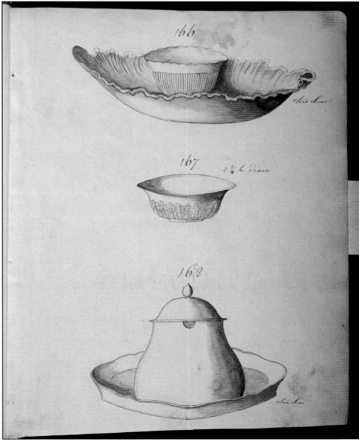

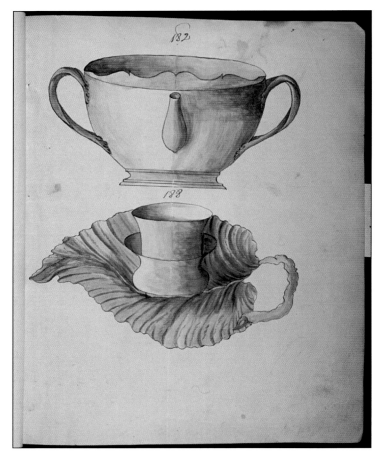

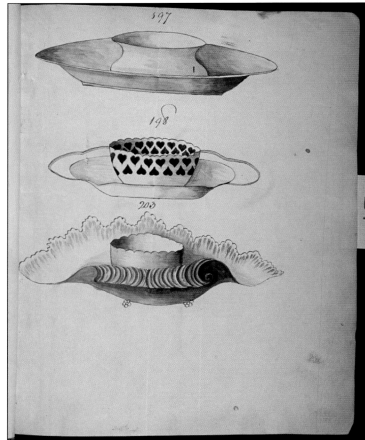

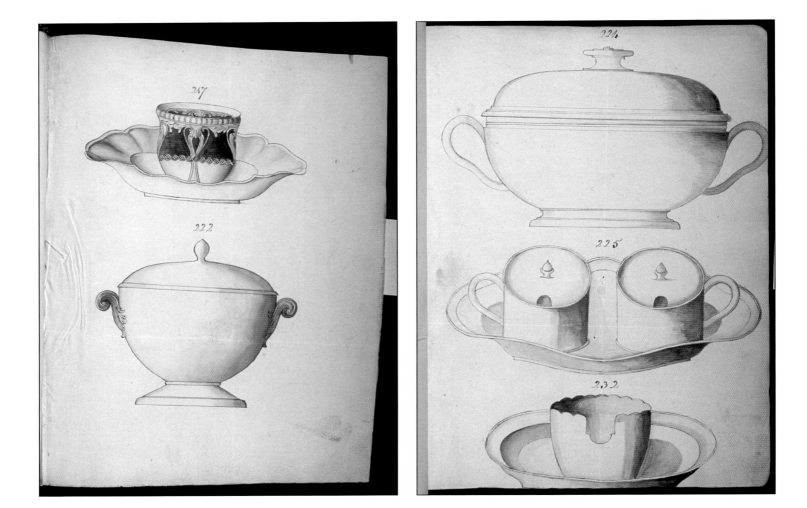

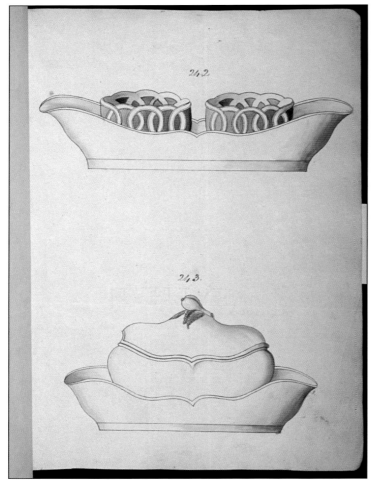

258

263

264

Stand Mellon or Dock Leaf 8 Inches

Stand Mellon Leaf 8 Inches

265

Stand Butter Plate 7 Inches

266

Stand Butter Plate 7 Ins

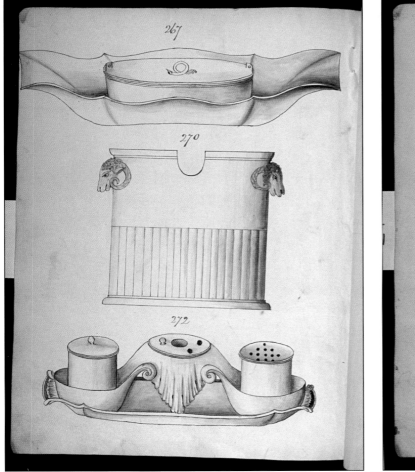

267

270

272

276

277

278

Nº 210   Nº 211

Nº 212   Nº 214

Nº 215

Nº 216   Nº 217

Nº 218   Nº 219

Nº 220   149

Title Page, Explanation of the Plates and the additional designs in the 1814 edition.

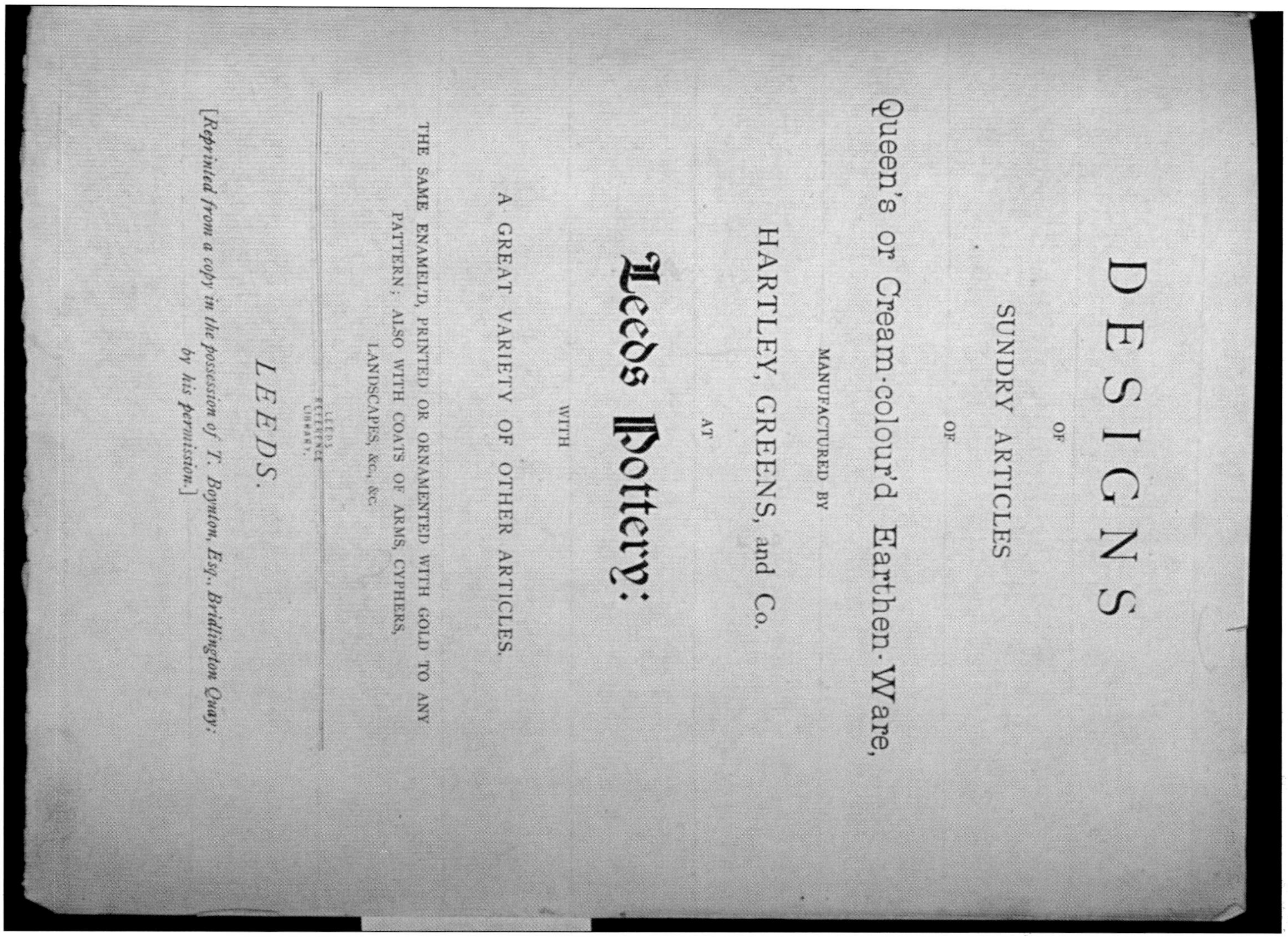

DESIGNS

OF

SUNDRY ARTICLES

OF

Queen's or Cream-colour'd Earthen-Ware,

MANUFACTURED BY

HARTLEY, GREENS, and Co.

AT

Leeds Pottery:

WITH

A GREAT VARIETY OF OTHER ARTICLES.

THE SAME ENAMEL'D, PRINTED OR ORNAMENTED WITH GOLD TO ANY PATTERN; ALSO WITH COATS OF ARMS, CYPHERS, LANDSCAPES, &c., &c.

LEEDS.

[*Reprinted from a copy in the possession of T. Boynton, Esq., Bridlington Quay; by his permission.*]

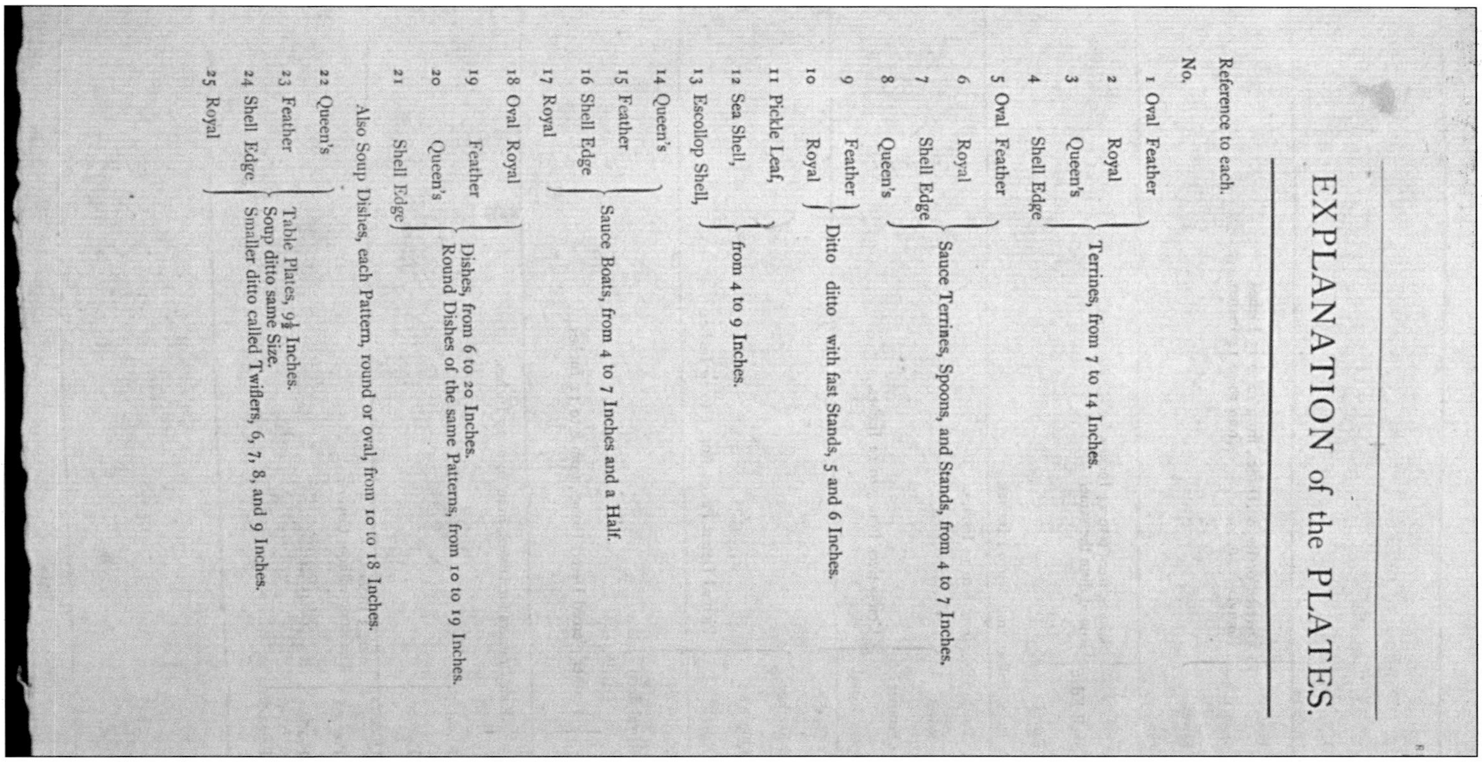

EXPLANATION of the PLATES.

Reference to each.

No.

1 Oval Feather
2 Royal
3 Queen's
4 Shell Edge
} Terrines, from 7 to 14 Inches.

5 Oval Feather
6 Royal
7 Shell Edge
8 Queen's
} Sauce Terrines, Spoons, and Stands, from 4 to 7 Inches.

9 Feather
10 Royal
} Ditto ditto with fast Stands, 5 and 6 Inches.

11 Pickle Leaf,
12 Sea Shell,
13 Escollop Shell,
} from 4 to 9 Inches.

14 Queen's
15 Feather
16 Shell Edge
17 Royal
} Sauce Boats, from 4 to 7 Inches and a Half.

18 Oval Royal
19 Feather
20 Queen's
21 Shell Edge
} Dishes, from 6 to 20 Inches. Round Dishes of the same Patterns, from 10 to 19 Inches.

Also Soup Dishes, each Pattern, round or oval, from 10 to 18 Inches.

22 Queen's
23 Feather
24 Shell Edge
25 Royal
} Table Plates, $9\frac{1}{2}$ Inches. Soup ditto same Size. Smaller ditto called Twiflers, 6, 7, 8, and 9 Inches.

No.		
26	Oval Queen's	
27	Feather	Covered or Ragou Dishes, from 10 to 15 Inches.
28	Shell Edge	Round ditto from 10 to 14 Inches.
29	Royal	
30	Queen's	
31	Feather	Sallads, from 6 to 14 Inches.
32	Shell Edge	Round ditto the same.
33	Royal	
34	Square Royal Sallad, from 6 to 14 Inches.	
35	Turtle Dish, from 8 to 13 Inches.	
36	Royal	
37	Feather	Compotiers, from 7 to 12 Inches.
38	Triangular Royal	
39	Feather	
40	Round Feather	
41	Queen's	Pierced Desert Plates, from 6 to 10 Inches.
42	Royal	
43	Shell Edge	
44	Royal deep	
45	Oval	
46	Round	Feather pierced Desert Dishes, from 8 to 11 Inches.
47	Round	
48	Oval	Fish Drainers for Dishes, from 10 to 20 Inches.
49	Oval Royal	
50	Pierced	
51	Queen's	Salts, 3 Inches.
52	Pierced	The same without Covers.
53	Feather	
54	Pierced	

No.		
55	Plain	
56	Fluted and pierced	Egg Cups.
57	Pierced	
58	Pierced double Salts.	
59	ditto with Covers.	
60	Plain Jug, from ½ Pint to 12 Pints.	
61	Fluted ditto, ditto ditto.	
62	Round Plain Salt.	
63	ditto, with Feet.	
64	Fluted Cover'd	
65	Plain Cover'd	Mugs, from ½ Pints to 4 Pints.
66	Fluted	Mugs, from ½ Pints to 4 Pints.
67	Plain	
68	Melon Terrine and Spoon, from 4 to 12 Inches.	
69	Round Terrine and Stand, from 6 to 12 Inches.	
70	Handled Cover'd Bowl, from ½ Pints to 8 Pints.	
71	Cover'd Bowl, without Handles, from ½ Pints to 8 Pints.	
72	Cover'd Desert, from 6 to 12 Inches.	
73	Ditto, with Partitions, 8 to 10 Inches.—A. The Cover.	
74	Oval Queen's	
75	Oval Feather	Butter Tubs, and Stands, from 4 to 6 Inches.
76	Oval Royal	The same, with pierced Covers.
77	Hexagon	
78	Round fluted	Butter Tubs and Stands, from 5 to 3½ Inches
79	Round plain	
80	Pepper or Sugar	
81	Mustard	Castors.
82	Oil and Vinegar	

No.			
83	Round fluted		
84	Round plain	Mustards.	
85	Square		
86	Round Strawberry Dish and Stand, 8 to 10 Inches.		
87	Oval ditto	ditto	8 to 12 Inches.
88	Platt Menage, 12 Inches high.		
89	Water Bottle and Bason, from 2 Pints to 6 Pints each		
90	Ice Cellar.		
91	Oval	Bakers, from 6 to 16 Inches.	
92	Round	Bakers, from 6 to 16 Inches.	
93	Plain	Ice Pails, for 1, 2, 3, and 4 Pint Bottles.	
94	Fluted	Ice Pails, for 1, 2, 3, and 4 Pint Bottles.	
95	Glass Tray for Ten or Twelve Glasses, 9 to 14 Inches.		
96	Double Pail and Ladle.		
97	Single ditto.		
98	Oval Water Dish for Dishes of all Sizes.		
99	Asparagus Shell.		
100	Escollop'd Nappy, from 5 to 16 Inches.		
101	Oval Octagon Sallad, from 8 to 13 Inches.		
102	Large Furnish'd Castor.		
103	Small ditto.		
104	Oil and Vinegar Stand.		
105	Grand Platt Menage, 17 Inches high.		
106	Grand Platt Menage, 25 Inches high.		
107	Small Composite Candlestick, 8 Inches high		
108	Dolphin	ditto	10 Inches high.
109	Toilet	ditto	6½ Inches high.
110	Ditto	ditto	6½ Inches high.
111	Ditto	ditto	6½ Inches high.
112	Ornamented	ditto	11 Inches high.
113	Griffin	ditto	10 Inches high.

114 Square Fluted ditto   10½ Inches high.
115 Corinthian Candlestick, 10 Inches high.
116 Vase Candlestick, 12 Inches high.
117 Large Composite Candlestick, 12½ Inches high.
118 Flatt   ditto.
119 Water Ewer, with Round or Oval Bason.
120 Shell Edged Oval Ewer and Bason.
121 Oval Chamber Pot, Four Sizes.
122 Round Chamber Pot, from 1 Pint to 6 Pints.
123 Spitting Pot without Handle.
124 Ditto   handled.
125 Oval Shell Edged Shaving Bason, from 9 to 16 Inches.
126 Round Plain ditto, from 9 to 16 Inches.
127 Table Spoon.
128 Sauce Ladle.
129 Tea or Mustard Spoon.
130 Pierced Sugar Spoon.
131 Pierced Fish Trowel.
132 Pierced Fruit Basket and Stand, from 5 to 12 Inches.
133 Ditto   ditto   ditto another Pattern.
134 Twig Fruit Basket and Stand, from 4 to 12 Inches.
135 Pierced Cover'd Fruit Basket and Stand, from 7 to 11 Inches.
136 Pierced Fruit Basket and Stand, from 5 to 12 Inches.
137 Chesnut Basket and Stand, from 6 to 11 Inches.
138 Ornamented Jarr or Potpourri, from 6 to 14 Inches.
139 Cockle Pot or Potpouri, from 15 to 18 and 22 Inches high.
140 Caper Jarr or Potpouri, from 6 to 12 Inches high.
141 Flower Cup, from 4 to 10 Inches high.
142 Quintal Flower Horn.
143 Ornamented deep Sweet Meat Cup, 3 Inches.
144 Ditto   shallow   ditto   4½ Inches.

145 Confectionary Basket and Stand, 4 Inches.
146 Pot Pourri, 10 Inches high, the Top being inverted makes a Candlestick, as at A.
147 Furnish'd Ink Stand.
148 Wafer Box.
149 Fountain Ink Stand.
150 Sand Box.
151 Common Ink Stand.
152 Cross, with Holy Water Cup, 8½ Inches high.
153 Oval Concave Terrine, from 8 to 14 Inches.
154 Oval New Royal Terrine, from 8 to 14 Inches.
155 Round Concave Terrine and Stand, from 6 to 12 Inches.
156 Handled Covered Bowl and Stand, from ½ to 8 Pints.
157 Oval Concave
158 Ditto Paris or Plain } Dishes, from 6 to 21 Inches; Round Dishes of same Patterns, from 10 to 19 Inches; also Soup Dishes, each Pattern, round or oval, from 10 to 18 Inches.
159 Ditto Bath
160 Oval Concave Covered or Ragou Dish, } From 10 to 14 Inches.
161 Round ditto   ditto   ditto ditto.
162 Oval Concave Vegetable Dish, from 10 to 12 Inches.
163 Oval New Royal Sallad, from 6 to 14 Inches.
164 Square Plain Covered or Ragou Dish of 12 Inches.
165 Bath } Table Plates, 9 Inches and a Half.
166 Paris or Plain } Soup ditto, same Size.
167 New Queen's } Smaller ditto, from 6 to 9 Inches.
168 Concave } N. B. A the Profiles.
169 Concave Sauce Boat and Stand, from 4 to 7 Inches and a Half.
170 Double Concave Sauce Boat and Stand, 8½ Inches.
171 Oval Plain Butter Tub and Stand, from 4 to 6 Inches.
172 Oval Concave Sauce Terrine, Spoon and Stand, from 4 to 7 Inches.
173 Oval Sugar Cup, pierced Spoon and fast Stand; the Sugar Cup 5½ Inches, the Stand 9 Inches.
174 Oval Butter Tub and fast Stand; the Butter Tub 5½ Inches, the Stand 12½ Inches.

175 Oval Radish Dish, 12½ Inches.
176 Mustard, Spoon and fast Stand; the Mustard 2¾ Inches, the Stand 6 Inches Diameter.
177 Double Mustards and Stand; the Mustard 2¾ Inches, the Stand 7½ Inches.
178 Double Egg Cups and Stand; the Stand 6½ Inches.
179 Ice Pot.
180 Cream Pot covered.
181 Glass Tray, 4½ Inches Diameter, and 4½ Inches high.
182 Ditto ditto, 4½ Inches ditto,   and 4½ Inches ditto.
183 Ditto ditto, 3½ Inches ditto,   and 3½ Inches ditto.
184 Bottle Stand pierced, 5 Inches.
185 Ditto ditto plain,   ditto.
186 Glass Stand plain, 3½ Inches.
187 Ditto ditto   pierced   ditto.
188 Fluted and plain randed Round Ewer and Oval Bason,
189 Oval plain Ewer and Bason,
190 Fluted and Shell Edged Round Ewer and Oval Bason, } Three Sizes to each Pattern.
191 Oval Shell Edged Ewer and Bason,
192 Oval Shell-Edged Covered Ewer and Bason; the Ewer 10 Inches high and Bason 14 Inches long.
193 Water Closet Pot, 12½ Inches Diameter and 14½ Inches high.
194 Stool Pot, from 6 to 14 Inches.
195 Bidet, 17 Inches long.
196 Oval Chamber Pot, Four Sizes.
197 Ditto   ditto   plain; Two Sizes.
198 Round Bowl for washing or bleeding the Feet in, 14 Inches Diameter.
199 Oval Shaving Bason from 10 to 15 Inches.
200 Round ditto ditto   11 and 12 Inches.
201 Furnished pierced Ink Stand, 8½ Inches long.
202 Furnished Ink Stand, the Stand 11 Inches.
203 Pot Pourri, or ornamented Vase, from 5 to 11 Inches.

B

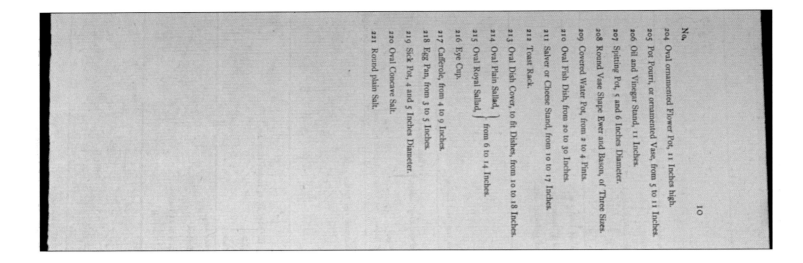

204 Oval ornamented Flower Pot, 11 Inches high.
205 Pot Pourri, or ornamented Vase, from 5 to 11 Inches.
206 Oil and Vinegar Stand, 11 Inches.
207 Spitting Pot, 5 and 6 Inches Diameter.
208 Round Vase Shape Ewer and Bason, of Three Sizes.
209 Covered Water Pot, from 2 to 4 Pints.
210 Oval Fish Dish, from 20 to 30 Inches.
211 Salver or Cheese Stand, from 10 to 17 Inches.
212 Toast Rack.
213 Oval Dish Cover, to fit Dishes, from 10 to 18 Inches.
214 Oval Plain Sallad,
215 Oval Royal Sallad, } from 6 to 14 Inches.
216 Eye Cup.
217 Cafferole, from 4 to 9 Inches.
218 Egg Pan, from 3 to 5 Inches.
219 Sick Pot, 4 and 5 Inches Diameter.
220 Oval Concave Salt.
221 Round plain Salt.

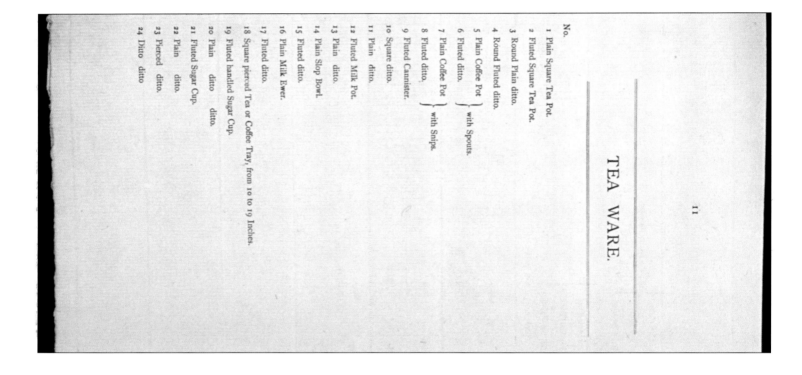

TEA WARE.

No.
1 Plain Square Tea Pot.
2 Fluted Square Tea Pot.
3 Round Plain ditto.
4 Round Fluted ditto.
5 Plain Coffee Pot
6 Fluted ditto. } with Spouts.
7 Plain Coffee Pot
8 Fluted ditto, } with Snips.
9 Fluted Cannister.
10 Square ditto.
11 Plain ditto.
12 Fluted Milk Pot.
13 Plain ditto.
14 Plain Slop Bowl.
15 Fluted ditto.
16 Plain Milk Ewer.
17 Fluted ditto.
18 Square pierced Tea or Coffee Tray, from 10 to 19 Inches.
19 Fluted handled Sugar Cup.
20 Plain ditto ditto.
21 Fluted Sugar Cup.
22 Plain ditto.
23 Pierced ditto.
24 Ditto ditto

No.
25 Square Chocolate
26 Common Chocolate } A; the Saucer for ditto.
27 Handled Tea Cup
28 Tea Cup not handled
29 Fluted Square Chocolate
30 Ditto common ditto. } A; the Saucer for ditto.
31 Ditto handled Tea Cup
32 Ditto not handled ditto.
33 Chocolate Stand, from 6 to 8 Inches.
34 Ditto ditto.
35 Ditto ditto.
36 Ditto ditto.
37 Ditto ditto.
38 Ditto ditto.
39 Ditto ditto.
40 Ditto ditto.
41 Ditto 8¼ Inches.
42 Ditto from 6 to 8 Inches.
43 Ditto ditto.
44 Ditto ditto.
45 Sugar Cup. 8¼ Inches Diameter.
46 Ditto.
47 Ditto.
48 Ditto.

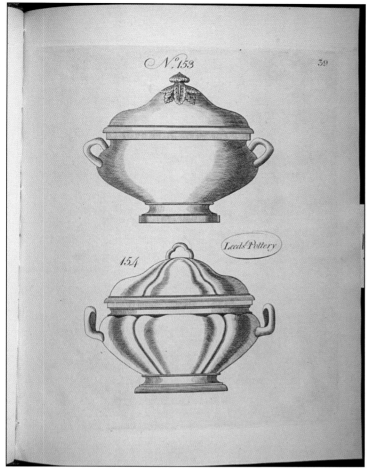

No. 153 - *Don 1.* **No. 154** - *Don 5.*

No. 155 - *Don 2, Wedgwood (1790) 4.* **No. 156** - *Don 110.*

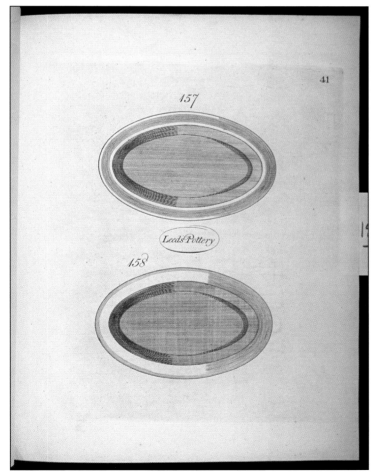

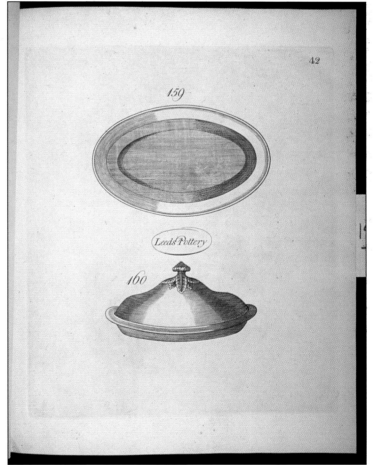

41

No. 157 - Don 31. **No. 158** - Don 32.

No. 159 - Don 33. **No. 160** - *Don 14, Castleford 77.*

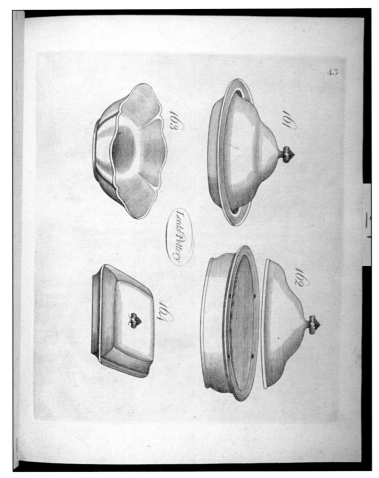

No. 161 - *Don 14*. **No. 162** - Don 49. **No. 163** - Don 51, Castleford 122. **No. 164** - Don 17, Sewell 10A.

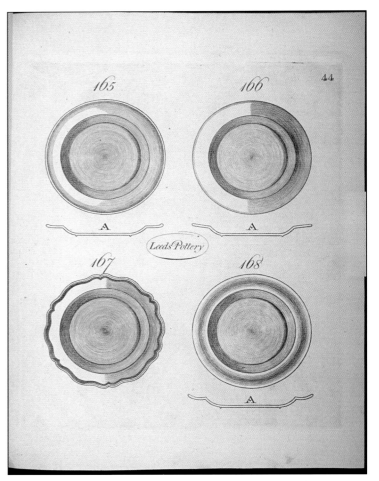

No. 165 - Don 40, Castleford 76, Whitehead 24. **No. 166** - Don 41, Castleford 81, Sewell 46. **No. 167** - *Don 45, Sewell 46, Whitehead 23*. **No. 168** - Don 43, Whitehead 22.

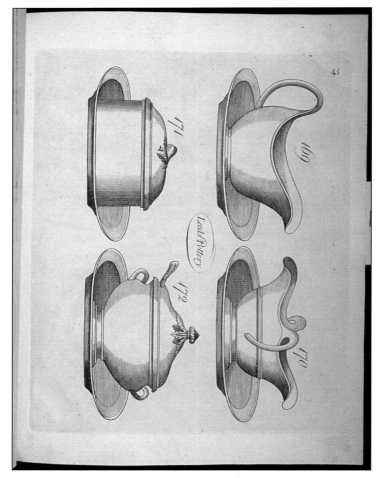

No. 169 - Don 26. **No. 170** - Don 25, *Whitehead 96*. **No. 171** - *Castleford 104*. **No. 172** - *Don 19*.

No. 173 - Don 17. **No. 175** - Don 117. **No. 176** - Don 130.

No. 177 - Don 129. **No. 178** - Don 116. **No. 179** - Don 24.

No. 181 - Don 165. **No. 182** - *Don 166*. **No. 183** - Don 167. **No. 184** - Don 168. **No. 185** - Don 169, *Castleford 231*. **No. 186** - Don 170. **No. 187** - Don 171.

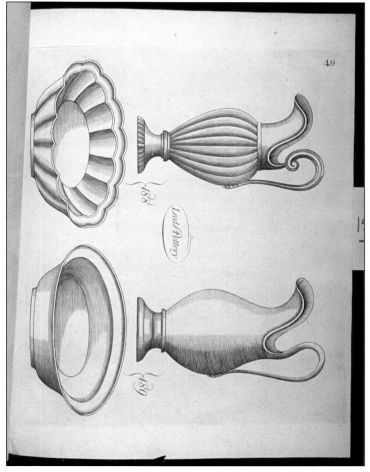

No. 188 - Don 192. **No. 189** - Don 193.

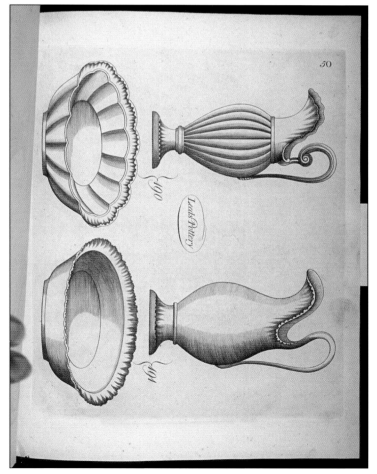

No. 190 - Don 194. **No. 191** - Don 195.

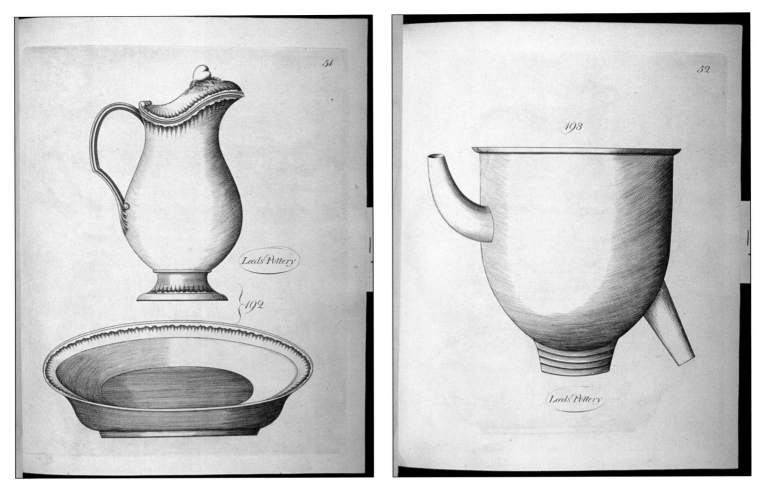

No. 192 - Don 196.

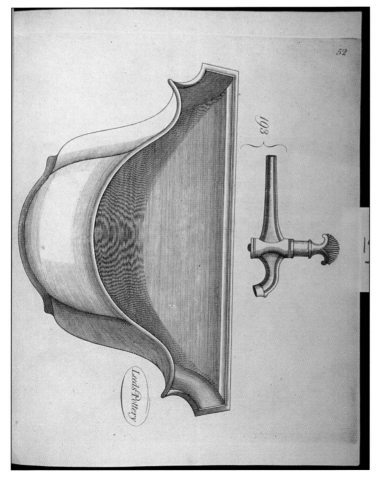

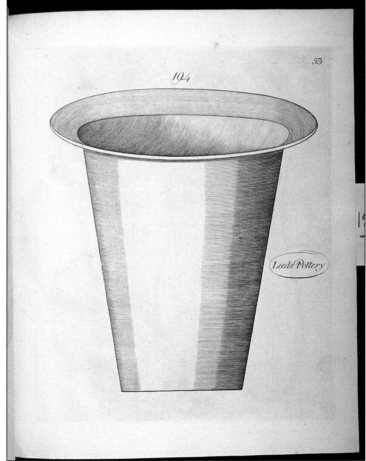

No. 194 - Don 184, Castleford 242, Sewell 41.

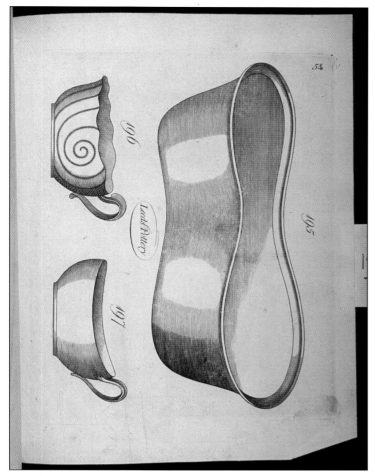

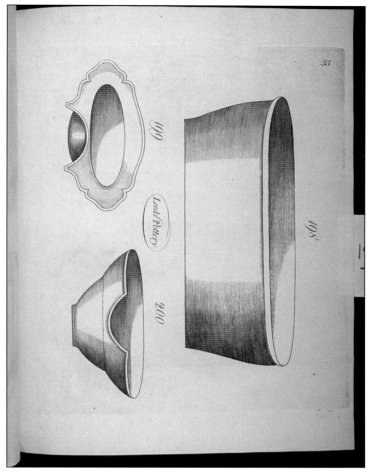

No. 195 - Don 203, Castleford 214, Sewell 39. **No. 196** - Don 204. **No. 197** - Don 205, *Wedgwood (1790) 38.*

No. 199 - Don 198. **No. 200** - Don 199.

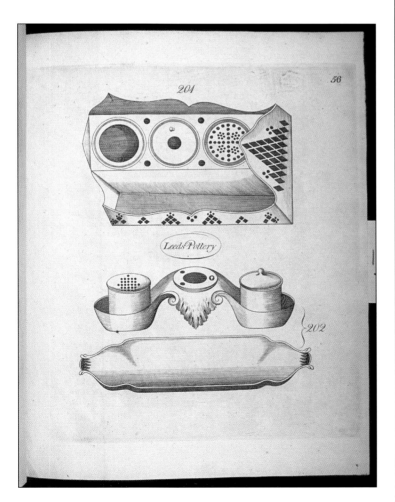

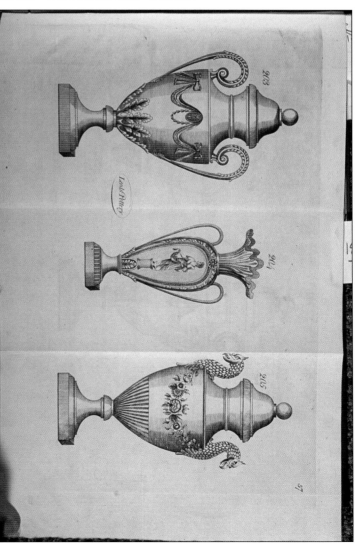

No. 203 - Don 225. **No. 204** - Don 226. **No. 205** - Don 227.

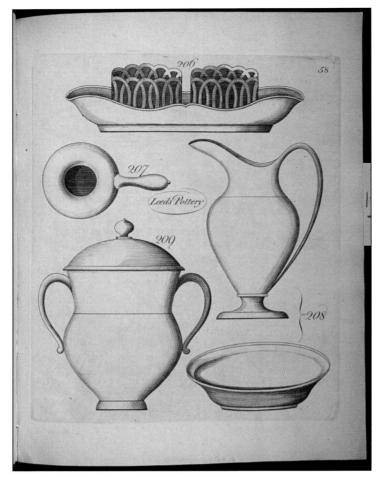

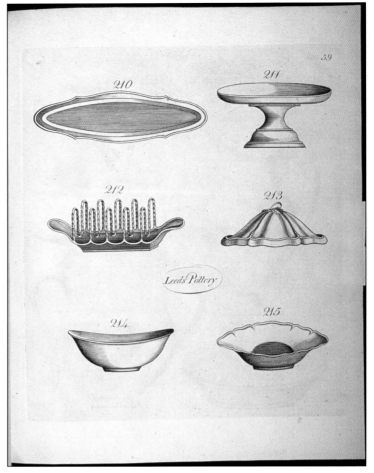

No. 206 - Don 128. No. 207 - Don 176. No. 208 - Don 191.

No. 210 - Don 46. No. 211 - Don 210. No. 212 - Don 146. No. 214 - Don 50, *Wedgwood (1790) 11*. No. 215 - Don 52, Whitehead 46.

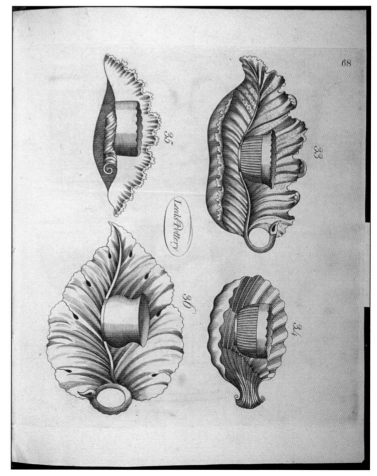

No. 216 - Don 220. No. 217 - Don 221. No. 218 - Don 174, Wedgwood (1790) 42. No. 219 - Don 147, *Castleford 239*. No. 220 - Don 109.

No. 33 (cup only) - Don 40, No. 34 - Don 40. No. 35 (cup only) - Don 38. No. 36 (cup only) - Don 37.

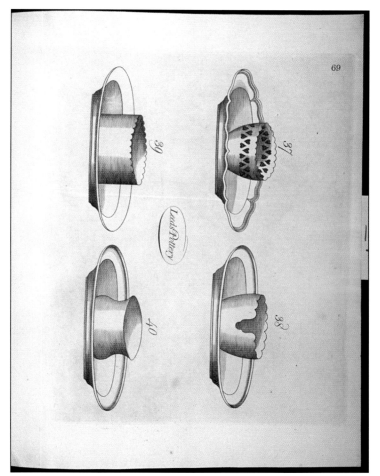

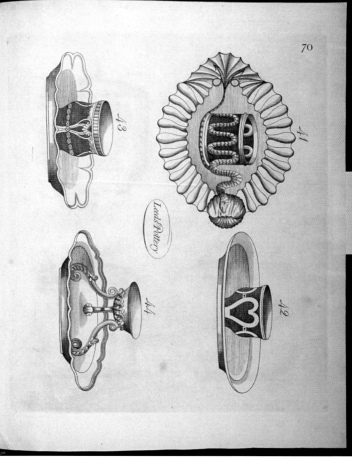

No. 38 - Don 42. **No. 39** (cup only) - Don 38. **No. 40** (cup only) - Don 37.

No. 44 - Don 41.

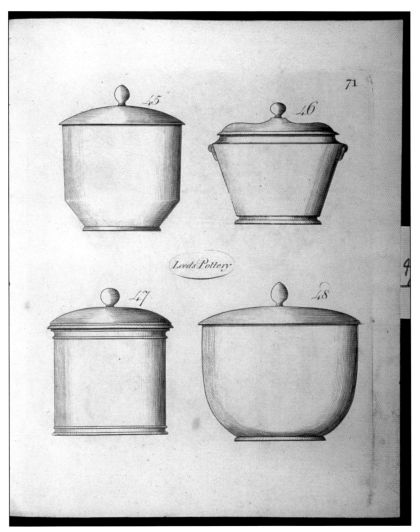

No. 46 - Don 14. **No. 47** - Don 15. **No. 48** - Don 16.

Block Moulds

Peter Walton, in his *Creamware and English Pottery at Temple Newsam House Leeds*, lists seventy-one glazed block moulds and eight hand-held formers used for forming the foot rings on circular plates. The majority of these items were acquired by Joseph R. and Frank Kidson in the 1890s from the derelict and deserted remains of the Leeds Pottery. The block moulds were the 'Master' moulds from which the working moulds were made. A small collection of spout moulds together with some hand-held formers are in the Holland Child Collection at the Harrogate Museum (see also under Sprig Moulds). Another small collection of moulds and forming tools are at the Yorkshire Museum, York; these were presented to the Museum by Joseph R. Kidson.

The following is the list of Moulds and Formers at Temple Newsam House as catalogued by Peter Walton. The letter/number code is the Museum's reference number and if printed in bold type indicates that that mould features in the illustrations which follow. Numbers in brackets refer to the design number in the *Design Book* of c.1814, or elsewhere as specified.

OVAL QUEEN'S TUREEN (3) – M64.

CIRCULAR NEW ROYAL TUREEN (154) – M63

OVAL SHELL EDGE TUREEN LID – M56.

FOOT OF AN OVAL SHELL EDGE TUREEN (7) – M110.

FOOT OF AN OVAL SHELL EDGE TUREEN – M109

FOOT OF AN OVAL ROYAL SAUCE TUREEN (6) – M22.

FEET OF SMALL QUEEN'S TUREENS OR SAUCE BOATS (8 & 14) – M92, M41, M 81.

FOOT OF A SMALL TUREEN OR SAUCE BOAT – M107.

LID OF A TUREEN – M21.

LID OF A TUREEN (6) – M43.

STAND FOR A TUREEN – M106.

STANDS, PROBABLY FOR TUREENS – M111, M95, M105, M112.

PICKLE LEAF DISH (11) – M101, M108.

SEA-SHELL DISH (12) – M99.

ESCALLOP-SHELL DISH (13) – M15, M16, M17, M62, M90, M93, M104.

ESCALLOP-SHELL DISH (*Drawing Book No.2* – 337) – M94.

ESCALLOP-SHELL DISH (*Drawing Book No.2* – 336) – M100.

PICKLE OR SWEATMEAT DISH – M23, **M24.**

'SHELL' SAUCE BOAT WITH FEATHER EDGE – **M113.**

'DUCK' SAUCE BOAT – **M32**, M53.

SAUCE BOAT WITH MOULDED DECORATION (15) – M33, M35, **M49**, M52.

SAUCE BOAT WITH MOULDED DECORATION – **M48.**

SAUCE BOAT WITH RIBBED MOULDING (17) – M30.

SAUCE BOAT WITH SHELL EDGE (16) – **M29.**

SAUCE BOAT WITH SHELL EDGE – **M47.**

SAUCE BOAT – M36.

SAUCE BOAT – M123.

SAUCE BOAT – M25.

SAUCE BOAT – M26.

EGG-CUP STAND (178) – **M97.**

FRUIT BASKET (132) – **M60**.

FRUIT BASKET STAND – M102.

CIRCULAR FRUIT-BASKET STAND (134) – M82, M122.

CIRCULAR FRUIT BASKET – M83.

OVAL, TWIG FRUIT-BASKET BASE (134) – M85.

CORNUCOPIA WALL VASES – M14, M13, **M44,** M45.

OVAL DISH OR STAND – M103.

FRUIT DISH – M51.

PLAIN CURVED SPOUTS –

M1 – incised "30".

M2 – incised "30".

M3.

M4 – incised "30".

M5 – marked "265" in black enamel.

M6 – incised "24".

M7 – incised "18".

M8 – marked "276" in black enamel.

PLAIN CURVED SPOUTS – the following two are in biscuit:-

M74 – incised – "12/March 28/1825".

M77 – incised – "12/March 28/1825".

spouts with moulded decoration – M9, M10, M11, M12.

PLATE FORMERS, *i.e.* – 'Hand-held jiggers.' :-

M27 – incised "11 Oval/con". *i.e.* – 11 in. Oval concave.

M28 – incised "R R 11". – *i.e.* Round Royal 11 in.

M31 – incised "18"

M34 – incised "Con 13". – *i.e.* Concave 13 in.

M37 – incised "RR 13". – *i.e.* Round Royal 13 in.

M38 – incised "Rod Royl 17". – *i.e.* Round Royal 17 in.

M39 – incised "Rd Royl 17". – *i.e.* Round Royal 17 in.

13/7 – incised "14".

Finally, while on the subject of moulded details, the collector is advised not to become too obsessed by counting the number of 'barbs' in the feather edge moulded decoration found on plates and dishes. It is far more reliable to observe overall mould shapes in detail and be able to recognise an identical match with a factory marked example than merely to rely on the number of barbs in a particular sequence.

BLOCK MOULDS – with only the Museum's reference number following the Plate number.

31. M29.

34. M113.

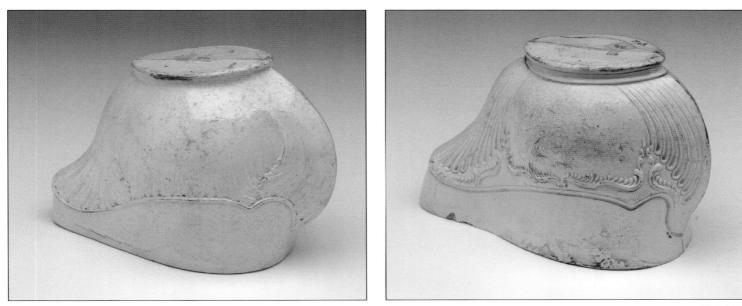

32. M47.

35. M49.

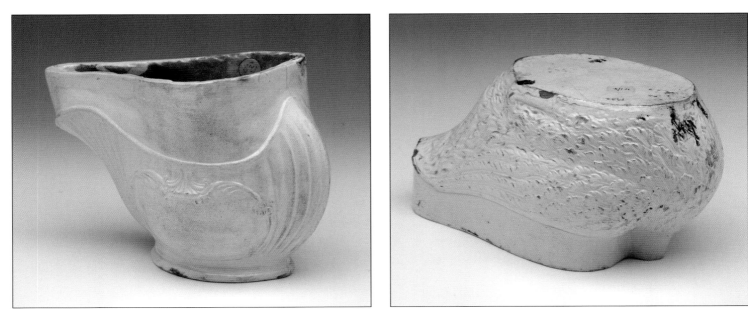

35. M48.

36. M32.

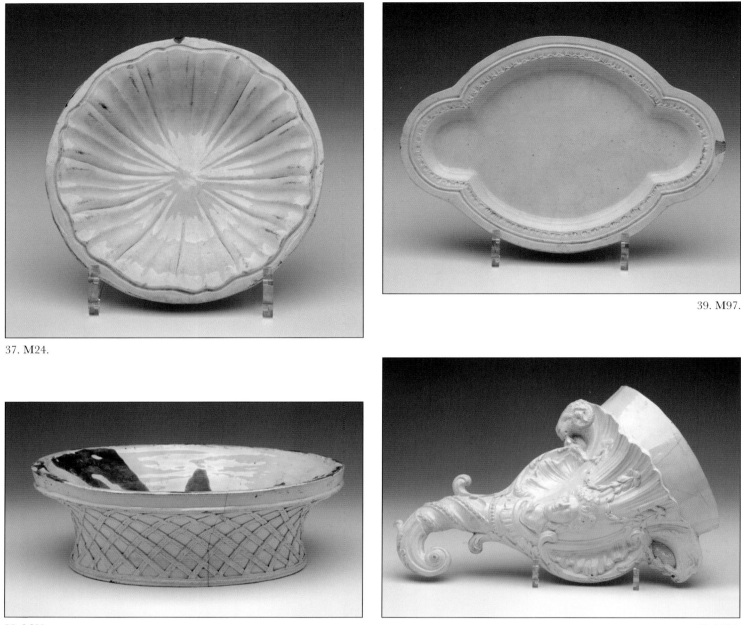

37. M24.

39. M97.

38. M60.

40. M44.

Sprig moulds – These will be dealt with in Chapter 9 and shown at Plates 353 to 377.

Shards

In the absence of detailed factory archives shards can be the most reliable material for revealing the range of wares produced by a pottery and also, in some instances, they can indicate a chronological sequence of their production. Before we consider the value and relevance of the shards held at Temple Newsam House, Leeds, it will be helpful if we try to put ourselves in the position of the manager of a pottery as large as the Leeds Pottery, *i.e.* John Green and his successors.

Shards, the broken and distorted remains of pots which for various reasons failed to come out of the kilns in a saleable condition, formed a considerable volume of waste material which had to be disposed of. A glance at the views of the remains of the Pottery buildings, Plates 6, 8 and 11, shows us the size of the hovels; the coal consumption, see page 87, indicates a considerable amount of work being produced. This is reinforced by the sale notice of the Pottery of 1849 which stated that it was "...capable of manufacturing 9 Gloss Kilns per week..." The sheer volume of waste could not therefore have been kept or disposed of on the Pottery site, neither could it have been allowed to accumulate there. Evidence from south Yorkshire shows that both the Don Pottery and the Swinton Pottery were able to sell loads of shards to the Highways Officers for road repairs, e.g. from the Don Pottery on the 13th of April 1811 there is an invoice for 260 loads of shards being sold at one shilling per load.[13] Some shards would undoubtedly go for drainage material to the site of Joshua Green's 'clay field', see page 22. Old mine workings, disused quarries or anywhere where such waste could be tipped, or used, would be used. However it must also be born in mind that at various periods in the history of the Leeds Pottery no fewer than twelve other potteries were working within a radius of just over half a mile from the Leeds Pottery – all needing somewhere to dispose of their waste. It is quite feasible therefore that some tipping sites may contain the waste from more than one pottery – moreover many of these other potteries are not known to have marked their wares.

The shards which are held at Temple Newsam House fall into two main categories :-

1. Shards recovered from the site of the Leeds Pottery and which can be subdivided into four groups :
   a. Gathered from the surface in 'Pottery Field' by Miss Joan Ella, an employee of the North East Gas Board in 1973 on land which had been dug up when transmission mains were laid in the late 1960s and early 70s. Streets and houses were built upon this area in the nineteenth century, see Plate 41.
   b. A trench dug by volunteers in 1977, known as Trench "B". On the map at Plate 41 it was across the Waggon Way, coloured blue, at a position just north of where Ivory Street ends (Trench "A" "having revealed nothing" – *P. Walton*.)
   c. A workman's trench, dug again across the Waggon Way near where it meets Jack Lane, coloured red on the map
   d. A collection of shards presented to Temple Newsam House by Mr. J.S. Fox, a well known former collector of Yorkshire ceramics[14] which he obtained from a private excavation towards the south end of the Pottery Yard.
2. Shards recovered from a trench dug to take new drains about 100 yards from Hunslet Hall, the site of another pottery which was established in 1800. This excavation was only possible because of the impending demolition of Kirkland Place, a street approximately 420 yards, as the crow flies, from the Leeds Pottery to the south west. A large cache of pottery shards was found here, mainly creamware, many fragments of which were impressed LEEDS POTTERY.

Needless to say a warning needs to be attached to, and always born in mind when assessing, the shards from (2) above. Some, of course, those marked Leeds Pottery or which obviously belong to such shards proclaim their identity. The same caution, however, must also apply to shards recovered from the site of the Pottery on Rushy Pasture, particularly any from the middle of the nineteenth century. The reader may recall that in the 1840s the Chappel brothers, Stephen and James, had been the proprietors of both the Leeds Pottery and the Leathley Lane Pottery which was situated on part of Dowbridge Close, being part of Pottery Fields and only 225 feet from the Leeds Pottery's nearest building. In 1849 the Leathley Lane Pottery was advertised for sale and the sale notice stated that it was capable of making four glost and two salt-glaze kilns per week. Any brown salt-glazed shards discovered in 1.a., and 1.c., could therefore be from the Leathley Lane Pottery as could any other unmarked and unrecognised shards from these areas.

The excavations and the material they produced were written up by Peter Walton in the *Transactions of the English Ceramic Circle*, Vol. 10 Part 4, and in *The Leeds Arts Calendar*, No. 82, 1978. Before an examination of relevant examples of the shards, which are illustrated here at Plates 42 to 63 and are commented on in the captions to each plate, I feel that it is important to assess their value, trench by trench, to our knowledge of the wares produced by the Leeds Pottery.

1.a. As noted earlier the Leathley Lane Pottery had also occupied a site on Pottery Fields, adjacent to the site of the Leeds Pottery since 1800. All this material, gathered from the surface, had been mechanically excavated and may not have been lying where it had been originally tipped. It is, therefore, not of significant value and could be misleading if used to justify a Leeds Pottery origin, unless particular shards are factory marked. Peter Walton dismisses trench A, as nothing significant was found.

1.b. Trench "B" is of interest on two counts. First, the sleepers of the Middleton Colliery's Waggon Way or Railroad were discovered at a depth of two feet; the excavation then continued for a further two feet. Secondly, in this layer, below the sleepers were found:

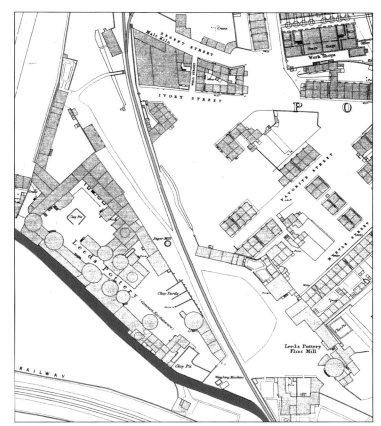

41. 1850 ORDNANCE SURVEY MAP OF LEEDS. This is a section from the 5 ft : 1 mile edition which was surveyed in 1847. The blue-coloured line shows the Middleton Colliery's waggon way and the red area indicates Jack Lane. Although more detailed and of a much larger scale it is worth comparing with the map of 1791 at Plate 2. The additions to the pottery's buildings, particularly near the south entrance from Jack Lane and the housing developments to the east of the Middleton Colliery's waggon way are the most obvious.

" ... thousands of ceramic fragments ... many being impressed with the Leeds Pottery's trade mark in many of its known forms. ... There was, of course, no stratification on the site and therefore the shards are of little use for the purpose of dating, although from external evidence most of them would appear to come from the 1780 – 1810 period. ..." (Peter Walton)

The Middleton Colliery first introduced a steam locomotive onto its railroad in 1812 (see page 85) and it would appear that because of this it was necessary to improve its track which may have involved evening out any undulations along its course which may either have existed from its first construction in 1758 or which may have developed over the years since then. *The Leeds Mercury* reported in an edition of early July 1812: " ...owing to a deficiency in the rail-way some of the waggons yesterday got a wrong direction ...". Then in a letter from Matthew Murray, the engineer, to a certain John Watson, dated the 8th of March 1813: " ... Mr. Blenkinsop has found it his interest to attend to his iron rails ... I have improved the mode of joining them together ..." and on the 10th of March 1813, Mr. Blenkinsop wrote to a Mr. Bevan: " ... I intend this summer to make a complete Rail Road."[15] The above three quotations would seem to suggest that possibly a completely new track might have been laid and if so this would have been a considerable undertaking as Brandling would still have had to abide by the stipulation, set forth in the last Act of Parliament, to deliver a specified daily amount of coal to Leeds. (See page 85.)

The workmen having the task of raising the track some two feet would need to build an embankment, above the old track level, on which to lay the new sleepers and new rails. It would appear that discarded pottery material, in the form of shards, broken saggars and discarded clay and kiln furniture, was used. My contention is that the quantity needed for such an undertaking could not have been that which was being produced on a daily basis but would have had to be transported there from some waste tip in the vicinity and which may well have contained waste from other potteries in the area as well as from the Leeds Pottery. If this was the case then it could account for the presence of salt-glazed examples, both white and brown and 'county-style' pottery shards, being present as well as marked examples of creamware and pearlware from the Leeds Pottery. I freely admit that this is only an assumption, but it is a possibility which future excavations, preferably from previously untouched areas, may be able to corroborate or dismiss. We must also remember that Peter Walton, in his report, has dated this material as being from what he estimated was the thirty year period from 1780 to 1810, without stratification and therefore conveyed to this position from elsewhere.

1.c. The 'Workmen's Trench' was dug in 1977 to renew existing mains. It was near to the boundary with Jack Lane and again in close proximity to the Middleton Colliery's railway. A number of pieces of marked LEEDS POTTERY and HARTLEY GREENS & CO/LEEDS POTTERY were discovered and the published reports, above mentioned, state that "...At one point they uncovered what must have been a Leeds Pottery dump and the foundations of the 18th century buildings ...". The shards discovered were judged to be from the period 1820-30 and included the backstamps for the patterns "New Star", "Eton College", "Forest", and "Elysium". Examples of banded, sprig decorated and Mocha ware were also found. From these pattern names I would suggest 1830s to 1850s as a more realistic period.

The Shards on the following Plates, Nos. 42 – 63, are in the keeping of Leeds Museums & Galleries.

42. SLIP-DECORATED. (B). The small quantity of this material which was recovered tells us little other than to proclaim its presence where found. Such complete wares, from other potteries, as do exist are very seldom factory marked. The small size of these fragments means that unless larger quantities of this type of ware, containing much larger shards, are eventually discovered in previously undisturbed and proven deposits of Leeds Pottery material then it may never be possible to positively identify complete examples, or to prove that such wares were ever made at the Leeds Pottery, particularly as the shapes are usually quite simple and the decoration 'drawn' in a naive, freehand style.

43. SALT-GLAZED WARES AND REDWARES. (B). The examples of salt-glazed wares do not indicate a style of decoration which would lead one to believe that it may be peculiar to one pottery. However the early partners may well have realised that, if such wares were still in demand in the early years, it would make business sense to produce them. Again. on the basis of present knowledge as cautioned in my introduction to this section, it is impossible to state with certainty that salt-glazed wares were made at the Leeds Pottery. It is claimed, by A. & A. Cox, *Rockingham 1745 – 1842*, that it was still in production until c.1775, at the Swinton Pottery. Wedgwood, however, according to Robin Reilly, *Wedgwood the New Illustrated Dictionary* suggests that Josiah Wedgwood had ceased making salt-glazed wares by 1762. However, judging by the specimens illustrated, if they were to be accepted as genuine Leeds Pottery products it would be virtually impossible to differentiate between them and those made at other potteries. With regard to the redware shards, we have the example, at Plate 64, of a redware coffee pot in Doncaster Museum and Art Gallery, which bears a mark which, in the light of present knowledge, may be accepted as having been used at the Leeds Pottery. There is also an order, from "BT", for redware cooking pots which appear to be engine turned. The order is dated c.1790 and is in the *Original Drawing Book No. 1*, see Plate 492.

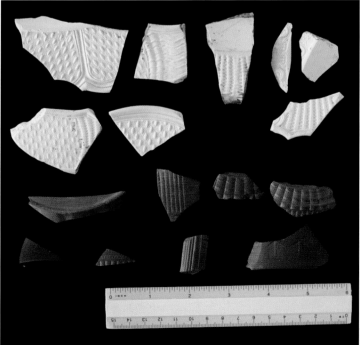

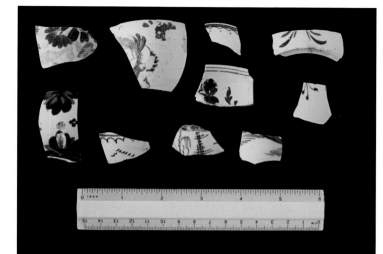

44. ENAMELLED AND PAINTED DECORATION. (B). The shards in this category are few in number and small in size. Although I am quite happy to accept the shards as being Leeds Pottery's products Such freehand decoration is totally inadequate to form the basis for attributing any entire, unmarked examples bearing such decoration.

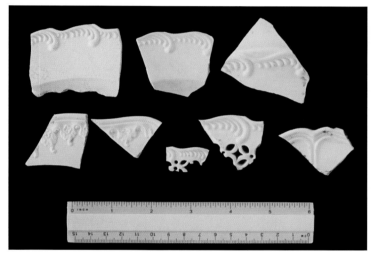

45. MOULDED PLATE BORDERS. (B).

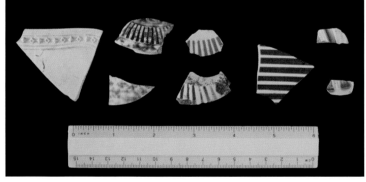

46. A SELECTION FROM THE J. S. FOX COLLECTION. (JSF). Compare with the coffee pot at Plate 106, and the plate at Plate 105.

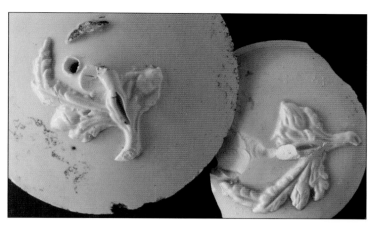

48. TWO LIDS. (B). These show very well the leaves and flower buds associated with the flower knops at Plate 47, top three. Notice the well known 'cut-stalk' feature running along the main stalk for a short distance; this feature is not unique to the Leeds Pottery.

49. FLOWER, FRUIT, ACORN AND SIMPLE KNOPS. (B).

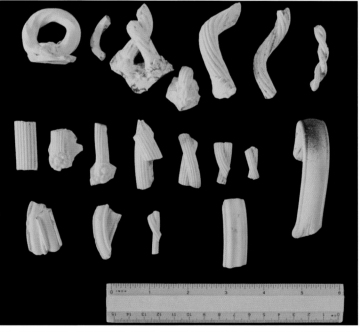

50. SQUARE, REEDED AND HEXAGONAL SECTION TWISTED HANDLES. (B). The reeded handles with 5, 6, 7, and 12 reeds. Two other sections are clearly visible on the bottom row. Some examples also showing the remains of their flower and leaf terminals.

47. FLOWER KNOPS. (B). Three sizes of two different designs. The one at top left measures 15/16 in. (24 mm) diameter. Many examples of flower knops, as are found on tea and coffee pots, etc., were discovered but what is of interest is that they are all of the two shapes shown here, as are those on marked wares that I have examined. See also the comments in Appendix X, under 'Batavian Ware'.

51. EXAMPLES OF LESS COMMON TERMINALS. (B).

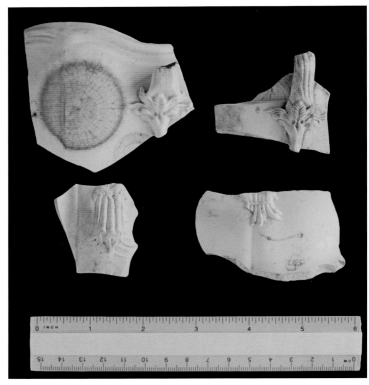

52. FRAGMENTS OF OTHER TERMINALS. (B).

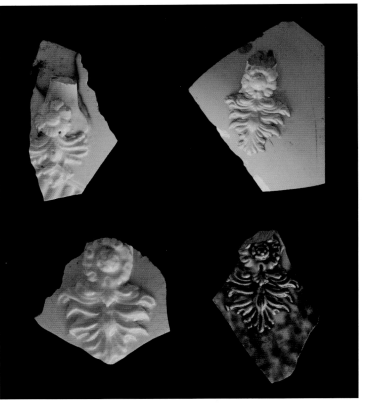

54. EXAMPLES OF THE 'CLASSIC' LEEDS TERMINAL SHOWN IN A RANGE OF SIZES. (B). It must be remembered that this is not unique to the Leeds Pottery as it has also been recorded, not surprisingly, at the Swinton Pottery by A. & A. Cox, see *Rockingham 1745 – 1842*.

The Don Pottery's *Design Book* also shows such terminals as many of the designs are straight copies from the Leeds *Design Book*. Attention is also drawn to *A Pottery by the Lagan* by Peter Francis where very similar terminals and other handle and knop details may be seen. I must, however, stress that an *exact* likeness is essential before any conclusions regarding a possible attribution can be made.

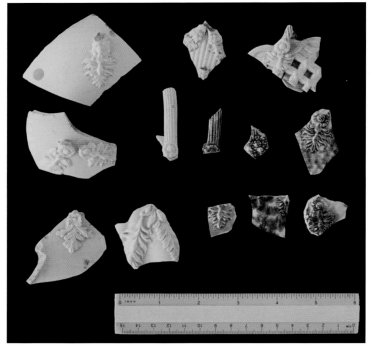

53. SMALL FLOWER AND LEAF TERMINALS. (B).

55. FRAGMENTS OF ASSORTED LEAF AND BUD TERMINALS, ETC. (B)

57.

56 & 57. It is very fortunate that this fascinating shard is impressed LEEDS POTTERY. This form of decoration has been given several names by modern writers, e.g: "Tessellated Slipware" and "Surface Agate" by Jonathan Rickard, "Granite Agate" by The Potteries Museum, Hanley. Dr. Minnie Holdaway, writing in the *NCS Newsletter* No. 91, Sept. 1993 at p. 36, quotes what this form of decoration was probably known as when in production at Ralph Wedgwood's Staffordshire Pottery from the sale notice of the contents of his London Warehouse at 35, St. Paul's Churchyard, in 1794, namely – "Terra Tersia". The word 'Tersia' is a corruption of 'Tarsia' from 'Intarsia'. Pierre Ramond states[16] :

> "The first incrustations (in marble) appear in Halicarnassus in the palace of King Mausole, 350 BC. Later, a type of marquetry called *Intarsia** developed in Italy during the Roman Empire... * Today, in Italy, marquetry is still called intarsio".

In other words the term, quoted above by Dr. Holdaway, implies a form of surface decoration, in this case not a pictorial form nor a regular geometrical arrangement, but an overall even but unarranged pattern of small irregular-shaped pieces of different coloured clays – many being in themselves composed of alternating layers of coloured clays – as agate ware. This decorative band is to be found let into the surface of pots in areas produced by the turner.[17]

As no contemporary records have so far been discovered which describe the process I will proffer the following suggestions :-

1. The body of the pot would have to be leather-hard before the shallow recess could be turned out.
2. Different coloured clays and lumps of 'agate' would have to be prepared – the alternating layers in the agate would have to be very thin, much thinner than when pots were made in solid agate ware. This material would then have to be dried until it became brittle so that it could be broken and crushed to form small particles, roughly less than a quarter the size of a match head. The fragments so formed would therefore be irregular in their shape. The dust would have to be sieved off and the larger particles also sieved off leaving fragments all roughly the same size and with the different coloured and agate particles thoroughly mixed together.
3. The turned-out recess in the pot could then receive a coating of slip and the fragments of clay and agate applied firmly to this surface in handfuls or by rolling the pot in the chips spread out on a bench or table. Another coating of slip could then be brushed or poured over this infill, its purpose being three-fold. First to further bind the particles together. Secondly to fill any voids between the particles and lastly, the water in the slip would be absorbed by the particles thereby reducing their brittle state towards the required leather-hard state. This would be necessary before the turner could re-mount the pot on his lathe and turn this 'inlaid' layer down to the level of the surrounding body.

A "Turners' List of Prices for Common Ware" which, although undated, does give us a clear picture of the comparative costs involved :-

"Dipt Ware. PER SCORE.	S.	D.
Banded, Cable, Mocha, and Self-coloured	3	6
Fancy Patterns	5	0
Inlaid ditto	6	8

. . . The Lathe-treader to have Fourpence in the Shilling." [18]

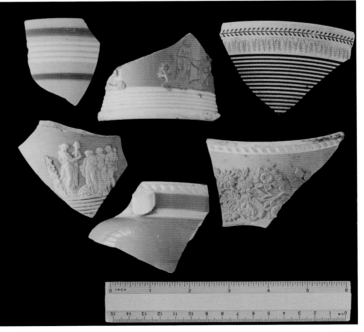

58. BANDED, ROULETTED & SPRIGGED DECORATION. (WT). This type of ware was produced by many potteries. The sprigged decorations may well be the same as is found on basalt ware.

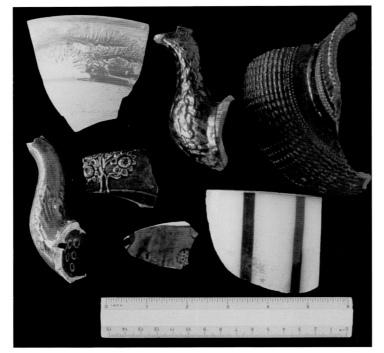

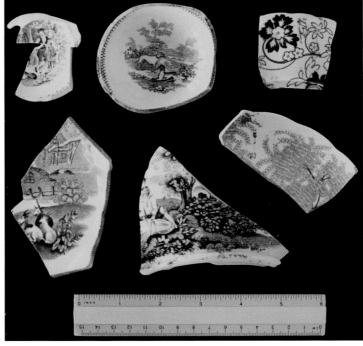

59. MOCHA, 'ROCKINGHAM' GLAZE, GREEN GLAZE, JACKFIELD AND STRIPED DECORATION. (WT).

61. BLUE AND WHITE UNDERGLAZE TRANSFER PRINTED WARES. (WT). The right-hand centre example is the pattern which is named "Forest" on another shard. See Chapter 8, p. 114 for shards with the initial "C". In the absence of factory records it is impossible to state whether this indicates 'Chappel' – at the Leeds Pottery or at the Leathley Lane Pottery – or at both.

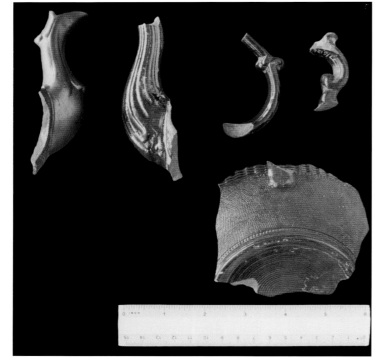

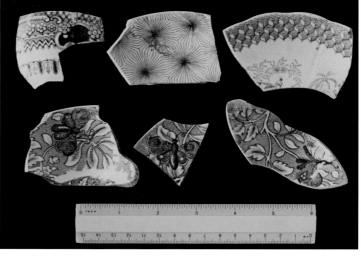

62. BLUE AND WHITE UNDERGLAZE TRANSFER PRINTED WARES. (WT). The example, top centre, is named "New Star" on another shard . See Chapter 8, p. 114.

60. JACKFIELD WARE. (WT). The right-hand spout is the same mould as found on the teapot at Plate 332 where the moulded details are more clearly defined.

63 PRINTED. (JSF). The prints are obviously of a humourous nature which, together with the *sans serif* lettering, would seem to have emanated from the same source as the registered pattern at Plate 444, which was registered on the 17th of September 1874.

1. *Historical Notices of the Leeds Old Pottery*, 1892, pp. 15 & 21.
2. *Reflections*, New York, 1979, p.70.
3. Letter by Donald Towner to Heather Lawrence dated 2nd of August 1972.
4. David Barker – *William Greatbatch a Staffordshire Potter*, pub. Jonathan Horne, 1991.
5. Cox and Cox – *Rockingham*, p. 54.
6. Robin Reilly – *Wedgwood The New Illustrated Dictionary*, p. 503.
7. Llewellynn Jewitt – *The Art Journal*, 1865, p. 309.
8. Geoffrey A. Godden – *Encyclopaedia of British Porcelain Manufacturers*, 1988, p.540.
9. J.R. & F. Kidson – *Historical Notices of the Leeds Old Pottery*, 1892, pp. 108/9. "...the old stamps with which the ware used to be marked remained in the Pottery until its final closure. They were made of a hard stoneware body, the face with the raised letters being semi circular."
10. A. Hurst – *A Catalogue of the Boynton Collection of Yorkshire Pottery*, p. 10.
11. The contemporary name by which its travelling representatives or salesmen were known.
11. Reproduced by Wolf Mankowitz in *Wedgwood*, 1953, pp.70–82, where it is erroneously given the date of 1774, an error which was corrected in later editions.
12. Finer and Savage – *The Selected Letters of Josiah Wedgwood*, pp.155/156.
13. John D. Griffin – *The Don Pottery 1801–1893*, p.34.
14. Jim Fox – *A Yorkshire Collector of Pottery and Porcelain*, Leeds City Art Galleries, 1986.
15. The above extracts taken from: *A History of the Middleton Railway Leeds*, p. 18.
16. Pierre Ramond – *Marquetry*, English Translation from the French, The Taunton Press, 1989, p.13.
17. See also *NCS Newsletters*, Nos. 89, p.16, and 91, p. 36.
18. In the collection of Keele University, Ref: HD 9612.4.T8. I am indebted to Rodney Hampson for bringing this to my attention.

CHAPTER NINE

The Wares
1770-1827

IN THE previous chapter I quoted from the writings of Llewellynn Jewitt and the Kidson brothers who had commented on the lack of knowledge concerning the early wares from the Leeds Pottery. In the same chapter I suggested that some of the designs illustrated in the first editions of the Pottery's published *Design Book* of 1783 could, on stylistic criteria alone, have been in production at the Pottery since its foundation.

The Leeds Pottery had not developed out of a smaller country pottery producing wares for a largely local market using local clays. This was a new purpose-built pottery which represented a considerable investment by the five founding partners, particularly Richard Humble. A total of £7,000 was advanced by the partners in 1770, see pages 27 and 573. this being equivalent to approximately £807,483 in 2003. Thus Richard Humble had advanced the equivalent of £403,742, John Green, Joshua Green and Henry Ackroyd had each invested the equivalent of £115,355 and John Barwick the equivalent of £57,677.[1] Business men, then as now, would not invest such sums of money unless they felt confident that first: such money would not be lost and secondly: that it would bring a good return on their investments. Their investment therefore showed that they had confidence, and an awareness of evidence, that the products of the pottery industry were being eagerly sought by a sufficiently large market both at home and overseas. The Leeds Pottery must therefore have been built and financed with such beliefs and confidence.

In 1770 the fashionable style was Neo Classical. Arguably the leading potter was Josiah Wedgwood with his, by this date, perfected creamware or Queen's ware. Thus it would seem obvious that the new pottery at Hunslet, under the " ... Direction and Management" of John Green, with the backing of sufficient capital from himself and a group of experienced local businessmen would seek to capitalise on the growing demand for creamware. Another consideration was the more advantageous geographical situation of Hunslet for the export of goods through the port of Hull to northern and central Europe, than was the case with the Staffordshire potters. In Chapter 7 I deduced, from the letter by Otto Setler to Josiah Wedgwood,[2] that the Leeds Pottery may well have been trading in Russia since its foundation and that certainly it was undercutting most other creamware manufacturers who were exporting to Russia at that time. However I also concluded, from the 'evidence' of some of the shards, that there is a possibility that some slip-decorated redware 'country style' pots as well as some white salt-glazed wares might have been made, so long as these were saleable and profitable and also so long as they could accommodate the requisite facilities and staff in the Pottery for their production. Once again it is important to remember that all potteries existed primarily to earn a return on invested capital for the partners. That some did produce objects of beauty resulted more from the demands of a discerning market, from within the fashionable taste of the period, than from any personal creative urge of the potter himself provided, of course, the individual skills of the employees and those who designed the wares were also present. Such wares would obviously sell for more money than crude, naive, slip-decorated redwares which would only be produced by potteries, like the Leeds Pottery, if the profit margin was sufficient to make their production worthwhile – but if it was, then I feel sure that they would certainly have been likely to produce them. Nevertheless I feel confident in asserting my belief that the production of creamwares would have been the main thrust of the partners' endeavours and vision when they formed their partnership.

The Pottery's agents or 'riders' would obviously report back to Hunslet any new styles or trends being supplied by other potteries or in demand in the areas where they operated. Such communications, in the form of sketches and drawings may be seen at Plates 445 to 567. Many of the articles are not of a design which, without their reproduction here, would readily be associated with a hitherto traditional Leeds attribution. Other wares than creamwares naturally followed: pearlwares, black basalt and later, coloured bodies, lustre decoration and printed wares.

It is my intention and hope that the reader will appreciate the quality of the *wide range* of wares produced by the Leeds Pottery and that this work will therefore give a fairer and more balanced account of Leeds pottery than just the creamwares, for which it is justly famous, on which other writers have concentrated. This has given a very biased picture by neglecting the full range of the other excellent wares produced in the late eighteenth and early nineteenth centuries. It is also my hope that, after reading the history of the Pottery, the myth which has unfortunately developed over the years whereby we were led to believe that the excellence of the wares was due, either solely or in part, to the person of the "corresponding clerk" William Hartley may now be laid to rest. It is very obvious that the wares produced after 1808, the year in which William Hartley died, were equally excellent compared with those produced before that date.[3] They may have been different but only because the fashions and styles of the period were changing – but they were of equal merit so far as quality of potting and decoration were concerned when appreciated objectively within their historical context.

Before going on to examine the wares which I have chosen for illustrations, may I once again draw the reader's attention to the following points as guidance for his or her attribution of unmarked wares.

1. Refer to factory marked wares only, making sure that the details correspond *exactly* to marked examples. Similar to is not good enough.

2. Refer to shards from the Leeds Pottery, (see Plates 42 to 63) and keep abreast of any new information which may be discovered from future excavations on the Pottery site.

3. Make use of the Pottery's Design, Drawing and Pattern Books which are reproduced here but also be aware that many of the examples shown were not peculiar to the Leeds Pottery.

4. Try to study and observe contemporary examples by other manufacturers, again marked examples only.

5. Be very wary regarding examples illustrated in any other books which, if unmarked, are not attributed to the Leeds Pottery by reference to marked examples or moulded details of marked examples fully quoted by the author.

6. Learn by handling, if at all possible, at antiques fairs and auction rooms, examples made by the Seniors and J.T. Morton. See Appendix IX for an account of their wares, many of which were produced using the original moulds from the Leeds Pottery. Remember that they too used an impressed LEEDS POTTERY mark; once you have seen a number of these marks you should be able to differentiate between the original ones and those by the Seniors and Morton.

7. Finally I fully appreciate that the following illustrations can only represent the 'tip of the iceberg' so far as the total output of the Pottery was concerned. However it will only be by using the above criteria that the collectors and students of this Pottery will be able accurately to extend the range beyond what is presently known.

Saltglaze

Although I am not, at the time of writing, aware of a single piece of saltglazed pottery which can be firmly attributed to the Leeds Pottery, nevertheless both Donald Towner and Peter Walton made valiant attempts to 'suggest' some such pieces. I feel that it is my duty to deal with these pieces within the exigencies of my previously stated self-imposed parameters for attributing unmarked wares.

1. Some saltglazed whiteware shards have been discovered on the Pottery site, see Plate 43. As stated earlier, they are not sufficiently distinctive in their moulded details to indicate a style other than that which was ubiquitous in the second half of the eighteenth century.

2. In the NCS *Newsletter No. 8*, January 1974 at p.5. Peter Walton wrote about a saltglazed dish in the collection at Temple Newsam House (Museum Ref. No. 20/73): " ... this curator has few doubts about labelling a saltglazed dish recently acquired for Temple Newsam House as being made at Leeds." The dish in question is illustrated in Peter Walton's *Creamware and other English Pottery at Temple Newsam House Leeds* at No. 73, pages 34/35 where it is more cautiously attributed "Perhaps Yorkshire, Leeds Pottery, 1770s." Its overall shape is not comparable with any known Leeds pieces. It has a feather edge with nine, eight and seven barbs depending on the spaces where used. The main decoration is piercing, some of which, in the larger areas is very similar to that on several pieces of marked Leeds creamware but which is not unique to the Leeds Pottery. The pierced decoration in the four smaller panels is not, to my knowledge comparable with any known Leeds work.

3. Donald Towner illustrates two saltglazed teapots at plates 4a and 4b. The one at 4b bearing the female figure named "Miss Pit" from this he extrapolates to the one at Plate 4a and then to a creamware example at Plate 26a.ii – the similarity being quite convincing. However at page 24 when discussing the said Miss Pit and in order to bolster up his claim for a 'Leeds' attribution he states: "This is further supported by the fact that 'Lady Pit Lane' (Pit also spelt with one 't') passed close to the Leeds Pottery and no doubt led to the residence of Lady Pit and presumably her daughter Miss Pit ..." Unfortunately the 'Lady Pit Lane' referred to a coal pit at Middleton of that name: "Lady Pit" as shown on the map in *The Middleton Colliery Railway*, 4th ed. 1968, revised by J. Bushell & M.D. Crew. Miss Pit(t) was more likely to have been the Ann Pitt a famous London actress of the late eighteenth century, *vide* DNB. If so such teapots were more likely to have been appreciated and purchased by Londoners and therefore decorated there than at Leeds where, of course, some may have been made and sold as plain creamware/saltglaze later to be enhanced by the purchaser taking them to their local London decorating establishment. I feel however that the style of the saltglazed teapots is too early for the Leeds Pottery. In this context we must always remember that when Towner was writing his *The Leeds Pottery* that he firmly believed the Leeds Pottery to have been founded c.1758.

Redware

I am only aware of one possible marked example of Redware which may well have been made at the Leeds Pottery. See my remarks in Chapter 8 under Marks No. 3.c. In the *Original Drawing Book No.1* a customer from France c.1790, with the code letters "BT", ordered some covered cooking pots – "*en terre rouge*" – with what appears to be engine turned decoration in a chevron pattern.

64. REDWARE COFFEE POT. Engine-turned decoration on body, lid and spout. See shards Plate 43 top right and compare with the lid of this pot. Ht. – 7 1/8 in. (180mm). Mark No.3c. *Doncaster Museum Service. DONMG. 1987.34.*

Plain Creamware

Queen's ware was the alternative name given to this ware by Josiah Wedgwood after his appointment as "Potter to Her Majesty" (i.e. Queen Charlotte) in 1766, following his supplying Her Majesty with a tea service late in 1765.

However, creamware had been produced in Staffordshire since the 1730s, being a fine bodied lead-glazed earthenware. Josiah Wedgwood had developed this class of ware and had succeeded in lightening it by 1763 no doubt in response to a market demand for a lighter coloured ware.[4] David Barker also states that William Greatbatch's creamware had changed to a light colour by 1770; he also records that the cargo of the ship *Ledbury* which sank off the coast of Florida in 1769 had both light and dark creamwares roughly in equal proportions.[5]

I have deliberately quoted the above in order to correct the popularly held erroneous belief, still being perpetuated by some writers, that creamwares did not become lighter until c.1775 following the relaxing of Champion's monopoly on the use of China Clay and China Stone. As I indicated in Chapter 7, the Leeds Pottery was purchasing its ball clay from the deposits near Wareham in Dorset which was a particularly fine white-firing clay on account of it not having iron in significant quantities to produce a darkening effect in the firing process. Moreover, when we examine any pot we only see the surface of it and if glazed, as creamware was, then the colour of the glaze and any impurities which it may contain determine the colour, *not* the body under the glaze. It is not denied that after 1775 that some china clay was incorporated into the body of earthenwares but this would not have had any effect upon the colour of that body if the clay had come from the Wareham district in Dorset.

Before leaving this topic of the colour of creamware it is worth recording that after Josiah Wedgwood had succeeded in gaining a foothold in the export trade to Russia following his first shipment in 1769, he was prevailed upon to intensify the yellow, i.e. darken the glaze. The following extracts from letters confirm this :

15th August 1769, from Alexander Baxter (later, the Russian consul in London) to Josiah Wedgwood :

" ... We enclose you an order for 4 setts of Queen's earthenware ... Should they give Satisfaction depend of receiving very considerable orders annually from our friends in Russia. They desire that the colour may not be <u>too light a yellow.</u>"

From Josiah Wedgwood to Bentley of the 18th of April 1772 in which Wedgwood comments on producing his creamware to suit the Russian trade :

" ... to make it yellower than it is at present, but not of the dull brownish yellow you see in the shops; I would aim at as bright a <u>Straw Colour</u> as possible – This would be just the thing the Russians and some of the Germans want ..."[6]

In 1857 when Joseph Marryat published the second edition of his *A History of Pottery and Porcelain* he added, at Appendix VII, some additional information on the Leeds Pottery which he had received from Edward Hailstone, see Plate 30, an eminent collector of the period :

" ... The cream-coloured ware was produced by an arsenical glaze which severely crippled the workmen, who were not able to follow the trade more than four or five years. The articles were almost entirely made for the Russian and north of Germany trade, and one of the partners in the works travelled in the north of Europe to push the trade there. There does not appear to be any other mark than that stamped 'Hartley, Green, and Co., Leeds Pottery,' or 'Leeds Pottery' only; ..."

The reference to one of the partners travelling in northern Europe may have been an easily made mistake i.e. – a confusion between William Barwick who was the nephew of the partner John Barwick, see page 53.

With regard to the 'arsenical glaze' Simeon Shaw (1837) has the following information[7]:

"ARSENIC

... It is employed in some Glazes to advantage; because while as a flux it promotes the fusibility of the components, its ready volatization capacitates it to dissipate and convey away any carbonaceous matter present in the alcalic employed. ... [&] ... *Arsenic*, is a very powerful flux in promoting complete vitrification, and with this advantage, that whatever carbonaceous particles it may be in contact with, it volatizes likewise with them during the fixation of the oxygen. It is very useful in the dipped ware for aiding the manganese."

It is recorded in Appendix VII that arsenic was still being used in some of the Leeds Pottery's glazes as late as 1842.

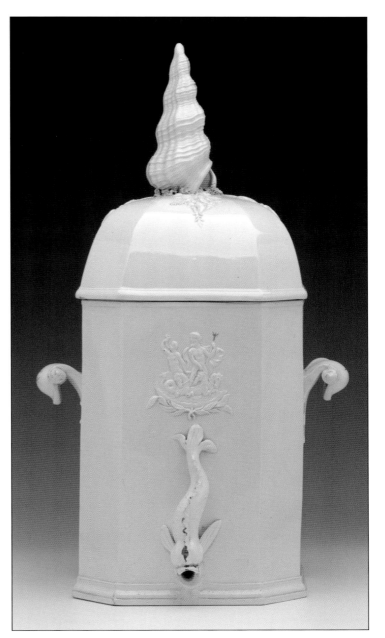

65. WATER CISTERN, LID AND BOWL. Ht. of body – 21 in. (533mm). Ht. of lid – 11 5/8 in. (295mm). W of bowl – 16 5/8 in. (422mm). Mark No.1 on body and bowl. No such object is illustrated in the published *Design Books*. However, in the Castleford Pottery's *Design Book* of 1796, at nos. 1, 2 and 4, two designs are shown and described as : "Lavemain fait à fontaine uni." This description is clear evidence that these were not for dispensing drinking water but for washing hands, hence the bowl which obviously matches the outline shape of the cistern, although it came into the collection at Temple Newsam with the one illustrated at Plate 66. *Leeds Museums & Galleries. LEEDM ZO 8120. & 16.1/47.*

66. WATER CISTERN AND LID. Ht. of body – 12 1/4 in. (311mm). Ht. of lid – 10 5/8 in. (270mm). Mark No. 1 on body. The design matches the one illustrated at No. 374 in *Drawing Book No. 2*, see Plate 719 and the caption to Plate 65. *Leeds Museums & Galleries. 16.1/47.*

67. EWER. Ht. – 12 in. (304mm). Mark No. 1. This design is No. 188 in the *Design Book* and was therefore not in the first edition of 1783. *Leeds Museums & Galleries. 4.17B/46.*

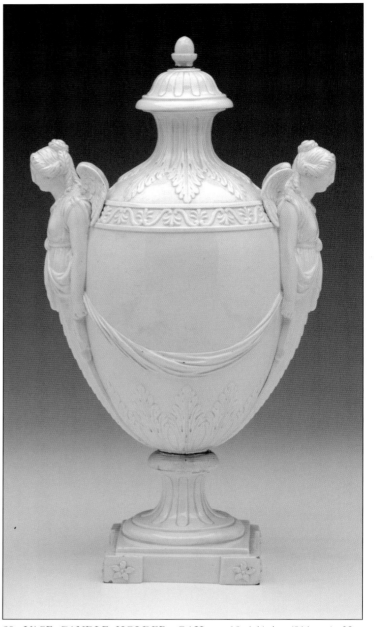

69. VASE CANDLE HOLDER. OAHt. – 12 1/4 in. (311mm). Not marked but the design is in the *Design Book* at No. 116 and Donald Towner illustrates an example in the Victoria & Albert Museum which has a scratched LP monogram under the base see Marks No.3b. Behind each angel's shoulders there is usually a hole in the top of the vase to receive the candle arms which presumably would have been in metal, probably ormolu. *Leeds Museums & Galleries. 16.89/47.*

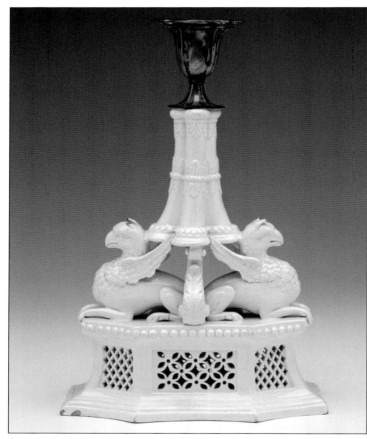

68. GRIFFIN CANDLESTICK, one of a pair. L. of base – 7 in. (177mm). Mark No. 1, impressed twice. The metal candle holder has replaced the original ceramic one indicating the value placed on this style of candlestick coupled with the obvious vulnerability of the original creamware. See the *Design Book*, No. 113 and the reference to a very similar model being made by the Castleford Pottery. *Leeds Museums & Galleries, T.N.19/P.*

70. INK STAND. L. – 8 1/4 in. (209mm). Mark No.1. The design is No. 201 in the *Design Book*, enlarged edition of early 19th century, where the pierced decoration differs from the one shown here. Notice the ink-stained rim of the inkwell. *Leeds Museums & Galleries. 16.45/47.*

71. INK STAND. L. – 7 1/4 in. (183mm). Mark No. 1. This design is not in the *Design Book* but may be seen at No. 326 in *Drawing Book No. 2*, at Plate 698. The function of the long tapering ceramic pegs which fit into holes in the tops of each inkpot is not understood. It contains a large and small inkpot, a wafer box with lid and a sanding box with perforations.

72. INK STAND. L. – 6 1/2 in. (164mm). Mark No. 2d. This version corresponds with No. 147 in the *Design Book*. where it is described as "Furnish'd Ink Stand." The hole for the ring handle is visible below the button finial. *York Museums Trust (Yorkshire Museum). YORYM 2001.2184.*

73. VASE. Ht. – 11 3/4 in. (298mm). Mark No.1. It is No. 138 in the first edition of the *Design Book*. This design was also produced at the Don Pottery but with minor differences in the proportions of the body. See *The Don Pottery*: Pl. 34 at p. 101 and compare the two illustrations. *York Museums Trust (Yorkshire Museum). YORYM 2001.526.*

74. QUINTAL VASE. Ht. – 8 in. (203mm). Mark No. 1. No. 142 in the *Design Book* in which it is described as: "Quintal Flower Horn." *Doncaster Museum Service. DONMG 1985.338.*

75. SHAVING BOWL. L. – 12 1/8 in. (307mm). Mark No.1. Notice the two small holes at the left-hand end to enable the bowl to be hung against a wall, suspended on a cord threaded through these holes.

76. WINE COOLER. Ht. – 9 3/8 in. (238mm). Mark No.2a. It is hard to tell whether the colour now seen is the original intended colour or the result of a general overall discolouration. From its mark I would date it post 1812, (see introduction to Marks No. 2). *York Museums Trust (Yorkshire Museum). YORYM 2001.533.*

77. SQUARE PIERCED TEA OR COFFEE TRAY. 14 in. x 11 1/2 in. (355mm x 292mm). Mark No. 1. No. 18 (Tea Ware section) of the *Design Book*. A larger example is in the same collection and which measures – 17 in. x 14 in. (432mm x 355mm). *Leeds Museums Galleries. 13.13/34.*

78. TEAPOT. Ht. – 5 3/8 in. (136mm). Mark No. 1. *Norfolk Museums Service (Norwich Castle Museum). NWHCM.1946.70.461*

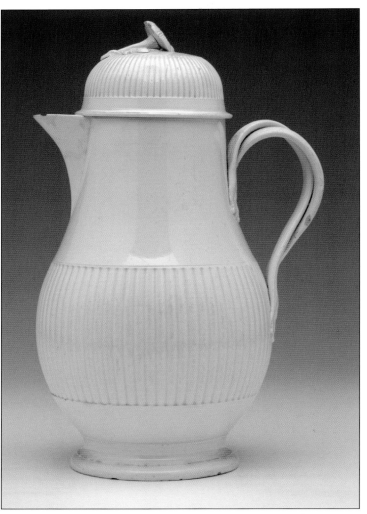

79. COFFEE POT. Ht. – 7 3/4 in. (196mm). Not marked. Nos 78 to 82 are *en suite* of which the milk jug at Plate 80 is the only marked piece. This is a variation of No. 8 in the *Design Book*, Tea Ware section where it is shown with a much flatter lid and is described as - "Fluted Coffee Pot with Snip." (See Reeding and Fluting in the Glossary, p. 629).

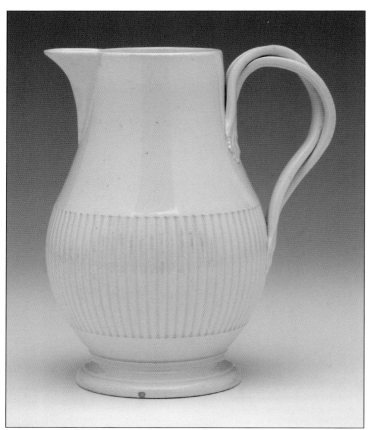

80. MILK JUG. Ht. – 6 1/4 in. (158mm). Mark No. 1.

81. FLUTED COMMON CHOCOLATE CUP AND SAUCER. Saucer D. – 4 7/8 in. (124mm). Not marked.

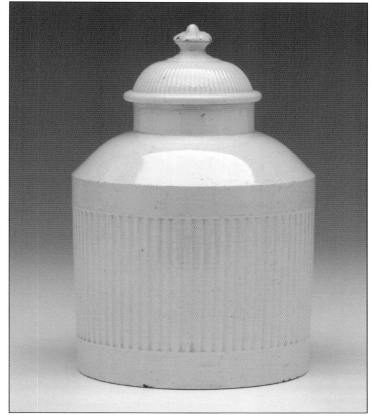

82. TEA CANISTER. Ht. – 4 in. (102mm). Not marked. No. 9 in the *Design Book*, Tea Ware section and described as "Fluted Cannister."

84. MELON TUREEN. OAL. – 12 7/8 in. (327mm). Mark No. 1 and impressed "6" or "9" and "S". No. 68 in the *Design Book*. The base of the tureen is fused to the leaf stand. *Leeds Museums & Galleries. 4.5/46.*

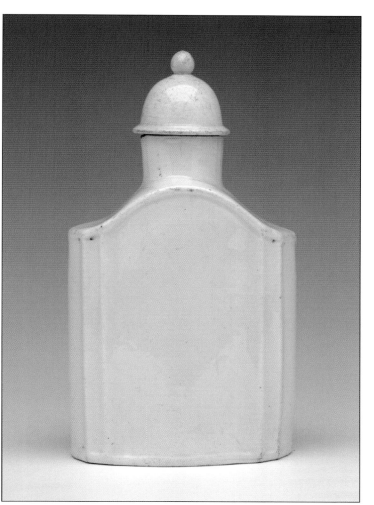

83. TEA CANISTER. Ht. – 5 in. (127mm). Mark No. 1b. No. 10 in the *Design Book*, Tea Ware section where it is described as "Plain Cannister." *York Museums Trust (Yorkshire Museum). YORYM 2001.5024.*

85. CHOCOLATE STAND. L. – 8 1/4 in. (209mm). Mark No. 1. These were not designed for invalids but to hold a chocolate cup, the vertical slot, seen in the example at Plate 36, was obviously designed to accommodate the cup handle. Very elaborate examples were made in silver and gold. See Marcia & Frederic Morton, *Chocolate, an Illustrated History.* pp. 31 and 32. *Doncaster Museum Service. DONMG. 1988.31.*

86. CHOCOLATE STAND. L. – 8 1/2 in. (216mm). Mark No. 1. See caption to Plate 85.

87. BOTTOM SECTION OF A PLATT MANAGE. D. – 10 1/2 in. (266 mm). Mark No. 1. A surviving component for design No. 88 in the *Design Book* where it is described as: "Platt Menage, 12 inches high." Observe that the moulded decoration on the surfaces of the divisions in the bowl are as shown in the *Design Book*. An alternative addition to cap the central column is to be seen in the sketch at Plate 499. *Leeds Museums & Galleries. 1928.101.*

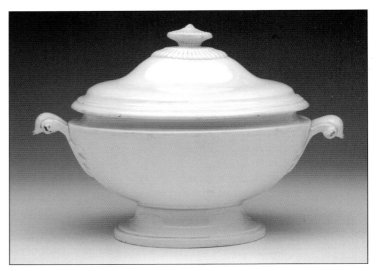

90. OVAL TUREEN AND LID. L. – 13 in. (330mm). Mark No. 2a. *Leeds Museums & Galleries. 1928.82.*

88. OVAL PIERCED QUEEN'S DISH. L. – 14 3/8 in. (365mm). Mark No. 1. A fine example of an oval Queen's-design dish with pierced border. *York Museums Trust (Yorkshire Museum. YORYM. 2001.5013.*

91. TRIANGULAR DISH. W. – 9 1/4 in. (235mm). Mark No. 1, and '3' impressed. It is shown at No. 38 in the *Design Book* where it is described as - "Triangular Royal Compotier, from 7 to 12 inches." *In the collection of: Hartley Greens Leeds Pottery Ltd.*

89. CIRCULAR TUREEN AND LID. D. – 8 1/2 in. (216mm) Mark No. 2a. It is No. 156 in the enlarged edition of the *Design Book*.

92. SHELL DISH. 7 1/8 in. x 7 in. (180mm x 177mm). Mark No. 1. No. 13 in the *Design Book* - "Escollop Shell, from 4 to 9 inches." Block moulds for this design survive in the Temple Newsam Collection.

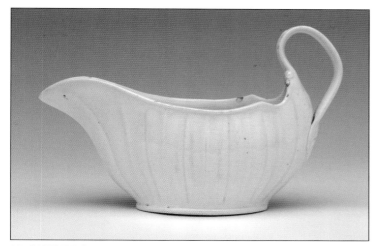

93. SAUCE BOAT. L. – 6 3/4 in. (171mm). Mark 1. No. 17 in the *Design Book* - "Royal Sauce Boat, from 4 to 7 inches and a Half." *York Museums Trust (Yorkshire Museum). YORYM 2001.5025.*

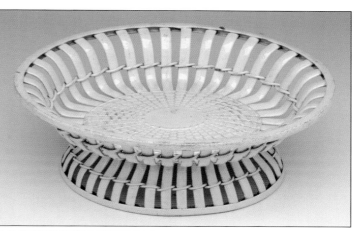

96. DOUBLE-TWIG FRUIT BASKET. L. – 9 1/4 in. (235mm). Mark No. 1. An interesting variation of the single twig fruit basket. *York Museums Trust (Yorkshire Museum). YORYM 2001.5019.*

94. OIL AND VINEGAR STAND. L. – 7 5/8 in. (193mm). Mark No. 1. No. 104 in the *Design Book. Leeds Museums & Galleries. 16.40/47.*

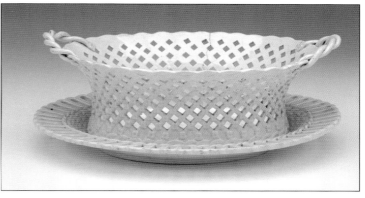

97. FRUIT BASKET AND STAND. Stand – 13 1/2 in. x 10 3/4 in. (343mm x 273mm). Mark No. 2a on both pieces. *Leeds Museums & Galleries. 16.252/47.*

98 FRUIT BASKET AND STAND. Stand, L. – 11 3/8 in. (288mm). Mark No. 1 on both pieces and '10' impressed on the basket. *Leeds Museums & Galleries. 16.54/41/1.*

95. STRAWBERRY-DISH STAND. 10 1/4 in. x 9 in. (260mm x 228mm). Mark No. 3a, and 'U' impressed. No. 87 in the first edition of the *Design Book* of which this is a very crisply moulded example. *Astley Hall Museum & Art Gallery, Chorley. 1934.A42.*

99. CIRCULAR CHESTNUT BASKET AND STAND. Stand D. – 10 5/8 in. (270mm). Mark No. 3a on the stand and the basket.

100. CIRCULAR CHESTNUT BASKET AND STAND. Basket D. – 10 1/8 in. (257mm). Mark No. 2a on basket and No. 1 on stand. The occurrence of the two marks suggests that the two pieces have been 'married', possibly by a dealer, collector or more likely by a member of the Pottery's warehouse staff when both marks were in use simultaneously after c.1812. See pp. 110 and 111. *Leeds Museums & Galleries. 1928.58.*

101. COCKLE/POT-POURRI POT. Not marked. A truly magnificent achievement of the potter's skill and a rare survivor in such good condition. Although not marked it matches very well with design No. 139 in the *Design Book*. Observe how the proportions shown in the engraving have been amended to produce a safer and more practical construction. The perforated lid would allow the scent from the *pot-pourri* to escape. Inside, however, there is a lower unperforated one which presumably would be used to retain the scent when not required to perfume a room and would have also retained the heat when used as a cockle pot. The sprigged assemblage of shells and seaweed between the perforated areas on the lid were produced from the mould illustrated at Plate 353/1. Another example is in the Harris Museum and Art Gallery, Preston which is unmarked and the outer lid has no piercings. *Garry Atkins, London*

170

102. COCKLE/POT-POURRI POT. Ht. – 10 1/2 in. (266mm). Not marked. The sprigged decoration between the perforated areas on the lid is taken from the ends of the swags around the body of the pot which is the same moulded detail as seen in this position at Plate 103. *Doncaster Museum Service. 1982.269.*

103. COCKLE/POT-POURRI POT. Ht. – 11 1/2 in. (292mm). Not marked. See the caption to Plate 101. *York Museums Trust (Yorkshire Museum). 2000.474*

Decorated Creamware

I must ask the reader's indulgence by prefixing my remarks, used several times before in this account with the following, *i.e*: "In the absence of factory records it is impossible to give a precise date for the introduction of ..." any form of surface decoration on creamware, or for that matter, on any other body. Such a lack of knowledge does not however prevent me from commenting upon what other writers have stated, or of offering opinions with reasons for so doing.

104. TEAPOT. Ht. – 3 3/16 in. (81mm). Although not marked the design is in the *Design Book* at Tea Wares No. 4. The flower knop and handle terminals match both shards and those on marked examples and the tortoise shell decoration also matches that found on shards. The base is flat.

105. PLATE. D. – 8 1/4 in. (209mm). Mark No.1, and 'S' impressed. It is quite rare to find such a plate marked.

107. LEAF DISH. 12 in. x 9 1/4 in. (304mm x 235mm). Mark No. 1 and 'N' impressed. The mottled glaze is quite rare. *York Museums Trust (Yorkshire Museum). YORYM 2001.4945.*

106. COFFEE POT. Ht. – 7 1/4 in. (183mm). Not marked. This pot is attributed by its overall design – see No. 6 in the *Design Book*, Tea Wares section where the spout details also match. The knop and handle terminals also match those on marked examples, – see also Plate 46 where shards match the engine-turned areas with the same additional colouring.

Printed Decoration on Creamware

This form of decoration had been employed by the porcelain manufacturers at Bow and Worcester as early as the 1750s. Josiah Wedgwood was doing business with the printers Sadler and Green of Liverpool from September 1761 and by the end of 1763 this business was worth £30 per month and had risen to £650 per month after ten years. It may seem strange that a pottery so well established and renowned as Wedgwood's should have its printed decoration carried out by a firm at such a distance from its own place of manufacture. However, the following reason tells us perhaps more about Josiah the astute businessman than it does about him as the potter and reinforces my contention that successful potters were first and foremost businessmen and secondly good potters.

The agreement between Wedgwood and Sadler and Green was that Wedgwood sold plain creamware to this Liverpool firm which then embellished it with transfer printed decoration, to Wedgwood's specification, and then sold it back to him. Sadler and Green were free to sell on to a third party any wares surplus to Wedgwood's requirements. Thus Wedgwood had his wares decorated and, more importantly, had secured an agreement that they would only decorate wares from Wedgwood thereby preventing other potters availing themselves of Sadler and Green's expertise.

Printing was well established at the Leeds Pottery by 1733 at the latest as it was proudly announced on the title page of the first published *Design Book* of that year, (see page 118). However, I feel sure that the Leeds Pottery was using on-glaze printed decoration quite early in its history; I make this assertion partially on stylistic grounds. If we look at the plate at Plate 110 we see a creamware plate of the Royal shape with an on-glaze, iron red, allegorical print and with the border decorated with six flower/foliage sprays of a very similar pattern to those used by Wedgwood on a plate of the same shape and decorated in the same colour, see Plate 108; Robin Reilly dates this plate c.1771–75,[8] thus indicating that such decoration was in fashion at that date. The Leeds Pottery was very obviously emulating Wedgwood or certainly producing the same type of ware in order to secure orders from a similar market. Of further interest is the fact that this Leeds plate is marked with the impressed "LP" mark which I feel could well have been an early mark, see page 112. Another piece of evidence for an early date for these plates is the print at Plate 109 which shows a fine view of Kirkstall Abbey which was situated only three and a half miles from the site of the Leeds Pottery. This view is taken from a print of 1747, by Francis Vivares after a painting by Thomas Smith, and therefore shows the central tower as a complete structure. However, on the 15th of January 1779 a large portion of the tower collapsed. After this date prints of the abbey showed the damage caused to the tower which is reflected in later views on Leeds pots, see Plates 348 – 350. I therefore believe that the printed mark, No. 1.c, was also used in the 1770s.

Apropos the subject of ruins, it should be born in mind that, from the middle of the eighteenth century, there had been an obsession with ruined gothic buildings forming an essential component in the landscape – even to the extent that if one was not present, or in the appropriate position, then a mock one was often built. This is born out by the following statement by the eminent historian, G.M Trevelyan in his *Illustrated Social History, Vol III*, page 108: "Before Pugin or Sir Walter Scott were born, and half a century before their influence was felt, ruined mediaeval castles were being erected as part of the 'landscape' ...".

Thus I feel confident in stating that after the partial collapse of the central tower of Kirkstall Abbey the Leeds Pottery would have depicted the tower in its more ruinous, and therefore more desirable 'picturesque' state.

Another group of early printed wares display bat prints associated with the Reverend John Wesley, see Plates 117 – 120. On these pots black bat prints of the founder of Methodism and figures and verses of a pious nature form the decoration. Peter Walton also recorded a teapot in the Hird Collection[9] with "Repentance" on one side and a portrait of "Cradock Glascott" on the other. The Rev Cradock Glascott of the parish of Hatherleigh (26 miles NNW of Exeter) was one of the Countess of Huntingdon's itinerants and an ardent evangelical and calvinistic clergyman. The Methodists held six conferences in Leeds in the 1770s and 1780s.

108 WEDGWOOD PLATE. D. – 9 11/16 in. (246mm). Mark – impressed "Wedgwood". This plate has been given a date of manufacture of 1771 – 1775 by Robin Reilly in *The Genius of Wedgwood* No. B20, pp. 28 and 30, V & A., 1995. *V & A. Museum, Schreiber Collection, Schr. II. 401(D).*

110. PLATE. D. – 9 5/8 in (244mm). Mark No. 3a. The allegorical decoration also appears, from a different copper plate, on the coffee pot at Plate 112, *q.v.* for an interpretation. *Leeds Museums & Galleries. 16.212/47.*

109. PLATE. D. – 9 7/8 in. (251mm). Mark No. 1c. In the introduction to this section at page 172, I put forward the opinion that this plate and the one at Plate 110 could have been produced in the 1770s purely on stylistic grounds – hence my inclusion of the Wedgwood plate at Plate 108; notice the similarity of the border decoration, colour of the print and that both plates are Royal shape. On this plate we have a printed decoration showing a view of Kirkstall Abbey (not Fountains Abbey as Donald Towner stated). It is copied from a print engraved by Francis Vivares and published in 1747 taken from a painting by Thos. Smith (d. 1767). If we examine the tower we see it to be intact, however on the 15th of January 1779 a large section of it collapsed leaving quite a ruinous appearance – see the Leeds Pottery's later view of this abbey at Plates 248,249 & 250 and my further remarks in the introduction to this section. *Leeds Museums & Galleries. 16.261/47.*

111 & 112. COFFEE POT. Ht. – 7 3/4 in. (196mm). Mark No. 1c. The scene used at Plate 110 is again used here at Plate 112 but from a different copper plate. The interpretation of the two scenes depicted on the coffee pot has been supplied by Liz Miller and Charles Newton of the Word and Image Department of the V & A Museum as follows: " ... it might be the case that in the scene with one female and two male figures, the woman is making a choice between the standing Apollo holding a book and a palm frond (symbolising Learning and Fame), and the flying figure of winged Cupid who is strewing the path with flowers. In the second scene Cupid (Love) has triumphed over Fame as Cupid and the woman are travelling together in a triumphal car ...".

113.a, and b. TEAPOT. Ht. – 3 3/4 in. (95mm). Mark No. 1c. The print at Plate 113.a shows Abraham about to sacrifice his son Isaac and at Plate 113.b is of Hagar & Ishmael.

114.a. and b. TEA CANISTER. Ht. – 4 1/8 in. (105mm), D. – 2 13/16 in. (72mm). Mark 1.c. bottom left of the print at 114.a. The design for this shape is illustrated in the first editions of the *Design Book* at No. 11, Tea Wares Section, where it is described as: "Plain Cannister". The two bat prints are from engravings produced by line engraving and etching. The style of the two engravings – their subjects and engraving techniques, together with the shape of the canister would indicate a date in the 1770s. The subject of the print at 114.b. is very reminiscent of one used at Worcester c.1776 – 80 (See Henry Sandon's *Worcester Porcelain 1751 – 1793*, Plate 126). The print at 114.a. is most likely from a French source as two *houlettes* are included, these being traditional implements used by French shepherds – see the Glossary for more details.

115 & 116. JUG. Ht. – 7 in. (177mm). Mark No. 1c. A fine jug with two large, clear prints. The one at Plate 115 of the pair of lovers needs no interpretation, however, the standing figure at Plate 116 seems somewhat sinister.

117. MUG. Ht. – 5 in. (127mm). Marks Nos. 1 and 1c. A number of such mugs are known with a religious theme. Just visible are the words 'Leeds' and 'Pottery' each being between the cherubs body and the oval cartouche – 'Pottery' being more obvious at Plate 118. The same applies to the teapot at Plate 119. *York Museums Trust (Yorkshire Museum) 2000.4753.*

118. MUG. Ht. - 5 in. (127mm). Mark No. 1c. See notes at Plate 117. The print is the same as shown on the teapot at Plate 119. *Leeds Museums & Galleries. 1928.86.*

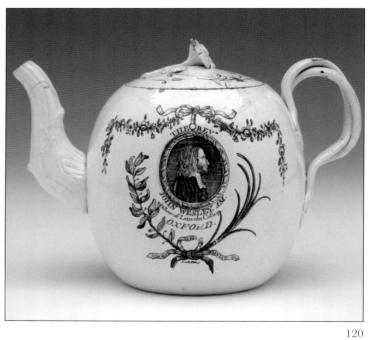

120

119 & 120. TEAPOT. Ht. – 4 1/2 in. (114mm). Mark No. 1c and 'X' scratched. See notes at Plate 117. At Plate 120 the words 'Leeds Pottery' are below the crossed stems of the fronds which encircle Wesley's profile. See also p. 173. *Leeds Museums & Galleries. 16.213/4.*

121. PLATE. D. – 9 in. (228). Mark No.2d and '10' impressed. This plate is sometimes seen with the decoration in a chocolate colour. It is not excessively rare unlike the one made to commemorate the Jubilee of George III in 1810 of which I have never seen an example. That such plates did exist is recorded by the Kidson brothers who had seen only one example. Leeds *Museums & Galleries. 1928.19.*

123

122

124

122, 123 & 124. JUG. Ht. – 8 in. (203mm). Mark No. 1c. A rare jug with a mask spout. The words 'Leeds Pottery' are at the lower centre part of the print at Plate 122. *Doncaster Museum Service DONMG. 1983.298.*

125 & 126. COFFEE POT. Ht. – 8 5/8 in. (219mm). Mark No. 1. Two bull-fighting scenes may indicate that this pot was either destined for the Spanish market or as a souvenir for a traveller who had visited such an event. It is not marked in the print as recorded by Towner. *York Museums Trust (Yorkshire Museum) YORYM. Ht: 5683.*

Enamelled Decoration

This is perhaps the most unreliable way of attributing a pot to a particular factory, yet some writers have done so. Such attributions have then led to moulded details and shapes being ascribed to the pottery in question and so on 'down the line'.

It is important to understand how painters and artists learned their skills until more recent times. They served an apprenticeship with skilled painters and this consisted of learning about the preparation of materials and acquiring the necessary skills in using them – almost entirely through the time-honoured tradition of *copying* examples of the type of work being undertaken by the master painter under whom they were working. Those readers who have read my Don Pottery book may recall that I illustrated two desert plates each with an enamelled copy of "Alpine Bell Flower" each done by a different artist both having copied it from the same print in Curtis' *Botanical Magazine*. I illustrated the two plates to show how difficult it would be to identify the work of either artist if confronted with an array of similar plates each with different flowers.

I have stressed this first point at some length in order to confront the reader with the difficulty in differentiating between the work of skilled painters who were so trained; even if one has the luxury of knowing signed work by any painter(s), particularly if there is a time gap of five or ten years between the signed example and another example under consideration. Finally we are all aware of the skill of the copyist in the world of fine art who, over the centuries, has deceived some of the top art dealers and museum curators with skillful fakes of the 'old masters'.

Great emphasis has been made by Donald Towner of the part played by the Leeds firm of Robinson and Rhodes – unfortunately now often referred to simply as "Rhodes decorated". This firm was established sometime before the 28th of October 1760 when it placed a notice in *The Leeds Intelligencer* .The following notice of the 11th of May 1761, in the same newspaper, gives a more detailed account of the firm's services :

"ROBINSON and RHODES,
Opposite the George, in Briggate, Leeds,
ENAMEL and BURN in COLOURS
and GOLD, FOREIGN and English CHINA; and match broken Sets of enamell'd
China Tea Ware, with Foreign or English, and make them complete to any Pattern
requir'd, either *India* or *Dresden*. They also enamel Coats of Arms, &c. and sell a
good Assortment of Foreign China, and great Variety of useful English China, of
the newest Improvement, which they engage to wear as well as Foreign, and will
change, gratis, if broken with hot Water. They also enamell Stone Ware, as cheap
as in Staffordshire, and sell Sorts of fine Earthenware. Likewise, piece all Sorts of
India Tea Ware, by melting it together in the Fire, so as to render it as useful,
without revitting, and to ring as well as before it was broken. Ready Money or
Goods for broken Flint Glass."

From this we learn that they were retailers of both foreign and English porcelain and "fine Earthenware", also that they undertook to repair damaged pieces and to add decoration to plain ware. Of particular relevance, however, is the fact that they offered to "match broken sets" and make them "complete to any Pattern" i.e. – they could copy any given pattern. I feel sure that a search through other local newspapers of the period would discover other chinamen offering very similar services.[10] The fact that this firm had been in existence for over ten years before the Leeds Pottery was founded demonstrates that it was not established because of its proximity to the Pottery and had obviously managed quite well without it.

The Leeds firm is on record as having bought wares regularly from Josiah Wedgwood from 1763, in which year David Rhodes took over the business in Leeds until 1768 when he moved to London, eventually managing the decorating establishment for Josiah Wedgwood in Chelsea from 1770 until his death in 1777.[11] Thus David Rhodes had left Leeds two years before the foundation of the Leeds Pottery. Unfortunately I have been unable to discover any pot which can be proved to have been decorated by David Rhodes personally. For Wedgwood he is known to have worked on the 'Frog Service' and to have supervised work on the 'Husk Service', neither of which bears any resemblance to the style of work which has been traditionally ascribed to him.

Confronted with the above facts it is obvious that David Rhodes personally could not have decorated Leeds creamware in Leeds. We must now consider how Donald Towner came to attribute some pieces of 'early Leeds' as having been decorated by Rhodes. The first point to make is that I am not aware of any of the pieces so attributed being factory marked. Secondly Donald Towner, when he published his *The Leeds Pottery* in 1963, believed that the Leeds Pottery was founded c.1758 and therefore on his erroneous dating it would have been possible for some pieces to have been decorated by David Rhodes. Thirdly the style of painting on the enamelled wares which have been *traditionally* attributed to Rhodes may be considered quite naive and would surely not have been beyond the scope of any reasonably-competent painter of the period to replicate if such a style of decoration was in demand. Fourthly, it would surely not have made commercial sense for the Leeds Pottery to produce undecorated wares, pack them in straw in casks or crates and then transport them down the road into Leeds, there to be unpacked decorated and repacked for transit back to Hunslet only to be unpacked, sorted and repacked for transit to their customers. Surely if such decoration was in demand it would have made much more sense to employ their own decorators or to poach or 'head-hunt' some from the establishment: "Opposite the George in Briggate".

The fifth scenario is, of course, that plain creamware could have been purchased from the Pottery by retailers or individuals who were then at liberty to take their wares to the independent decorating establishments in Leeds or in any other town or city nearest to them.

Finally the following quotations add weight to my own views on this subject :

1. Robin Reilly, 'The Pursuit of Perfection', *The Genius of Wedgwood*, page 28: " ... The enamelling is in a style associated with David Rhodes ... The several types of enamelled decoration traditionally associated with his name were probably common to a number of creamware painters working in Leeds and London, and presumably elsewhere."

2. A.A. Eaglestone and T.A. Locket, *The Rockingham Pottery*, page 32, – quotation from a letter from Thomas Brameld dated the 23rd of April 1809., in the WWM : " ... Elizabeth Barraclough went off last Sunday However, you need not hesitate to take orders for her work, as James Bullough, Abraham Nicholson and Shaw, the painters, all say they can do it, and wish to have it ... However, my present intention is to have Anne Hodgson brought to do it ...". From this we learn that it had been the custom "to take orders for her work"; what is of significance, therefore, is that no less than four other painters were capable of doing the same work.

As a tailpiece to the above it is worth recording that Jasper Robinson, David Rhodes' erstwhile partner took over the firm after David Rhodes had departed for London but had retired from the concern by the 18th of May 1779 when the following notice was placed in *The Leeds Intelligencer* of that date :

"Leonard Hobson, Glass & China-Man, At the GOLDEN-JARR, in Briggate,
Leeds, *(Successor to Mr. J. Robinson)* Respectfully begs Leave to acquaint Ladies,
Gentlemen, and Others, both in Town and Country, That he has a Good
ASSORTMENT of CUTT and PLAIN GLASSES; Also Foreign and English
CHINA, compleat Sets of Nankeen TEA CHINA, and of Colour'd Ditto.
He returns his sincere Acknowledgments to his Friends for the many Favours
conferr'd upon him, and hopes for the Continuence of the same; and all who
please to favour him with their Commands, may depend on being well served,
so as to merit their future Favours, which will ever be gratefully acknowledg'd,
by L. HOBSON.
N.B. He continues to mend broken Foreign China, by burning, in the
neatest and strongest Manner. Gentlemen in the Country, who send a
sufficient Quantity together, will have the Carriage gratis. He having a very
great Quantity of China already mended by him, desires the Owners to
send for it the first Opportunity; and by so doing they will very much
oblige him."

179

It is interesting to note that the above notice does not include any hint that decorating was still one of the services being provided, or any hint that it had been *recently* discontinued.

Leonard Hobson died on the 21st of April 1799, the event being announced in *The Leeds Mercury* of Saturday the 27th of April :

"On Sunday last Mr. Hobson of this town china mender."

The jugs and mugs illustrated at Plates 158 to 173 are, if dated, all 1802 or 1803. Moreover they all display a type of decoration, not seen on other wares from the Leeds Pottery, which may be described as being naive yet often exhibiting quite an exuberant flare; see the decoration around the name at Plate 159 and below and around the names at Plates 165 and 166, 171 and 172. Spelling and the use of upper and lower case letters do not imply that either the decorator or the person supervising his or her work was particularly literate. In short they all belong to a class of their own and are far removed from other personalised wares to be seen at Plates 129, 131, 252, 255, 257 and 284.

127. MUG. Ht. – 5 in. (127mm). Mark No. 1. The simple enamelled decoration round the top is a typical feature of Leeds mugs. *Leeds Museums & Galleries. 4.61/46.*

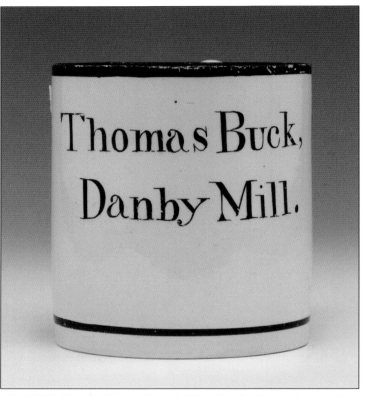

129. MUG. Ht. – 3 3/4 in. (95mm). Mark No. 2a. Danby is a parish in North Yorkshire 2 miles east of Middleham where in 1823 a Peter Buck was listed as a 'corn miller' – see Edward Baines, *History, Directory and Gazetteer of the County of York*, Vol. II, East & North Ridings.

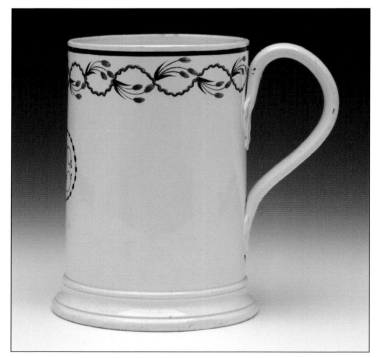

128. MUG. Ht. – 5 7/8 in. (149mm). Mark No. 1. Out of sight, opposite the handle, are finely drawn initials "RFC" as a monogram in the same style as at Plate 131.

130. TUREEN AND DISH. Dish L. – 10 5/8 in. (270mm). Mark No. 1 on both the dish and the tureen base. *Leeds Museums & Galleries,* – Tureen: *1890.14;* Dish: *1928.106.*

131. DISH. 7 1/4 in. x 5 3/4 in. (183mm x 145mm). Mark No. 1.

134. PLATE. D. – 6 3/4 in. (171mm). Mark No.1 and 'G' impressed.

132

135. TEAPOT. OAHt. – 4 1/2 in. (114mm). Mark No.1. Bohea Tea was regarded as the finest black tea in the early eighteenth century but by the middle of the nineteenth century it was ranked with the lowest grades. It took its name from the Bohea hills where it was cultivated, an area north of Fuhkien, China. *Law Fine Art, Hungerford, Berkshire.*

132, 133. PLATE. D. – 7 1/4 in. (183mm). Mark No.1. SAUCE BOAT. OAL. – 8 1/4 in. (209mm). Mark No.1. This pattern of stylised flower groups is pattern No. 247 in the *Enamelled Table-Service Drawing Book.*

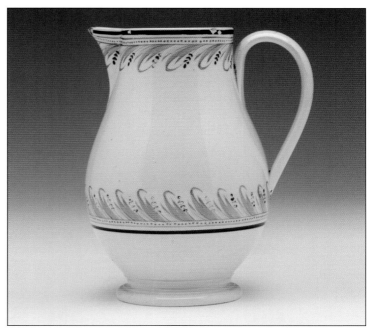

136. JUG. Ht. – 5 1/4 in. (133mm). Mark No. 1. Pattern No. 233 in the *Enamelled Table Service Drawing Book. Leeds Museums & Galleries. 1928.11.*

137. BUTTER TUB. D. – 3 3/4 in. (95mm). Mark No. 1. Unfortunately the decoration has lost much of its enamelling. *Leeds Museums & Galleries. 16.121/47.*

138. TEAPOT. Ht. – 3 5/8 in. (92mm). Mark No. 1. This style of decoration is known as 'Dutch Decoration'. It is rare to find a piece so decorated on a pot which is factory marked. I feel certain in stating that such wares would have been purchased from the Leeds Pottery undecorated by a Dutch merchant who would then have had them decorated for resale. Another possibility is that individuals could have taken single pots, purchased undecorated, to an independent decorating establishment for the same purpose. It would therefore be unwise to attribute any unmarked examples with such decoration to the Leeds Pottery unless shape and moulded details correspond exactly with proven marked wares as the decoration has no connection peculiar to the Leeds Pottery. *Leeds Museums & Galleries. 16.137/47.*

139. MUSTARD POT ON FIXED STAND. OAL. – 6 1/4 in. (158mm). Mark No. 1 and '11' impressed. *Leeds Museums & Galleries. 16.105/47.*

140. DISH. 14 3/8 in. x 11 in. (365mm x 279mm). Mark No. 1 and '2' impressed. Pattern No. 106 in the *Enamelled Table Service Drawing Book*, with slight variation colour wise.

141. PLATE. D. – 9 5/8 in. (244mm). Mark No. 1. *Doncaster Museum Service. DONMG. 1985.328.*

142. PLATE. D. – 9 1/2 in. (241mm). Mark No. 2a.

143. PLATE. D. – 9 5/8 in. (244mm). Mark No. 1. Pattern No. 156 in the *Enamelled Table Service Drawing Book*.

144. DISH. D. - 16 5/8 in. (422mm). Mark No. 1 and '5' impressed.

145. PLATE. D. – 9 3/4 in. (248mm). Mark No. 1b. impressed three times. A very elegant and restrained border pattern which is No. 209 in the *Enamelled Table Service Drawing Book*. A rare example of the mark being impressed three times.

146. DISH. D. – 14 3/4 in. (374mm). Mark No. 1 and '15' impressed. This genuine Leeds dish is included as a warning as the central decoration is cold painted! Most period plates and dishes show surface knife scratches and this dish is no exception. However, on close examination some scratches extend from the undecorated area and go **under** this 'recent' decoration. The painting is 'soft' to a sharp steel pin or point of a pocket knife, this would not be the case with fired-on decoration which is virtually as hard as the surrounding glaze. The owner removed this decoration with one application of paint stripper. See also comments on p.192 with reference to the "Vicar & Moses" jug.

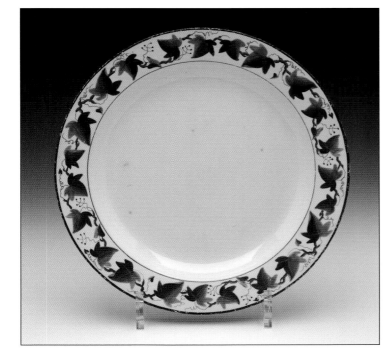

147. PLATE. D. – 9 1/4 in. (235mm). Mark No. 1, pattern No. '298' enamelled, and impressed workman's mark: "**⋮⋮⋮**". Pattern No. 298 is in the *Enamelled Table Service Drawing Book*, at Plate 933. The marking with a pattern number is not common on Leeds Pottery.

148. PLATE.. D. – 10 in. (254mm). Mark No. 2d.. therefore c.1820–27. *Astley Hall Museum & Art Gallery, Chorley. CHOAH 1934:E9d.*

149. SOUP PLATE. D. – 9 7/8 in. (251mm). Mark No. 3a and 4e This decoration is represented by pieces in the Doncaster Museum & Art Gallery and the Yorkshire Museum as well as at Temple Newsam House. The arms belong to the family of Fenton of Underbank, Penistone, near Sheffield. *Leeds Museums & Galleries. 1928.50.*

150. PLATE. D. – 9 7/8 in. (251mm). Mark 1b. The same pattern as in the *Enamelled Table Service Drawing Book* No. 260, but here it is shown in brown – in the book it is green. Unfortunately the crest of a lion rampant with two tails cannot be identified as Fairburn lists no fewer than seven families which used this crest.

152. FRUIT-BASKET STAND. 11 1/4 in. x 8 1/2 in. (285mm x 216mm). Mark No.1. The arms and crest are most likely for the Ellison family. *Doncaster Museum Service. DONMG. 1980.153.*

151. FRUIT-BASKET STAND. 11 1/8 in. x 9 1/4 in. (282mm x 235mm). Mark No. 1.The initials 'JCR' in the monogram are encircled by two fronds tied with a ribbon where they cross, a feature quite common on Leeds and some Don wares. *Leeds Museums & Galleries. 16.267B/47.*

153. FRUIT BASKET. 8 7/8 in. x 7 1/2 in. (225mm x 190mm). Mark No. 1. Unidentified armorial in the centre. The enamelled border pattern is No. 197 (at Plate 915) in the *Enamelled Table Service Drawing Book*, this pattern was used in a printed form by the Don Pottery, see *The Don Pottery 1801-1893*, Plate 139, p.131. Wedgwood also used an enamelled version.

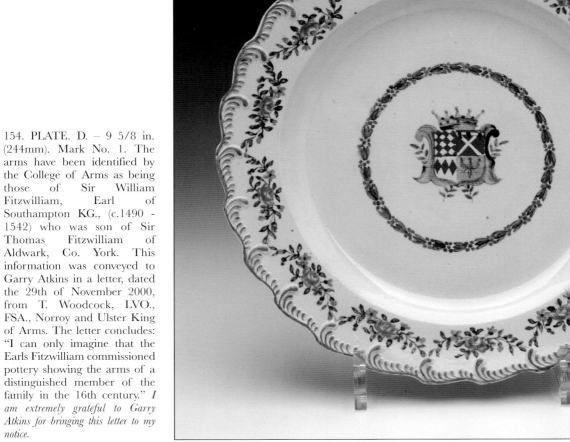

154. PLATE. D. – 9 5/8 in. (244mm). Mark No. 1. The arms have been identified by the College of Arms as being those of Sir William Fitzwilliam, Earl of Southampton KG., (c.1490 - 1542) who was son of Sir Thomas Fitzwilliam of Aldwark, Co. York. This information was conveyed to Garry Atkins in a letter, dated the 29th of November 2000, from T. Woodcock, LVO., FSA., Norroy and Ulster King of Arms. The letter concludes: "I can only imagine that the Earls Fitzwilliam commissioned pottery showing the arms of a distinguished member of the family in the 16th century." *I am extremely grateful to Garry Atkins for bringing this letter to my notice.*

155. PLATE. D. – 9 3/8 in. (238mm). Mark No. 1. The plate shows traces of gilding on the beaded edge and on the edges of the shallow fluting leading from the rim to the well. This is perhaps the most splendidly decorated Leeds creamware plate known to me. Like the specimen at Plate 154 it is something of a mystery. I am extremely grateful to Jirí Louda of Prague, one of the leading authorities on the heraldry of the Royal Families of Europe for the following information: The plate shows the arms of Poland-Lithuania with those of Saxony in pretence. The last person to have been entitled to bear such arms was Frederick Augustus II of Saxony and III of Poland who died in 1763 after which his son Frederick Christian became Elector of Saxony, in 1763, without any pretension to the Polish throne; he had four younger brothers. Jirí Louda concluded his letter as follows: "... it is quite possible that the Polish arms were not forgotten completely among the Saxon rulers and this could be an explanation why they appeared on the Leeds Pottery." – It is also possible that replacement plates were made for an earlier service or, maybe, this plate was done simply as a sample to show the quality of work available to prospective customers? *I am indeed grateful to Graham Beck for his help with this matter and also to J. Michael Phillips of the Heraldry Society.*

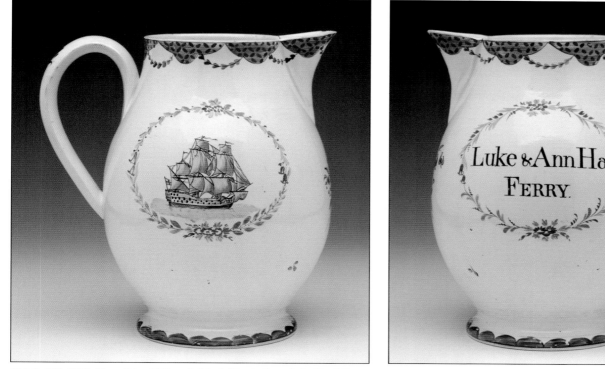

156 & 157. JUG. Ht. – 9 in. (228mm). Mark No. 1. Ferry is in Norfolk, two miles north of Wisbech.

157

158

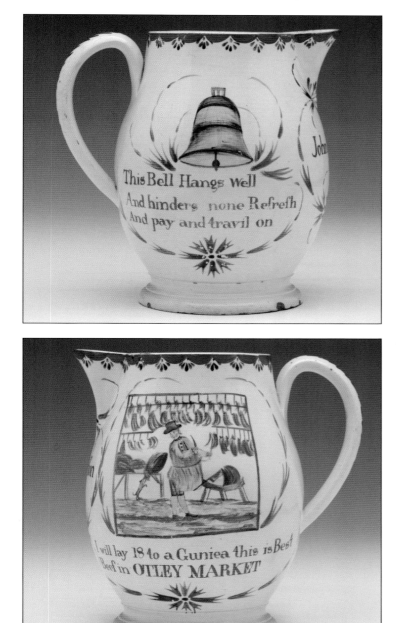

159

158, 159 & 160. JUG. Ht. – 6 1/2 in. (164mm). Mark No. 1. *Leeds Museums & Galleries. 46/84.*

160

161. JUG. Ht. – 6 3/4 in. (171mm). Mark No. 1. "John & Mary Young 1802/Wighill/The loss of A. friend is much./loss of time is more lost of/Christ is such that no man/can restore". Wighill is a village two and a half miles north of Tadcaster, Yorkshire. *Doncaster Museum Service. DONMG. 1985.321.*

164. MUG. Ht. – 4 7/8 in. (124mm). Mark No. 1. "Look to the Lord/& he will be[a] tender/Father unto the". *Leeds Museums & Galleries. 4.45/46.*

162. MUG. Ht. – 3 5/8 in. (92mm). Not marked.

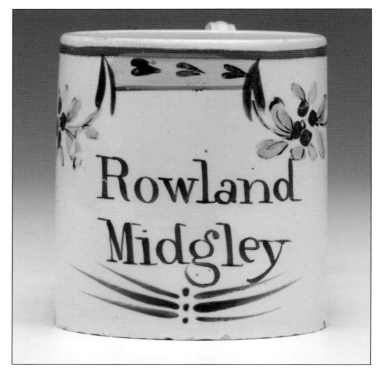

165. MUG. Ht. – 2 5/8 in. (67mm). Mark No. 4e.

163. TWO JUGS. Left, Ht. – 5 1/8 in. (130mm). mark No. 4d. Right, Ht. – 7 1/2 in. (190mm). Mark No. 1 & Mark No. 4d. Left: "William Rowlinson/Gelder[*] 1803/Virtue alone is happiness/below & all our knowledge/is our selves to know". Right: "James Stevenson Aged/31 Kippax 1802". [*] Gelder – A man who gelds or castrates animals. Kippax is a village nine and a half miles south-east of Leeds. *Leeds Museums & Galleries. – Left, 16.181/47; Right, 4.44/46.*

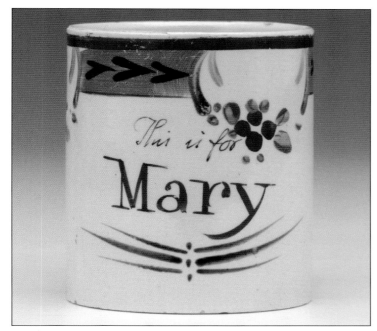

166. MUG. Ht. – 2 3/8 in. (60mm). No mark

169. JUG. Ht. – 9 in. (228mm). No Mark. On the other side: "Nancy Riley/Sleep on blest creture in/thine urn my sighs & tears/shall never a wake thee ille/stay behind untill my turn/& then with you i will Overtake/thee

167. MUG. Ht. – 6 in. (152mm). Mark No. 1 and No. 4d. Wighill is a village two and a half miles north of Tadcaster, Yorkshire.

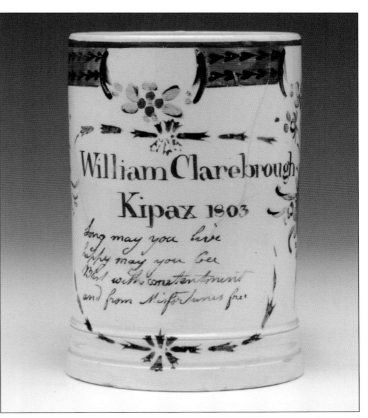

170. MUG. Ht. – 4 7/8 in (124mm). Mark No. 4d. A strange mixture of lettering and long hand writing. The verse on this mug tells a sad story. A William Clarebrough was baptised at Kippax on the 23rd of November 1796 and died the 9th of January 1797. As was often the custom another son, also William, was baptised on the 8th of November 1802 and who also died young on the 25th of June 1809. Both boys were the sons of William. *IGI*.

168. JUG AND MUG. Pearlware. Jug: Ht. – 5in. (127mm). Mark No. 1. Mug: Ht. – 5 in. (127mm) No Mark. Although they are both pearlware they are included in this section because of their decoration. On the jug: "Grace Silson/Remember time will come/ When you must give an Account/To God how you on Earh/do Live. 1802." *Leeds Museums & Galleries. Jug: 4.37/46. Mug: TN 69.*

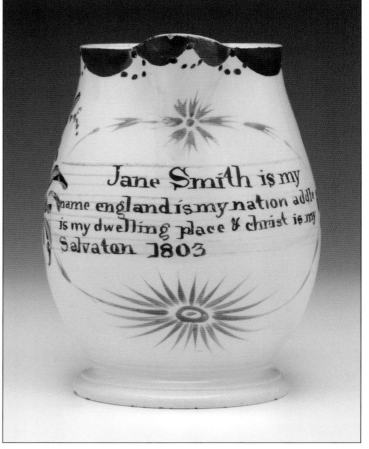

171. MUG. Ht. – 5 in. (127). Mark No. 1. The verse reads: "A Contented mind makes aneasy/heart where love is fixed never/to part 1803". Netherdale is in Banfshire, five miles west of Turriff.

172. JUG. Ht. – 5 in. (127mm). Mark No. 4d. The guide lines for the lettering are clearly visible – surely a mistake. Adel is a parish four and a half miles north west of Leeds.

173. JUG. Ht. – 5 in. (127mm). No mark. "Hannah Fleetwood/is my name & England is my Nation/Holbeck is my Dwelling place/& Christ is my Salvation 1803". Holbeck is now in the City of Leeds, south of the river Aire and west of Hunslet. *York Museum Trust (Yorkshire Museum). YORYM. 1971.282.*

174. MUG. Ht. – 3 1/8 in. (79mm). Mark No. 1.

175. MUG. Ht. – 4 1/2 in. (114mm). Mark No. 1. "This is for/John Thompson/1809". This is a very interesting piece as in 1809 the Leeds Pottery was officially closed and was being carried on at a greatly reduced scale by Ebenezer Green, see Chapter 3. *Leeds Museums & Galleries. 4.48/46.*

176. MUG. Ht. – 5 in. (127mm). Mark No. 1. The style of lettering and decoration on this mug matches that on the one at Plate 175. *York Museums Trust (Yorkshire Museum). YORYM 2000.4763.*

Pearlware

What we now call Pearlware was introduced by Josiah Wedgwood in 1779 and which he termed "Pearl White"; it has also been claimed that other Staffordshire potters had introduced what they called "China Glaze" as early as 1775.[12] Whatever it was, or is now called, it satisfied the market demand for a type of ware which resembled as far as possible the imported Chinese porcelain which was in great demand by those able to afford it. It is a white firing earthenware body with a clear glaze to which about a quarter of one percent of cobalt oxide has been added. It is readily identified by the bluish-grey glaze which shows more obviously where it may have pooled near the footring or in the depressions in moulded areas of decoration.

Leeds pearlware often seems to have had a slightly more generous proportion of cobalt added to it as the bluing effect is more pronounced than many such wares produced by other potteries. Not surprisingly the same may also be said regarding the pearlware produced at the Don Pottery and the Swinton Pottery. This characteristic has the effect of making more obvious the moulded details of the plain pearlware figures, see Plate 306, and is therefore a definite advantage on such wares. However I feel that it is not so successful when used under some enamelled decoration where either a plain creamware or ideally a whiteware would have lent an altogether cleaner appearance and shown the enamelled decoration off to better advantage.

The introduction of underglaze blue transfer-printed decoration, with which we are all familiar, has been a staple product of many earthenware potteries since its introduction c.1780. Again I must confess that the exact date of its introduction at Leeds is not known but I would expect that the partners at Leeds would have been very keen to exploit any new demand from the market particularly if messages came back from their 'riders' that their competitors were securing good sales for such wares.

Llewellynn Jewitt recorded, in his article in *The Art Journal* of 1865, that he had examined some of the Leeds Pottery's original account books and that in 1791 the copper plates "then in use" were valued at £204. Geoffrey Priestman, in his *An Illustrated Guide to Minton Printed Pottery 1796 – 1836* at Plate 2.3 on page 17, publishes a valuation of Minton's copper plates in 1817, in which 331 copper plates are listed in sets for printing eighteen different patterns to the total value of £392. Jewitt also recorded that, at the time he was writing his article for *The Art Journal* (c.1865) the value of the Leeds copper plates was £1000.

It is virtually impossible for the layman to evaluate the current value of sums of money from previous periods without a great deal of specialist knowledge. However, with the aid of tables published by the Office for National Statistics in its *Economic Trends* of March 2004 at pages 41 and 43 "Composite Price Index 1750 to 2003", the task of arriving at a present-day value is comparatively simple, thus: Minton's 331 copper plates for eighteen patterns, valued at £392 in 1817, would have been worth £21,239 in the year 2003, or **£1,180.** per pattern. Leeds Pottery's £204 in 1791 would have become £19,453 in 2003 which divided by **£1,180.** would indicate approximately sixteen patterns on approximately 303 copper plates. Leeds Pottery's £1000 in 1865 would have become £74,466 in 2003 which if divided by **£1,180.** would indicate a holding of approximately sixty-seven patterns on approximately 1,160 copper plates.

It is stressed that the above figures can only be approximations so far as the numbers of patterns and plates are concerned, nevertheless they are reasoned calculations based on a precise figure from another pottery. The Minton's plates were for patterns then being used on table wares, tea wares, ewers and jugs, basins and chamber pots – very similar to the range of wares being produced at Leeds. However, the fact that Llewellynn Jewitt specifically mentioned the value of the copper plates, at the above two dates, signifies the importance which he attached to them.

I have not recorded any backstamps for the period prior to 1827 when the Hartley Greens & Company partnership ended. Names which we now give to some of the printed patterns from this period, for example: "Great Wall of China", "Wanderer" and "Jar and Fisherman" are recent names deemed necessary since the comparatively recent phenomenon for studying and collecting underglaze blue-printed earthenwares has become popular.

The production of underglaze printed wares was not a cheap alternative compared with most other forms of decoration. See page 97 where I reproduce the price list of Messrs Hartley Greens & Co., for 1796. Under teawares are listed the prices for the alternative types of decoration for each size, thus: Plain, flute[ed], Enamelled, Queen's Blue painted, Nankeen Blue printed, Brown China and Egyptian Black, the blue printed being the dearest option at approximately 166% above the plain, undecorated, option. Ironically the present mania for collecting blue and white transfer-printed wares has, for some items in this genre, maintained a similar or even higher differential.

By the 1820s, the blue printing was used on a very white body with a glaze which was virtually devoid of cobalt and which gives a very clean appearance to the pieces so made, (see Plates 223, 225 and 229). Another underglaze colour used extensively at Leeds and not found significantly elsewhere is the grey/brown colour, see Plates 187 – 191 for examples.

There is one pearlware jug which was originally in the collection of the nineteenth century collector, Edward Hailstone, see Plate 30, and was commented upon by Llewellynn Jewitt before passing into the collection of Thomas Boynton until it finally came to rest in the collection of the Yorkshire Museum, York. It was illustrated by A. Hurst in his *A Catalogue of the Boynton Collection*, then by Oxley Grabham, in his *Yorkshire Potteries, Pots and Potters* and finally by Donald Towner in his *The Leeds Pottery*. I refer, of course, to the famous example of the "Vicar and Moses" jug. The six previous writers and collectors had each accepted this jug as being a product of the Leeds Pottery, presumably because below the spout there is an image of the Leeds symbol of the suspended sheep ('the tup in trouble') and the wording "Success to Leeds Manufactory", also the initials JB. All the previous writers, except Oxley Grabham, stated that the initials SB were also present, Donald Towner going so far as to suggest that they were "probably for John Barwick, a partner of the Pottery, and his wife". (Even the most superficial of searches would have revealed that the name of John Barwick's wife was Margaret.) There was no sign of the presence of the initials SB in 2002 when I examined the jug, moreover the decoration just mentioned does not bear any resemblance either in style or quality to the image of the Vicar and Moses or the text of the poem of that name which appears on the other side of the jug. Indeed I believe that it is cold-painted decoration and not fired-on enamel as there is no evidence of any disruption of the surface of the glaze where such letters and other parts of this decoration are missing. This last 'feature' led me to question very strongly the attribution of this jug to the Leeds Pottery. My assumption was vindicated when I examined an identical specimen when it was recently offered for sale, the same size, shape, prints and colouring, but without the 'tup in trouble' etc. On this jug the print was signed "John Ainsley Lane End".

Because of the close proximity of the Pottery to the town of Leeds it may have made more economic sense to use the services of one of the firms of engravers working there than to employ their own engravers. We know that one of these firms, Livesey later Butterworth & Livesey, engraved the billheads for the Pottery, see Plates 22 and 24, which are 'signed' by these firms; we also know that C. Livesey advertised "Plates for Potteries, either Black or Blue ware." – see Plate 177 where his trade card is shown.

177. ENGRAVER'S TRADE CARD. The reference: "Plates for Potteries, either Black or Blue Ware." which appears on this trade card of c.1800, implies that Christopher Livesey was supplying stipple engraved plates for bat-printing (Black Ware), for use in on-glaze printing, as well as the line engraved plates for 'Blue Ware' for use in under-glaze printing. The method of engraving used to produce each type of plate did not, however, limit its use for printing any specific colour. *I am grateful to Paul Holdway, Design Engraver at Spode Ltd., for confirming this interpretation.*

At Plates 252 to 261 is a group of dated and personalised mugs, jugs and loving cups – all, if dated, being 1801, 1802 and 1803. These should be compared with the group, of the same period, illustrated at Plates 158 to 176 which show a much more naive standard of decoration.

It must be remembered that creamware continued to be made, alongside pearlware, well into the third decade of the nineteenth century. The collector must also bear in mind that the revivalists, Senior and Morton, did not make pearlwares, see Appendix IX.

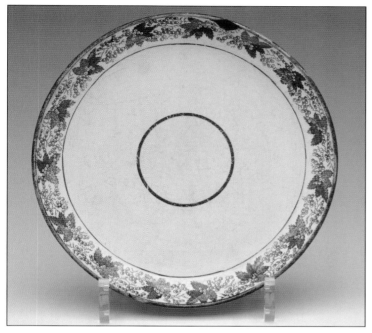

178. PLATE. D. – 7 1/2 in. (190mm). Mark No. 1. Overglaze printed decoration on pearlware. *York Museums Trust (Yorkshire Museum) YORYM. 1971.217.*

179. SAUCER DISH. D. – 7 1/2 in. (190mm). Mark No. 1. Overglaze printed decoration on pearlware. *Leeds Museums & Galleries. LEEDM. E/1933.255.*

180 & 181. MUG. Ht. – 4 3/4 in. (120mm). Mark No. 2a. See FOBB 46/6 where a jug with this print is illustrated. *Leeds Museums & Art Gallery. 1928.46.*

182. TEAPOT. Body: L. – 6 3/8 in. x 5 in. (161mm x 127mm). Mark No. 1 and '1' impressed. *York Museums Trust (Yorkshire Museum) YORYM 1971.271.*

183. PLATE. D. – 9 1/8 in. (232mm). Mark No. 1b. *York Museums Trust (Yorkshire Museum). YORYM. 1971.222.*

186. COFFEE POT. Ht. – 8 in. (203mm). Mark No. 2a.

184. COFFEE POT. Ht. – 8 1/8 in. (206mm). Mark No. 2a. *Leeds Museums & Galleries. 4.48A/46.*

187. PLATE. D. – 8 1/4 in. (209mm). Mark No. 1. *Doncaster Museum Service. DONMG. 1985.325.*

185. SOAP BOX. 3 7/8 in. x 3 1/8 in. (98mm x 79mm). Mark No. 2a (in the lid only). *Doncaster Museum Service. DONMG. 1986.25.*

188 PLATE. D. – 8 1/4 in. (209mm). Mark No. 1.

189. PLATE. D. – 8 1/4 in. (209mm). Mark No. 1. *York Museums Trust (Yorkshire Museum). YORYM. 1971 221.*

190. SAUCER. D. – 7 in (177mm). No mark. See also Plates – 201, 202 and 203, none of which is marked. However, marked examples are illustrated by A.W. Coysh in his *Blue-Printed Earthenware 1800 - 1850*, at Plates 48 and 48a.

191. PLATE. D. – 8 1/4 in. (209mm). Mark No. 1. *Doncaster Museum Service. DONMG. 1985.326.*

194

192

195

193

192, 193, 194 & 195 – All *en suite.* COFFEE POT. Ht. – 8 1/4 in. (209mm) No mark. SUGAR BOX & TEA POT. Tea pot Ht. – 4 1/8 in. (105mm) No mark on either piece. SAUCER, TEA BOWL AND PLATE. Plate D. – 6 1/2 in (164mm). Mark No. 1, impressed twice. TWO MILK JUGS. Right hand jug Ht. – 5 1/4 in. (133mm). Neither is marked. *Leeds Museums & Galleries. 4.28/46.*

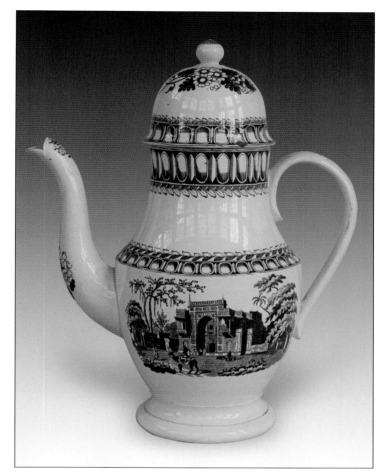

197

196, 197 & 198 – All *en suite*. COFFEE POT. Ht. – 8 in. (203mm) Mark No. 2a. BOWL. D. – 6 3/4 in. (171mm) Mark No. 2a. JUG. OAHt. – 5 1/4 in. (133mm) No mark. See FOBB 93/6 and 88/8. *Astley Hall Museum & Art Gallery, Chorley. CHOAH. F12 - 2, 5, & 4.*

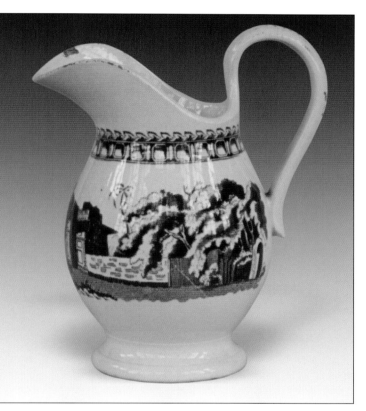

198

199. PLATE. D. – 8 3/8 in. (213mm). Mark No. 1. This pattern is well known as a product of Rogers of Staffordshire. See also Plate 228. *Doncaster Museum Service.DONMG. 1985.327.*

200. PLATE. D. – 6 3/8 in. (161mm). Mark No. 1. See Plate 216.

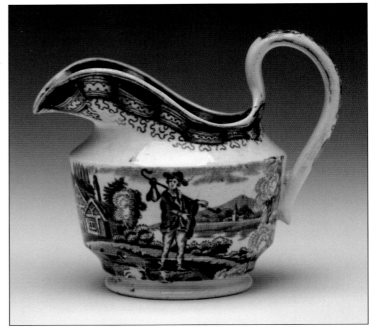

203. CREAM JUG. OAHt. – 4 1/4 in. (108mm). No mark, see caption to Plate190.

201 & 202. BUTTER TUB AND STAND. Butter tub: L. – 8 1/8 in. (206mm). Stand: L. – 9 1/4 in. (235mm). Neither piece is marked. See Plate 190.

204. PLATE. D. – 9 7/8 in. (251mm). Mark No. 3a. By the blue/black colour of this print I would presume that it was probably such a colour which persuaded the partners to cease preparing their own cobalt oxide and to purchase it ready prepared, see Appx. IV. B, p. 583. This is an early line-engraved print. See FOBB 23/8 where a marked jug is illustrated.

205. PLATE. D. – 10 in. (254mm). Mark No 1. The ubiquitous standard Willow Pattern. It is, however, very rare to find a piece which is marked as this one is. Connie Rodgers, of the USA, who has been collecting and studying this pattern for many years and who recently published the results of her studies has reported never seeing a piece marked Leeds Pottery. Many shards of standard Willow Pattern have been excavated on the Pottery site which belong to the period after the end of the Hartley Greens & Co's period. *Collection of Graham Oliver.*

206. TEA CANISTER. D. – 3 1/2 in. (89mm). Mark No. 1. POTTED MEAT DISH. L. – 5 1/2 in. (139mm). Mark No. 1.e. and '4' & 'W' impressed. The Leeds version of the 'Conversation' pattern with its distinctive inverted 'V' shaped bridge. *Leeds Museums & Galleries. 1928.29 & 16.226/47.*

207. TEA CANISTER. Ht. – 5 in. (127mm). Mark No. 1b. *York Museums Trust (Yorkshire Museum). YORYM. 1971. 252.*

208, a,b & c. MUG. Ht. – 5 in. (127mm). Mark No. 1. Yet another chinoiserie pattern, a larger image of which may be seen on the smaller jug at Plate 209.

209. TWO JUGS. Left: Ht. – 7 5/8 in. (193mm). Mark No. 1. Right: Ht. – 9 1/8 in. (232mm). Mark No. 1.e. *Leeds Museums & Galleries. 10.16-18/38.*

210. TWIG BASKET. 9 7/8 in. x 8 1/4 in. (251mm x 209mm). Mark No. 1b. Leeds standard 'Long Bridge' pattern – see Plates 211, 212 and 213 for its use on different shaped wares.

211. SAUCE TUREEN AND LID. Ht. – 4 1/8 in. (105mm). Mark No. 1 and '18' impressed. *Leeds Museums & Galleries. 10.73/38.*

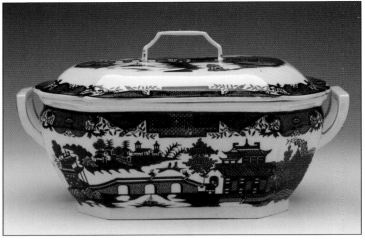

212. TUREEN AND LID. OAL. – 14 1/2 in. (368mm). Mark No. 1 impressed twice. *Leeds Museums & Galleries. 16.282/47.*

213. DISH. 11 5/8 in. x 7 3/8 in. (295mm x 187mm). Mark No. 1 and 'M' impressed. *York Museums Trust (Yorkshire Museum). 2001.4962.*

214. PLATE. D. – 7 1/8 in (180mm). Mark No.1 and 'U' impressed. Notice the three different concentric border patterns.

215. PLATE. D. – 7 in. (177mm). Mark No. 1 and '5' impressed. The Leeds version of the 'Tall Door' print. *York Museums Trust (Yorkshire Museum). 1971.239.*

216. PLATE. D. – 6 3/8 in. (161mm). Mark No. 1 and '8' impressed. See also Plate 200 for a brown version of this print.

217. TEA POT. Ht. – 4 1/2 in. (114mm). Mark No. 1b. Heather Lawrence called this pattern 'Cottage and Vase'. *York Museums Trust (Yorkshire Museum). 1971.270.*

218. PLATE. D. – 8 in. (203mm). Mark No. 1. *Doncaster Museum Service. DONMG. 1985.343.*

219. COFFEE POT. Ht. – 7 in. (177mm). No mark, see Plates 217 & 218.

220. SUCKLING POT. Ht. – 3 7/8 in. (98mm). No mark, see Plates 217 & 218.

221. PLATE. D. – 10 1/8 in. (257mm). No mark, see Plate 222. This pattern was also used by the Don Pottery and has been called 'Jar & Fisherman'. See *The Don Pottery 1801-1893*, Plate 45 and FOBB 80/6.

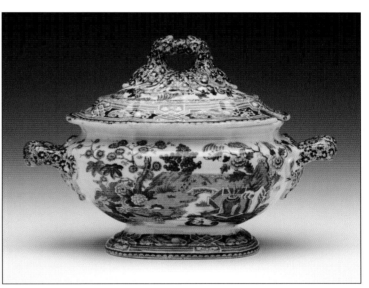

222. SAUCE TUREEN AND LID. Ht. – 3 1/2 in. (89mm). Mark No. 2a.

223. PLATE. D. – 9 5/8 in. (244mm). Mark No. 2a. A well printed pattern on a white-ware body and glaze.

224. SAUCER. D. – 5 3/8 in. (136mm). Mark No. 2d. This pattern has recently been recorded on a marked Don Pottery cup and saucer. See FOBB 11/3 where two parts of this print have been used on a bowl.

226. DISH. 13 1/2 in. x 10 1/4 in. (343mm x 260mm). Mark No. 1b. and '3' impressed. This is 'The Great Wall of China' print.

227. SAUCE BOAT. OAL. – 6 3/4 in. (171mm). No mark, see Plate 226. Interestingly the Pottery had this print engraved the same size mirror image, thus enabling the print to be applied twice, symmetrically, to pots such as this sauce boat. *Collection of Graham Oliver.*

228. PLATE. D. – 8 1/4 in. (209mm). Mark No. 1.e.

225. PLATE. D. – 9 in. (228mm). Mark No. 1b. This print is taken from Thomas Daniell's *Oriental Scenery*, Part I, Pl. 21, a view entitled "Near Currah, on the river Ganges", published as an aquatint in November 1796. Leeds also produced this print in the gray/brown colour seen at Plates 187 – 190. See FOBB 83/3. *York Museums Trust (Yorkshire Museum). YORYM 1971.231.*

229. PLATE. D. – 9 1/2 in. (241mm). Mark No. 2a and '2' impressed. Known as 'Scene after Claude Lorraine'. It is fortuitous that this plate has been personalised and dated 1819, showing that the Pottery had, by this date and probably under the influence of Thomas Lakin, taken to printing on a fine white earthenware in place of the earlier pearlware which often is seen to have had an over-generous addition of cobalt oxide. This plate and the one at Plate 230 show the use of two different border prints to the main scene. Six different border prints so far have been recorded, all of which are composed mainly of rural English scenes together with some in which palm trees are included. A version of this print was used by Riley of Staffordshire. See FOBB 80/6. *Doncaster Museum Service. DONMG. 1985.330.*

230. PLATE. D. – 8 3/8 in. (213mm). Mark No.1. See the caption to Plate 229.

231 & 232. MUG. Ht. – 6 1/8 in. (155mm). Mark No.1. The significance of the swan in the oval surround and 'No. 3' cannot at present be explained. *York Museums Trust (Yorkshire Museum).YORYM. 1971.266.*

233. PLATE. D. – 8 1/4 in. (209mm). Mark No. 1. 'Flowers and Butterflies' pattern. *York Museums Trust (Yorkshire Museum). YORYM 1971.218.*

234. PLATE. D. – 8 1/4 in. (209mm). Mark No. 1 and 'C' impressed. 'Flower Groups' pattern. *York Museums Trust (Yorkshire Museum). YORYM 1971.220.*

235. PLATE. D. – 8 1/4 in. (209mm). Mark No. 1 and '7' impressed. 'Shell' pattern. See FOBB 23/8.

236. CREAM JUG. OAL. – 5 5/8 in. (142mm). Mark No. 1 and '1' impressed. 'Shell' pattern.

237. SOAP BOX. 3 1/2 in. x 2 5/8 in. (89mm x 67mm). Mark No. 1b. 'Shell' pattern. *York Museums Trust (Yorkshire Museum). YORYM. 1971.255a and b.*

238. MUG. Ht. – 4 1/8 in. (105mm). Mark No. 2.a. Blue printed wares which have been enamelled over are quite rare from the Leeds Pottery. *Leeds Museums & Galleries. 16.237/47.*

239. PICKLE DISH. L. – 7 1/4 in. (183mm). Mark No. 1b.

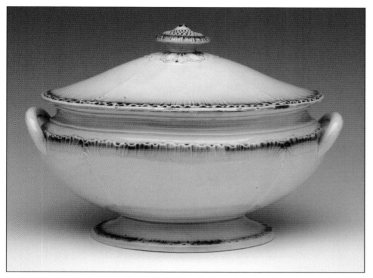

240. TUREEN. 13 in. x 9 in. (330mm x 228mm). Mark No. 1. *York Museums Trust (Yorkshire Museum). YORYM. 2001.2322.*

241. PLATE. D. – 9 3/4 in. (248mm). Mark No. 1. *Doncaster Museum Service. DONMG. 1983.228.*

242. PICKLE DISH. L. – 5 1/4 in. (133mm). Mark No. 1b. *York Museums Trust (Yorkshire Museum) YORYM. 1971.261.*

243. TEA CANISTER. Ht. – 4 1/2 in. (114mm). Mark No. 1 and 4g. This painted pattern was used by many potteries. *York Museums Trust (Yorkshire Museum). YORYM. 1971.251.*

244. PLATE. D. – 8 1/8 in. (206mm). Mark No. 1. See Plate 292 for a similar version enamelled in pink, blue and green.

245. PLATE. D. – 9 1/2 in. (241mm). Mark No. 1. Pattern No. 293 in the *Enamelled Table Service Drawing Book*. Shards with this pattern have been recovered from the Swinton Pottery site indicating its manufacture there, most likely during the Greens Bingley partnership. It was also used by Spode, see Robert Copeland, *Spode's Willow Pattern and other designs after the Chinese*, p. 15.

246. PLATE. D. – 8 1/4 in. (209mm). Mark No. 1 and '7' impressed. Such underglaze painted patterns were common to many potteries. *Leeds Museums & Galleries. TN79/P*

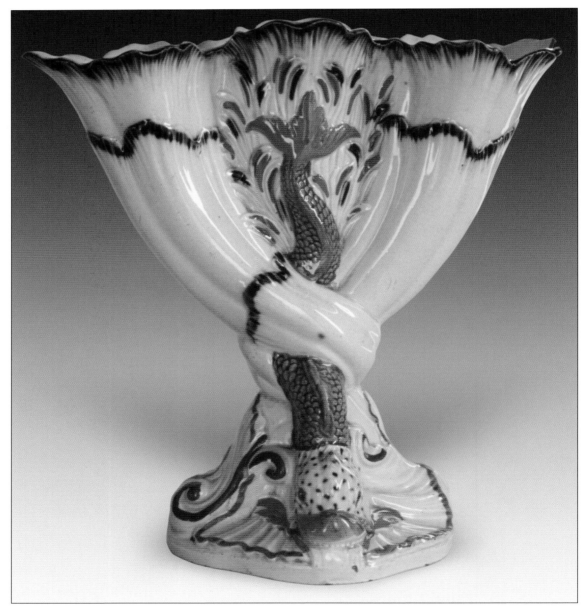

247. VASE. Ht. – 7 1/8 in. (180mm). Mark No.1. *Tyne & Wear County Museums Service. TWCMS. E2436.*

248. VASE. Ht. – 7 in. (177mm). Mark No. 1 and '18' impressed. *Leeds Museums & Galleries. 16.127/47.*

250. TEAPOT. D. – 5 3/8 in. (136mm). Mark No.1. Dipped and engine turned decoration as we see here may be seen in many variations in both geometric designs and other single or multiple colour patterns at Plates 972, 983, 996, 1013 to 1015 and 1018 to 1020 which are just three of the groups of such decoration in the *New Teapot Drawing Book. Victoria & Albert Museum. 3558-1901.*

249. SAUCE BOAT. OAL. – 6 1/4 in. (158mm). Mark No.1. The underglaze pattern is No. 388 in the *New Teapot Drawing Book. Victoria & Aibert Museum. C.40-1967.*

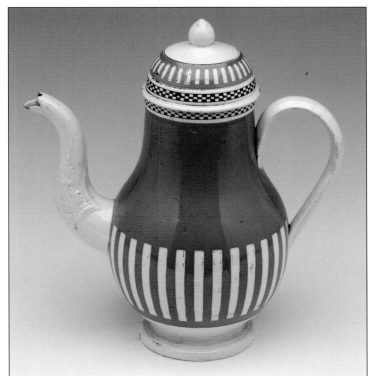

251. COFFEE POT. Ht. – 7 5/8 in. (193mm). Mark No.1. See caption to Plate 250. The moulded design on the spout is, I believe, peculiar to the Leeds Pottery. Block moulds survive for it in the Temple Newsam Collection. *York Museums Trust (Yorkshire Museum). YORYM 2001.2228.*

252 & 253. MUG. Ht. – 5 1/8 in. (130mm). No mark. See edge decoration at Plate 127 and lettering at Plate 255. *Leeds Museums & Galleries. 2000/0018.*   253

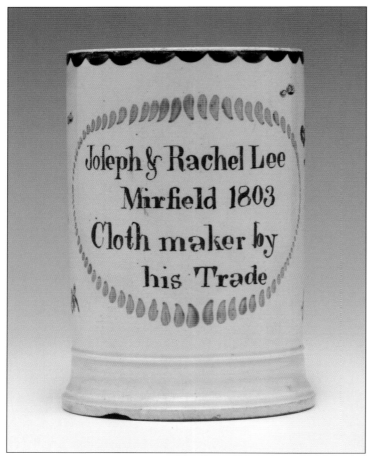

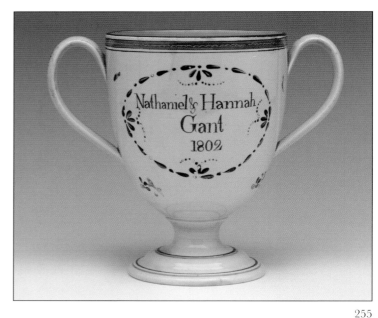

255

254. MUG. Ht. – 6 1/8 in. (155mm). No mark. Joseph Lee had married Rachel Brook at Mirfield on the 6th of April 1797. *IGI.* Mirfield is a town four and three-quarter miles north east of Huddersfield which is famous for its woollen cloths. Another mug whose style of lettering has a dotted surround to the inscription, very similar to that at Plate 174, has been recorded; it is personalised for "John & Sarah Mitchell Kighley 1802". Keighley is a market town in Yorkshire nine miles north west of Bradford. *Leeds Museums & Galleries. LEEDM. ET.3.900.140.*

255 & 256. LOVING CUP. Ht. – 6 5/8 in. (168mm). Mark No.1. Nathaniel Gaunt had married Hannah Wheatley on the 1st of October 1792 at St. Peter's Church, Leeds. *IGI.*

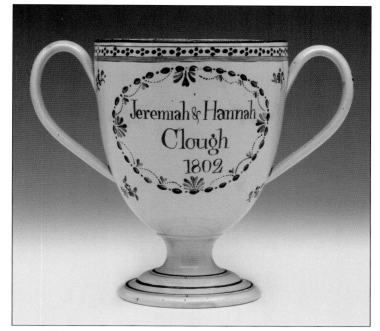

257. LOVING CUP. Ht. – 6 5/8 in. (168mm). Mark No.1. Jeremiah Clough had married Hannah Gaunt on the 13th of March 1791 at St. Peter's Church, Leeds. *IGI. Leeds Museums & Galleries. 4.38/46.*

258.a & b. JUG. Ht. – 6 1/2 in. (164mm). Mark No.1. This jug must rank as one of the most delightful jugs ever produced in this genre. It is well proportioned with two names and dated, which, with the two gardeners striking an almost ballet-like attitude, must have given satisfaction to its decorator and joy to its first and subsequent owners. Unfortunately I have been unable to trace either Elias or Elizabeth Wate.

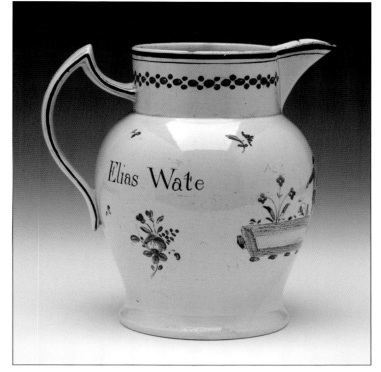

258a

259. JUG. Ht. – 6 in. (152mm). Mark No. 1. The writhen moulding of this jug could not have been the ideal surface for lettering. The following appears on the other side of the jug : "Who rail not at Kings/Nor Politick things/Nor treason will speak when he's mellow/But takes A full glass/to his Country Success/This is an honest brave fellow." The IGI records the marriage between a Benjamin Dean and Martha Worsnop at Calverley on the 27th of January 1794. Calverley is a parish 5 3/4 miles west-north-west of Leeds.

260 & 261. JUG. Ht. – 7 1/2 in. (190mm). Mark No.1. This is another fine and very interesting jug about which much more is now known. It was included in the NCS's 1997 exhibition *A Celebration of Yorkshire Pots*, No. 57 in the catalogue, for which I was fortunate to discover the following: It was first illustrated by the Kidson brothers in their monograph on the Leeds Pottery of 1892 at pl. 21 and referred to at p. 79 - "... It was said by the late owner to have been brought from America by a captain of a ship. ..." I am indebted to William Eldridge Miller, Genealogist, of Bowie, Maryland, USA., for researching and supplying the following information: General Hugh Mercer was the only General Mercer in the US Army in the period 1775 – 1801. A native of Scotland and a veteran of the battle of Culloden, he migrated to Pennsylvania and subsequently fought, with his troops, alongside Washington. He was one of the lead American officers in the battle of Princetown on the 3rd of January 1777 during which battle he received wounds from which he died on the 12th of January. During the same battle a Captain James Moore led a group of US troops which captured 194 British troops. Capt. James Moore commanded the First Regiment, Middlesex County, New Jersey militia. In the 1790 census, taken at Federal level, there was a James Gant living in South Huntingdon Township, Westmoreland County, State of Pennsylvania. Gant/Gaunt was quite a common name in the Leeds Area in the late 18th and early 19th centuries. *Leeds Museums & Galleries. 4/47/46.*

262. BIN LABELS. 5 1/4 in. x 3 1/4 in. (133mm x 83mm). All marked with mark No. 1b. except 'SHERRY' which has no mark. These are the only recorded bin labels marked Leeds Pottery. *Leeds Museums & Galleries :*
CLARET – *LEEDM . E.T.3.900.249.*   MADEIRA – *LEEDM .E.T.3.900.247*
SHERRY – *LEEDM .E.T.3.900.246.*   PORT – *LEEDM . E.T.3.900.248*

263. COFFEE CAN & SAUCER. Saucer D. – 5 in (127mm). No mark. See Plates 264 to 268. This pattern and the variation at Plates 264 – 268 are in the 'New Teapot Drawing Book', pattern No. 274 which is a copy of New Hall pattern No. 83 (see David Holgate *New Hall*, pl. L, opp. p. 116). The shape of the coffee can and saucer is what the Leeds Pottery called 'Grecian'. See the named handle shapes in the *Drawing Book No. 4* at Plate 795, and the thumbnail sketch of such a can and handle at Plate 507, dated the 28th of November 1790, in the *Original Drawing Book No. 1.*

264

265

267

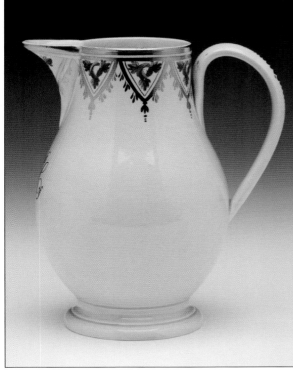

266

268

264, 265, 266, 267 & 268. COFFEE POT. Ht. – 8 7/8 in. (225mm). Mark No. 1. TEAPOT. OAL. – 11 in. (279mm). Body: 5 5/8 in x 5 1/4 in. x 4 1/8 in. high. (142mm x 133mm x 105mm) Mark No.1 and 'S' impressed. MILK JUG. Ht. – 5 3/8 in. (136mm). Mark No.1. BASIN. D. – 6 in. (152mm). No mark. SUCRIER. D. – 4 3/8 in. (111mm). No mark. A rare survival of such simple yet elegant forms coupled with a first-rate quality of decoration, not only of the border pattern but also the execution of the monogram 'MFC', all of which shows the excellency of the best work from this Pottery. These pieces have survived in almost pristine condition.

269. TEAPOT. Ht. – 5 1/2 in. (139mm). Mark No.1. This teapot is exactly the same mould as the porcelain example at Plate 334. The monogram is 'JMW'. *York Museums Trust (Yorkshire Museum). YORYM 1971.267.*

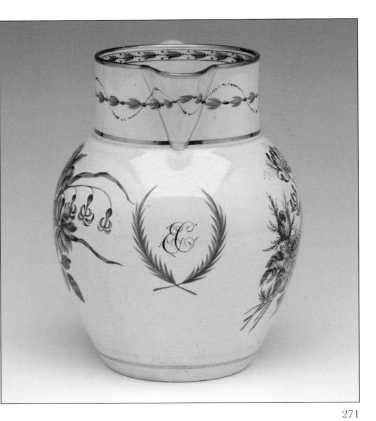

271

270

270, 271 & 272. JUG. Ht. – 6 5/8 in. (168mm). Mark No. 1 impressed twice and '8' impressed, also Mark No. 1d. Three views of another jug with excellent potting and top quality decoration. This shows that had the decision been made to move to large scale porcelain production they would have had the requisite skill, in house, to decorate to the standard which would have been required to hold their own with any competitor. This is the only example so far recorded with the enamelled mark, an indication of the importance attached to this jug by the Pottery. *York Museums Trust (Yorkshire Museum). YORYM. 2001.2233.*

273. JUG. OAHt. – 7 3/4 in. (196mm). Mark No. 1. The other side is decorated with a well executed painting of a spray of roses. Below the spout is "AP" as a monogram and, on a ribbon, the words "Alles um Liebe" – translation: "Everything for Love's Sake". *Victoria & Albert Museum. C.62-1932.*

274. TEA CANISTERS. Left: Ht. – 5 3/8 in. (136mm). Mark No. 1b. Centre: Ht. – 4 3/4 in. (120mm) Mark No.1. *Doncaster Museum Service. DONMG. 1989.163 & 1989.164.* Right: Ht. – 4 7/8 in. (124mm). Mark No. 1b. *Leeds Museums & Galleries. 16.46/47.* In the *Design Book* this shape is No. 10 in the Tea Wares section of the first edition and is described simply as "Square Cannister".

275. PUZZLE JUG. Ht. – 7 1/8 in. (180mm). Mark No.1 impressed twice and 'Wood 1803' inscribed. *Leeds Museums & Galleries. 4.59/46.*

276. PUZZLE JUG. Ht. – 10 3/8 in. (263mm). Mark No.1 and '4' impressed. Surely this is a de luxe version of this type of ware. It would have been quite a complicated item to construct. An added feature of this model is the well-moulded swan within the central 'cage'. This jug once belonged to Alfred Britton, one of Richard Britton's sons. It is described and illustrated by Llewellynn Jewitt in his *Ceramic Art* at Fig. 857 on p. 480 of Volume I. *Leeds Museums & Galleries. 16.134/47.*

277. COFFEE POT. Ht. – 8 1/8 in. (206mm). Mark No. 1. Although this decoration is not included in the extant pattern books there are several painted chinoiserie scenes in a similar vein. This is the only one of this kind which I have so far recorded. The knop on a small fragment of the original lid is also shown.

278. PLANT POT HOLDER AND STAND. Stand: D. – 6 in. (152mm). Mark No. 1 impressed twice. Plant Pot Holder: Ht. – 5 5/8 in. (142mm). Mark No. 1. It is a great pity that some of the yellow area has become discoloured yet it does not take too much imagination to visualise it as it was intended to look. The design of this piece is in the *Ornamental Drawing Book No.1*, at No. 16 which is illustrated here at Plate 815. *York Museums Trust (Yorkshire Museum). YORYM 1971.273.*

279. CRUET. L. – 9 1/8 in. (232mm). Mark No. 1. *Leeds Museums & Galleries. 4.23/46.*

281. TEA CUP AND SAUCER. Cup Ht. – 2 1/4 in. (57mm). Mark No. 4b on the saucer only. This is pattern No. 573 in the *New Teapot Drawing Book* and which is annotated "DP No. 561". It has been given the name 'propeller-blade pattern' on account of the three yellow parts of the top central flower. Several patterns on the same page are annotated "DP" indicating that the artist entered several Don Pottery patterns at the same time. This was a very common pattern used at the Don Pottery. To differentiate the Don from the Leeds version examine the flower standing apart at 4 o'clock on the saucer and notice that the two red flowers face the centre of the saucer and invariably downwards when on the sides of cups. On the Don version these always face outwards on flatware and upwards on the sides of cups, as shown in the pattern book. The Leeds Pottery seems to have deliberately altered this small feature. See *The Don Pottery 1801 - 1893*, p. 50 and Plates 10, 146, 147 & 148.

282. TEAPOT. Body L. – 6 3/8 in. (161mm). Mark No. 1. *Norfolk Museums Service (Norwich Castle Museum). NWHCM. 1992.226.468.*

280. CHOCOLATE STAND. L. – 6 3/4 in. (171mm). Mark No. 1b. This design is in the tea wares section of the *Design Book* at No. 33 and described as "Chocolate Stand, from 6 to 8 Inches". It is decorated with pattern No. 170 from the *Enamelled Table Service Drawing Book. Leeds Museums & Art Gallery. 1928.55.*

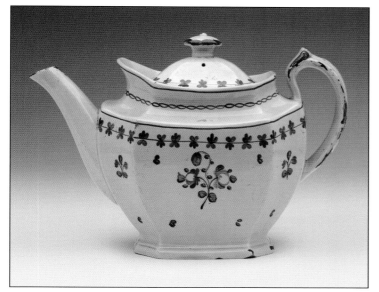

283. TEAPOT. OAL. – 9 1/2 in. (241mm). Mark No. 1. *Norfolk Museums Service (Norwich Castle Museum). NWHCM. 1992.226.472.*

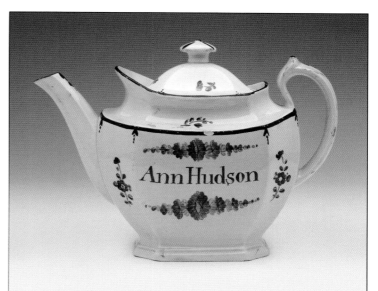

284. TEAPOT. OAL. – 9 1/2 in. (241mm). No Mark. (See Plates 283, 285 & 286/7). *Norfolk Museums Service (Norwich Castle Museum). NWCHM. 1992.226.470.*

285. TEAPOT. OAL. – 9 1/2 in. (241mm). Mark No. 1.

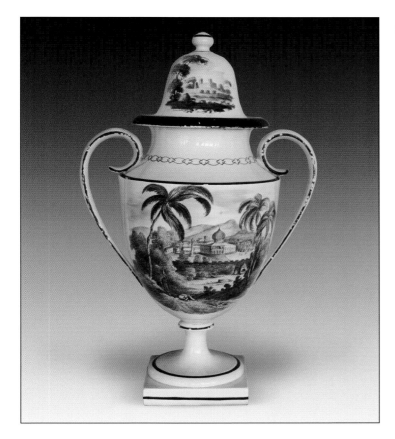

286 & 287. TEAPOT. OAL. – 9 5/8 in. (244mm). Mark No. 1b. A goat seems an incongruous creature to adorn the side of a teapot. The three ostrich feathers issuing from a coronet has, from the time of the accession of the House of Stuart up to the present day, been the special badge of the Prince of Wales. The monogram 'RML' is very well executed like other examples in this style. *Leeds Museums & Galleries. LEEDM E.3.1996.4.*

288. VASE. Ht. – 10 1/4 in. (260mm). Mark No. 2a impressed on the outside vertical surface of the base. Under the base in red script, enamelled: "Jerusalem in its Present State". The other side of this vase is finely enamelled with flowers, see the *Frontispiece*. The scene on the lid is not named. *Leeds Museums & Galleries. 1928.10.*

289. PLATE. D. – 8 3/8 in. (213mm). Mark No. 1.

292. PLATE. D. – 8 3/8 in. (213mm). Mark No. 1. This pattern is a variation of the one more usually seen in underglaze blue, see Plate 244.

290. PLATE. D. – 7 1/4 in. (183mm). Mark No. 1 and 'G' impressed. *Doncaster Museum Service DONMG. 1985.324.*

293. PLATE. D. – 8 7/8 in. (225mm). Mark No. 1.

291. PLATE. D. – 7 3/8 in. (187mm). Mark No. 1 and '8' impressed. *Yorks Museums Trust (Yorkshire Museum). YORYM. 1971.219.*

294. PLATE. D. – 8 1/4 in. (209mm). Mark No. 1. A very similar pattern in monochrome is in the *Enamelled Tea Ware 1819* book at No. 25. Seen here in polychrome one cannot help but admire the skill required to produce such an even effect. *Doncaster Museum Service. DONMG. 1992.214.*

295. PLATE. D. – 8 7/8 in. (225mm). Mark No. 2d. *York Museums Trust (Yorkshire Museum). YORYM. 2001.4946.*

296,297 & 298. SIX PLATES. All Plates D. – 8 3/8 in. (213mm) and all marked with Mark No. 1. *Leeds Museums & Galleries.* The specimens are named in enamel under each plate and were copied from Curtis' *Botanical Magazine,* Plate number and year of publication being shown in square brackets :

296. – Left, (10.55/38) – Two Leaved Lady's Slipper. [192, 1792]. – Right, (10.50/38) – Everlasting Pea. [unknown*].

297. – Left, (10.48/38) – Sweat Pea. [60, 1788]. – Right, (10.49/38) –Yellow Lupine. [140, 1790].

298. – Left, (10.53/38) – Verginia Lungwort. [160, 1791]. – Right, (10.51/38) – Periwinkle. [248, 1793].

* After extensive searches in both the index and the plates of Curtis no specimen of either this name or appearance has been found. I am also very grateful for the work carried out by James Kay, Assistant Illustration Curator, of the Royal Botanic Gardens Library at Kew who has also searched *Curtis* and other publications and indexes, but in vain.

297

298

299. PLATE. D. – 8 1/2 in. (216mm). Mark No. 1. The specimen named on the base "Winged Passion Flower", copied from Curtis' *Botanical Magazine*, Plate No. 66, pub., 1788. The most heavily gilded decoration on pearlware so far recorded from the Leeds Pottery. *Leeds Museums & Art Gallery.44/79.*

300. BOUGH POT. L. – 9 1/2 in. (241mm) Ht. – 6 in. (152mm). Mark No. 1. Creamware. This is the only marked Leeds Pottery bough pot which I have recorded. The design is to be found at No. 21 in the *Ornamental Drawing Book No.1* which may be seen at Plate 820. This pot is only glazed on the inside and unfortunately the exposed biscuit creamware body, between the painted decoration, has become quite dirty over the last two centuries. However, when it was new, the contrast between the unglazed near-white body and the red and black decoration enhanced with gilding would have produced a splendid object to grace the mantlepiece of its original owner. A considerable proportion of the original gilding has disappeared which may indicate that it might have been leaf gilding, (see p. 537). The original pierced lid is missing. *Courtesy of Salford Museum and Art Gallery.*

301. THREE-PIECE JARDINIÈRE. Bowl: Ht. – 10 3/4 in. (273mm), D. – 14 1/4 in. (361mm) no marks. Socle: Ht. – 5 in. (127mm), D. – 10 1/2 in. (266mm) Mark No. 1. Dish: D. – 14 1/2 in. (368mm) Mark No. 1. There is a central drainage hole in the bowl and the socle. The vertical blue striped decoration, in two bands round the bowl and in one round the dish has been enhanced to create a three dimensional appearance to the stripes – each of which is on a sharply formed facet. The continuous floral and leaf decoration around the base of the socle is similar to Pattern No. 82 in the *Enamelled Tea Ware 1819* book, illustrated at Plate 1058. *Leeds Museums & Galleries. 41/252 LH..*

Figures

The Leeds Pottery produced quite a range of figures of different sizes. They were made in plain creamware, which is very rare, and plain or enamelled pearlware. The figures are frequently factory marked, LEEDS POTTERY, impressed but the prospective buyer needs to be aware that marked plain creamware figures, from the same moulds, were made by the revivalist Senior, see pages 612, 613.

Two features of the figures of the type illustrated at Plates, 305 to 308 are :

1. All the heads give the impression of being made from the same mould, whether male or female.
2. The figures and their bases are both hollow right up into the body of the figure. If the base is square then one frequently finds a vertical line up the inside corners where it is presumed that the modeller had pressed the clay into the corner of the mould with the fine edge of one of his tools, see Plate 302.

The large figure of the horse at Plates 322 and 323 is in itself something of an achievement of the potter's skill in that such a large body is supported on the four slender, well-moulded, ceramic legs. These figures were also reproduced by the Seniors in creamware, the originals only being in pearlware with the ears set almost vertical in an alert attitude. See page 608 & Plate 1125 for further comments regarding Senior's horses.

302. VIEW UNDER THE BASE of the figure of Venus illustrated at Plate 319, right, to show the construction of Leeds figures. Notice that the figure is hollow and that there are incised marks in the corners of the base, also that the figure is glazed inside. *Leeds Museums & Galleries. 16.194/47.*

303. FIGURES OF MINERVA & MARS. Ht. of Minerva – 10 1/2 in. (266mm) with Mark No. 1 impressed twice. Ht. of Mars – 10 1/4 in. (260mm) with Mark No.1. *Leeds Museums & Galleries. 16.198/47 and 16.200/47.*

304. FIGURES OF THE SEASONS. Ht. of Spring – 6 1/4 in. (158mm). All have Mark No. 1 except Autumn which is unmarked. *Leeds Museums & Galleries. 16.193/47; 16.202/47; 16.203/47 & 16.208/47.*

308. FIGURE OF A FALCONER. Ht. – 7 1/2 in. (190mm). Mark No.1.
Leeds Museums & Galleries. 14.20/48

305, 306 & 307. PAIR OF FIGURES in three different finishes their heights ranging from 7 3/8 in. (187mm) to 7 5/8 in. (193mm). The pair of creamware figures at Plate 305 are very rare and are unmarked. They are from a private collection. The figures at plates 306 and 307 show the same figures with different finishes, plain pearlware and pearlware enamelled. It is also instructive to study the details bearing in mind that although the components of these figures would have come from the same moulds, they were assembled by the 'repairers' and therefore some details do not always match exactly, e.g. observe the height and angle at which the male figure is holding the tambourine. Plates 306 and 307 – Mark No. 1 on each figure.
Leeds Museums & Galleries. 16.305/47 & 16.206/47.

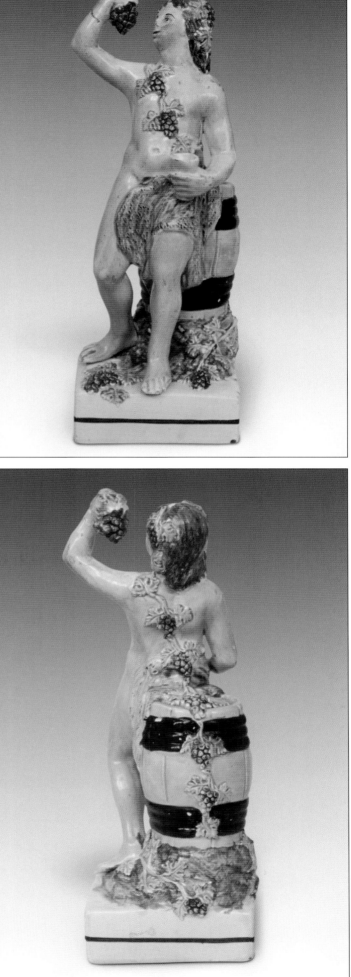

309 & 310. FIGURE OF A HARVESTER. Ht. – 7 3/8 in. (187mm). Mark No. 1. The only example of this figure so far recorded. The remains of what may be presumed to be his scythe stail and the position of his hands would indicate a plausible reason for the name given to this model.

311 & 312. FIGURE OF BACCHUS. Ht. – 7 5/8 in. (193mm). Mark No. 1.

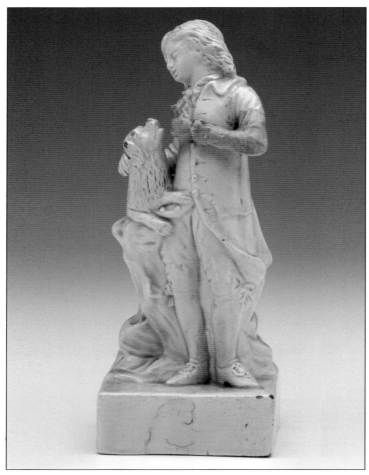

313. FIGURE OF A BOY WITH A DOG. Ht. – 6 1/4 in. (158mm). Mark No. 1. See also Plate 315. *Leeds Museums & Galleries. 16.205/47.*

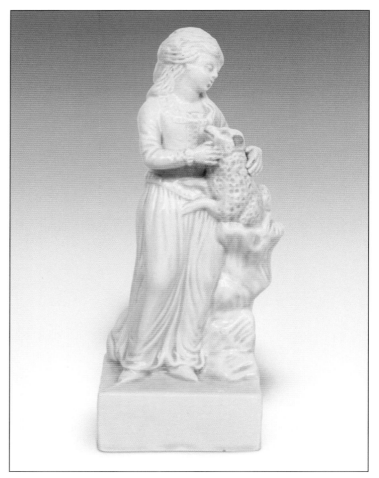

314. FIGURE OF A GIRL WITH A LAMB. Ht. – 6 1/4 in. (158mm). Mark No. 1.

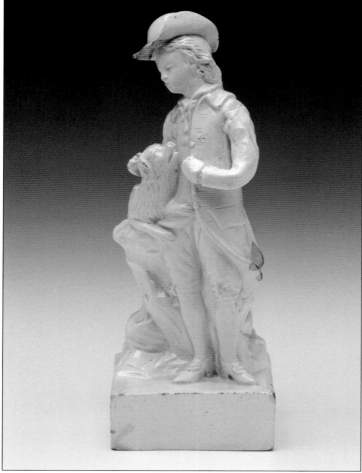

315. FIGURE. Ht. – 6 5/8 in. (168mm). No mark. A very rare figure being one of only three plain creamware figures presently recorded. It is also rare in that no other figure is known with a hat of this style. However everything about this figure proclaims it to be a Leeds figure – compare the details with Plate 313. The figure's left arm is a replacement.

316. FIGURE OF ISAAC NEWTON. Ht. – 10 1/8 in. (257mm). Mark No. 1 impressed twice. Strangely the figure does not show him with a Newtonian reflecting telescope. *Leeds Museums & Galleries. 16.199/47.*

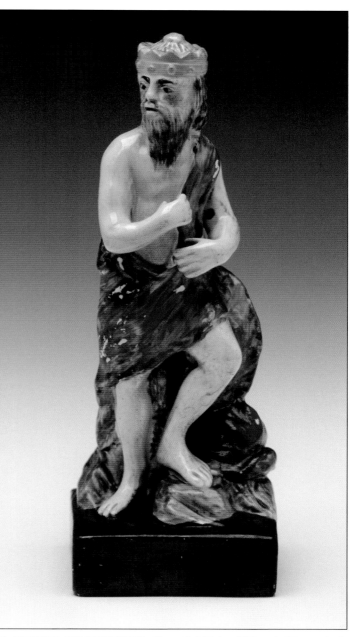

317. FIGURE OF VENUS. Ht. – 7 1/2 in. (190mm). No mark but see Plate 319 for two marked examples. See also the caption to Plate 318.

318. FIGURE OF NEPTUNE. Ht. – 7 3/8 in. (187mm). No mark. It makes a pair with Venus at Plate 317, again unmarked. Two marked examples of Venus are illustrated at Plate 319. This example and that at Plate 317, its pair, illustrate a less common heavily enamelled base. *Doncaster Museum Service. DONMG. 1998.20.*

319. FIGURE OF VENUS. Ht. of both – 7 5/8 in. (193mm). Both figures with mark No. 1. The figures arranged to show both sides, see also plates 309/310 and 311/312. Figures which are well modelled all round indicate that they were made to decorate the table where such modelling could be appreciated. Such ceramic figures had replaced the more transient sugar figures which, at an earlier date and in wealthy households had been made by the confectioners. See. Philippa Glanville & Hilary Young, *Elegant Eating.* Victoria & Albert Museum Publication, 2002. *Leeds Museums & Galleries. 16.207/47 & 16.194/47.*

320 & 321. FIGURE OF ANDROMACHE. Ht. – 12 1/2 in. (317mm). Pl. 320 has Mark No. 1; Pl. 321 is not marked. Figure 320 only, *Leeds Museums & Galleries. 16.196/47.*

322 & 323. FIGURE OF A HORSE. OAL.– 14 1/2 in (368mm). OAHt. – 17 in. (432mm). Mark No. 3d. on the rear bottom square of the saddle cloth on the horse at Plate 322. Please note that all genuine Leeds horses were only made in pearlware and that any encountered in creamware were made by the Seniors, see Appendix IX. G.W. Senior recorded, in an interview with Peter Walton, of which transcript notes were kept, that the Seniors' horses had the angle of the ears altered to point forwards in order to make them appear as "Wild horses of the field". Pl. 322: *York Museums Trust (Yorkshire Museum).YORYM. 2001.420.* Pl. 323: *Leeds Museums & Galleries. 16.180/4.*

Lustre Decoration

Included under this heading are both pink and 'silver' lustre as well as tinselling.

Pink Lustre. This form of decoration is well known from the countless examples which have survived, many of them erroneously attributed to the potteries of the North East.

It is produced from a mixture of gold and tin; reducing the amount of tin results in a stronger purple colour. Marked examples from the Leeds Pottery are few in number. The salt, at Plate 324, with overall coverage is sometimes called 'oil-splat' lustre. The very fine fruit basket and stand, at Plate 327, shows the plain pink lustre used as a border line decoration. W.D. John and Warren Baker in their *Old English Lustre Pottery* illustrate a pair of salts: Illustration 56A – from the "Mrs.Holden Collection, Sibdon Castle, Shropshire." See also comments on "Persian Gold" at page 566.

Silver Lustre. This is the modern name for a decorative effect which, although it resembles silver, is produced by the use of platinum. When it was first introduced regularly by John Hancock in 1804, it was called 'Steel' lustre, no doubt on account of it resembling very closely the appearance of the cut-steel jewellery which was then very fashionable. It was used either as an overall coating as on the mug at Plate 328 or more decoratively by means of the 'resist' process, as at Plates 330 and 331. The technique consisted of covering the areas not to be 'silvered' with a resist medium which would burn off in the kiln leaving the 'silvered' areas to fuse with the underlaying glaze. the 'silvered' areas did not require burnishing when the wares came out of the kiln. Please see pages 615, 616 for the use of silver lustre decoration as used by the revivalist Senior.

Tinselling. The appropriate definition in the OED. "Tinsel v^2 1.b. to embellish (ceramic ware) with metallic effects ... Hence Tinselling."

Some patterns in the Leeds pattern books are annotated with the instructions "tinselling" (see Plates 1048 and 1049). It is impossible to state precisely what was meant by this term when written. Did it infer any metallic lustre decoration or perhaps the sort of effect which is seen on the drab-ware dish at Plate 338 where the red flowers, unlike all the other enamelled pattern, have been given a definite metallic sheen? Llewellynn Jewitt gave the following definition in his article in *The Art Journal* of 1865 at page 308:

"...'Tinselling,' it must be understood, is the peculiar process by which a part of the pattern is made to assume a metallic appearance by being washed here and there over the transfer or drawing. Examples of Leeds ware of this kind are in the possession of Mr. Manning and of Mr. Davis.*

*These examples are plates, and cup and saucer. They are marked with the curved mark to be hereafter described [*i.e.* the 'horseshoe' mark No. 2.d]. ... The cup and saucer in Mr. Davis's possession have flowers and rude landscape in colours and copper-coloured 'tinsel.' "

324. SALT. L. – 3 1/2 in. (89mm). Mark No. 2d. *York Museum Trust (Yorkshire Museum). YORYM 200.4711.*

325. PLATE, CUP & SAUCER. Plate D. – 7 3/8 in. (187mm). Mark No. 2a and '12' impressed on plate only. This style of decoration is usually associated with wares produced for sale in the USA. *Leeds Museums & Galleries.* 51.2/86 & 51.3/86.

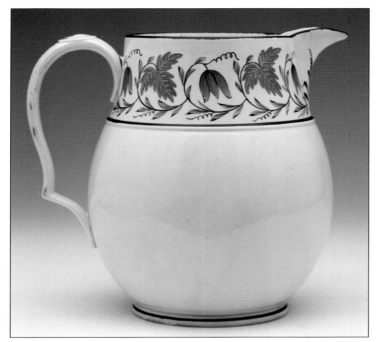

326. JUG. Ht. – 7 3/8 in. (187mm). Mark No. 2a. The very distinctive handle design with an oval raised thumb pad on top is represented, with minor alterations to its proportions, in the *Handle Drawing Book* – No.25 at Plate 805.

327. FRUIT BASKET AND STAND. Stand: 10 1/4 in. x 8 1/2 in. (260mm x 216mm). Mark either No. 2a or No. 2d. As the body of this basket is probably the same as shown at Plates 340 to 347 I would guess that it will be Mark No.2d. *Image supplied by the Antique Collectors' Club with the kind permission of Mrs. Dorothy Gibson, widow of the late Michael Gibson in whose book "19th Century Lustreware" it was published at p. 156.*

328. MUG. Ht. – 3 7/8 in. (98mm). Mark No. 2a. Overall silver lustre on a redware body. *Leeds Museums & Galleries. 16.217/47.*

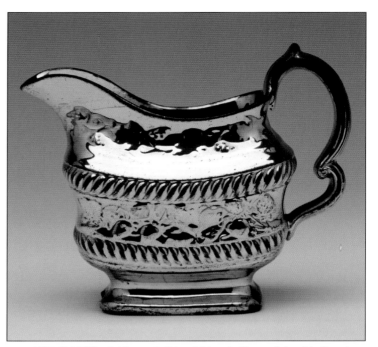

329. CREAM JUG. OAL. – 5 3/8 in. (136mm). No mark but I believe it to be Leeds on account of the marked examples of Black Basalt ware of this design, both body and handle. The only other factory that I am aware of which did similar strawberry-moulded tea wares was Riley. However the characteristics of this piece clearly indicate a Leeds rather than a Riley origin. See further information at Plate 393. Attention is also drawn to *19th Century Lustreware* by Michael Gibson, Colour Plate 68 on p. 79, where a pearlware cream jug is illustrated with enamel and pink-lustre decoration on the same body-moulded decoration as on the Leeds design but with a different handle, unfortunately it is un-marked. *Leeds Museums & Galleries. E.62.61.3*

330. DISH. D. – 14 3/8 in. (365mm). Mark No. 1 and '15' impressed. A very similar piece is in the Fitzwilliam Museum and is illustrated in the *Catalogue of the Glaisher Collection*, pl. 74 A. *Leeds Museums & Galleries. LEEDM.ET.3.900.012.*

331. DISH. 16 1/4 in. x 12 1/4 in. (412mm x 311mm). Mark No. 1. Silver resist lustre-decorated jugs with this same decoration have also been recorded. See W.D. John & Warren Baker, *Old English Lustre Pottery*, where they illustrate a three-gallon jug with the same lion decoration. A smaller jug of one-gallon capacity, of the same shape and again with the same decoration, is illustrated by W.T. Lawrence and H.C. Lawlor in "Silver Lustre, Part II", *The Connoisseur*, July 1904 at p. 151. Both the above jugs are unmarked. *The Nelson-Atkins Museum of Art, Kansas City, Missouri (Gift of Mr. & Mrs. Frank P. Burnap) ref: 41-23/546. Photograph by Jamison Miller.*

Felspathic Stoneware

I am only aware of one marked example of this type of ware; it is illustrated by Diana Edwards and Rodney Hampson in their *English Dry-Bodied Stoneware*, at Fig.173, page 138. The piece in question is a plain, smear-glazed, sucrier and lid with Mark No. 2.a., – see the introductory notes to this mark on page 111 where I have reasoned that this mark was not introduced until 1812. The two unmarked teapots illustrated below at Plates 332 and 333 are both from the same designs as Basalt examples which feature in the *Drawing Book for Blackware*, post 1812 section.

332. TEAPOT. Ht. – 4 1/2 in. (114mm). No mark. This teapot matches exactly No. 86 in the *Drawing Book for Blackware 1806*, post 1812 section, see caption to Plate 390.

333. TEAPOT. OAL. – 10 in. (254mm). No mark. This teapot matches exactly No. 87 in the *Drawing Book for Blackware 1806*, post 1812 section, see caption to Plate 393. *Norfolk Museums Service (Norwich Castle Museum). NWHCM. 1946.70.274.*

Porcelain

I am only aware of one piece of marked porcelain from the Leeds Pottery, see Plate 334. Interestingly this teapot matches in its moulded details a marked pearlware example in the Yorkshire Museum which I have illustrated at Plate 269.

The overall appearance of this solitary example of porcelain gives the impression that it is what we now term 'hybrid hard paste'. Although the enamelling and the gilding are very competently executed the body shows several stress cracks indicating that the maker had not fully mastered the technicalities of working in this medium. I have only come across one other reference to a possible piece of Leeds porcelain. In the catalogue of an exhibition held in Leeds in 1868, in "Section V English Porcelain", at No. 2368 was listed a "Leeds ware Coffee Pot". As there was a separate section for Pottery and also the fact that the coffee pot in question was loaned by that eminent nineteenth-century collector of ceramics Emerson Norman I feel confident that this pot would have been in the appropriate section – but was it correctly attributed to the Leeds Pottery?

I have often been asked the question in respect of both the Leeds and the Don Potteries which both made some porcelain: "Why didn't they make more?" To answer this question we must revert to some comments which I have made earlier, namely that a potter's sole *raison d'être* for being in business was, and still is, to earn a living, i.e. to make a reasonable profit above the overheads of running the pottery. The proprietors of the Leeds and the Don potteries, having experimented and then realised

what would be involved in providing: workers skilled in a different medium, separate working space and higher firing temperatures, therefore more fuel – all of which would amount to higher production costs. When all these factors were considered, and no doubt the potters simultaneously realising that their earthenware business was in a healthy state – why bother changing horses if they were already riding a winner? We must also bear in mind that until the Bramelds started to make bone china in c.1826 that there was not another nearby pottery from which to entice workers skilled in this branch of the trade.

334. TEAPOT. Ht. – 5 1/8 in. (130mm). Mark No. 1. and 'P' in script scratched on the base. The monogram is 'RMG'. This is the only presently known piece of porcelain from the Leeds Pottery. There are several stress cracks on the inside surface and it gives the impression of being what we now call 'hybrid hard paste'. A pearlware example of exactly the same mould is illustrated at Plate 269. *Leeds Museums & Galleries. 2/75.*

Coloured Glazes and Drabware Bodies

The Leeds Pottery, like other potteries, had to produce what the market demanded and, moreover, to produce it quickly before such a 'taste' went out of fashion and therefore became unsaleable. As the Pottery was catering for an extensive export market as well as the home market this may well have entailed the production of a wide range of styles simultaneously.

Coloured Glazes

Yellow-glazed wares were obviously produced very successfully, see Plates 336 and 337 and the *Enamelled Tea Ware 1819*, book: Nos. 42 to 47 at Plates 1051 and 1052. The reader's attention is also drawn to J.Jefferson Miller's *English Yellow Glazed Earthenware*, where at Plate 45 is shown, unfortunately in black and white, a two handled bowl of diameter: 8 3/4 in. (222mm), mark No. 2a or d. It is decorated with weapons, trophies and flags commemorating Brazil's independence from the Portuguese in 1822 (present whereabouts unknown). In the same work two yellow-glazed melon tureens are illustrated, both carrying Mark No.1. These are further decorated with light green lines to the edge of the leaf stand and to the stems and foliage on the lid.. Their length is given as 8 in. (203mm). However at Plates 42 and 43 Jefferson illustrates a dish with a pierced lid and an oval medallion, each impressed LEEDS POTTERY. From the illustrations I would attribute both to the Revivalist Senior, see Appx. IX. The covered dish is illustrated in Slee's catalogue at No. 604, we also know that Senior did produce several such oval medallions as the one shown and some very good yellow-glazed wares, see Plates 1090, 1091, and 1120.

Green-glazed wares which were produced in large quantities by most other earthenware potteries, must have been made at the Leeds Pottery, see the shard at Plate 59. Unfortunately I have never seen a marked piece of green-glazed ware, neither has Barbara Tomkins who has been collecting and studying this class of wares for many years. The mottled green/brown glazed leaf dish at Plate 107 being the nearest.

The two ornamental vases at Plate 335, each one of a pair, are the only ones known of these shapes and colour. Their size indicates that they were intended for the decoration of large rooms where their colour and restrained yet rich gilding would certainly have made very bold statements.

335. TWO ORNAMENTAL VASES. <u>Left</u> (one of a pair): Ht. – 7 3/4 in. (196mm) Mark No. 1 and impressed "18". Creamware body with coloured glaze/slip. The handles are of red clay which is clearly visible on a broken handle on the other matching example. The design corresponds to No. 12 in the *Ornamental Drawing Book No.1* (see Plate 814) where it is shown with a high ogee-shaped lid surmounted by an acorn finial. <u>Right</u> (one of a pair): Ht. – 12 1/4 in. (311mm) D. – 8 7/8 in. (225mm) Mark No. 1 impressed twice. Creamware body with coloured glaze/slip. This design corresponds to No. 22 in the *Ornamental Drawing Book No. 1* (see Plate 821). Unfortunately the handles are broken and missing on both vases of this shape but, from the *Drawing Book*, they would have been large hanging ring-handles. On the vases there is no evidence that they were fused to the body at their lower edges. From the *Drawing Book*, it would appear that the rings were intended to be very slender which could indicate that they might have been made of brass, bronze or ormolu, rather than ceramic. Both the above vases are of bold impressive design which is accentuated by their colour enriched by the addition of the gold bands. The colour is a darker version of what Davenport and the Don Pottery produced as a body colour for a short period in the early nineteenth century and which is known as Chalcedony. *Leeds Museums & Galleries.*

336. PLANT POT & STAND. – Plant Pot D. – 4 3/8 in. (111mm). Stand D. – 5 in. (127mm). No marks. Attributed by the pattern on the yellow ground, see Pattern No. 47 in the *Enamelled Tea Ware 1819* book *at Plate 1052 York Museums Trust (Yorkshire Museum). YORYM 2001.2276 a and b.*

337. LOVING CUP. Ht. – 5 in. (127mm). No mark. Attributed by the pattern on the yellow ground, see caption to Plate 336. *National Museum of American History, Smithsonian Institution, Washington, DC . Catalogue No. 67.161*

Drabwares

Two colours were produced under this heading. First, the appropriate one illustrated at Plates 338 and 339 which is indeed quite a drab colour which one cannot imagine being fashionable for very long, hence the comparative rarity of extant examples. Enamel colours would not be seen to their best advantage against such a background and therefore the introduction of the 'lustre' effect on the red flowers was no doubt an attempt to liven up the overall appearance.

The second, and to my mind, much more pleasing colour is that illustrated here at Plates 340 to 347. This colour I believe to be peculiar to the Leeds Pottery and does form quite a pleasing background for the decoration, when done in monochrome and with the dark-green mat line edging to be seen on the above Plates.

All the Drabware examples which I have examined and which have been marked have all carried the horseshoe mark No. 2.d, illustrated on page 112. It is tempting to surmise that they may well have been introduced by Thomas Lakin, see below, who is known to have worked with and perhaps introduced such wares elsewhere before his move to Leeds.

Finally, in the *Enamelled Tea Ware 1819*, pattern book, some patterns have the wording – "On a fawn body" and others – "On a drab body"; as I have not yet seen any pieces decorated with the patterns shown it is not possible to differentiate between these two descriptions. However any such differentiation is made more difficult because in Thomas Lakin's book of ceramic recipes is one for a "fawn or drab body"!

338. DISH. OAW. – 8 7/8 in. (225mm). Mark No. 2d and '3' impressed with 'Nr 29' in iron red enamel near the foot ring. The pink flowers have a metalic lustre which may indicate that this is an example of 'tinselling' see p. 225.

339. STAND FOR A CREAM TUREEN. 7 1/2 in. x 6 1/8 in. (190mm x 155mm). Mark No. 2d with '3' impressed. See caption to Plate 338, also Peter Walton, *Creamware and other English Pottery at Temple Newsam House, Leeds,* No. 834 – and – Donald Towner, *The Leeds Pottery,* Plate No. 47.b.i. *York Museums Trust (Yorkshire Museum). YORYM. 1971.241.*

340. PLATE. D. – 8 3/4 in. (222mm). Mark No. 2d.

342. CREAM TUREEN. 5 3/4 in. x 4 1/2 in. (145mm x 114mm). Not marked. This would have originally been *en suite* with a stand of the shape illustrated at Plate 339. *Leeds Museums & Galleries. 16.321/47.*

341. COMPORT. 11 in. x 9 in. (279mm x 228mm). Mark No. 2d. *Leeds Museums & Galleries. 4.34/46.*

343. DISH. OAW. – 9 in. (228mm). Mark No. 2d and '3' impressed. Enamelled decoration.

344

345

347. DISH. 10 in. x 8 3/4 in. (254mm x 222mm). No mark it is *en suite* with the plates at Plates 344, 345 & 346. *Leeds Museums & Galleries.*

344, 345 & 346. PLATES. D. – 8 3/4 in. (222mm). Mark No. 2d on each one. Enamelled decoration. *Leeds Museums & Galleries. 1928.20 B, A & D.*

Thomas Lakin I (1769 - 1821)

We owe a debt of gratitude to Harold Blakey for his research, and subsequent piecing together of that research which resulted in the account of the life and career of Thomas Lakin, most of which was spent in his native Staffordshire.[13] By the time he came to the Leeds Pottery, most probably in 1818, he had certainly had considerable experience in the pottery trade, having been employed by John Davenport as "principal manager", during which time he was also promoted to the rank of Captain in the Longport Volunteers. He had also worked with his son as an independent potter and also as an independent enameller to the trade as "Lakin & Son".

The surviving partners in the Leeds Pottery had thus secured the services of a very experienced potter with the added experience of having managed a large pottery under John Davenport. Sadly he died on the 27th of January 1821, *The Leeds Mercury* of Saturday the 3rd of February carrying the following announcement :

"On Saturday last, aged 51, of *angina pectoris* Mr. Thos. Lakin, one of the principal managers in the higher departments of the Leeds Pottery, to whose skill and ability the valuable improvements recently made in the ornamental department are mainly to be ascribed. The remembrance of the rectitude of his principles, and the integrity of his conduct, will be long cherished by a respectable circle of friends; but the loss to his numerous and afflicted family is irreparable."

The Staffordshire Advertiser of the 10th of February added the following :-

" ... He resided in the Staffordshire Potteries to within a few years of his death, where he had long been distinguished for his taste, judgement and ingenuity as a potter: by his unremitted exertions some valuable improvements were introduced which greatly assisted in the raising of china and earthenware to their present elevated station in this country."

His son, also Thomas, (1799 – 1824) did not survive him by many years, *The Leeds Mercury* of Saturday the 5th of June 1824 carrying the following notice :

"Same day, [*i.e.* Tuesday the 1st of June] at his mother's house, in Meadow Lane, Mr. Thomas Lakin, superintendent of the Leeds Pottery. He was, by the sudden death of his father, at a very early age, placed in this very important and confidential situation, the duties of which he discharged in a manner that secured him the confidence and esteem of his employers. His loss to his widowed mother and orphan sisters will be irreparable."

Later, in 1824, Catherine, widow of Thomas, senior, advertised and in the same year published a book of ceramic recipes together with some for glass staining these being a collection which her late husband had collated and was preparing to publish at the time of his death.[15] The work was sold at £5-5-0d a copy and was published by Edward Baines of Leeds. In the advertisement flyer for this publication Catherine described her late husband as: " ... manager of the Leeds Pottery of Messrs Hartley Greens & Co. ...". It will also have been noticed that when Thomas junior died, his obituary seemed to imply that he had succeeded his father as superintendent of the Leeds Pottery which is somewhat at variance with his father's obituary which only claimed that he had been: "one of the principal managers of the higher departments of the Leeds Pottery."

Whatever the precise description of Thomas senior's position may have been it is recalled that after the departure of John Green from the partnership that the remaining partners had had to employ a person, with practical potting experience, to take his place in the management of the Pottery and the direction of the work and the appointment of the workmen. Thomas Lakin's background would certainly have qualified him for such a position which, from the above quotations, he may well have held. That his son at the young age of 21 could adequately have fulfilled such a role is somewhat difficult to appreciate.

We must now try to decipher the meaning of that part of Thomas senior's obituary :

" ... to whose skill and ability the valuable improvements recently made in the ornamental department are mainly to be ascribed ...".

If we review what is presently known about the work of Thomas Lakin prior to his move to Leeds two aspects come to mind. His name is associated with drabwares and monochrome landscapes. I will therefore draw the reader's attention to this class of wares, just previously dealt with, see Plates 338 to 347, produced at Leeds, both monochrome landscapes and floral decoration. Of more interest, however, is the class of wares under the next sub heading.

Crystal Ware

It was Harold and Clarice Blakey who first brought a group of wares to our attention in which each example has the words "Crystal Ware" pencilled in red enamel underneath it.[14] Examples of known Crystal Ware pieces are illustrated here at Plates 348 to 352, with the reasons for their attribution to the Leeds Pottery given in the captions. In addition to these examples it is known that a garniture of vases passed through Phillips', New Bond Street, Saleroom on the 7th of December 1983, lot No. 199 :

"AN INTERESTING GARNITURE OF THREE 'CRYSTAL WARE' VASES of shield shape with waisted necks and circular feet, applied with oval false-ring handles, painted with a background of flower heads and palmettes in pale underglaze blue and gilding, reserving panels of coloured birds in sepia landscapes, the reverses with ripe fruit sprays. *19.5cm. and 16.5cm., one marked 'Crystal Ware' in red script* (R)"

Then followed a postscript drawing the reader's attention to the plate in the Victoria and Albert Museum, illustrated here at Plate 351, and going on to state that "The distinctive handle form appears on Davenport porcelain" and adding that "a Swansea attribution cannot be ruled out". Unfortunately the vases were not illustrated in the catalogue.

A probable connecting link with Thomas Lakin is that in his book of 'Receipts' there is the following :

PROCESS 40.

To make a fine Crystal Glaze.

Take 105 Parts of Cornish Stone.
  90 - - of Borax.
  60 - - of Flint.
  50 - - of Red Lead.
  12 - - of Crystal of Soda.
  10 - - of Oxide of Tin.
  ¼ - - of Blue Calx.

This glaze produces very superior white earthenware, and, for the purpose of enamelling, the colours, lustres, and burnished gold appear to considerable advantage ; it is also adapted for iron stone, and makes superior blue printed earthenware ; it has a singularly striking effect on printed brown and mulberry. When used for dipping it must be considerably diluted, and requires but little shaking from the hand of the operator ; it requires the heat of a china glazing oven, but to answer the earthenware oven it will require a small addition of white lead, according to the temperature of firing. The materials must be mixed and calcined as before stated, and the ware fired in lime and slip seggars, well washed.

I feel confident in confirming the Blakeys' original attribution of Crystal Ware to the Leeds Pottery and therefore venture to date its manufacture to c.1820. The quality of the decoration seen on the pieces illustrated, together with that on the paler drabware would also seem to bear out the claim made about Thomas Lakin senior, in his obituary notice, regarding his contribution to the achievements made in the Leeds Pottery's "ornamental department".

348. PLATE. D. – 9 in. (228mm). Mark No. 6. The central decoration on this and the pieces at Plates 349 and 350 is enamelled. "Kirkstall Abbey" is written (*i.e.*,scratched) through the decoration at Plate 350, bottom centre. This plate has the same section as the one illustrated at Plate 340.

349. CREAM TUREEN. 5 3/4 in. x 4 1/2 in. (145mm x 114mm). Mark No. 6. Compare the body shape with the cream tureen at Plate 342. *Leeds Museums & Galleries. 1998.0012.*

350. DISH. 9 1/2 in. x 8 1/4 in. (241mm x 209mm). Mark No. 6. Compare the outline shape with the dish at Plate 347, the section through both dishes is also the same.

351. PLATE. D. – 8 7/8 in. (225mm). Mark No. 6. The section through this plate is exactly the same as those at Plates 344 to 346. Also the mat-green enamel matches that on the plate at Plate 340 and the dish at Plate 342. *Victoria & Albert Museum. 2556/1901.*

352. DISH. OAW. – 9 in. (228mm). Mark No. 6. Compare the outline shape with the dish at Plate 343, the section through both dishes is also the same. The holly leaves with their mat-green enamel match those on the pieces at Plates 340 to 342.

Black Basalt

The Leeds Pottery produced large quantities of black basalt, judging by the frequency with which marked examples appear on the market and are represented in collections both public and private. That such wares were in demand in the late eighteenth and early nineteenth centuries is born out by the fact that Diana Edwards has recorded more than 150 different manufacturers of basalt who are presently known.[16] The following comments by Josiah Wedgwood, although repeated many times by other writers, are nevertheless worth quoting again; both the following extracts are from letters addressed to his partner Thomas Bentley in London :[17]

26th of December 1772.

"... I hope <u>white hands</u> will continue in fashion, and then we may continue to make <u>black teapots</u> 'till you can find us better employment. ..."

5 March 1774.

" ... The Black is stirling, and will last for ever. ..."

The enthusiasm shown by Wedgwood in these quotations is proof that "Egyptian Black" wares were very much in demand in the early 1770s. I would, therefore, find it hard to believe that the partners in the Leeds Pottery would not have tried to satisfy such a demand. A perusal of the designs in the first, 1806, section of the Leeds *Drawing Book for Blackware* reveals several which could have answered the taste of the 1770s and 1780s, for example – Nos. 18, 21 and 41, these, together with others from this 1806 section, could well have been in production for many years prior to their entry in the *Drawing Book for Blackware*. Proof that the Leeds Pottery had been producing Egyptian Black Teawares since at least 1796 and earlier is their presence in the *Prices Current List* of the 1st of February 1796 and which "differe[d] not materially from the Old One". See Chapter 8, under Mark No. 2, for observations pertinent to the dating of wares, based on the division of designs in the two sections of the *Drawing Book for Blackware*.

I am not aware of any examples of Leeds Blackware which would fall in the category of decorative or ornamental wares as opposed to useful wares. Several plaques which are known and which are impressed LEEDS POTTERY were produced by the revivalist Senior, see Appendix IX.

Sprig Moulds

The Kidson brothers in their chapter on "The Black Egyptian Ware"[18] stated, at page 93 :

"It has fallen to our lot to become possessed of a number of the intaglios or working blocks used by the Leeds Pottery in the ornamentation of the ware."

A selection of forty-two from this collection was illustrated at Plate 20, facing page 93, in their above-mentioned book. It is our great fortune that the collection of sprig moulds which the Kidsons acquired from the ruins of the Leeds Pottery and which amounts to approximately one thousand six hundred moulds is now in the safe keeping of Temple Newsam House, Leeds.[19] Another small collection of approximately fifty-four moulds is in the Holland Child Collection at the Harrogate Museum, all but six are duplicates of those held at Temple Newsam House. The Castle Museum, York, also has a small selection which are replicated by those at Leeds.

The Temple Newsam collection has been examined and sorted into groups, for illustrating here, according to the type of decoration represented by each mould. They are illustrated below on Plates 353 to 377.

Master Moulds, for sprigged decoration, have the decoration standing proud of the surface of the mould and therefore represent the image as seen on the pot; these are referred to as CAMEO. The moulds made from the master moulds are therefore INTAGLIO indicating that the design is below the surface. The clay would be pressed into these *intaglio* moulds which appear as a mirror or reversed image of the sprigs which they produce. Obviously where the design is symmetrical the appearance of the sprig remains the same as the appearance of the mould which has produced it.

There are, however, some master moulds which were made *intaglio* in order to produce a tool for impressing numbers, letters or other devices into a pot. See Plate 375 where numbers 1,2 and 5 were for making such stamps. At number 6 is another master mould for making the "HARTLEY GREENS & CO. LEEDS POTTERY" stamp which is illustrated as Mark No. 2.a. (See page 111).

Almost all the moulds are made in a fine ceramic body with just a few in the much softer plaster of Paris. In the illustrations which follow I have, as far as the condition of the moulds would allow, included an example of every design in the collection and every size within each design. All the moulds shown in the Kidsons' book are represented in the plates which follow.

In the examples which are illustrated will be found moulds for most of the sprigged decoration indicated in the Blackware Drawing Book and also on the examples of the Basalt Wares which are illustrated at Plates 378 to 421. It is not, therefore, deemed necessary to give a commentary on all the examples which are illustrated. The following points are, however, worth making:

– Not all sprigged decoration was done in black basalt: see the shards at Plate 58 and the creamware examples at Plates, 101, 102 and 103.

– Although some of the moulds have dates inscribed *verso*, all of which range from 1800 to 1822, there are some which obviously belong outside this period. The two moulds of cricketers at Plate 360 Nos. 1 and 2 undoubtedly refer to a jug produced c.1846 which was decorated with the images of W. Clark, Fuller Pilch and Thomas Box, which jug was produced again much later by the Seniors c.1913 and appears in Slee's Catalogue of that date at No. 550. It is illustrated here at Plate 1126.[20] At Appendix IX it will be seen that the Seniors revived the production of earlier Leeds Pottery using many of the original moulds.

– At Plate 354 Nos. 3 to 7 and Plate 356 Nos 1 to 4 will be seen moulds which match precisely the decoration in the designs for the tureens in the *Drawing Book No. 3* - Nos. 403 (Plate 724) and 435 (Plate 741). The sprig moulds are inscribed : "On Tureen August 26 1819" – and – "On 10 Tureen August 27 1819"
This gives us a precise date when this design of tureen was being introduced.

– The style of dress of the topers/peasants at Plate 361 Nos. 6, 7 and 8 surely indicates a continental, perhaps Germanic style and again most likely were in use later in the nineteenth century.

– Among the miscellaneous moulds at Plate 375 will be seen, at No 6, the intaglio mould from which the stamps would be made for the HARTLEY GREENS & CO/ LEEDS POTTERY mark; an identical mould is in the Harrogate Museum. The neatly formed cameo mould for the bell at No. 7 is clearly visible in the group illustrated by the Kidson brothers. However I am unaware of any pot with a sprigged decoration matching this mould which is the only one in the collection with this motif.

The following is a complete listing of all the inscriptions which it has been possible to read on the moulds. With reference to this I have to point out that at some time in their history many have been stuck, with animal glue, to a display board. This has resulted in the destruction of many potentially informative inscriptions as, at some unknown date when they were removed from wherever they were glued, the strength of the glue has removed the back surface layer of these moulds. The remains of many inscriptions are evident by half a letter or part of a number etc.

– The inscriptions on moulds not illustrated are entered against the numbers of identical moulds which are illustrated.

– Where more than one inscription is found on different moulds of the same design, such inscriptions are separated by a comma.

– If more than one mould of the same size has the same inscription, this is indicated by a number in square brackets.

– (Y) - indicates that the mould is in the collection at the Castle Museum, York.

– (H) - indicates that the mould is in the Holland-Child collection at the Harrogate Museum.

– A question mark indicates a missing or illegible part of the inscription.

– Numerals. It is not always easy to explain the significance of all the numbers in the following inscriptions. Sometimes where the numerals follow "No." the number does refer to the design in the *Drawing Book for Blackware*. At other times the number may refer to a size, see *Prices Current List* at pages 95-98, or they may refer to a size by the potter's dozen.

Mould Number	Illustrated Examples	Moulds which are not Illustrated Cameo	Intaglio
Plate 353.			
3		? September 2 1814	
4	44		
12			LP
Plate 354.			
1	On		
3	13 & 14		
4	&13, ? August ? 1819		
5	12 Jany 21 1820		
6	10 Jany 21 1820		
7	? August 1819		
11		JB 1806 September 19th	
17	December 1816		
23			18 [or81]
Plate 355.			
3	2nd		
4	3		
5	2		
7	4		
9	2 Siz		
Plate 356.			
1		On Tureens August 26 1819	
2	On 10 Tureens August 27 1819		
3	9 Jny 21 1820		
Plate 357.			
2	2 Siz		
6			1 Siz, 2, Siz
7			2 Siz
14		On Jockle 2 May 12 1817	
15	4		
16	24		
17	2		On 2 Siz Jocklet EB May 10 1817 (Y)
18			1
19	12 & 18 Milk Pots		
21		18 [2]	
22	2nd	24	2 Size
23			Butter Pot
24			Butter Pot
25			Butter Stands, Butter Tub Stands,4
28	2		
30			Coffee Pots, 4 & 6 Coffee [2],
31			9 & 12 T Pots, Decer 31 1814, 12 Tea Pots Prest [2]
32	9 & 12 T Pot		
33			Milk Pot
Plate 358.			
4		JB Second size	2
9	On Pitcher Block		
10	2		
11	On Pitcher Block		
12	On 1 size		
13	On 4 size		
14	3 siz		
18	Coff 4 & 6		
19			Coffee covers
21			Milk Pot covers
22	1		
23			2
24	3		
27	Tureens 4 & 5		
30	On Royal Sauce Boat		
Plate 359.			
1	On 3		
5	B No 1		
7	On ? 1816		
9	On 10 inch New ? ing		
Plate 360.			
6	? O Teapot No 2 Pearl		
9	? Block		

Mould Number	Illustrated Examples	Moulds which are not Illustrated	
		Cameo	Intaglio
Plate 365.			
5	on		
6	1 size		
9		18	24
19	12		
Plate 366.			
16	WM		
21	4		
Plate 367.			
1	1 size Working Block		
2	24	On 3rd siz November 24,, 1814 (H)	2
3	24		
4			4
6	2 size Working Block		
7			3
9			1
12	4		
Plate 368.			
3		On 1 siz, No 9 T Pots, No 79, Round	
4			[On a mould larger than this, 123 x 105 mm]- On Coffey E Black Feby 7-1822 Flood at Leeds Feb 3 1822. (Y)
6	On Ewer		
7	30 TP		
8			[On a mould smaller than the example illustrated]- No 46 On 18 Milk Pots 12 x 18 Milks 1822 Decbe13 1822 (Y), (H - not dated)
Plate 369.			
3	On Ewers No 5 May 1st 1817		On Ewers No.35 EB May 10th 1817 (H)
5	18 Bowls No 35	November 30 1815	
7		First size piller for 12 Bowls for No 29	
8	24 Bowls		
Plate 370			
16	Smallest		
17	1 siz		
18	3rd size on Decer 17 1817		
Plate 371.			
1	On 2 siz		
2	1 siz		
4	5 siz		
10	Best Baul Clay		
11	Dinner basket Jan 5 1813		
Plate 372.			
2		For 24 Bowls August 29 .. 1814	12 Milk Pots [2], 24 Bowls [4], 18 Milk Pots & 18 Bowls, 18 Milk Pots [2], 18 Bowls [2], 12 Milk Pots & 6 ? Pots, 12 & 18 Milk Pots 18 Bowls [2]
3	18 & 24 bowls		30 TP, 18 & 24 Sugars [3]
4	Coffee boddams		
5	Bowls boddoms		
6	Coffee 4 & 6	On coffee sprigd 6 & 4 boddoms	Coffee 4 & 6 [4]
7	18 & 24 Bowls		
8		Milk pots 18 & 24 boddams spridge	
11		On coffee pots	4 & 6 Coffee, 18 & 24 Milk Pot cover
15	on		
19	Milk covers		
20		On 24 & 30 Teapot round No 35	
29		Milk pot cover sprigd 18 & 24 bowls boddams siridge	Coffee covers
30		On 18 & 24 milk pot covers (&H)	18 & 24 milk pot covers [2], No 3[2], 18 & 24 milk pot, 3 cov sprig, 1st cov sprig, 18 & 24 milk pot No 41

| Mould Number | Illustrated Examples | Moulds which are not Illustrated | |
		Cameo	Intaglio
33		On 24 & 30 No 35 covers ?, On small size	3 [2]
Plate 373.			
1			30
2	2		1824 30 SD (Y)
3			30 Teapots
5	4 ? coffee		18 & 24 teapot, 18 & 24 TP, 9/12 [2], 9 & 12 TP [3]
7			30 [3], 36 [2]
9	Saucers		Saucers [2]
10	30 TP, 18 & 24 sugars		
19	On ewers No 79 June 21 1817		
21	On 18 & 24 milk pot boddoms		
22			2, 1 siz
23	2	on, 12 Teapot Nr 19 round Ju? 16 1817 [or 1811]	2 [2]
24	3		3
Plate 374.			
5			WM
10	2		
12			1813
14	Smallest		
15	12 Teapot fluted		12 Teapot fluted
17	47		
20			9·12
21			2 [3], 18 & 24
22			36 [2]
28	1 size		
30	1 siz Ewers		
31	1st clay	1 siz original	1 siz [4], 1 size [2]
32			2nd F
33		On Butter Tubs Stands	
34	? 7		4 & 6 Coffee
37		On Ewers No 35 May 10th 1817	
Plate 375.			
6	August 30 1817		
14		4 siz	
17	1		
24		T Pots D? 1800	
25	Butter Tub Stands No 15 1816		
32	On 1 siz		
33	2nd Siz		
Plate 376.			
1	WB 12 & 11 inches Tureens 1818		
3	30 ? Butter Tubs		
4	4 & 5 in ?? Tureens November ? 1814 & Butter Tub		
Plate 377.			
5	Original sprig for Milkpots 12 & 18 Egyptian Black (H)		

The Sprig Moulds on the following Plates, Nos. 353 to 376, are in the keeping of the Leeds Museums & Galleries. Those at Plate 377 are from the Harrogate Museum.

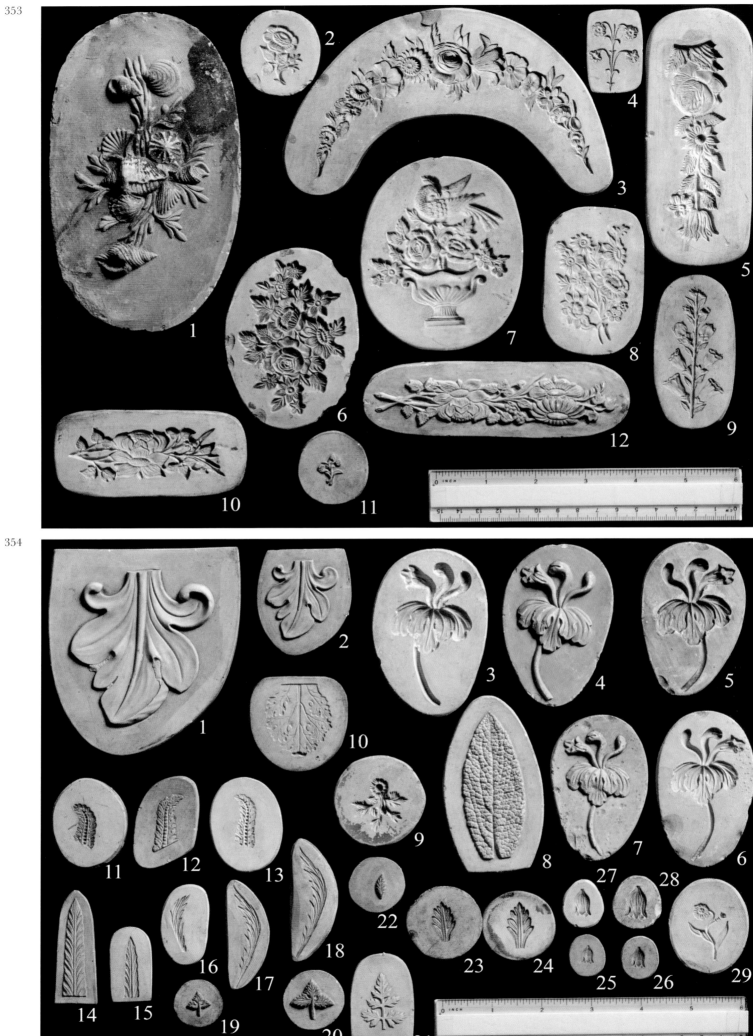

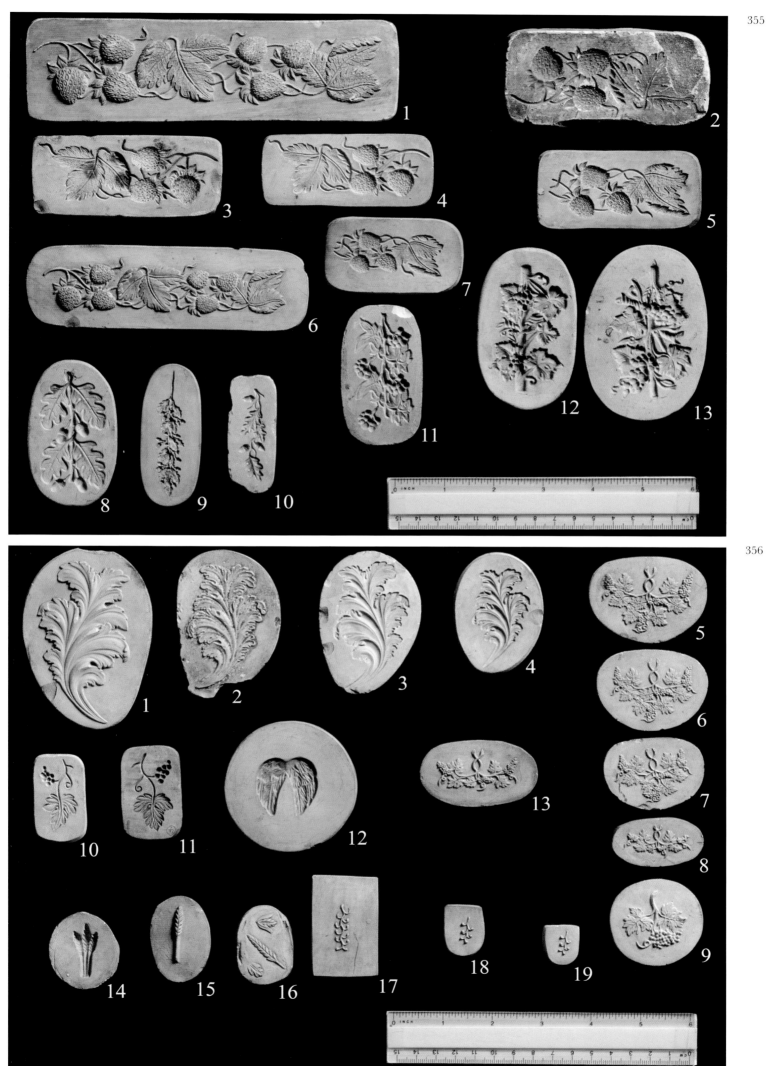

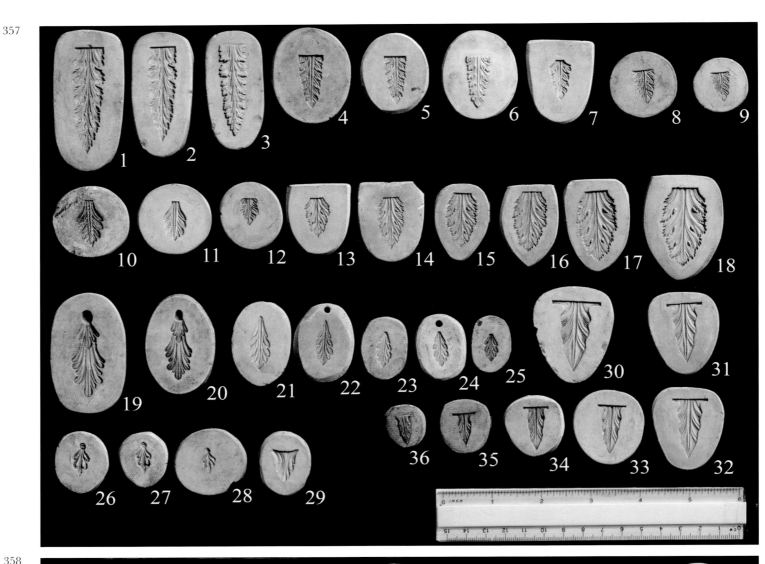

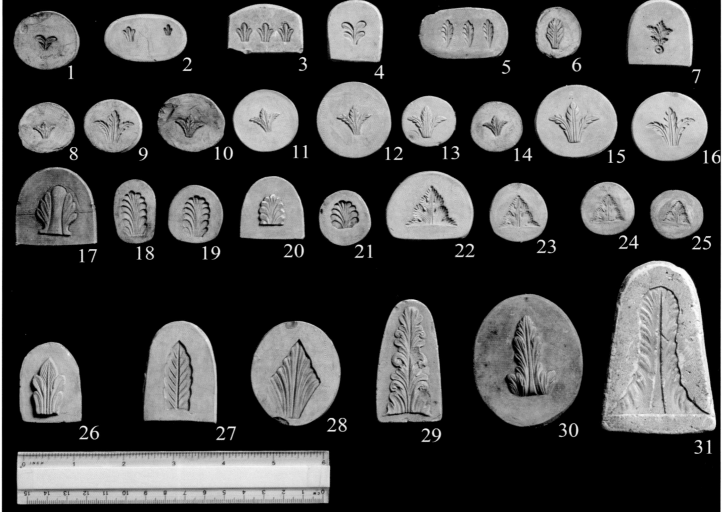

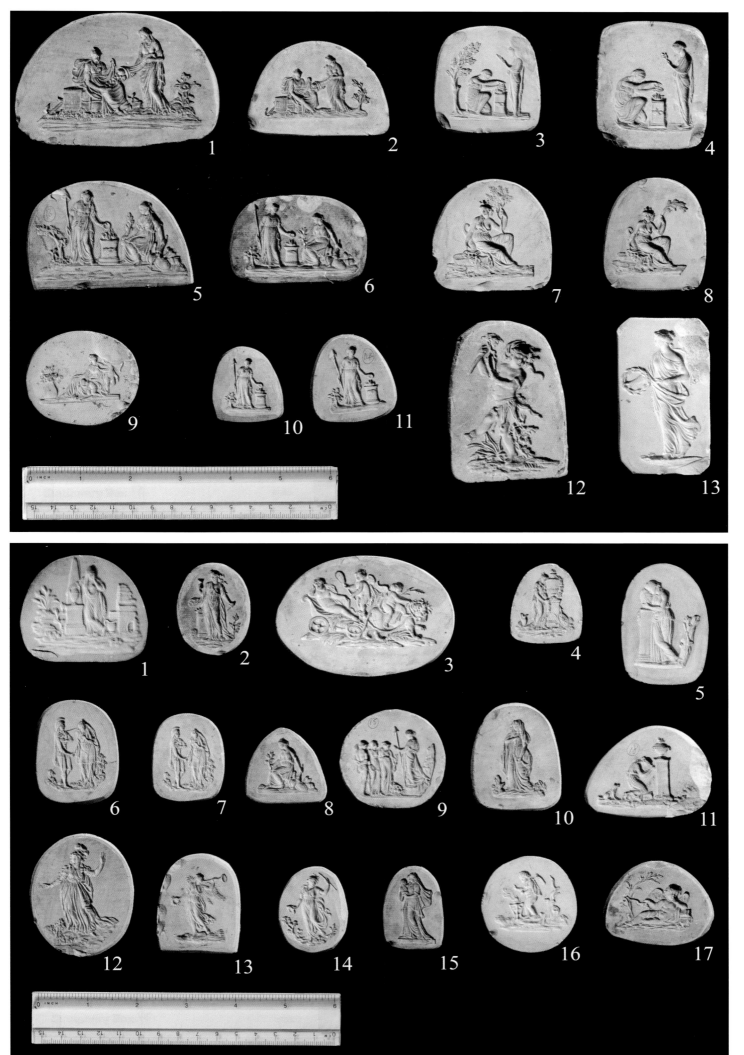

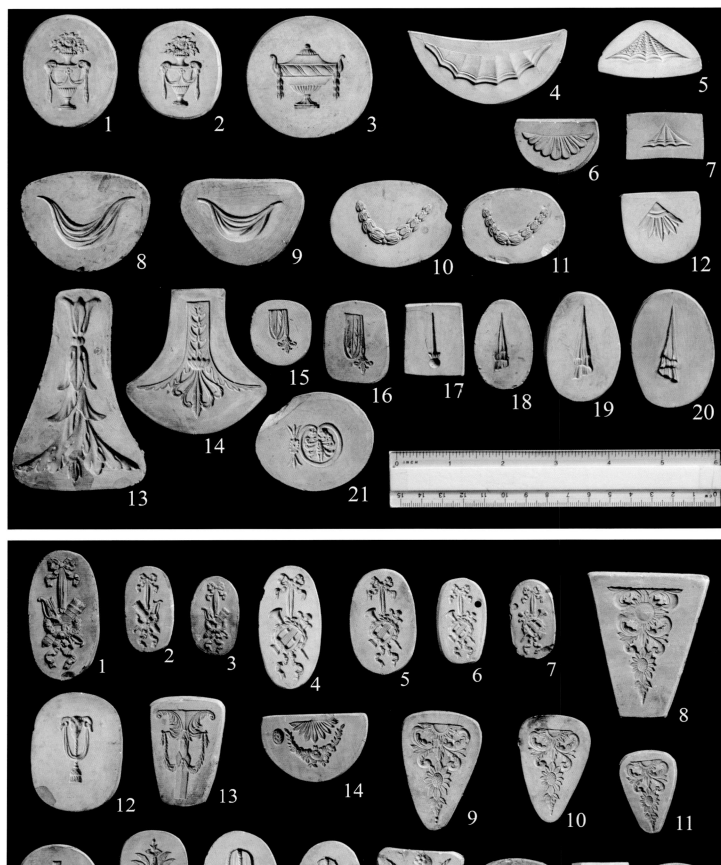

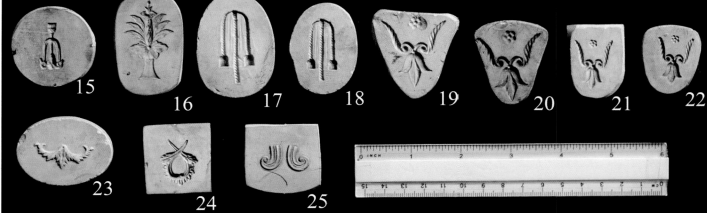

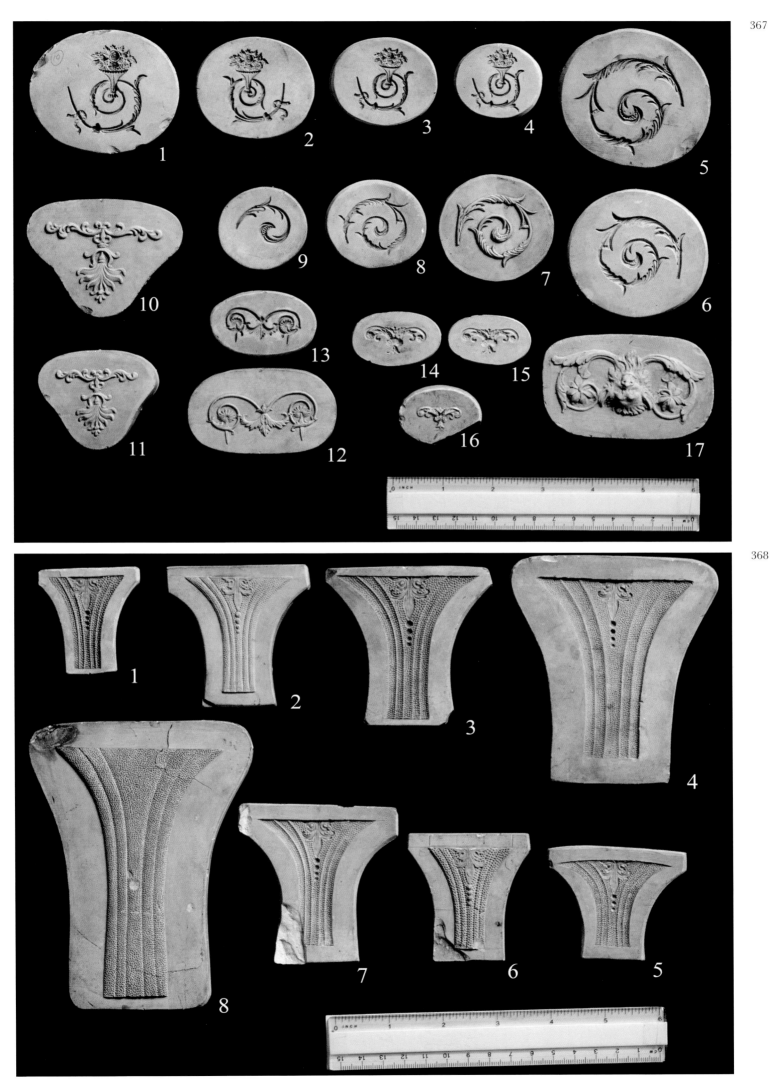

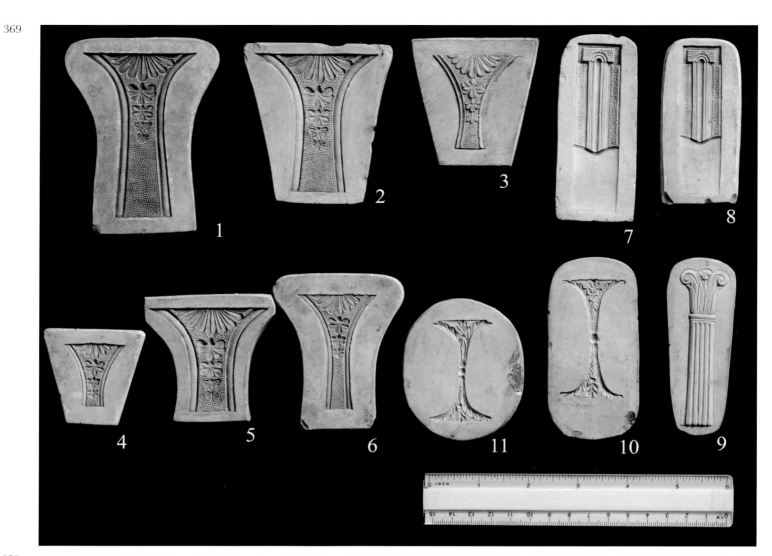

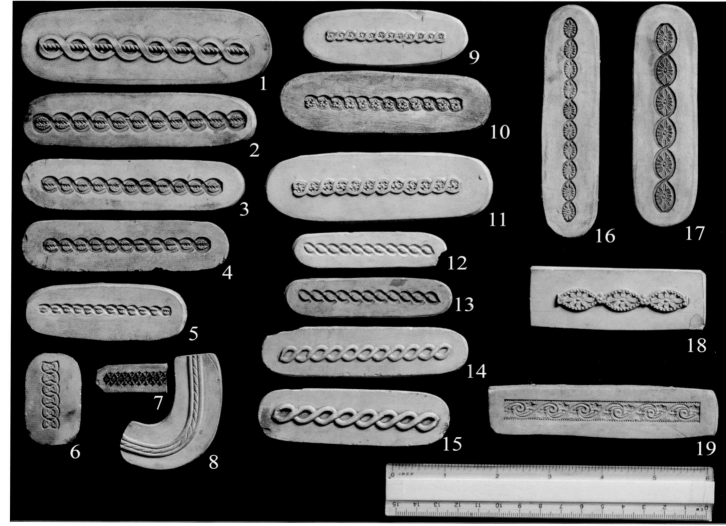

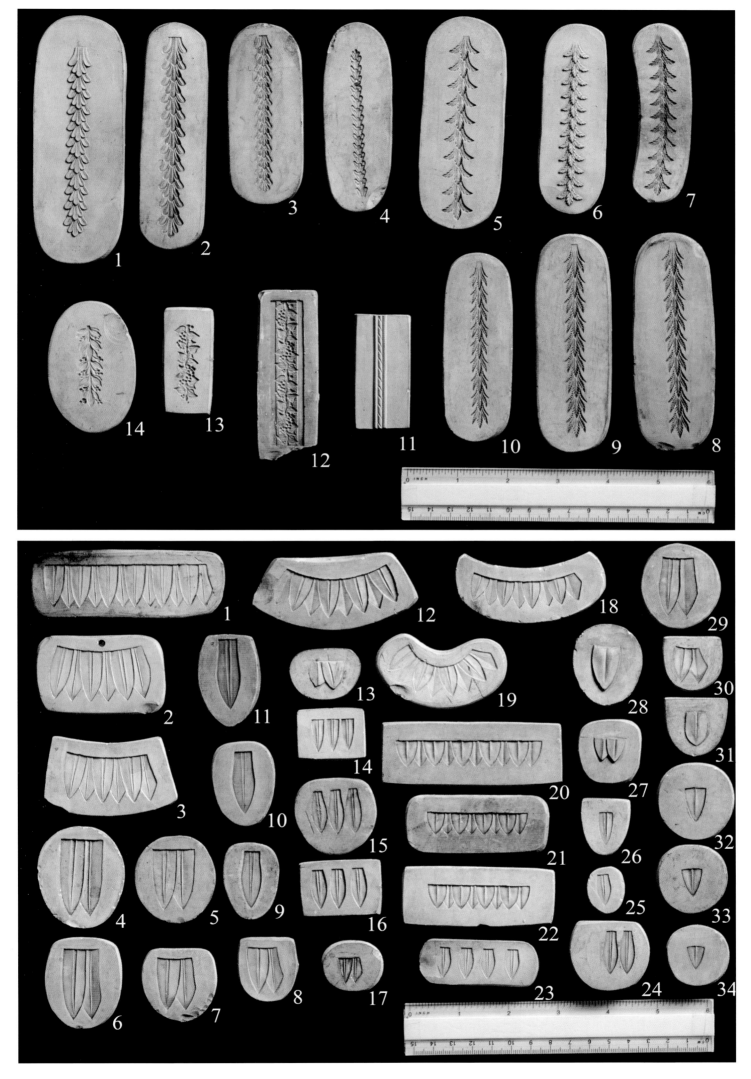

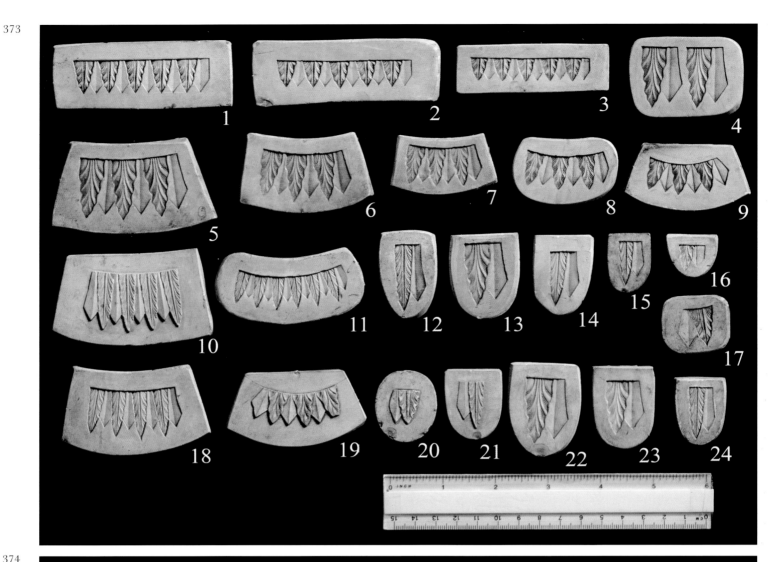

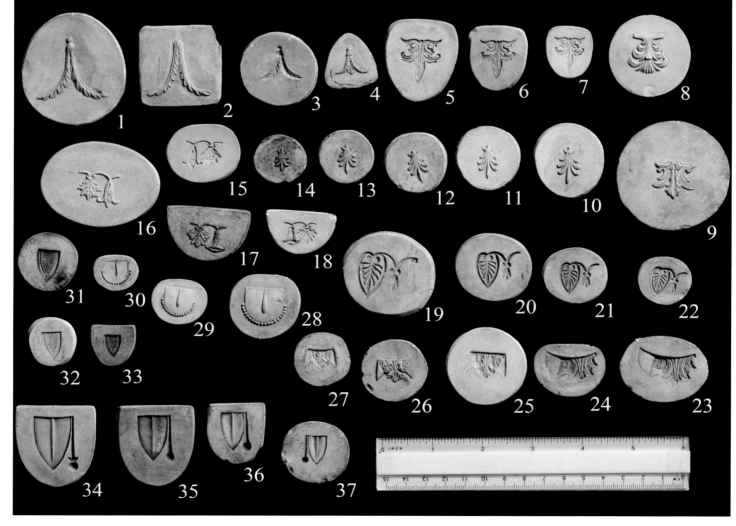

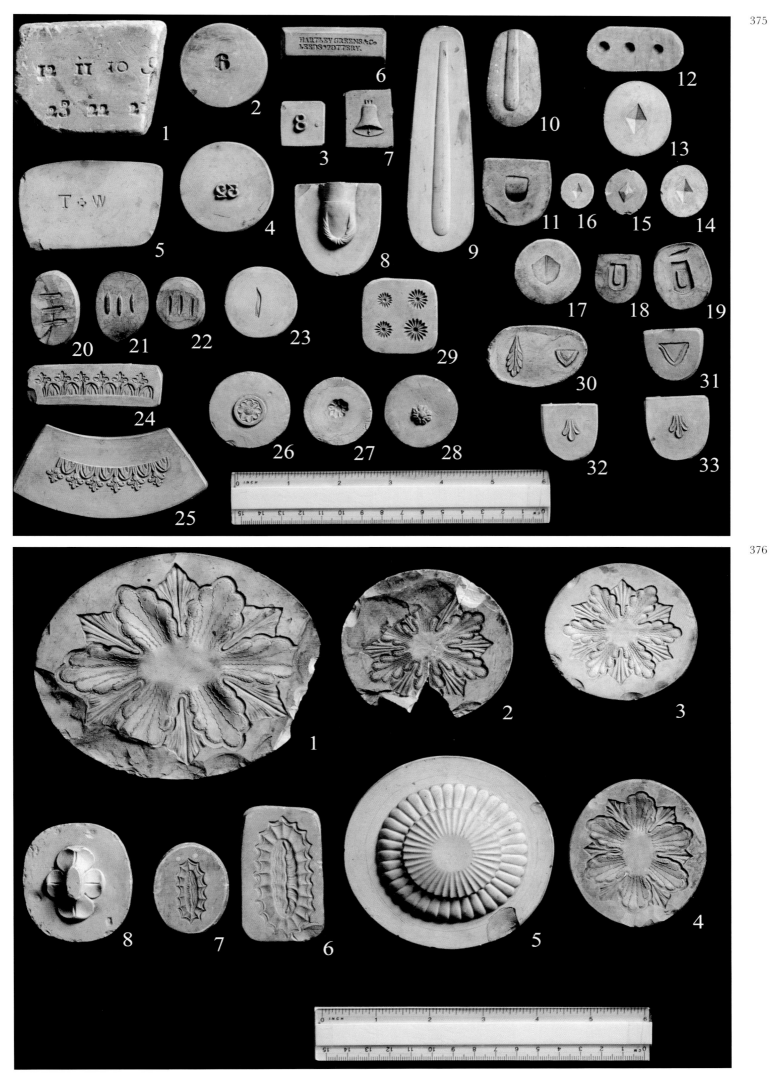

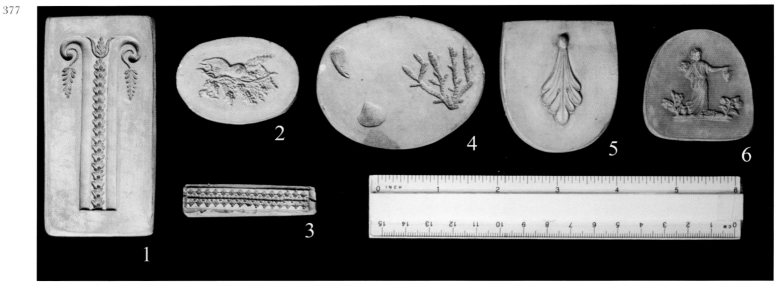

In the captions to the examples of Basalt wares which follow, if a number is seen in brackets following the heading e.g: COFFEE POT (25) – this would indicate the number of that design in the *Drawing Book for Blackware 1806* (see Plates 825 to 885). If that number is in italics, however, this indicates that the design is similar but not exactly the same.

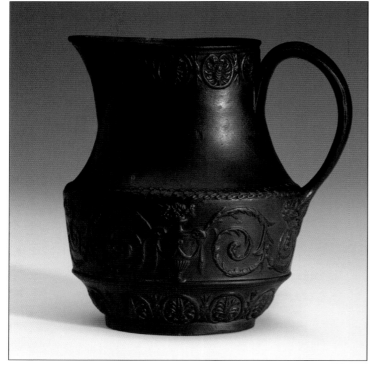

378. MILK JUG (17). Ht. – 5 in. (127mm). Mark No. 1. *Leeds Museums & Galleries. 4.94/46.*

380. SUCRIER (28). L. – 5 1/4 in. (133mm). Mark No. 1 and '4' impressed. *York Museums Trust (Yorkshire Museum). YORYM 209.2260.*

379. TEAPOT (22). Ht. – 3 1/4 in. (83mm). Mark No. 1. *Leeds Museums & Galleries. 4.103/46.*

381. COFFEE POT (31). Ht. – 8 in. (203mm). Mark No. 1 on the vertical outer surface of the foot ring below the spout. *Leeds Museums & Galleries. 4.79/46.*

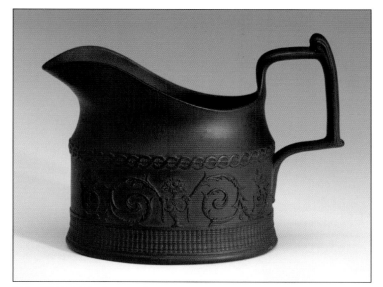

382. CREAM JUG (31). OAL. – 6 1/4 in. (158mm). Mark No. 1. *York Museums Trust (Yorkshire Museum). YORYM 2001.2677.*

385. SUCRIER (46). L. – 5 7/8 in. (149mm). Mark No. 1 on bottom edge of the foot ring. *Leeds Museums & Galleries. 4.62/46.*

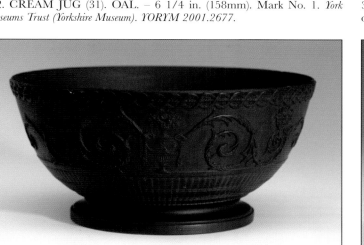

383. BOWL (31). D. – 6 3/4 in. (170mm). Mark No. 1. *York Museums Trust (Yorkshire Museum). YORYM 2001.5007.*

386. SUCRIER (47). Base – 4 1/2 in. x 3 1/4 in. (114mm x 83mm). Mark No. 1 on outer vertical side of the foot ring at one end. *Leeds Museums & Galleries. 4.84/46.*

384. SUCRIER (38). L. – 5 1/8 in. (130mm). Mark No. 1. *Leeds Museums & Galleries. 4.96/46.*

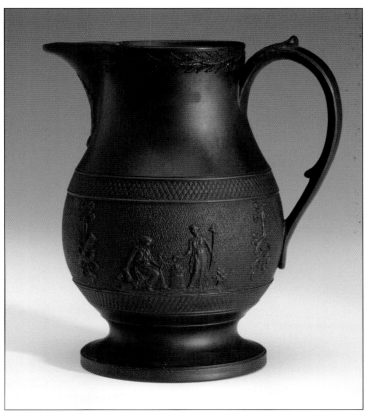

387. MILK JUG (77). Ht. – 5 1/8 in. (130mm). Mark No. 1. *Leeds Museums & Galleries. 4.105/46.*

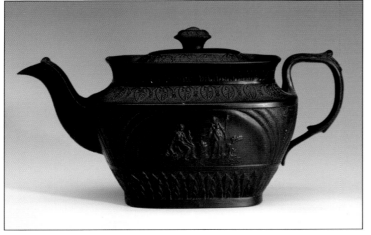

388. TEAPOT (79). OAL. – 11 3/8 in. (288) Mark No. 2a below the spout. *York Museums Trust (Yorkshire Museum). YORYM 2000.4724 a & b.*

389. TEAPOT (81). OAL. – 11 1/2 in. (292mm). Mark No. 2a. *Norfolk Museums Service (Norwich Castle Museum). NWHCM.1992.226.679.*

390. SUCRIER (86). Ht. – 4 in. (102mm). Mark No. 2a. This body and spout design was also used at the Don Pottery in the 1870s in pearlware and buff-coloured ware. See *The Don Pottery 1801 - 1893*, Plate 280, p. 208. *York Museums Trust (Yorkshire Museum). YORYM. 1996.383*

393. TEAPOT (87). OAL. – 10 3/8 in. (263mm). Mark No. 2a and '6' or '9' impressed. A similar design was used by John & Richard Riley of Staffordshire. See Roger Pomfret: "John & Richard Riley" in the *Journal of Ceramic History*, Vol. 13, pl. 21, for a basalt sucrier. The overall design and shape are very similar except for two features: first, the knop is different and secondly the sprigged/moulded decorative band round the top of the body consists of a straight line of alternating large and smaller daisy-like flowers. The Leeds version has a meandering, continuous stem with alternating vine leaves and bunches of grapes. See also the caption to Plate 329. *Leeds Museums & Galleries. 4.107/46.*

391. CREAM JUG (86). OAL. – 4 7/8 in. (124mm). Not marked it is *en suite* with Plate 390.

392. CHOCOLATE CUP (86). Ht. – 2 1/2 in. (63mm). Mark No. 2a. *Leeds Museums & Galleries. 4.70/46.*

394. TEAPOT (87). OAL. – 12 in. (304mm). Not marked. *Leeds Museums & Galleries. 4.102/46.*

395. BOWL (87). D. – 6 1/8 in. (155mm). Mark No. 2a and '6' or '9' impressed. *Leeds Museums & Galleries. 4.87/46.*

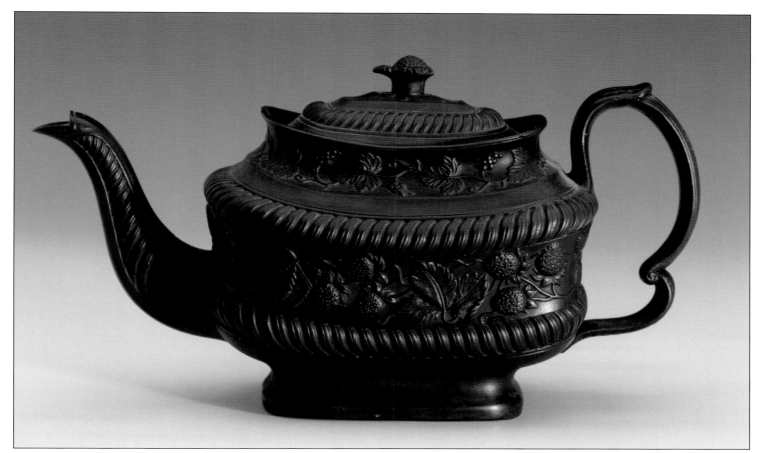

396. TEAPOT (87). OAL. – 10 in. (254mm). Mark No. 2a, only the top line of the mark is visible. *Norfolk Museums Service (Norwich Castle Museum). NWHCM. 1992.226.677.*

397. CREAM JUG (87). OAL. – 5 3/4 in. (145mm). Mark No. 2a. *York Museums Trust (Yorkshire Museum). YORYM.2001.2675.*

399. COFFEE POT (20). Ht. – 8 5/8 in. (219mm). Mark No. 1. *York Museums Trust (Yorkshire Museum). YORYM.200.4723.*

398. MILK JUG (2,3 & 5 - 14). Ht. – 4 1/2 in. (114mm). Mark No. 1.

401. TEAPOT (21). Ht. – 3 in. (76mm). Mark No. 1. *Norfolk Museums Service (Norwich Castle Museum). NWHCM. 1946.70.638.*

400. HOT-MILK JUG (21). Ht. – 4 3/4 in. (120mm). Mark No. 1. *Leeds Museums & Galleries. 4.104/46.*

402. TEAPOT (26). Ht. – 2 3/4 in. (70mm). Mark No. 1. The body shape is a copy of a popular silver honey-pot shape of the period. A silver-gilt example by Paul Storr, hall marked for 1799, is illustrated by Brian Reade in *Regency Antiques*, 1953, pl. 111, p. 155.

403. TEAPOT (*29*). OAL. – 9 in. (228mm). Mark No. 1. *Norfolk Museums Service (Norwich Castle Museum). NWHCM.1992.226.393.*

404. COFFEE POT (*29*). OAH. – 8 1/4 in. (209mm). Mark No.1. *Leeds Museums & Galleries. 4.81/46.*

405. MILK JUG (*29*). Base – 2 3/4 in. x 2 in. (70mm x 51mm). Mark No. 1 and '∷' impressed. Part of the pouring lip is missing. *Leeds Museums & Galleries. 4.66/46.*

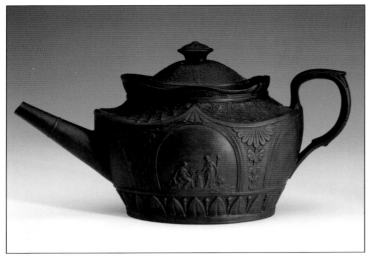

406. TEAPOT (*35*). OAL. – 11 1/2 in. (292mm). Mark No. 1 and 'X' scratched. *Leeds Museums & Galleries. 4.91/46.*

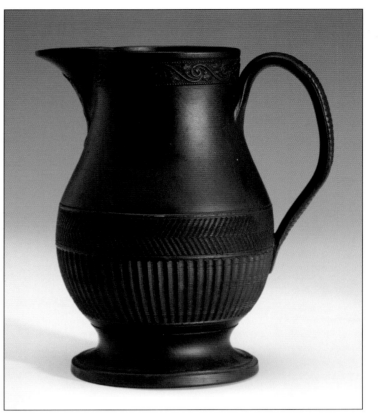

409. MILK JUG (*45*). Ht. – 5 1/4 in. (133mm). Mark No. 1. *Leeds Museums & Galleries. 4.95/46.*

407. CREAM JUG (*37*). OAHt. – 3 7/8 in. (98mm). Mark No.1. *York Museums Trust (Yorkshire Museum). YORYM.2001.2676..*

408. TEAPOT (*41*). Ht. – 4 in. (102mm). Mark No. 1 impressed twice and 'O' impressed. *Leeds Museums & Galleries. 16.290/47.*

410. COFFEE POT (*61 & 73*). Ht. – 7 5/8 in. (193mm). Mark No. 1. *Leeds Museums & Galleries.4.97/46.*

411. MILK JUG. Ht. – 4 5/8 in. (117mm). Mark No. 1. *Leeds Museums &
Galleries. 4.106/46.*

412. MILK JUG. Ht. – 4 3/4 in. (120mm). Mark No. 1.

413. COFFEE POT. Ht. – 7 3/4 in.
(196mm). Mark No. 1. *Leeds Museums &
Galleries. 24.14/67.*

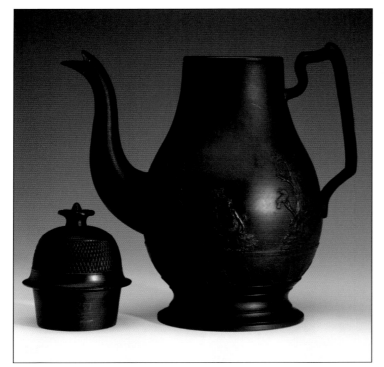

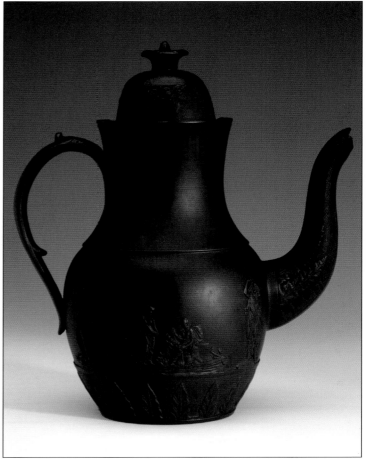

414. COFFEE POT. Ht. – 8 3/4 in. (222mm). Mark No. 1. *Leeds Museums & Galleries. 1928/57.*

415. COFFEE POT. Ht. – 7 7/8 in. (199mm). Mark No. 1. *Leeds Museums & Galleries. 4.80/46.*

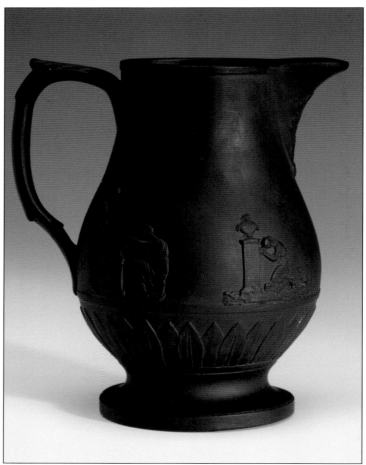

416. JUG. Ht. – 6 3/4 in. (171mm). Mark No. 1 impressed below the spout just above the base. *Leeds Museums & Galleries. 4.100/46.*

417. MILK JUG. Ht. – 5 1/8 in. (130mm). Mark No. 1. *Leeds Museums & Galleries. 4.93/46.*

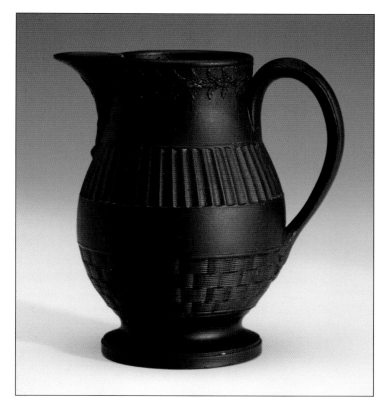

418. MILK JUG. Ht. – 4 1/2 in. (114mm). Mark No. 1. *Leeds Museums & Galleries. 11.103/69.*

420. PLATE. D. – 6 1/4 in. (158mm). Mark No. 1. *Leeds Museums & Galleries. 4.88/46.*

419. BOWL. D. – 5 7/8 in. (149mm). Mark No. 1. *Leeds Museums & Galleries. 4.108/46.*

421. PLATE. D. – 6 3/8 in. (161mm). Mark No. 1. *Leeds Museums & Galleries. 4.89/46.*

1. O'Donoghue, Goulding and Allen – "Composite Price Index 1750 to 2003", *Economic Trends,* Office for National Statistics, March 2004, pp. 41 and 43.
2. See p. 91 & Appx. IV p. 586.
3. See p. 29-31 where I give evidence to show that William Hartley was never employed in the production/management side of the Pottery, except for the possibility of one or two years of shared responsibility after the departure of John Green in 1801.
4. Robin Reilly – *Wedgwood the New Illustrated Dictionary,* pp. 122/3.
5. David Barker – *William Greatbatch a Staffordshire Potter,* p.176.
6. Gaye Blake Roberts – 'Wedgwood in Russia', *Ceramics,* July/August 1986, pp. 77 – 85.
7. Simeon Shaw, LL.D. – *The Chemistry of the Several Natural and Artificial Heterogeneous Compounds, used in Manufacturing Porcelain, Glass, and Pottery,* London, 1837, at pp. 308 & 488.
8. Robin Reilly – *The Genius of Wedgwood,* B20, pp. 28 &.30.
9. Peter Walton – *Creamware and other English Pottery at Temple Newsam House Leeds,–* notes under Ref No. 989.
10. Angela Cox – *NCS Newsletter,* No. 38, p.9.
11. Robin Reilly – *Wedgwood the New Illustrated Dictionary,* p. 367.
12. George L, Miller and Robert Hunter – "How Creamware got the Blues: The Origins of China Glaze and Pearlware", *Ceramics in America,* The Chipstone Foundation, 2001. pp.135 – 161. Rodney Hampson – The China Glaze, *NCS Newsletter No. 37,* pp. 11/12.
13. Harold Blakey – *NCS Journal No. 5,* 1984, pp. 79 – 114.
14. Clarice and Harold Blakey – *NCS Newsletter No. 90,* pp. 16,17.
15. *The Valuable Receipts of the Late Mr. Thomas Lakin, with proper and Necessary Directions for their Preparation and Use in the Manufacture of Porcelain Earthenware and Iron Stone China … ,* Leeds: Printed for Mrs. Lakin, By Edward Baines, 1824.
16. Diana Edwards – *Black Basalt,* p. 26.
17. Ann Finer & Geo. Savage – *The Selected Letters of Josiah Wedgwood,* pp. 142, 159.
18. *Historical Notices of the Leeds Old Pottery,* 1892.
19. After examining these moulds I have to state that there are approximately 1600 and not "over 6000" as recorded in Peter Walton's *Creamware and other English Pottery at Temple Newsam House Leeds,* at p. 257.
20. See Ron Morley – "A Provincial Pot & a Metropolitan Cricketer", *NCS Newsletter No. 91,* pp. 21 – 24, Sep. 1993.

CHAPTER TEN

The Wares
1827-1881

ALTHOUGH it has been possible to write an accurate account of the history of the Pottery throughout this period because of the wealth of archive material which I have been privileged to consult, I feel a great sense of frustration at not being able to match it with an equally full account of the wares produced over the same period. There are several factors, however, which account for the paucity of examples from this phase of the Pottery's history and which I can offer to justify this acknowledged weakness.

The first is summed up in the words 'pottery' and 'earthenware'. Fine creamwares and early pearlwares were undoubtedly bought by the middle classes in the eighteenth and early nineteenth centuries but, as the nineteenth century advanced and the production of porcelain became more plentiful and affordable, those who could afford to deck their tables with porcelain would no doubt have jettisoned their 'old fashioned' earthenware. Pottery tea wares in particular were probably the first class of wares which would have been exchanged for the finer qualities of simple and modestly decorated porcelain. There is, however, evidence that earthenware dinner services continued to be used by this strata of society long after earthenware had been replaced by porcelain for the tea table.[1]

The second phenomenon, of relevance to the ceramics industry, which characterised the advancing nineteenth century was the population explosion :

Year	UK Population	Hunslet	Leeds (including its townships)
1801	15,900,000	3,825	53,776
1841	26,750,000	15,852	152,054
1881	34,940,000	46,942	309,119

The greater proportional increase of Leeds and Hunslet over the United Kingdom's figures is evidence of the migration from the rural areas to the growing industrial centres, most of this being skilled and unskilled workers and their families.

There was therefore a rapidly increasing market, not only for housing but for all the requisite furnishings and household goods which inevitably included a selection of the wares which only the potters could provide.

In Yorkshire only the Rockingham Works, under the Bramelds, ventured into porcelain, i.e. bone china production from c.1826 to 1842, but it still continued to produce earthenware alongside its porcelain until its closure. The Leeds Pottery, as we saw in the last chapter, had produced some porcelain a quarter of a century before the Bramelds but had deemed its production not to have been commercially worthwhile pursuing. The partners had thus chosen to confine the output to their tried and tested eathenwares and, *ipso facto*, to supplying a lower strata of society less demanding in its needs than the more affluent customers might have been.

After the demise of the old firm of Hartley Greens & Co., in 1827, the Pottery traded as "The Leeds Pottery Company" with Samuel Wainewright II as tenant until his death in October 1834, and then under the partnership of Stephen and James Chappel from 1842 until 1847.

Virtually nothing is known regarding the wares produced in this period save the obvious fact that the Hartley Greens & Co.'s mark would not have been used although the simple impressed "LEEDS POTTERY" mark would, in all probability, have continued in use, (see page 74, where it is recorded that some new stamps were purchased). The only presently known marked piece from the Stephen and James Chappel period is the "Eton College" printed plate illustrated at Plate 426. The three very well painted plaques at Plates 427, 428 and 429 are a mystery (see their captions for more details). The shards illustrated at Plates 58 to 63 may indicate further types of wares being produced.

The only marks so far recorded from this period are illustrated in Chapter 8, pages 113, 114 bearing in mind that the earlier impressed LEEDS POTTERY mark may also have continued to be used. It must also be borne in mind that the Chappel brothers had had an interest in the Leathley Lane Pottery, see, page 76.

A little more is known about the products under Richard Britton and his partners, Samuel and William Henry Warburton and Richard Britton's sons, Alfred and John Broadbent, from 1850 to 1878. Joseph Marryat, in his second edition of *A History of Pottery and Porcelain*, published in 1857, at page 435, quotes notes supplied to him by Edward Hailstone, see Plate 30 :

"The Pottery ... after passing through many hands, and declining in the quality of the work and in estimation, is now having considerable knowledge applied to it by the present proprietors, Messrs Warburton and Britton. The present manufactury makes chiefly toilet services, mugs, pitchers, &c., employing about 400 hands, men, women and children; the greater portion of their trade is in the printed transfer ware ...".

From the above we learn that the workforce had remained constant since the time of the last Census in 1851.

Llewellynn Jewitt, in his article in *The Art Journal* of 1865, at page 309, gives us a fuller picture, in words, of the Pottery at that time :

"The Leeds Pottery is, as I have said, at the present time carried on, as it has been for some years, by Mr. Richard Britton, who employs more than two hundred hands. The wares produced are the ordinary descriptions of earthenware for domestic use, consisting of dinner, tea and coffee, toilet, and other services, jugs and mugs, screw jugs[2], bowls and basins, and indeed, all articles in general use. The white earthenware is of the same quality as the ordinary run of Staffordshire ware, and has a good glaze. it is produced in the usual styles of blue printing, painting and edging. In this, the principal branch of his manufacture, Mr. Britton successfully competes with some of the Staffordshire houses.

In Rockingham ware, tea and coffee pots and other articles are still made at these works in considerable quantities, as they are also in Egyptian black glazed ware. Yellow earthenware made from native clays procured from Wortley, and pearl white of good quality, both plain and decorated, are also manufactured. Thus it will be seen that the Leeds potteries of the present day – of the very existence of which but few persons are aware – are of considerable size and importance, and are doing a large business – a business which, unlike that of the olden times, is principally confined to the supplying of the home markets, where, not being marked, the ware usually passes for that of Staffordshire."

The last sentence answers the question: "why can't we identify any wares from this period?" The following advertisement from Jones's *Mercantile Directory of Leeds*, 1863, page 282, may give an inkling of some of the wares listed by Jewitt :

The advertisement for the following year in Charlton & Anderson's Directory shows Richard Britton trading on his own account and without any pictorial enhancement :

If the plaques from Stephen Chappel's period begged more questions than they answered then surely the pair of *pot-pourri* jars illustrated at Plates 438 to 442 take the mystery a stage further. From the letter which verifies their manufacture it is evident that some other pieces of similar decoration and quality were produced. What is of even more significance is the fact that there were potters and artists capable of such quality work at the Pottery in 1857 – who were they and would they have been there unless such work was being produced alongside the "... ordinary run of Staffordshire ware ..." ? When one of these pots was displayed in the NCS Exhibition, *A Celebration of Yorkshire Pots*, in the Clifton Park Museum, Rotherham, in 1997, a highly respected member of the staff from Hanley Museum remarked, pointing to it, "I can tell that I am not looking at Staffordshire Ceramics because that decoration would have been on porcelain if it had been made in Staffordshire!". See the caption for more details.

Among Heather Lawrence's ceramic papers is the following which has obviously been copied from a sale catalogue, unfortunately no date or auctioneers name was recorded with it :

"Lot 81. Interesting porcelain jug of baluster shape decorated with sprays of garden flowers and inscribed 'A Present For Mr. Joseph Boywater Salesman, at Leeds Old Pottery, as a token of respect 1855.' 7 inches high".

It would be strange indeed if the pottery where Joseph worked could not have presented him with a piece of its own making. This therefore poses the following questions none of which I am able to answer :

1. Was the jug incorrectly catalogued, *i.e.*- was it good quality earthenware and not porcelain?
2. Was porcelain being bought in the white and decorated at the Leeds Pottery at that period?
3. Was porcelain being made at the Leeds Pottery in the 1850s?
4. Did those making the presentation regard Joseph so highly as to warrant something better than was at that date being made at the Leeds Pottery?

The font at Plate 443 was obviously produced from a mould. One other identical with it is in the Leeds Museums' Central Store and a note with it informs us that it was from the Methodist New Connection Church in Dewsbury Road, Hunslet, which was built in 1861.

The six registered designs and patterns reproduced at Plates 431, 433, 435 to 437 and 444 show a good range of the types of wares being produced. Unfortunately only three pieces have so far been identified, see Plates 430, 430.a and 432. The transfer print at Plate 444 seems very much in the same vein and with the same *sans serif* lettering as seen on the shards at Plate 63. It should be pointed out that under The Designs Act of 1842, a period of only three years protection was given to a registered design.

Llewellynn Jewitt in his *Ceramic Art of Great Britain*, under Leeds Pottery, at page 484 does record two curious and novel products:

"This pearl body ... is also being introduced for washing-machines, substituting earthenware bottoms for wood; also for patent machines for cloth manufacturers. These were first shown at the Leeds Exhibition of 1875."

I have searched the catalogue for this exhibition but have not found any specific reference to the components mentioned. The following are the only references to washing machines in the exhibition which were made by Leeds manufacturers :

Page 14. – Thomas Briggs, Improved Patent Washing Machine.
Page 86. – Thomas Briggs, Woodhouse Lane Leeds, – Cottage Washing Machine.
Page 85. – William Hill, 2 Benson St., North St., Leeds, The Excel-All Washing Machine.

The only marks recorded from this period are illustrated in Chapter 8.

I am not aware of any wares peculiar to the short period when the Pottery was in the occupation of the Taylor Brothers.

In concluding this all too brief chapter on what is currently known about the products of the Pottery's last fifty-four years, I can only state that one day a design and/or pattern book may come to light or an excavation may reveal a wealth of shards – hopefully previously undisturbed and with convincing evidence of their origin. The quality of potting of such wares as I have been able to examine and illustrate are of a standard as good as any similar wares manufactured elsewhere and, in the case of the two *pot pourri* jars, I believe could not be bettered for quality of both potting and surface decoration – ground colour, glaze, gilding and enamelling when compared with other earthenwares of the period.

422, 423 & 424. MUG. Ht. – 4 3/4 in. (120mm). Mark No. 1 and ':.' impressed, ex. Edward Hailstone's Collection. It is impossible to state precisely how long the Pottery continued using mark No. 1. The Orange Order which is commemorated on this mug was founded in 1795, taking its name from William Prince of Orange, with the purpose of supporting the Protestant Faith against Roman Catholicism. On a ribbon round the outside of the print are the names of the signs of the zodiac. On a ribbon near the top: "Protestant Ascendancy Holiness to the Lord" and at the base of the print: "May the Orange Institution stand as firm as the oak/and its enemies fall off like the leaves/in October". From 1813 to 1828 the Orange Order was entirely suspended in its native land. *York Museums Trust (Yorkshire Museum). YORYM.2001.4957.*

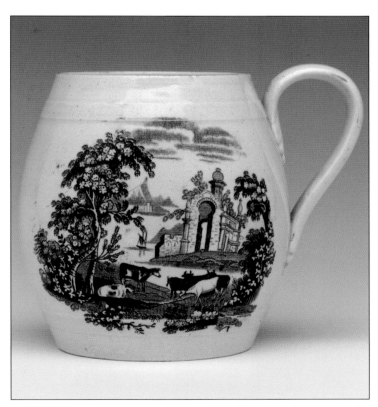

425. MUG. Ht. – 4 3/8 in. (111mm). Mark No.1. Another mug in the Yorkshire Museum, of identical size and form, has the same print in blue. *York Museums Trust (Yorkshire Museum). YORYM.2001.2695.*

426. PLATE. D. – 9 1/8 in. (232mm). Mark No. 7a.i. and 'S' impressed. This print is called 'Eton College', as nothing in this print resembles the famous public school one wonders why it is so called. Perhaps, at an earlier date, a potter had supplied Eton College with wares decorated with this print which then became very popular and was produced by many potters. The backstamp has been discovered on shards from the Pottery but without the initials and is illustrated at Marks No. 7.a.ii.

427

428

429

427, 428 & 429. THREE PLAQUES. 427 – 8 1/4 in (209mm) square. 428 – 8 3/4 in. (222mm) square. 429 – 9 1/8 in. x 8 7/16 in (232mm x 214mm). They are porcelain and each bears a glued-on label as follows :-

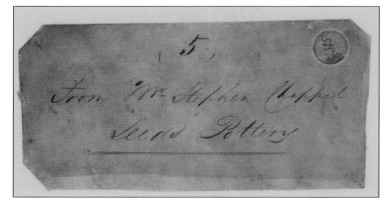

I have absolutely no evidence to claim that these were made at the Leeds Pottery and had it not been for the label, reproduced here, they would not have been considered for including in this work. As will be seen the label bears the writing of Stephen Chappel (compare with his signature on page 73). They were, therefore, once in his possession and I presume either consigned by him to an auction house – hence the possible lot No. 385 on a small circular label stuck top right on the large label, or perhaps to an exhibition. Many exhibitions are recorded as having taken place in Leeds throughout the nineteenth century. Unfortunately after searching extant catalogues for the period up to Stephen Chappel's death, nothing relevant has been found. I have therefore decided to include them as they do tell us something about the taste of their owner and, of course, leave the door a little ajar to the possibility that they could have been decorated at the Leeds Pottery. See the quality of flower painting at Plates 270, 272, 273, 299, 334.b. and 352 and the *Frontispiece* and also Plates 439 and 441. Please read the captions to the last two from which it is obvious that decorators with considerable ability were at the Leeds Pottery as late as 1857.

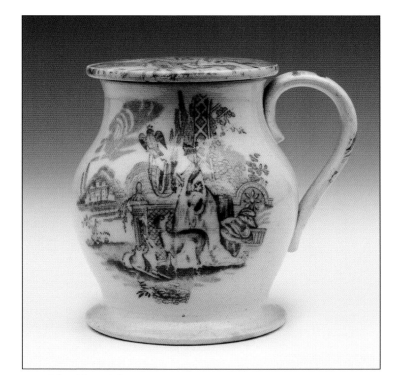

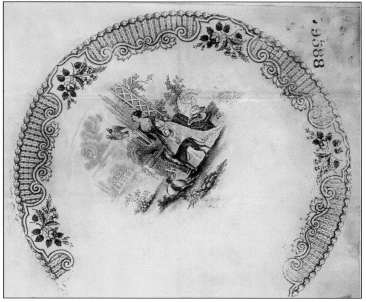

431. REGISTERED DESIGN No. 79588, registered by R. Britton & Co. on the 10th of July 1851. © *The National Archives; Public Record Office BT 43/65 No. 79588.*

430. TREACLE POT WITH A SIMPLE SCREW-THREADED LID. Ht. – 5 in. (127mm). Not marked, '107' is scratched under the base and inside the lid. See Plate 431 which shows that the transfer printed pattern was registered by R. Britton & Co., on the 10th of July 1851. Owners of such pots would have taken them to shops to be filled with treacle as and when needed. See also p. 263.

430.a. PLATE. – D. – 7 1/2 in. (190mm). Kite mark for 10th July 1851 and impressed 7. See plate 430 & 431.

432. JUG. OAHt. – 7 7/8 in. (199mm). Marks - raised moulded 'Kite' Registration Mark which corresponds with the registered design shown at Plate 433, also '3' impressed. *Leeds Museums & Galleries. LEEDM. Z.O.8119.*

433. REGISTERED DESIGN NO. 86857, registered by Warburton & Britton on the 27th of September 1852. ©*The National Archives: Public Record Office BT 43/66 No. 86857.*

434. WASH BOWL. D. – 12 5/8 in. (320mm). Mark No. 7c.i. The pattern is called "Elysian". Please note that very similar patterns were used, at the Don Pottery, named 'Syrian' and at the Middlesbrough Pottery where it was called 'Arabian Nights'.

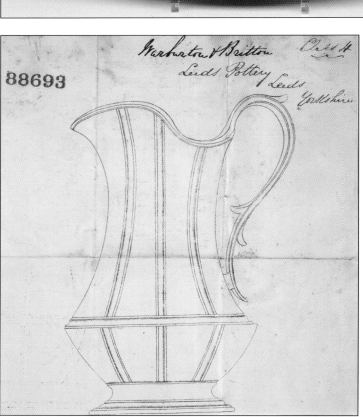

435. REGISTERED DESIGN NO. 88693, registered by Warburton & Britton on the 27th of December 1852. © *The National Archives: Public Record Office BT 43/66 No.88693.*

436. REGISTERED DESIGN NO. 95646, registered by Warburton & Britton on the 21st of April 1854. © *The National Archives: Public Record Office BT 43/66 No. 95646.*

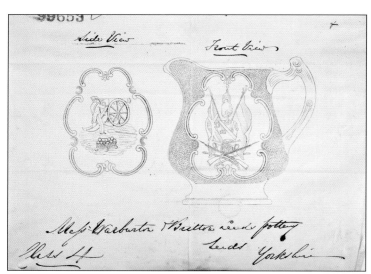

437. REGISTERED DESIGN NO. 99653, registered by Warburton & Britton on the 13th of March 1855. © *The National Archives: Public Record Office BT 43/66 No. 99653.*

438

439

440

441

442

438, 439, 440, 441 & 442. PAIR OF POT-POURRI JARS AND COVERS. Ht. – 7 1/2 in. (190mm). Neither is marked but they are authenticated by the following: This pair of vases entered the Yorkshire Museum with the Boynton Collection which was presented to the Museum in 1916 and 1920. They were first recorded by J. & F. Kidson in their *Historical Notices of the Leeds Old Pottery*, 1892, pl. 18 and pp. 83 – 84: " ... a pair of vases or pot-pourri jars, made by Messrs. Warburton & Britton about 1857 ... They were purchased by the late Mr. Edward Bond, in 1879, from Mr. Richard Britton, the then proprietor of the Pottery, who gave the following certificate:

'Leeds Pottery, 6th May, 1879.

I certify that the pair of blue and gold Globular Vases, painted with fruit on the one side and flowers on the other side, sold by me to Mr. Bond, were manufactured at the Leeds Pottery by Warburton & Britton, and have never been out of my possession, and that only one other such pair was made.

[signed] Richard Britton.'

These vases were purchased at Mr. Bond's sale in October 1884, by Mr. T. Boynton, of Bridlington Quay, in whose hands they now remain."

See also *A Catalogue of the Boynton Collection* by A. Hurst, 1922, pp. 52/3, where we learn that the other two vases, above referred to, were then believed to be in the possession of two daughters of Mr. Warburton. A. Hurst also recorded that he had heard of only two other examples of similarly decorated pieces, these being a pair of bottle-shaped vases with a maroon ground. The above quoted documentation is particularly interesting in that it is proof that there were decorators then at the Pottery capable of such work; would they have been there if their skills were not being regularly employed ? *York Museums Trust (Yorkshire Museum). YORYM 1997.16.*

443. FONT AND COVER. OAHt. – 18 1/2 in. (470mm). Inscribed under the base: "George Brook/Hunslet Leeds/Joseph Bury Leeds Pottery 1864/June 28 1864." Another identical example is also in the Leeds Museums' collection and contains a piece of paper recording that it was from the Methodist New Connection Church in Dewsbury Road, Leeds, built in 1861. *Leeds Museums & Galleries. 3.4/1990.*

444. REGISTERED DESIGN NO. 285322, registered by Richard Britton & Sons on the 17th of September 1874. See the shard at Plate 63 where prints in a very similar vein and with the same style of lettering can be seen. © *National Archives: Public Record Office BT 43/70 No. 285322.*

---

1. Caroline Davidson – *The World of Mary Ellen Best*, p. 107.
2. Presumably what we now refer to as treacle jars/jugs, see Plate 430.
3. Mus. Ref. No: LEEDM.E.1964.48.

END OF VOLUME ONE